WITHDRAWN

A PASSION FOR JUSTICE

A PASSION FOR JUSTICE

*Emotions and the
Origins of the
Social Contract*

ROBERT C. SOLOMON

Rowman & Littlefield Publishers, Inc.

ROWMAN & LITTLEFIELD PUBLISHERS, INC.

Published in the United States of America
by Rowman & Littlefield Publishers, Inc.
4720 Boston Way, Lanham, Maryland 20706

3 Henrietta Street
London WC2E 8LU, England

British Cataloging in Publication Information Available

Library of Congress Cataloging-in-Publication Data

Solomon, Robert C.
A passion for justice : emotions and the origins of the social
contract / Robert C. Solomon
p. cm.
Originally published: Reading, Mass. : Addison-Wesley, 1990.
Includes bibliographical references and index.
1. Social justice. 2. Social contract. I. Title.
HM216.S585 1995 303.3'72—dc20 95-22282 CIP

ISBN 0–8476–8087–8 (pbk.: alk. paper)

Printed in the United States of America

♾™ The paper used in this publication meets the minimum requirements of
American National Standard for Information Sciences—Permanence of
Paper for Printed Library Materials, ANSI Z39.48–1984.

For Jem, Jesi, Danyal
For Rachel and Carrie
and for Alexander K.

This book and,
I hope,
a decent world to live in.

Justice, the mistress and queen of all virtues. . .
CICERO, DE OFFICIIS

Justice is the first virtue of social institutions, as truth is of systems of thought.
JOHN RAWLS, *A THEORY OF JUSTICE*

CONTENTS

PREFACE

As a wound infects the finger, a thought the mind.—ETHIOPIAN PROVERB

For twenty-five cents you can call the weather bureau to satisfy your curiosity about the temperature today, or you can save an Ethiopian child from starving to death tomorrow. (For the price of a call to Dial-a-Joke, you can save two.) We are told that, for a dollar, less than the price of that Big Mac Snack that you don't need or really even want, you can feed an African family for a week. For the price of a late-night pizza, you can save an Indian from blindness. These are the thoughts that explode in our complacent minds—and we cannot wait to get rid of them.

One recollects the magazine photo of a two-year-old child—could he really be seven?—the arms and legs as thin as the limbs of a spider, the stomach bloated in the now too-familiar paradox of starvation. But the sinister fact is that even if we are moved—and how could we not be?—we have an obscene ability and readiness to rationalize. A million starving children is a statistic that the mind cannot grasp. (It was Stalin, remember, who pronounced that one death is a tragedy but a million is a statistic.) And statistics are worse than lies, especially when true. They numb us to the facts even while informing us. They reduce that benign natural impulse, "we have to do something!" to a mere gasp of horror, or worse, an argument about the validity of the methodology of the statistician. Some recent studies of poverty in this country, for example, seem to be intended as weapons in an ideological argument rather than as part of an effort to promote justice. Our natural compassion for that single child and others like him is dulled over by a meticulous network of figures and theories, and we do nothing.

An acquaintance of mine recently bought a new Mazda RX-7 for the price of 250,000 Ethiopian dinners. He said, "What's the point?

Whatever we might give, it would just be a drop in the bucket." The argument (I supposed) was that saving one or five or even a hundred children from the horrible fate of starvation didn't amount to much, considering the millions that were dying and had already died. In fact, those same children we save today would most likely starve next week or next month.

But, of course, he didn't actually say this. The same insensitivity, without the inhibition or tact, is illustrated in a high school principal who, upon hearing that one of his pupils had AIDS and had been barred from attending school, declared "The kid will be dead in a couple of months. What's the point?"

I brought the subject up with a colleague who had just sold a modest house in Austin for a $150,000 profit. She said, "What's the point? The money never goes to the right people anyway."

The argument, I supposed, was that some 30 or 40 percent, or in some cases even 60 or 70 percent, of relief funds goes to administrative costs, inefficiency and waste, or in the case of Ethiopia, to the military expenditures of a hostile, hateful government, instead of to relief. That would mean a five percent (tax-deductible) share of her profits on the house would save only seven or eight thousand lives, instead of ten or twenty thousand.

But, of course, she didn't say this.

A politically radical friend replied that nothing short of a revolution would help these people. He wasn't clear about when or how that might happen.

A politically conservative colleague started talking about the virtues of the free enterprise system and the "magic of the market," adding the predictable corollary that "these people must have brought it on themselves."

These are all good people, considerate at work, generous on birthdays, kind to their friends, just going about their business. But part of their "business" seems to be rationalizing, and the premises are none too pretty. There is the megalomania: if my gift won't make all the difference, then what's the point? There is the fear of being ripped off: some of my money is going to people I don't like at all. (Why should I accept such a limit to my control?) There is the nagging but negative image of charity that is so tied to pity and, consequently, to a certain sense of superiority and the idea of being "patronizing." As good egalitarians, therefore, we avoid seeming superior by not giving. And, finally, there is a straightforward hypocrisy: people who praise "individual generosity"—but always leave bad tips (ask any waitress) and find something wrong with every charity.

Our failure is not so much greed or selfishness as it is a stubborn, infantile insistence on blocking out the nastiness of the world, even when our awareness might make some difference. How much of the violence and ugliness on television is designed (not by anyone in particular) to make us more callous and uncaring, in the recognition that the world is so bad that there's just not much that we could do to change it? (Isn't "realism" just another name for resignation, cynicism, and despair?) Then there is that Sunday School lesson that says, "Remember that others are worse off" and even "There but for the grace of God go I." But these words of wisdom have been reduced to platitudes, simple nonnegotiable facts about the world. And instead of feeling gratitude we just feel lucky, or, we pretend that we have earned our good fortune. Or we rationalize, even at the cost of considerable self-deception. We blame the victims for their own plight, citing their "laziness" or suggesting the unthinkable, that "they choose to live that way," even "they're happy the way they are." And then we feel put upon. What we don't seem to feel is moved to act with dispatch.

It is true that time spent wallowing in the miseries of the world helps no one, but neither do bad rationalizations and neglect. This is not a just world, and there is no point in pretending that it is. But in the end, we really are the world, there are no excuses, and justice, if it is to be found anywhere, must be found in us.

ACKNOWLEDGEMENTS

This is obviously not a book for my colleagues, but I nevertheless owe a large number of debts to those philosophers and social thinkers who have once again made the concern for justice an essential topic and cause of concern. More personally, I want to thank Lee Bowie and Meredith Michaels and the "Propositional Attitudes" group in Amherst, Massachusetts, who listened to my first crude rumblings with interest and offered their encouragement; David and Jenny Armstrong for their hospitality in Sydney, Peter and Renata Singer in Melbourne; and several friendly philosophy departments in Australia and New Zealand—especially at the University of Auckland. Closer to home, I owe a very special debt of gratitude to Mark Murphy, who wrote his senior thesis on justice and gave me assistance all along the way (especially with the wolves and apes in Chapter 3), and to Kathleen Higgins, whose support has become the "without which not" of my work. Melanie Jackson's wisdom has been helpful and encouraging throughout the project. Most of all, I want to thank my friend and editor Jane Isay who originally encouraged me to do the book and suffered with me through its various versions. And most important for all of us, there were the people at Amnesty International, the ACLU, Greenpeace, Oxfam, Save the Children, CARE, the Humane Society, and all of those other sometimes much abused and misunderstood organizations who kept reminding me that a defense of personal passion for justice was no futile or merely academic exercise but the imperative for our times and the only moral response to our own good luck and affluence.

INTRODUCTION

These abstract terms which abound in democratic languages and
which are used on every occasion without attaching them to any
particular fact, enlarge and obscure the thoughts that they are
intended to convey; they render the mode of speech more succinct
and the idea contained in it less clear. But with regard to language,
democratic nations prefer obscurity to labor.

ALEXIS DE TOCQUEVILLE, DEMOCRACY IN AMERICA

YOU ARE ON YOUR way to a luxurious dinner at Chez
Nous when a homeless panhandler approaches you and
politely asks for spare change. What do you do? Ignore him? Apologize? Reach for your wallet? Look for a policeman? What do you feel?
Pity? Indignation? Contempt? Fear? Self-righteous superiority? Does
some political indictment race through your mind? ("Why doesn't the
government . . . ?" or "Why don't these people . . . ?") Do you wax
theological? ("There but for the grace of . . . " or "How could a beneficent, all-powerful God . . . ?") How should you act? (Spare some
change? Share your dinner? Join him in the street? Write your congressman? Campaign for socialism?) How should you respond and
what should you think? Or should you just ignore the situation and
just go on and enjoy your boeuf bourguignon?

This is a book about *justice*. But let me say quickly that it is not
yet another tract on the fate of liberalism, not yet another grand
theory; nor is it a footnote to a theory, an attack on a theory, or
another of those brilliant philosophical displays of technical virtuosity
that employ all of the latest tricks of econometrics and game theory
to leave even professional colleagues aghast with consternation if not
awe. It is rather, I hope, a book on justice that is easy for the intelli-

gent reader to read and understand. It is simply a plea for compassion, a plea for justice.

Justice is today the "hottest" single topic in social philosophy, debated daily in Washington and in prominent think tanks as well as in the graduate seminars of our leading universities. But, accordingly, I find it irresponsible that this most important philosophical issue of our day has not yet found an audience much wider than the readership of the *New York Review of Books* and the *National Review*. Here is a topic that is crucial to our everyday well-being and our sense of our place in the world. Justice is each and every citizen's personal responsibility, and yet discussions of it have become so specialized and so academic and so utterly unreadable that it has become just another intellectual puzzle, a conceptual Gordian knot awaiting its academic Alexander. Brilliant thinkers spend their lives attached to a twig on a branch of an isolated tree of knowledge, spinning a cocoon of embellishments and rejoinders in defense of an idea that they may have had in graduate school. The result has been, as in so many important public issues, that public discussion, care, and concern have been put on hold. Meanwhile, the experts become so obsessed with their *theories* of justice that they have very little time for—justice.

This is a book about how we live, and how we feel that we ought to live, about the kind of people we are, and the kind of people we would like to be. My central claim is that justice—or, more accurately, a keen sense of injustice and the urge to do something about it—is an essential ingredient of the good life, and that it is, accordingly, the concern and responsibility of each and every one of us. This thesis is opposed not to any particular theory or conception of justice but to all of those abstract and impersonal schemes that stifle our natural compassion and stymie action. This book, therefore, is not a blueprint for yet another perfect but nonexistent society; it begins by accepting (more or less) this society. It is not a defense of some great cause or a venting of ideological spleen, nor is it a book about prophets, saints, and heroes. It is rather a book about ordinary people and their feelings about justice. It is about perfectly familiar human emotions and justice, not an obscure abstraction or an exquisitely complex process, not an eternal verity, not a grand plan or an ideal society designed by yet another philosopher-king intending to shake up the world or to justify once again the unearned advantages of the few. I do not try, in the pages that follow, to summarize or begin to do justice to the millions of thoughtful and sometimes insightful words that have been penned in the past two decades or so, but I do try to deal with the basic issues without academic complexities.

At the same time, I want to challenge the entire tradition that those academic complexities both disguise and express—the overbearing emphasis on a very specialized notion of rationality and the wholesale neglect of our more ordinary feelings of fairness and fellowship. I want to shift the focus from impersonal institutions and government policies to individual people and their personal passions. Justice is not, as the tradition presumes rather than argues, an ideal to which our society (or any other) more or less badly conforms. Justice is first of all a function of personal character, a matter of ordinary, everyday feeling rather than grand theory. Thought naturally tends to celebrate thought, but sometimes thought ought to do obeisance to feeling. As Rousseau says in the essay that is more than any other the inspiration and background of my own work, "one is not obliged to make a man a philosopher before making him a man."[1] We have over-intellectualized our feelings about justice, with the result that our feelings have become as confused as our theories, if indeed they have not been eclipsed by them.

Accordingly, this is not another theory of justice but a complement to those theories of justice that now populate our intellectual universe. It is a book with a single point to make, in different ways and from different perspectives. It is, to mention one of my favorite composers but least favorite pieces of music, much like Ravel's *Bolero*: one deliberately simple theme, played over and over again, with lots of embellishment and varying orchestration but little development in the usual sense. That theme is, again, that justice is not a utopian plan for the perfect society but a personal sense of individual and collective fellow-feeling and responsibility. It is not an abstract theoretical ideal but a constellation of feelings and a perfectly ordinary virtue of character. We are not, as so many progressive but cynical thinkers have suggested, essentially or naturally selfish. We are essentially and naturally social and sociable creatures, and the relations, contrasts, and comparisons between us are far more important than some artificial sense of "one's own interests."

I should add, even at the beginning however, that this constellation of sociable feelings does not just consist of such praiseworthy sentiments as care and compassion, although they are, of course, essential to justice. We are participants in the social world, not just observers of it, and the emotions that make up our sense of justice cannot be just the sensibilities of the benign spectator. Justice also involves envy, resentment, and vengeance and all of the other passions that we feel when we are deprived or cheated. In other words, true human justice involves real human passions, not just a special saintly distillation of them. But neither is the human soul divided into parts, one dark and selfish, the other enlightened and compassionate, with the two (or more) sides warring against one another for mastery of the soul. Nor are we divided into masculine and feminine philosophical camps, as has been recently charged with great fanfare, with an ethic of rigid rule-defined justice on the one hand and a nurturing sense of caring on the other. We are much more complicated than that, and so, too, is justice.[2]

WHAT IS JUSTICE?

Justice, under various names, governs the world—nature and humanity, science and conscience, logic and morals, political economy, politics, history, literature and art. Justice is that which is most primitive in the human soul, most fundamental in society, most sacred among ideas, and what the masses demand today with most ardour. It is the essence of religions and at the same time the form of reason, the secret object of faith, and the beginning, middle and end of knowledge. What can be imagined more universal, more strong, more complete than justice?

PROUDHON, *DE LA JUSTICE DANS LA REVOLUTION ET DANS L'EGLISE*

WHAT IS JUSTICE? SOCRATES asked that question at the beginning of Plato's *Republic*, and we have all been asking ever since. It was, perhaps, the first great philosophical question, and it is still the most important and unavoidable philosophical question, embracing as it does not only those essential questions about what we deserve in life and some disturbing questions about how we should punish those who hurt us but also all of those basic questions about the good life—what it is, how to find it, how to live it. Should we feel envious because people with less talent prosper more than we do? Should we feel guilty when we have so much and others have so little, not even a home or enough to eat? Should we allow ourselves to feel vengeful when other people seriously harm us? Should we think of ourselves competitively, as living in a "zero-sum" or a "dog-eat-dog" world, gaining our self-esteem at the expense of others, or is the good life to be found elsewhere, in a world already rich with invaluable and not usually competitive opportunities such as (nonromantic) love, friendship, and beauty?

Our answers to such questions differ, in part because we differ, and different societies may well have different conceptions of what is fair and what is not. What we call justice would not have been recognized as such in Homeric Greece or in the Athens of Plato and Aristotle four hundred years later. It is very different from the sense of justice that one would find in feudal France, in the Florentine renaissance, or in the bourgeois London society of Jane Austen. It is very different, indeed, from the sense of justice one finds in contemporary Japan or Iran and it may well differ from New York City to Dallas, Texas. Nevertheless, *justice* (like *truth*) is not the kind of concept that easily admits of variation. Conceptions may differ but the concept of justice seems to be one. Indeed, it has the connotations of an almost religious notion, incontrovertibly grand, cosmic, universal, and necessary for the very existence of human life as such. And so, the very word *justice* tends to awe us, transfix us, mislead us. It so obviously refers to something undeniably honorable, perhaps heroic, but in any case enormous, awesome, perhaps even divine. It seems to refer, at the very least, to an ideal system of world government or of economic distribution, or to the criminal justice system as it "should" be—not a criminal unpunished and not an innocent wrongly abused—or to some utopian state of the world, with plenty and happiness for everyone, the Will of God conscientiously applied to the ways of humanity.

But the most striking and immediate result of any such conception of justice is that it is always *at a distance*, something *other*, a state to be hoped for, prayed for, or perhaps desperately worked for, but not as such something already "in us," something very much our own. Justice is out of our hands, a matter of personal concern perhaps but not a matter of individual responsibility. Justice is blind, not the way that love is blind (love has an extremely keen grasp of personal particulars) but as the lady in the statue is blind, intentionally blindfolded, oblivious to particulars and standing in judgment over us, with her impersonal, scientific scales. We assume that justice will happen, or that it won't, depending on whether we employ faith or cynicism as a means of coping with the world. Meanwhile, we go on with our affairs, cursing and lamenting the headlines, allowing ourselves to become furious at the latest atrocity or political scandal and maudlin about the most recent "little girl saved from the well" story. But justice has little or nothing to do with us, except, of course, that our salaries are lower than we really deserve, and there is still that uncollected apartment deposit from three years ago, and that unfair traffic ticket ("the light was really yellow, and, besides, the bicyclist went through it too."). Justice will be done, we hope, but not by us.

The problem is that, except in special cases (as a judge or as a character in a Clint Eastwood movie), we do not see justice as our own responsibility. Instead, we think of justice as the responsibility of others, out of our hands. We see ourselves only as potential victims of injustice—of higher taxes, an unsympathetic magistrate, or a violent crime. We refuse to see ourselves as the actual agents of justice. Of course, we all have our opinions, and we play our little role in the determination of justice every two or perhaps only every four years, punching out the little dots in a neighborhood voting booth. (That is, about half of us do so for national elections, far fewer for local offices; but only a demagogue would identify this minimal public behavior with citizenship and confuse voting behavior with a sense of justice.) We probably hold some strong opinions about the ultimate justice of that gigantic system of economic distribution called capitalism, but this too is more a matter of deferral than a concern for justice. Indeed, it is the main target of much of my argument to follow: One praises the "magic of the market" and goes one's own way, making money and living well, satisfied in the expectation that the market will take care of justice. Or, one condemns "the system" and declares that its very nature is such that it could never produce justice. Then one goes one's own way, making money and living well, thoroughly convinced that nothing short of total social change would establish a truly just society.

In other words, we talk about justice, and we may indeed have strong feelings to accompany our opinions and arguments, but we do not see justice as our own, as something everyday and ordinary that we ought to do something about. Instead, we think of Justice (like God) as a cosmic force to be appealed to and prayed to, an object of hope rather than a spur to action. This distant, grand, and impersonal sense of justice can be traced, as an ancient idea, at least back to Plato. In *The Republic* and elsewhere he presented us with a mind-boggling but ultimately ethereal suggestion that justice is a divine Form, an other-worldly ideal that is at best badly approximated (and rarely even that) in this world. But Plato played a rather schizophrenic, even if central, role in the history of justice. He also thought of justice as a personal virtue, indeed, as *the* virtue that defined the good life. His teacher Socrates was not only the teacher of the divine Form; he also exemplified it (if imperfectly) in his own life. And so we got not only the idea of justice as a grand abstraction, but also the idea that justice is a personal virtue, a way of living and thinking and feeling, not an idea or a theory. (In fact, Plato's own conclusions are rather murky, and readers of *The Republic* have long struggled in vain to summarize Socrates' own conception of justice.) We argue about justice, but justice personified seems to wait for another Socratic hero, or at least a heroic politician.

In the struggle between Socrates' conception of justice as a personal virtue and the other-worldly ideal of justice as an abstract Form, it was the idea of justice as a grand abstraction that finally won, and the idea of justice as a personal virtue has since been all but lost. Philosophers today tend to argue that the very idea of justice as a personal virtue is a kind of conceptual confusion. Yet it is important to remember that our current conceptions of justice are, for the most part, only a few decades or at most a century old, and they are very much in flux. Many of them date from the New Deal in the thirties, more recently augmented in an uncomfortable alliance of free market fetishism and a distinctively American version of the old republican civic virtues. But all of this is very new, and we can hardly expect one single ideal to emerge from it all. Indeed, the contemporary discussion didn't really start up until 1971, when John Rawls published his *Theory of Justice*, a truly epoch-making book that we shall often mention in the pages that follow. But in that work, the grand abstraction suggested by Plato becomes definitive. "Justice is the first virtue of social institutions," Rawls tells us, and then he makes justice into a noble but very abstract defense of equality and an equally abstract concern for "the least advantaged" in our society. It is not as if Rawls entirely denies the passions, but he says that our sense of justice is nothing but our "effective desire to apply and to act from the principles of justice.³ In other words, our emotions, insofar as they are relevant to justice at all, become as impersonal as our theories.

THE HISTORY OF JUSTICE

"Eye for eye, tooth for tooth, hand for hand, foot for foot, burning for burning, wound for wound, stripe for stripe."

EXODUS 21:24–5

JUSTICE AND OUR SENSE of justice have changed dramatically through history, and since one of the main themes of this book is that justice is inextricably contextual it is important to appreciate the nature and direction of these changes. I think that the history of justice, simply stated, is an ever-increasing sense of the importance and dignity of the individual and the radically expanding scope of our concern for others. All of this is, I believe, to the good, but there are costs which are just beginning to be appreciated—the loss of our sense of community and, consequently, the (I hope temporary) loss of a larger sense of self, the extraordinary emphasis on abstract reason and the resulting diminution of both confidence in and respect of our basic feelings for and about each other. In this book, I would like to pursue a modest corrective to these grand historical trends, arguing for a sense of individualism that does not deny this larger social sense of self and, in order to do this, insisting on a renewed emphasis on the passions, educated and expanded to include the now global scope of our sense of justice.

Looking back again to ancient times, we find that the original meaning of justice, in Homer and in much of the Old Testament, clearly lies in the realm of the personal passions, especially in our sense of vengeance. It is not uninteresting, therefore, that today vengeance is almost always excluded from considerations of justice, and is in fact considered to be opposed to justice. ("I don't want revenge: I want justice!" is a familiar, even obligatory cry when one has been grievously wronged.) Even Plato opposed the idea of vengeance as part of justice, arguing in effect that two wrongs don't make a right. But several centuries earlier, however, in the brutal world of *The Iliad*, justice meant little other than revenge, and the concept of justice could even be coupled with wholesale genocide, as when Agamemnon reproaches his brother Menelaus for taking a hostage and urges him, "No, let us not leave even one of them alive, down to the babies in their mothers' wombs," and Homer, commenting, tells us that "he turned his brother's heart, for he urged justice."[4] Justice, in this sense, isn't even getting even, for one is instructed to punish the offender far more savagely than one was offended. Justice, in this sense, is simple self-assertion, the unqualified insistence that one's honor and integrity must be defended, and that any offender deserves the worst. It is the justice of the warrior, the victor, the justice of the strong. Odysseus, Homer tells us, killed all of his wife's suitors, without exception, just because, assuming that he was dead, they presumed to woo his wife (unsuccessfully). The idea that justice should be tempered with compassion and mercy was still a millennium away, and vengeance was a legitimate passion.

It is in this brutal context that we should reconsider some of those seemingly brutal lessons from the Old Testament. "An eye for an eye, a tooth for a tooth" sounds horrifying to our innocent ears, but in the context of the ancient world this dictum was not so much a cry for vengeance as a civilizing revision of vengeance. One should *only* extract an eye for an eye, rather than kill the offender and his entire family. Justice demands balance, restraint, limits.[5] But what is evident in this ancient sense of justice as vengeance is that justice is not at all an ideal, much less abstract. It is retaliation for a particular offense.

It is, in other words, a more-or-less measured response to an injustice, not an attempt to apply some general theory about how the world ought to be. It is decidedly personal, whether involving individuals, a whole family or tribe, or perhaps even a whole nation or people. It makes no claims about "the good society" as such except to say that particular sorts of action will not be tolerated. Justice as vengeance may not be what we are seeking in this book, but it is an ineliminable part of justice. Furthermore, it has the indisputable virtue of being readily comprehensible, wholly concrete, and thoroughly established throughout the whole of human history.

By the time of the Athenian Golden Age of the fifth century B.C. and in the philosophizing of Socrates, Plato, and Aristotle, the concept of justice became much more lofty, less concerned with vengeance and much more concerned with the harmonious working of the community and the well-being of the citizens of the city-state. It was no longer the satisfaction of that primitive tribal emotion but the exercise of the civic virtues. Justice became "the sum of all virtue" (the phrase is from Theognis)—a mark of urbane civilization instead of a warrior's hunger for getting even.[6] In the Old Testament, the ancient passion for revenge had been rationalized, modified, and moralized. With the New Testament, the thirst for revenge became further removed from the core of justice, and the element of mercy—in the Old Testament often a matter of Jehovah's whim—became a systematic promise, albeit with conditions. Justice became more akin to love and caring than revenge, though the distinctions between justice, love, and mercy were already being put into place. With the further development of Christianity and the birth of Islam, the Old Testament prophets were still in view, but justice moved further and further away from its tribal and personal origins and got more and more involved with new abstractions about theology and religious morality. But justice still had its source in personal feeling, although perhaps the personal feelings were those of Jehovah or Allah rather than (or as well as) our own. What was new was the infusion of theory and the increasing scope that the abstractions of theory both allowed and encouraged.

One of the most important implications of this increased scope and abstraction was the fact that questions of justice increasingly became concerned with social injustice rather than just personal and family offenses. The sufferings of the poor and the oppressed became a matter of concern. The gross inequities between the very rich and the very poor became a matter of some embarrassment; indeed, the very fact of being rich or even well-off could put a devout believer on the defensive, and by the time of St. Francis, for example, the idea of giving all of one's possessions to the poor—which would have seemed utterly foolish to Aristotle, for example—became something of an ideal. But as justice got increasingly tied up with God's will and social conditions in general, it was thought of less and less as personal motive or a personal virtue. Finally, that still specific concern for injustice turned into the very modern, very abstract conception of "social justice," an idea which prescribed governmental rather than divine intrusion into the economy in order to assure some semblance of equity if not equality. Many social thinkers are still rightly suspicious of this concept. Friedrich von Hayek, for example, calls the idea "intellectually disreputable, the mark of demagogy or cheap journalism."[7] The idea that *we* can make a real difference, without dreaming the impossible dream and without destroying our free society in the process, is still not wholly convincing. But notice that both sides of this now-classic debate (sometimes summarized by the misleading terms "liberal" and "conservative") affirm the legitimacy of impersonal systems rather than the personal sense of justice (or injustice) that gave rise to these concerns in the first place.

It is not until the mid-nineteenth century that the question of justice takes what is now its dominant form, in which it is concerned not at all with revenge or personal virtue but almost single-mindedly with the distribution of wealth in society as a whole. In our particularly materialistic age, justice has become entirely secular and largely economic in its focus. The question is how the goods produced (or otherwise acquired) by society should be distributed such that no one gets too much and no one too little. Of course, Aristotle—plausibly our first economist—discussed these issues at some length in his *Nicomachean Ethics* well over two thousand years ago, but he certainly had no general scheme in mind and emphasized justice as a personal virtue, especially for statesmen. Justice, like all of the virtues, was mainly a matter of good judgment (*phronesis*). It was not, as Rawls tells us, a virtue of institutions but a virtue of particular individuals; and of particular importance, of course, was the good judgment and sense of fairness of the rulers—the statesmen or the king. Throughout most of history, it was assumed (at least by the king) that the king could keep just about anything. All lands were essentially his, and the "wealth of the nation," if we can apply Adam Smith's radical phrase to precapitalist society, was measured by the size of the royal treasury. (This was still true in seventeenth-century "mercantilist" society, which Smith criticized at length in his *Wealth of Nations*.)[8] Today, of course, the king (if there is one) will probably receive a salary that is negotiated according to established standards of merit and responsibility, just like any other employee. (In fact, in Sweden, he does not even get special parking privileges.) But the abstract idea of equality, and especially equality in material wealth and well-being, has moved from the mouths of a few neglected prophets to the center social stage.

Our new individualism and concern with equality and fairness have not resulted in an increasing personal sense of justice. Just the opposite. Today, the attention all turns away from individual responsibility and a sense of fairness in particular cases to questions about the nature, functions, and legitimacy of governments and other state institutions. The all-important notion of personal "merit"—whether this means the aristocratic concern for who a person is, or the criminal concern for what a person should be blamed for, or the achievement-oriented concern for what a person deserves and has earned—tends to drop out of the picture in favor of much more impersonal questions: How should the wealth be distributed? How should incomes be equalized? Does the government have the right to interfere with private enterprise? Does the government have the right to violate the rights of citizens, particularly the right to private property? Of course, the goods of society (food, clothing, shelter) have always been in some sense "distributed," and so there was always some scheme in place, even if it was just "whoever gets there first" or "whoever can keep it owns it." These were hardly theories of justice, however, and they were rarely questioned, except by a few clever eccentrics who learned to be envious and resentful rather than simply disappointed or grateful for whatever they got. Distribution in most established societies was simply settled by tradition, or by luck, or by force. And except for the case of outright theft (a personal injustice, not a "crime against the state"), the question of justice did not arise. Today, distribution is *the* question of social philosophy and policy, and with it, paradoxically, our sense of justice has been compromised even where it has not been eclipsed.

There have always been the very rich. And of course there have always been the poor. But even as late as the civilized and sentimental eighteenth century, this disparity was not yet a cause for public embarrassment or a cry of injustice. Adam Smith hardly talked about it, for example, in *Wealth of Nations*, (1776), a book that more than any other in history expressed confidence and optimism in the possibility of general prosperity. Poverty was considered just one more "act of God," impervious to any human solution except mollification through individual charity and government poorhouses to keep the poor off the streets and away from crime. It wasn't until the late nineteenth century that Dickens shook the conscience of his compatriots with his riveting descriptions of poverty and cruelty in contemporary London, and it is really just within the past several decades that the problem of poverty and resistance to its solutions has become the central question of justice. This is an extremely important historical fact for us to digest, for while I want to argue that our sense of justice is to a certain extent inborn and thus universal, our vision has to be cultivated along with our emotions. People may have always had compassion and pity, but the scope of those sentiments depends upon our philosophy—who counts and who does not, what is "natural" and inalterable and what is not. The idea that poverty is a tragedy that we can and should do something about is just now becoming part of our sense of justice. Its neglect for so much of human history underscores not human callousness or hopelessness but rather the remarkable (if belated) development of a truly universal moral sense, not through the abstractions of practical reason but by way of increasing global exposure and the personal empathy made possible by modern communications, travel, and shared experience. The poor and oppressed are no longer "other," and we no longer have the luxury of either ignorance or despair.

JUSTICE AND DESPAIR: HOW NOT TO THINK ABOUT JUSTICE

Every revolution, every war, every overthrow has always been effected in the name of Justice. And the extraordinary thing is that it should be just as much the partisans of a new order as the defenders of the old who invoke with their prayers the reign of Justice. And when a neutral voice proclaims the necessity of a just peace, all the belligerents agree, and affirm that this just peace will come about only when the enemy has been annihilated. . . . Each will defend a conception of justice that puts him in the right and his opponent in the wrong. . . . Every antagonist . . . has always declared and has done his best to prove, that justice is on his side; . . . justice is invoked every time recourse is had to an arbiter—and at once one realizes the unbelievable multiplicity of meanings attached to the idea, and the extraordinary confusion provoked by its use.

CHAIM PERELMAN, *THE IDEA OF JUSTICE AND THE PROBLEM OF ARGUMENT*

TAKING UP A GLOBAL perspective, the sheer awfulness of the world is more than sufficient both to stimulate our sense of justice and to overwhelm it. If we are really serious about justice, all but the most hopeful among us are likely to be overcome by despair. The numbers are overwhelming: six million Jews murdered in the Nazi camps, five million babies dead of starvation in the East Africa famine of 1985, twenty million people living below the poverty line in America this year, one out of four children without the opportunity of decent schooling or a career. Just a few days ago, ten thousand people were killed or maimed in an earthquake in northwestern China. (I catch myself staring at the headline and breathing a sigh of relief: no one I know. China, thankfully, is so far away.) Today there are twelve million refugees in the world, people who have to sneak from border to border in search of a place they might be allowed to live in their dire poverty.[9] Meanwhile, six thousand political prisoners rot in their cells without trial in South America.[10] But South America too is so far away, and it is easier not to think about it. What can we do? We need only remind ourselves of Stalin's cynical observation: "One death is a tragedy; a million is a statistic." How do we cope? What should we think? Wouldn't it be better not to *feel* about global tragedies, to be tough and "realistic"? Isn't it so much easier to argue abstractly about our "national interest" or, domestically, the efficiency or the failure of the Great Society?

What can we do, in a world so violent, so full of hate and deprivation? Our natural reaction is to turn our glances away, to look to home and the details of life. But once our eyes are open and our sensibilities alerted, we see injustices here at home too, and our practiced self-deception allows us to turn away here too. It is enough, my friends and colleagues tell me, to be a "decent" person, good to one's family and conscientious at work, and, besides, "if we were to get involved, wouldn't we just make matters much worse?" Overwhelmed by the injustice in the world and seduced by an abstract, otherworldly ideal of justice, we lose or more properly give up our sense of justice altogether. It is out of our hands. Thus the theme of this book is that justice is and must be first of all a matter of personal concern and an individual virtue, not just a quality of anonymous institutions, systems, and governments. It is a matter of our feelings, intentions, and attempts and not just a question of results. We have so elevated justice to the status of a lofty, abstract, awesome concept which (if properly implemented) will solve all problems, and we have so relegated and delegated the execution of justice to institutions and systems (if not to God), that personal responsibility for justice has all but disappeared, even among those who are elected or appointed in its name. Accordingly, the idea to be defended here is that justice is basically not an ideal state or a scheme for the way of the world or a perfect government system, but rather the way that one *lives*, the way that one *feels*, the way that one acts and responds and seeks out situations in everyday life. We don't know what effects our efforts may have, and we certainly won't solve the world's problems. But justice is and must be the fabric of our lives, not a dream of the perfect society and not an abstract system of rewards and punishments in which we are all mere recipients. Justice must be found, if it is to be found at all, in the outlook and responsibilities of every individual, not deferred to the market (which is itself our joint creation and responsibility), not postponed until the revolution, and not handed over to the government or the president's Council of Economic Advisors.

How not to think of justice: as the way the world ought to be, as a grand scheme that, ideally, ought to be imposed "from the top"— by the government or by God. To think of justice just in terms of policy is already to slip into this illusion, to think that if things were only run right there would be no injustice and, moreover, no further need to worry about justice. Justice would then really be out of our hands, no longer our responsibility because it would no longer be a problem or a question. But my thesis here is that there is no such grand, coherent scheme, no policy or set of policies that would set everything right, no possible perfect world in which our responsibilities would miraculously be canceled. The world is imperfect, of necessity, and injustice is inevitable. That means that the abstract concern for justice—the search for a single blueprint that will (or should) satisfy everyone—is misplaced, and that the real concern should be to rectify particular injustices, perhaps even thousands or millions of them, not to search in our studies for justice as such. And it means that justice is, and always will be, in each of our individual hands. There is no escape from it, no appeal to a higher court. Governments will do what governments are made to do, and God will do as He will. We, however, are the ultimate instruments of justice—and injustice. To despair about the awful state of the world and hope for something better are just two more of the many ways in which we evade and deny our responsibilities.

This is not to say, of course, that justice has nothing to do with the overall scheme of things, or that the structure of society has no effect or influence on personal attitudes and responsibilities. The ancient Greeks used to say that to live a good life one had to live in a great city. We would modify that observation (allowing now for suburban and elegant rural living and excluding certain neighborhoods of even the greatest cities) but the sentiment remains intact. A great nation produces great citizens, and a spiritually impoverished one produces spiritually impoverished citizens. A just system produces just individuals. But great nations and just systems do not just pop into existence, and from an existential point of view it is essential to insist that compassionate and fair-minded individuals are primary and prior to any system of justice. Historically and causally, society precedes and produces the individual, but from the personal point of view and the perspective of responsibility, it is the individual who commands our attention. It is each and every one of us who has to decide, on the basis of feelings that we have cultivated or quashed, what the society and the world we live in is going to be like. Contemporary theories of justice emphasize the importance of rules and policies and delight in the most recent mathematical models in the social sciences, but the real importance of our sense of justice emerges precisely when the rules and policies are unclear or uncertain, when personal responsibility and not public rationality (or irrationality) is at issue. As Jean-Paul Sartre often wrote, it is our individual freedom—the sort of person that one decides to be—that is always at stake, and this freedom is just what the impersonal presumptions of current theory tend to deny or ignore. To believe in justice is not to hold up an impossible optimism, nor is it to despair of the world. It is to enlarge our personal vision and concerns, to allow ourselves to be moved by injustice wherever we find it and, most important of all, to do what we can.

THE RHETORIC OF JUSTICE

Justice, in the only sense in which it has a meaning, is an imaginary personage, feigned for the convenience of discourse, whose dictates are the dictates of utility, applied to certain particular cases.
JEREMY BENTHAM, *AN INTRODUCTION TO THE PRINCIPLES OF MORALS AND LEGISLATION*

. . . it is in relation to an audience that all argumentation is developed.
CHAIM PERELMAN, *THE IDEA OF JUSTICE AND THE PROBLEM OF ARGUMENT*

WE ARE SO USED to declarations of rights, accusations of injustice, insistence on equal treatment, that we naturally tend to think that such words as *rights, justice,* and *equality* actually stand for something, perhaps not an actual state of affairs but at least some sort of standard, some sort of ideal, some sort of precise equation against which the world can be measured. And, as if to prove the point, we do on happy occasion find that the world indeed conforms to the ideal: the Supreme Court upholds an individual's right to privacy against government intrusion, an evasive criminal or abusive despot is given his due, the underdog stands up and fights and wins. Nevertheless, I want to suggest that the language of justice is rhetorical rather than logical or descriptive. The terms do not refer to an ideal standard but rather play a central role in political discourse. One need not say, with Edmund Morgan (*Inventing the People*), that they are "made up," as he claims that the notion of "the people" was the "invention of the people in American and England." This makes it sound too much as if we've bamboozled ourselves, whereas in fact rhetoric, like politics, is not a negative notion or a dishonest concept except by comparison with some other, over-idealized concept. But there is no coherent ideal of justice. Justice claims are always contextual and presuppose a local set of conditions and considerations. Where there are no clear criteria, which is often the case when contexts collide or overlap, the language of justice is not (as the philosophers hope) a vehicle for rational calculation but a medium of persuasion. It is not our reasons but our emotions that are moved when we are persuaded to "see" one point of view rather than another.

If justice claims are always contextual and presuppose a local set of conditions and considerations, then it also follows that the all-embracing principles that are so often thought to define justice will themselves be open to negotiation and persuasion. Our pity for a people who seem to us to be living in poverty is mollified when we find out (and not just as our rationalization) that they actually prefer to live so, in accordance with ancient tribal rites, perhaps, rather than accept what they see as the drab, routine existence of the affluent urban population nearby. What we celebrate as the work ethic has been greeted with derision in societies where work is unnecessary and ambition is thought (probably rightly) to be a kind of psychosis. In Russia today, *perestroika* and the urge to individual initiative run headlong into the established sense of justice—and that means equality rather than individual reward.[11] Whatever we think of indentured labor and the abuses and injustices of feudalism, it is clear that our ideas would wreak total disaster in feudal societies and that an advocate of the free market system would, quite correctly, be hanged (or worse) as an enemy not only of public order but of justice too. Even our horror of torture evaporates when we find out, for example, that the prisoner is being interrogated to find out where he has set a nuclear explosive to go off in a heavily populated city. Justice as rhetoric means that justice is not the attempt to match reality to some abstract ideal but rather the struggle within ourselves to come to terms with the way the world is and persuade both ourselves and others to attack this particular injustice and adopt that specific course of action. Our sense of justice is our persuasion to do what we can.

Elizabeth Wolgast, in her recent *A Grammar of Justice*, seems to hit the nail right on the head. She also argues that justice is not an ideal, that questions about justice always begin from some particular problematic circumstances, so that the key concept is injustice, not justice. But injustice too is a largely polemical term, subject not only to interpretation but to very different and opposed viewpoints. The Arab-Israeli debate is (or at least was) routinely described in terms of injustice on both sides and, in a more civil context, most marital and tax disputes hinge on injustices allegedly perpetrated by each side. Wolgast's conclusion, and the conclusion of several other authors, is that there is no ideal state or agreed upon standard of justice and no single set of violations that define injustice. As Professor E. Dupreel concluded some years ago in his *Treatise on Morals* (Vol. II), "there does not exist an ideal of justice. . . . There are multiple forms of the ideal of justice, and each one has a content which is never, by itself, pure justice." Chaim Perelman adds that "justice is a prestige-laden and confused idea."[12] I would say not confused but dislocated and, consequently, over-idealized and falsified.

To insist that justice is rhetorical is not to say that it is not real (the cynic's position, also that of the moral skeptic). Justice is certainly real; we are just looking for it in the wrong place. Justice is in the sensibility, not in the standard. "We want to see justice done," but it is the seeing and the wanting that constitutes that sense of justice; and there is no guarantee, and in fact little likelihood, that the cauldron of conflicting sensibilities and demands in the world today will allow for a single, sensible solution. The problem is that the search for what is sensible becomes just as problematic as the claim that one or another solution is rational, in other words, just another rhetorical device which may posture as a neutral overseer but in fact almost always lends a hand to one set of interests or ideologies rather than another. A sense of justice may be one of the most important attributes of a good person, but there is no guarantee, except in carefully controlled "spheres of justice,"[13] that a sense of justice will ever result in a state of affairs recognized by all as justice. In the world at large, all we can do is to press our case, fighting against injustice where we find it but without the illusion that the end we seek is in any way prefigured in the heavens.

NOBLESSE OBLIGE: IS IT WRONG TO BE RICH?

 . . . *in France, a rich man is a rich man and everybody is de-lighted to defer to the considerable powers that his wealth com-mands. Nobody begrudges that. Nobody questions that. But nobody would think that the rich man, by definition, because he is rich, is also either good or wise. That is a confusion and a mistake that a Frenchman would never make, and one we often make.*   LEWIS LAPHAM, *MONEY AND CLASS IN AMERICA*

"Virtue is better than wealth."   KENYAN PROVERB

JUSTICE IS A MATTER of personal character, not a state of the world. But what this means in practical terms is that what counts for justice is ultimately what we do, not the way the world is. Many people confuse the natural inequities and inequalities of the world with injustice, but there is all the difference in the world between being born into an advantageous position in life and stepping on other people in order to get ahead. What is wrong with being rich in this world is not having luxuries and advantages that others do not; it is having a certain attitude that denies good fortune in favor of arrogance and ignores the special obligations of those who are well off, which used to be called *noblesse oblige.*

A friend of a friend of mine is a twenty-six-year-old multimillionaire. (Mere millionaires don't seem to count much anymore.) He has the obligatory Porsche (Carrera, 4-liter, 305 h.p., sexy black, spoilers), condominiums at two exotic beaches, and about a million in the bank for every year of his life. (He doesn't invest in the stock market.) He has retired, essentially, and doesn't know quite what to do. Making money now bores him. Spending money bores him. The *idea* of making and spending money bores him even more, and he talks about his wealth and accomplishments in a disarming, self-abasing way. And yet, there is no doubt that he feels quite superior, even anointed, not because of his cleverness or his wealth as such but rather as if they themselves were rewards for some special status. He occasionally suggests that he has been lucky, but there is not an ounce of gratitude or humility in his voice or gestures, and he certainly feels no obligations that might go along with such spectacular good fortune. His politics, if one would call them that, are quite "conservative"—but in fact a complex of paranoia, selfishness, and seething resentment glossed by crude rationalization. He blames the poor for their plight and wonders, contemptuously, why they don't do something about it. He gives very little to charity or, for that matter, to the politicians he supposedly supports. Ultimately, he admits to being a cynic and a pessimist, "just holding onto what I've earned." In his opinion, those of us who are over thirty and not yet rich are at best misguided idealists, or worse, proven failures. Needless to say, he has never held a job for any substantial period of time (his four years as an investment banker were divided between almost as many firms). He has no plans to do anything in particular now, and certainly no financial need to do so. And yet he becomes defensive when people, especially his elders, point out that he hasn't really worked for his money, that he is in fact a spoiled but lucky whiz kid who happened on Wall Street at a flukey time in history, that he has somehow missed out on or perhaps circumvented the sorts of necessities that make life meaningful for most of the people he so despises.

What do we make of such a case? Well, to begin with, that depends whether you too are an under-thirty multimillionaire, but most people treat my friend's friend as a symptom of a social disease. His wealth is not itself the issue, for there are and always have been many wealthier men and women. Nor is it his age, for there are and always have been young people with large, unearned fortunes, thanks to their parents or grandparents or ancestors. Of course, one might object to the idea of anyone's having so much wealth at any age in a country where nearly twenty percent of the children do not have enough for food and clothing, but at least half of the detractors and diagnosticians of my friend's friend would not argue that line at all. They believe in wealth, whether earned or inherited. Some of them also have it. Others hope for or dream about it. What they object to in my friend's friend is the way that his wealth fits into, or doesn't fit into, his life as a whole. Or, put differently, how his extremely fortunate circumstances seem to inspire in him no moral or social response other than just holding onto what he has. No sense of good fortune. No sense of generosity. No sense of community obligation. Of course, it can always be charged that such objections are no more than disguised expressions of resentment, but what is so striking is not that so much more is expected of him, rather that so much less is forthcoming. The robber barons of yesteryear may have been ruthless in the boardroom, but they prided themselves on their philanthropy; indeed they justified their good fortune and wealth on the basis of it. The Bourbon kings and the great aristocrats of prerevolutionary France, the Medicis of Florence, and the great feudal lords were not just being presumptuous when they attributed their wealth and power to God; they were recognizing the need for gratitude and the very real social obligations that such wealth placed upon them. Plato and Aristotle too were addressing the sons of the very rich. They did not preach against wealth but presumed it as a precondition of the good life. But the very essence of the good life was to use such prestige, power, status and wealth to free oneself from financial worry so that one could turn one's attention to the higher things in life—art, religion, philosophy, politics and justice—not out of ambition or for the sake of achievement, but as community awareness and service. That is what's missing from my friend's friend's vision of life. It isn't a rich life at all; it is merely the life of the rich.

To defend justice by attacking wealth, however, is to abandon the case for justice from the outset. The mistake is to confuse our keen sense of injustice at the gross disparity between the very rich and the very poor with an otherworldly ideal of justice which requires that there be no inequality at all and that people have at most modest material concerns. But this is not our world, and the fact is that we are a materialistic society—whatever else we may be, a consumer society in which status depends at least in part on what one has and what one earns, in which a color television set is considered one of life's necessities, not a mere comfort or a luxury. What is wrong is not our obsession with material goods and comforts but the moral perspective within which we enjoy them. Along with wealth and affluence come obligations and responsibilities (and anyone who can afford to buy this book is, in global terms, wealthy). But it will not do to insist on a sense of justice that requires us to give up the good life just to fulfill the impossible dreams of a few philosophers. It is Socrates' provocative questions and his cleverness that impress us, not his poverty. Indeed, not only Aristotle but even Kant argued that poverty makes a man mean, while wealth makes possible generosity and justice. Our own well-being is (quite reasonably) the premise of any sense of justice we may have. To attack American life as such, to campaign against wealth and consumerism and business as such, is often to betray not so much a sense of justice as the motives of envy and resentment— envy of those who have more and resentment of those who are happy with what they have.

The attack on material success, we might add, is as old as America, as old as Christianity, as old as philosophy and the concept of justice. In fact, it is probably as old as wealth itself, dating back to the first Neanderthal who accumulated more than the usual number of mastodon carcasses. We should not be concerned, therefore, about the sociological messages we are always receiving, about the current epidemic of greed or the predictable reaction against it, about America's unbounded awe of wealth and "the lives of the rich and famous." De Tocqueville commented on the American love of money back in 1835, and John Adams complained about the crass commercialism of New York City back in the 1780s. Thus, when *The New York Times Magazine* announced, back in October of 1986, that we have an "increasing preoccupation with wealth as a measure of achievement," we should not be all that impressed. Robert Samuelson makes the nice point that our current "discovery of money" only makes sense against the background of the rather innocent notions about money nourished by the so-called baby boomers a few years ago.[14] But, as Samuelson points out, to like money or creature comforts does not mean that one has surrendered to "crass materialism," and the "new" emphasis on wealth does not necessitate a shift to conservative politics. Material comfort and success are not irrelevant to justice, but neither are they in themselves proof of one's righteousness, exemptions from the usual demands for community involvement and humanitarian concern. Our consumer society does not eclipse but rather reorients and ought to accentuate our sense of justice.

A sense of justice is one of concern, not self-sacrifice or self-imposed poverty, and the problem is not so much that whatever one does it will only be a drop in the bucket but rather that one decides to do nothing, except perhaps to soothe one's conscience. Indeed, the wealth of rationalizations that we employ in order to avoid thinking or doing anything about justice while we ourselves are in such a privileged position is what we find so offensive. For most of us, the inequities and inequalities of wealth and freedom are not as objectionable as the cavalier, uncaring, and insensitive attitudes towards the poor and the desperate and the needy on the part of those who have so much. Justice must be considered part of the good life, which for us is largely a life of consumption and material success, and it should not be presented as an alternative or an obstacle to the good life. In this light, we should be very suspicious of those theories of justice that tend to harp on the evils of wealth and capitalism as well as those that bang again and again on the sonorous gong of "rights"—not in order to promote but rather to block any effective sense of justice and concern for those who are much worse off than we are.

WHO IS JUST? (HEROES, SAINTS, AND SINNERS)

As my grandfather taught, it is not necessary for everyone to sacrifice our lives for others. We [just] need to take a little time from our lives to help.

ARUN GANDHI, QUOTED IN THE MARCH 4, 1989, ISSUE OF NEWSWEEK

PLATO DREW A PROTRACTED analogy between the just society and the just individual, noting that each depended upon the "harmony" of its parts and insisting that neither was possible without the other. But what Plato meant by *justice* (*dikaiosyne*) was not at all the abstract rules and policies that so obsess us. Justice was nothing less than "the good life," the way for us all to live well together. Plato's teacher and hero Socrates was the model and not merely a theoretician of the good life. Condemned to death for "corrupting the minds of the youth," he allowed himself to be executed rather than, as he put it, "corrupt his soul" for the sake of a few more years of life. But I don't want to give the impression that living for justice means sacrificing oneself and dying for justice either. Socrates, who died at seventy-one, was no ascetic and no martyr. He lived notoriously well, fully indulging in the good things in life. In the last twenty-four hundred years, we've somehow gotten the idea that, insofar as any one of us might be called to stand up for justice, it is inevitably a position of martyrdom or, at the very least, extreme self-deprivation and sacrifice. So the choice becomes, saint or sinner, champion of justice or selfish slob. Plato turned Socrates into a saint, and so we too tend to think of acts of justice as rare and spectacular, appropriate only to saints and heroes and not at all a part of our everyday lives.

Buy why? Why don't we have even a vocabulary of goodness, honor, and virtue for ordinary life? The reason is that we tend to think of a person who represents justice only in terms of some special role (as judge or administrator, for example). We do not think of justice as a virtue we all share, a virtue that is not only part and parcel of but more or less coextensive with a full life. Indeed, some of our best philosophers have argued that the ancient ideal of the *just person* is a kind of category mistake, that *justice* applies only to institutions, not to individuals.[15] Justice has been separated from personal character and turned into a special skill, a political and not a personal concern. As a result we don't even have a proper way of talking about it as a personal virtue, and the cry for justice becomes instead an appeal to the heavens or the powers that be, often a plea for a bigger government.

If justice is an ordinary virtue, then we should understand it as an ordinary human configuration of feelings and thoughts, not in terms of the purified ideals of sainthood. Saints are rare birds, and I confess to being suspicious of those periods long ago that we now seem to think were full of them. There may be a few living saints—Mother Theresa comes first to mind—but that is not the ideal that I am concerned with in this book. I am concerned with the ordinary business-person, the average husband and wife, the regular college student, even the routine bureaucrat—but as a person and not as a functionary. I am interested in the nature of the good life, not the spectacularly extraordinary life. I'm not interested in the hero but rather in what Montaigne called "the hero of everyday life." (The former tends to look too much like Rambo these days). The problem with sainthood is that it is so often used not as an ideal to emulate but rather as a lesson in how morally corrupt we are by comparison. Saints are supposed to represent our own everyday ideals in purified form, but there is a very real question whether one can possibly have such purification, that is, have the virtues without the vices, have such "nice" emotions as love and compassion without the "nasty" emotions, like jealousy and resentment.

Philosophers these days don't talk much about sainthood, but they do talk in much the same way about the philosophical virtues of objectivity and detachment, and in a dozen different ways they celebrate that hypothetical character once called "the ideal observer"—detached, dispassionate, with all of the right attitudes (like sympathy and compassion) and none of the wrong ones (like envy and greed). But one should ask whether one can be ideal and still be human, or even still understand the human. Against all of our idealized conceptions of justice, I want to argue that justice requires (and does not just tolerate or try to get around) the nastier passions, such unflattering emotions as envy, jealousy, resentment, and vengefulness. And against our idealization of saints and heroes, I want to argue that justice is up to all of us. Whether or not there are perfect people, and whether or not a perfect world would allow or require us all to be perfect, we live in an imperfect world and we are surrounded by injustices that we can correct, sometimes even easily.

A PASSION FOR JUSTICE: AN EDIFYING DISCOURSE

For this command which I am enjoining upon you today is not too difficult for you; neither is it far off. It is not in heaven, that you should say, "who will go up for us to heaven and bring it down to make us hear it, so we may do it?" . . . No, the word is very near you in your life and in your heart in order that you may do it.   DEUTERONOMY 30:11–14

JUSTICE IS A TOPIC that has been studied by some of the best minds of our times. The positions have been drawn, defined, refined, and redefined again. The qualifications have been qualified, the objections answered and answered again with more objections, and the ramifications further ramified and embellished. But the hope for a single, neutral, rational position has been thwarted every time. The attempt itself betrays incommensurable ideologies and unexamined subjective preferences, and, contrary to Proudhon we get no universal, strong, and complete system of justice. On the contrary, as the various theories become more sophisticated and more tightly defined, the argument becomes a professional obsession and the gap between the professional speculations about justice and the ordinary intelligent citizen's ideas and feelings about justice gets wider and wider. What I want to do here, accordingly, is to approach justice from the street level, so to speak, postponing those high-level policy questions and those complex questions about methodology to turn instead to the personal feelings that make us creatures who care about justice. My aim, in other words, is to assure that the cynical phrase *bleeding heart* will never again be an effective put-down but rather, as it should be, a symptom of virtue.

My thesis in this book is that these feelings are essentially social. They are both natural in origin and cultivated and developed in society. People are not essentially selfish but, of course, we can cultivate (and we have cultivated) attitudes and ideologies that make us overly self-interested and, paradoxically, endanger our larger self-interests. Going one step further, we can too easily imagine an Ik-like existence,[16] a culture in which the sentiments of compassion and fairness,

and even such feelings as envy and jealousy, serve no perceivable purpose. But it turns out that even the notorious Ik aren't really like
this—they wouldn't have survived as a people if they were. Contrary
to the host of social critics who insist that in contemporary America
society is already like this—that compassion is already eclipsed by nar-
cissism and everyone looks out for number one—I want to argue that
few societies have ever been so alive with a concrete sense of justice.
Where we go wrong is in our penchant for abstraction, our rationalizations in the name of "reason" and our love of leaping from the
particular context, in which our sense of justice is keen and healthy,
to what the French postmodernist Lyotard calls "totalizations"—
empty but dangerous generalizations about "communism" and "national security." My argument is that we should be suspicious of these
grand generalizations and theories and think of justice as a personal
virtue, an open and receptive but (com)passionate mind toward the
world. In fact, the pluralism and unprecedented international awareness of our own society makes us particularly keen to understand the
legitimacy of differences and ready to share with other societies. Our
unique sense of power and affluence, even as it encourages arrogance,
also provokes in us a deep sense of concern (underscored by guilt) for
the millions of people in the world who are much worse off than we
are.

This book is, first and foremost, an attempt to be edifying. It is a
plea for the passions and, in particular, for compassion, but without
turning this virtue into something unreasonable, something benign
but silly, a fragrant whiff of benevolence that has virtually nothing
to do with the world and all but ignores the darker facets of our
contemporary character. I like to think that this book is about the
moral strength that has made this country flourish, but it would be
dishonest not to sound a warning as well. Let's remind ourselves that
a *free country*, like the *free market*, is an experiment, and that there is
very little in the history books to give us any assurance about the
long-term feasibility of such experiments. If our remarkable freedom
and prosperity are not accompanied by a sense—no, a passion—for
justice, then it must be said that the fate of our society is in doubt.
It is true that many (by no means all) other cultures envy our prosperity and our inventiveness, and that few people on earth will shy away

from making a buck when they can, as the advocates of universal commercialism keep telling us. But if our political promises are perceived as sheer self-serving hypocrisy—if our talk about "human rights" turns out to be just another facade for our financial interests—if our domestic efforts at justice continue to display to the world a society in which twenty percent of its children live in poverty and a million adults live in the streets—then it is not at all clear that we have anything to teach the world. We are then just one more society with an unfair proportion of the world's goods without deserving them according to the only measure that is relevant, that of justice. There is the very real danger that while our leaders base our security on multibillion dollar military gadgets and insist on the need for a minute of silent prayer in the schools, our reputation for indifference if not injustice spreads like tomorrow morning's news across the world. The word is out that Americans care about very little besides their own material interests and their collective "national security." If we can't develop a national and personal character that conforms to our best rhetoric—if we are not the model for humanity that we claim to be but just a lucky bunch of rich people, like those ancient dynasties and ambitious warlords who enjoyed their undeserved rewards as if they were entitled to them by God—then we too will soon find that neither the earth nor the heavens will any longer support our uncaring arrogance.

My activist friends will no doubt complain that I do not actually tell people what to do in this book, and radicals will complain that I simply accept our status quo without advocating its overthrow. Conservatives will no doubt complain that I am far too liberal, and liberals will argue that I have given far too much away to the conservatives. But choosing between ideologies is not my worry here, and advocating some bold, grand scheme of action would once again turn the pursuit of justice into a specialized career instead of a personal concern that everyone ought to have and practice in their everyday lives. It is just that gap between the personal and the impersonal that I wish to fill here. My argument is that if justice isn't personally felt, then there can be no justice at all.

A SENSE OF JUSTICE: FEELINGS AND THEORIES

"No man is devoid of a heart sensitive to the sufferings of others. . . . Whoever is devoid of the heart of compassion is not human, whoever is devoid of the heart of shame is not human, whoever is devoid of the heart of courtesy and modesty is not human, and whoever is devoid of the heart of right and wrong is not human.   MENCIUS

JUSTICE, I WILL ARGUE, consists first of all of a constellation of feelings, which alone can provide the psychological soil in which our grand theories can take root. But it should be obvious that there are several quite different and often conflicting feelings involved in our sense of justice—a sense of pity and compassion for those in dire need, a sense of righteous indignation when one's hard-earned property is taken away, just to name two. It should also be evident that these very different feelings can come into conflict, notably when the government taxes away your hard-earned income to help those who are in need. Which feelings should take priority, your compassion or your indignation? Of course, part of the question is whether you think that the government has the right to take away your hard-earned income or that you should be left to your own sense of charity to give what you like to the poor. But how one answers this political question already depends on the legitimacy and relative strength of one's feelings. Is there a right way to feel? How do we solve such conflicts? Is there no solution, just the clash of personalities? Or can a solution be found in the cultivation of shared emotions, providing a general agreement not by way of a "social contract" or a set of arguments and beliefs but by way of a shared sense of what's right and proper, a shared sense of justice?

This is not, of course, the usual suggestion. Emotions are taken as nonnegotiable and undependable, and it is taken as obvious that personal feelings, often short-sighted and frequently self-centered, will not produce social harmony. And so what we seek with some desperation in this pluralistic and violent world, is an "objective" sense of justice that extends beyond our limited horizons and embraces everyone. It is not enough to follow our feelings, no matter how honorable or intense; we need some sort of guidance. It is not enough just to "tend one's garden" and be a 'decent' person; we live together and share a world that is already too small to have gardens for all. It is not enough to do no wrong. We need a larger perspective, a picture of how we each fit into the world and how we should live in it with others. Philosophy should not just calculate; it should expand our horizons, enrich our emotions, tell us stories, make us movies, educate us, and move us. It is the emotions and not just reason that provide us with this larger perspective.

In response to this need for perspective, social thinkers and political philosophers since Plato have devised one theory of justice after another in their efforts to transcend the merely personal and impose an objective, invariant, and universal conception on all of us— whether in the name of God, or reason, or nature, or simple fairness. The nobility of the intent is undeniable, but our grasp falls far short. We want to transcend ourselves and the luxuries and frustrations of our own little world, but it is the philosopher's mistake to leave all feeling behind.

The problem with this lofty theoretical approach is that it seems to descend upon us from nowhere, and consequently it tends to ignore the very human emotional foundations of justice and to neglect those passions in us which make justice both necessary and possible. As in so much philosophical thinking, the leap is from strictly personal and subjective feelings to universal, utterly impersonal, "objective" principles. What gets left out are all of those intermediate levels of living, defined by affection and affiliation but by no means merely personal or subjective: families, communities, even whole nation-states. Justice is not, first of all, a set of principles or policies; it is first of all a way of participating in the world, a way of being with other people, a set of feelings of affection and affiliations that link us—not through "reason"—with other people. Without the cultivation of these feelings—and some of them are by no means attractive—the principles of justice are nothing but abstract ideals, and the policies that would make us just, however justified, seem overambitious and even irrelevant, but in any case unsuited for application in "the real world," people being—as cynics and skeptics of all varieties so readily remind us—"the way they are."

But how are we? The reigning assumption, at least since Thomas Hobbes's classic characterization of human life in the "state of nature" as "solitary, poor, nasty, brutish, and short" is that we all basically fend for ourselves, perhaps with an occasional streak or whim of benevolence. If we are caring or generous at all, it is only for those closest to us. Toward strangers and foreigners we feel only defensive malevolence, and so we need something else, some authority that will force us to cooperate, or at least keep us from murdering one another. Society is thus formed out of prudence, by way of a "contract" agreed upon by all. Society is a voluntary association of individuals who in their natural state would be more likely to kill one another than cooperate with each other. Theories of justice, accordingly, are cooperative plans that appeal to our self-interest in order to give us reason to help one another and support public institutions, even if (on the short view) doing so runs counter to our own interests.

Throughout this book, I will have much to say about this hardly flattering model of "natural" humanity and the formation of society by way of a mutually agreed-upon contract. It is this model, in its many variations, that forms the foundation for just about every theory of justice now in the books or on the drawing boards. For now, however, I just want to point out the viciousness of the dichotomy it presumes—our natural inclinations (most of them selfish) on the one side, our social and contractual obligations and expectations on the other. It is, to begin with, a dubious distinction—between inclinations and obligations, between our natural existence and our social existence, between the natural disposition of our feelings and the rationality that allows us to form society and then live in it. But it is a vicious dichotomy, emotion versus reason, and these two classic metaphors—the "state of nature" and "the social contract"—have a dangerous appeal for us. They make us distance ourselves from our emotions (falsely conceived of as "natural" and presocial) and encourage us to entertain the appealing fiction that we live in society by voluntary choice rather than just because we happened to be born and raised here. The metaphors suggest a convenient way of defusing unwanted obligations not of our own choosing and defending the most unreasonable expectations as "rights." They provide a flattering way of fooling ourselves into thinking that we are above nature and smarter than our emotions, rational creatures who have taken our existence—and especially our social existence—into our own hands. In these two metaphors we can already appreciate the considerable myth-making power of philosophical theories of justice, no matter how precise and putatively hard-headed their formulation. Theories of justice can serve as articulate and systematic expressions of our emotions, but they can also serve as rationalizations, as obfuscations, as obstacles to our emotions. That is why it is important to look at our emotions and that too easily dismissed gut level sense of justice and cast a suspicious eye not just on this or that theory of justice but on the very idea of a theory of justice. The emotions are not just evidence or "intuitions" that will (or won't) support one or another theory of justice; they are the very substance of our sense of justice.

The argument of this book is that justice is a passion to be cultivated, not an abstract set of principles to be formulated, mastered, and imposed upon society (with or without our acknowledgement of their rationality). Justice begins not with Socratic insights but with the promptings of some basic emotions, among them envy, jealousy, and resentment, a sense of being personally cheated or neglected, and the desire to get even—but also, of course, those basic feelings of sharing, compassion, sympathy, and generosity that cynics have forever refused to acknowledge. Whatever one's principles of justice, they are utterly meaningless without that fundamental human sense of caring and the ability to understand and personally care about the well-being of other human beings and other creatures who may be very far away and personally quite unknown to us. Aristotle and others have argued that justice takes over where friendship and family end on the grounds that one doesn't need a sense of justice where one has love; but it is just as true that a sense of justice would be impossible for a person who was incapable of love.

So much emphasis has been placed on the nature of justice in states and institutions that it has all but been denied in more intimate circumstances, in families and relationships, for example. John Rawls excludes justice from family relationships, and Robert Nozick parenthetically comments that any such concerns would be intolerably intrusive.[1] But what sort of concern should dictate the distribution of family resources (including love and attention) if not justice? Why should justice be only—or even primarily—a feature of states, governments and institutions? Indeed, shouldn't the family serve as an ideal model for justice (as it did, for example, with Rousseau, who never had one)? Against the usual (and now institutionalized) practice of talking only about policy and institutions, I shall be moving back and forth between interpersonal relationships, families, communities, and the larger society and humanity. After all, what is more essential to our ultimate sense of justice than the metaphor of fraternity, of brotherhood and sisterhood? (And is it just a metaphor?)

One of the more controversial aspects of my argument is the idea that "negative" emotions such as vengefulness, outrage, and resentment have an essential place in the cultivation of justice. Their role has often been denied or neglected. The idea that justice requires emotional detachment, a kind of purity suited ultimately only to angels, ideal observers, and the original founders of society has blinded us to the fact that justice arises from and requires such feelings as resentment, jealousy, and envy as well as empathy and compassion. It has often been said (by Konrad Lorenz, for example) that there can be no love without aggression, and so too there can be no justice without a keen sense of injustice, and injustice done to oneself in particular. So, then, the "negative" emotions may not be so negative at all. Isn't hating evil, for instance, in fact rather one of the most positive emotions, as Shula Sommers often argued?[2] And isn't reacting "negatively" to personal violation essential to our very sense of ourselves, and as such a virtue rather than a vice? Righteous indignation is an emotion appropriate even to saints, and jealousy, no matter how painful, is the emotional price of possession. It has been argued that envy is itself an important emotion, propping up capitalism and the consumer society by encouraging us to want more and be competitive.[3] It is widely known that Friedrich Nietzsche argued at length that resentment is the main ingredient in much of what we call morality. The argument that I want to pursue here is that our sense of justice cannot ignore and to some extent even develops out of these rather vile emotions. This is not to deny that justice requires and presupposes compassion, respect, and a sense of duty as well, but these too cannot be understood in terms of abstract rational principles. They are, as Adam Smith and others recognized, "moral sentiments," whose origin ("natural" or not) must be located in the individual human soul, and it is from these sentiments, not from reason alone, that our sense of justice develops.

THE FEELINGS OF JUSTICE AND THE SENSE OF ONESELF

Any doctrine that eliminates or even obscures the function of choice of values and enlistment of desire and emotions in behalf of those chosen weakens personal responsibility for judgment and for action.   JOHN DEWEY, COMMENTARY, JULY, 1946

TO SAY THAT JUSTICE is a personal virtue rather than an abstract policy or theory is to say that justice is first of all a sense of one's self, a sense of one's place in the world, and especially in the social world. But we fragment the self into pockets or "faculties"— emotion and reason. We split ourselves into mind and body (and then wonder why it is so hard to fit the emotions in). We falsely distinguish our motives in life as "selfish" or "altruistic" or "rational" and we use our various roles in life (e.g., "private" and "public" or "professional") and dozens or hundreds of other categories to chop ourselves into little pieces and confuse ourselves. But though the self may have many features (and, in rare cases, several personalities) it is not a conglomerate of incompatible parts, and justice is not just a virtue of just one supposed part of the soul—that is, having the right *beliefs*. When I insist that our sense of justice must first of all consist in feelings, therefore, I am not arguing for the revolt of emotion or the ascendancy of passion over reason. I am only arguing that such feelings as compassion, indignation, pity, gratitude, guilt, resentment, envy, and even spite have an essential role in an understanding of justice. No matter what thoughts or theories one may hold, if one is not moved by emotion there is no role for justice to play. No matter what brilliant and persuasive theory of justice one may have worked out, if it is not motivated by passion it is not an expression of justice, but at most perhaps a manifestation of managerial efficiency and insight.

Plato and Aristotle, because they recognized that the sense of justice must be wholly integrated with one's sense of the good life, insisted that justice is a product, at least in part, of the passions. One could not possibly be considered a good man, much less a happy man, unless he acted not against his feelings but in harmony with them. This holistic view of the self will be central to the account defended here as well, however opposed it may be to the frequently dualistic and combative accounts of the moral self we find in more modern theories. Plato and Aristotle knew, and I want to insist that the most important element in moral education is not the teaching of moralistic bromides and abstract commandments but the cultivation of the emotions. Human beings are not naturally selfish (neither are most animals), and though we are born sociable, the shape of our social sentiments is the product of the society (and more immediately, the family) we grow up in. So too, we might add, Christian authors from Anselm and Abelard to Kierkegaard and Barth insisted that their religion could not possibly be understood merely as a matter of ritual and belief but rather should be understood as *faith*, that is, feeling and not mere routines and rationalizations. But somewhere along the line we got sidetracked and began overemphasizing performance and the merely cognitive while neglecting or dismissing the affective and the emotional. Indeed, the concept of justice itself became corrupted and identified merely with policies and beliefs, cut off from its roots in the social psyche and the passions that make us human. There are books and articles by the thousands on the theory of justice but only an occasional note on the importance of the passion for justice. So that is what I want to talk about here.

In one sense, it is ironic that our concern for justice should now be so cerebral, so impersonal and theoretical, for if there has been any single major transformation in our conception of ourselves since the days of the ancient Greeks it is the much-celebrated turn to the subjective, the personal, the individual. Indeed, our current way of thinking about ourselves and our minds only dates back to the seventeenth century, at most, with Descartes's dramatic subjective turn to the *cogito* and Bacon and Locke's radical empiricism. Plato and Aristotle and the early Christians may have stressed the importance of the passions in justice while we do not, but it is only in the past two centuries that we, in other matters, have put so much emphasis on the "inner" emotional life of the individual, holding that it is what a person feels, not actions or thoughts, that is the single most important facet of his or her character. What has come about in the past two centuries or so is the dramatic rise of what Robert Stone has called "affective individualism," this new celebration of the passions and other feelings of the autonomous individual. Yet, ironically, it is an attitude that has become even further removed from our sense of justice during that same period of time. We seem to have more inner feelings and pay more attention to them, but we seem to have fewer feelings about others and the state of the world and pay less attention to them. And so we get this wrong-headed idea that feelings as such are generally selfish while reason and reason alone can account for and promote a sense of justice. Philosophers like Hume and Rousseau emphasized the importance of the passion for justice back in the eighteenth century, but the subsequent history of the subject has seen such references almost all but ignored, and even Hume and Rousseau are reinterpreted along more legalistic lines by philosophers who claim them as predecessors but in fact seem to be opposed to their most fundamental insights.

The explanation for this shift goes far beyond philosophical considerations, of course, to the bourgeois attack on decadent aristocratic sentimentality and dangerous sansculotte mob passions, to the almost paranoid psychological visions of Freud and many of his followers and a renewed distrust of emotion and sentiment in general. So, too, one should look at the distinctively modern emphasis on legality as such, with its curious notions that the law actually determines (or at any rate is the primary means of enforcing) morality. But philosophers have certainly had much to do with this shift as well, and one cannot even begin to understand the current debates in social and political thought without some fundamental appreciation both of the principles propounded by Immanuel Kant in opposition to the passions and all other "inclinations" and also of the scientific approach to ethics of the various utilitarians, who may have respected the emotions as causes for happiness and unhappiness but gave them no credence whatsoever as measures of utility or justice. Then, too, there was the rich literature on the abstract nature of human and civil rights that flourished, not coincidentally, about the time of the American and French revolutions. These abstract principles were powerful intellectual weapons, and they became powerful defenses too against the ambitions of particular men or groups in increasingly complex societies. But the language of "rights" was not conducive to appreciation of the passions (except insofar as these were symptoms or signals of the violation of rights), and the personal sense of justice was again taken over by the legal apparatus and delegated to governments and institutions (whose purpose was now redefined as the protection of individual rights).

I do not want to argue against that legalistic and principled tradition but rather to insist that by itself it is ethically vacuous. The law is essential, of course, but it is time that we looked with a bit of suspicion at our Founding Fathers' central article of faith, that ours should be a society governed by "laws, not men." The law is, as its worst as well as its best, the expression of the beliefs and passions of people. As Hegel argued so convincingly (if obscurely) a century and a half ago, social morality and justice first of all need some substance or content as well as a legal form, and this content must be found in our originally inarticulate, unreasoned existence as essentially social and emotional beings. But we have neglected our emotions, and our overly legalistic and overly principled sense of justice has consequently lost sight of its underlying source. This is not to say that having the right feelings alone makes one a just person, but feelings lead not only to action but to thought, and any emotion worthy of the name demands both expression in action and articulation. The passion for justice is not just an aimless, unintelligent fulmination of feeling; it is nothing less than an intelligent, sensitive, compassionate, and personally engaged view of the world. The divorce of justice from benevolence, of ethics from emotion, of reason from passion, is one of the great philosophical tragedies of modern times.

In this book I want to say something about how this passion for justice is cultivated, to reintroduce these lost but still essential ingredients in justice and defend a holistic sense of the self and society in which the passions play a central role. I want to mend the split between the now antagonistic Platonic parts of the soul and reintegrate our thoughts and our feelings about justice. It will be objected, no doubt, that I am thereby attacking the very meaning of the word, "justice," which—whatever it may have meant (in Greek) for Plato and Aristotle, means something quite different now. Justice is now opposed to compassion and benevolence, but I want to argue that they can and they must be put back together, for justice is the expression of these (and other) sentiments and it is a mistake to pull them apart. But today, in so much of social and political theory, all questions become questions of rationality alone. I recently sat in bewildered fascination listening to a conversation between some of our brightest political theorists who were arguing, without any sense of absurdity or embarrassment, about whether it was rational to vote in the recent presidential election. The question wasn't whether one approved of the candidates on the ballot or whether one would be protesting by not voting. It was rather whether (according to "rational choice theory") the effort of casting a vote would be worth the trouble, given the millions of other people also voting, the traffic on the way to the polls, and so forth. When citizenship becomes a matter for rational deliberation rather than spontaneous participation in one's own political process, something has gone very wrong indeed.

THE PROBLEM OF VENGEANCE AND THE NEGATIVE EMOTIONS

As for the thief, both male and female, cut off their hands. It is the reward for their own deeds, an exemplary punishment from Allah.   THE KORAN

PERHAPS NOWHERE IS THIS odd phenomenon of our deny-
ing what is most human about us (that is, our personal passions) more
apparent than in the various debates and concerns that surround the
problems of punishment in criminal justice. The ongoing dispute between the "utilitarians" (who believe in a "deterrence" theory of punishment) and the "retributivists" (who believe that punishment is
necessary in order to satisfy the demands of justice as such) not only
neglects but explicitly dismisses any mention of the passion which
alone would seem to give some fuel to the notion of punishment,
namely *vengeance*. This is not to say that punishment should serve
only to revenge, but it is to say that punishment is in part the satisfaction of the need for vengeance and makes no sense without this com-
ponent. Several years ago, Susan Jacoby argued (in a book entitled
Wild Justice) that our denial of the desire for vengeance is analogous
to the Victorian denial of sexual desire, and that we are paying a
similar psychological price for it.[4] I would not go quite so far but I
would say that our current disputes and theories about punishment
are emotionally banal (for all the heat that gets generated) and naive
about the nature of vengeance.[5]

There are few motives so readily understandable as the motive of
vengeance. This is not to say, of course, that this motive is therefore
legitimate or the action of revenge always justified. But to seek vengeance for a grievous wrong, to revenge oneself against evil: that seems
to lie at the very foundation of our sense of justice, indeed, at the
heart of our sense of ourselves, our dignity and our sense of right and
wrong. We may not be like those ancient Greek warriors for whom
the sense of personal honor was everything, but neither are we mere
observers or victims of the moral life. The desire for vengeance seems
to be an integral aspect of our engagement in life and, more morally,
in our recognition of evil. Vengeance is the "undoing" of evil, "getting
even" for wrong. Vengeance is an inescapable part of our psychology,
perhaps it is even an instinct. It forms the foundation of Old Testament justice in the measured guise of the *lex talionis*, "an eye for an
eye, a tooth for a tooth." And the New Testament does not reject
vengeance; it only transfers it to God. Retribution is the point (even
if it is not the only purpose) of punishment. Indeed, a punishment

would not be punishment if retribution were no part of it, and the desire for retribution is the desire for vengeance.[6]

What is vengeance? It is not just punishment, no matter how harsh. It presupposes personal, emotional intensity, not just an abstract sense of obligation or rationality. Yet, it is not just aggression and self-assertion either but, in a deep philosophical sense, getting even, putting the world back in balance, supplying the retribution or retaliation that will put things right and pay back the offender. It is not first of all a thought, much less a theory, but rather a feeling, a primal sense of the moral self and its boundaries. By denying the reality or the legitimacy of vengeance we deny this sense of the moral self and moralize away those boundaries of the self without which it makes no sense to talk about dignity or integrity. But these boundaries do not define just the individual. To the contrary, they for the most part enclose one's family and friends and the world that one cares about. Not to feel vengeance may therefore be not a sign of virtue but a symptom of callousness and withdrawal, a diminished sense of self and an amoral "not my problem" attitude to the world.

Of course, there is a danger. Violence, even when justified, leads to more violence; one act of revenge results in another offense to be righted. And when the act is perpetrated not against the same person who did the offense but another who is related to him—part of the same family, tribe, or social group (as in a vendetta)—the possibilities for escalation are endless. In Sardinia, according to an ancient code of vengeance (*Su sambene no est abba*, "Blood is not water"), family feuds can last for centuries without recourse to any "third party," such as the state. "An action is offensive when the event from which depends the existence of such offense is foreseen in order to damage dignity and honor."[7] In New Guinea, according to Buck Shiefflin, an anthropologist who has worked there, every death used to be attributed to some enemy from another family, who was then accused of witchcraft (now banned by law) and peremptorily clubbed to death.[8] Again, the feuding could go on for generations. Accordingly, we can readily appreciate the need to limit or eliminate the escalation of revenge through institutionalization, but if punishment no longer satisfies vengeance, if it ignores the emotional needs of the victims of crime, then punishment no longer serves its primary purpose, even when it succeeds in rehabilitating the criminal and deterring other crime, which, in general, it evidently does not.[9] The restriction of vengeance by law is entirely understandable, but the wholesale denial of vengeance as a legitimate motive may be a cultural and psychological disaster. If we suppress vengeance in favor of acquiescence to the legal system, is it not possible that we will thereby suppress our sense of care and compassion too?

In the current state of the discussion, with so much of the emphasis on justice shifted to questions of distributive justice, what are we to make of such "uncivilized" emotions as vengefulness in the overall scheme of justice? Socrates and Plato rejected vengeance as just another instance of doing harm, and so, they concluded, it is always wrong. But do we—can we—accept this suggestion, and deny what is surely (if our movies and literature are any indication) one of the most powerful sensibilities we possess? And if justice omits all mention of vengeance, how many other passions will be eliminated as well? Can one have a sense of justice without the capacity and willingness to be personally outraged? Can one fight evil without being motivated by hatred? Can one care without being protective? Can we, then, really understand distributive justice without some appreciation of envy, jealousy, and resentment? Indeed, would there be any call for redistribution of goods (beyond basic, vital needs) if no one envied the rich, or felt cheated by life and resentful? Would there be any problem in the idea of redistribution if no one felt possessive or a sense of ownership? (What would "distribution" mean?) Of course, the questions that we have just raised about vengeance and the negative emotions apply just as well to such generous emotions as compassion, pity, and even love. Would we care about justice if we didn't care about people (and other living things)? And (to complete the circle) don't we feel vengeful just because we care about ourselves and our self-esteem, about others and about that delicate balance in our lives that is so easily shattered by offenses (casual or malicious) and losses that can or should be blamed on others?

Vengeance may be primitive, but it is still the conceptual core of justice. A sense of justice requires engagement, not detachment. It requires a keen sense of what it is to be offended, not just an abstract sense of fairness. It involves that basic sense of protective selfhood (again, including one's family and tribe as part of the self) and the felt need to retaliate (by getting even or evening the score) that marks our place in the social universe. Without these feelings, without the capacity to be offended or outraged, would most of us have any sense at all of dignity, of morality? To be sure, there may be a few of us sufficiently saintly, sufficiently sure of themselves or on top of things, to practice only mercy and forgiveness and not feel hatred, resentment, or vengeance; and we must all transcend our sense of personal place in order to apprehend and appreciate other people and their flaws and vulnerabilities. It is therefore necessary to expand and modify our sense of justice so that it is more aware of the general dangers, the cost, and ultimately the fairness of revenge. But a system of legal principles that does not take such passions into account is not—whatever else it may be—a system of justice. Moreover, any theory of retribution based only on "reason" (for example, that of Immanuel Kant)[10] or on deterrence or compensation isn't a theory of punishment, whatever else it may be. Brilliant theories for making society more efficient and egalitarian and eliminating conflict and crime are certainly desirable but nevertheless are not theories of justice. Justice presupposes caring and concern and consequently indignation and revenge, personal relationships and not a merely rational relationship with the law.

What I have just suggested with regard to vengeance is even more true with reference to such hostile emotions as moral indignation and outrage. It is all well and good to argue that morality consists of a rational willingness to obey the moral law, but the truth seems to be that what provokes us (and the defenders of that view) is the sight of someone breaking the law or violating the bounds of justice. Whether or not it is possible to develop a vision of a world in which all is fair, our sense of justice begins and moves through our indignation and outrage at injustice, concerning not just ourselves, of course, but also those close to us and, with cultivation, virtually all of the peoples and creatures of the world. But this is to say that our sense of justice and the "moral sentiments" that make it up cannot be understood just in terms of the benign emotions of sympathy and compassion. We need fire and fuel for our sense of justice as well as warmth, and I want to suggest that the traditional moral sentiment theorists did not have adequate faith in the efficacy of the sentiments, not just the sympathetic sentiments but the antipathetic, hostile passions as well.

EMOTION AND REASON

As if every passion didn't have its own quantum of reason.
NIETZSCHE, *GAY SCIENCE*

THERE IS, NEEDLESS TO say, a thesis about emotions that is embedded in everything I say: Our emotions, or at least some of our emotions, make us human, make life meaningful, make us what we are and can be. What makes justice so special is not the complexity of our theories about it so much as our passionate feelings of concern. Philosophers and psychologists often give the impression that the ideal human life is purely rational, dispassionate, and without a care in the world. But the truth is that our emotions, and care in particular, are not intrusions into but rather the stuff of our lives. Emotions are not as such brute irrational forces; they are often intelligent, sensitive, beneficial, and even wise. This is the mistake of so many traditional theories: they take emotions at their worst and most irrational and reason at its best, usually as a corrective to emotion. But every emotion has its own "quantum of reason," as Nietzsche said, and even vengeance—contrary to its usual depiction as endless and wholly destructive—includes a conception of its own satisfaction and limits. It is true that we may fall in love and care for those who do not deserve our affections, but it does not follow that love and care are themselves irrational. Indeed, without them, what would serve as the basis of any rationality?

Rationality is not opposed to emotions but is rather an intrinsic part of them. Emotions are not opposed to judgment; they invoke and require judgment. Indeed, emotions are judgments, emotional judgments, if you like, but no less judgments and no less dependable for that. We have placed so much emphasis on what is calculative, impersonal, and dispassionate in us that we have lost much of our ability to appreciate the importance of what we generically call "feeling." Or we disparage that essential aspect of our being as a matter of self-indulgence, perhaps just a sense of cheap thrills as in the feelings manufactured in horror films and soap operas, the vicarious emotions enjoyed in fascist cop-killer and slasher movies and thrillers. Our feelings are seen as upsetting intrusions that, in a properly rational life, occasionally serve as recreations. They are incidental to our being, purely secondary to our definitive quality of reason. But now that computers, and even lap-top and hand-held calculators, can do what we so long thought to be uniquely human, it is time to rethink our old notion of ourselves as rational animals. What distinguishes us not just from animals but from machines are our passions, and foremost among them our passion for justice. Justice is, in a word, that set of passions, not mere theories, that bind us and make us part of the social world.

We routinely oppose our emotional reactions to our rational calculations, but the emotions are not essentially irrational. Some are irrational. Some are not. But also, reason (paradoxically) is not as such rational. It sometimes is, but sometimes is not. I confess to a deep distrust of reason. Hermann Kahn's "thinking the unthinkable" gave me the willies long before I was willing to attack the pretense of "rationality" in which it was formulated. More recently, I have seen one of the most brilliant philosophers of our time suggest a defense of the Spanish Inquisition from a utilitarian point of view as if he were weighing the ingredients for a chocolate torte. I am similarly suspicious when Robert Nozick declares, at the beginning of *Anarchy, State and Utopia*, that he was at first reluctant to defend the libertarian view because it seemed "callous towards needs and sufferings of others," but was eventually argued into it. First, he says, he was persuaded to take libertarian arguments seriously, and then he became convinced of them. Finally, he had "grown accustomed to the views and their consequences" although he disliked the company he found himself keeping.[11] I find all of this tremendously upsetting. Given a choice between feelings of repugnance and reluctance and clever, even irrefutable arguments to the contrary, I would hope to have the courage to go with my feelings. And when John Rawls invokes the persuasive notion of "reflective equilibrium"—the idea that we should go back and forth between our feelings ("intuitions") and our theory, adjusting each in the light of the other—I get suspicious, because the feelings all but drop out of the picture, or get regularly chastised (where they disagree with the theory) as irrational. What upsets me is that so many theorists and ideologues, convinced of the rationality of their ideas about justice, manage to ride roughshod over tender feelings of compassion and deride those who take them seriously as "bleeding hearts" and "do-gooders." I suggest that instead we distrust all theories and give some renewed credence to our passions.

If emotion is the protagonist of our account of justice, reason— that is, a particular kind of reasoning—is our antagonist. It is that abuse of our rationality that we call "rationalization," and it gives rise to some of the most sophisticated philosophical and judicial theories as well as the run-of-the-mill excuses for not giving to charity ("It would be a drop in the bucket," "What can I do?", "Life isn't fair," etc.). It is, especially, that obsession with quantification and calcula- tion that gets spelled out in some of the most sophisticated techniques in philosophy, decision theory and the social sciences, all but destroy- ing those disciplines in some instances and rendering them utterly irrelevant in others. Economists (more accurately, econometricists) re- duce consumer spending to a formula and then decry "irregularities in the market" when their calculations run awry. (Does an astronomer cry "irregularities in the heavens" when her calculations don't pan out?) Or else they point to the "irrationality" or "emotionality" of consumers, or work in a margin of error to account for "human fact- ors." Rationality is always right, and if people's emotions get in the way (because they actually *care* about something) then that only shows that emotions—and people—are irrational.

It is not a question of whether people are predictable or not (they are), but rather a matter of an extremely impoverished view of human behavior, which is, from a more personal and unscientific point of view, both falsifying and offensive. Such abstract exercises in rational- ity readily lend themselves to the attack on welfare programs and to the most fraudulent tax schemes ("voodoo economics" and "the trickledown effect"). Conservatives loudly complain about liberals who approach every social problem by throwing money at it, but they rarely say what we are supposed to throw instead. Abstract liberal constructions encourage government policies that are oblivious to real human needs and are responsible too for so much regulation that has no real understanding of the enterprises "regulated." And then, let us not forget how much inhuman cruelty and destruction such theoretical constructions as modern Marxist theory have wreaked on the modern world. To be sure, the abstract promises and appeal of Marxism have given many people hope and the intellectual apparatus to fight against oppression and injustice, but the rigidity of Marxist theory has led to consequences as disastrous as those of any otherworldly religious war. This so-called reason, not as enlightened thinking or an expanded awareness of the world but as a carefully restricted and quantified (rather than qualified) frame for thinking, has proved to be a way of blocking even our most basic emotional reactions to other people. Accordingly, much of what I have to say is going to be critical of abstract belief and, especially, of that encrusted and inflexible form of belief called "ideology." This sort of rationality is not the stuff of which justice is made, but its very antithesis.

Given the controversial and possibly dangerous direction of this argument, however, let me make it very clear that I am not attacking reason, reasoning, and intellect as such. There is an obvious and essential role for logistics and calculation, and no one would argue that an understanding of justice—including its articulation in a theory—is antithetical or antagonistic to a keen personal sense of justice. In larger social and policy matters, such an understanding is, of course, indispensable, and even in the most intimate and purely personal situations, reason has the essential function of promoting mutual appreciation and thus the resolution of conflicts. But whether in policy or in personal matters, reason in justice is never simply a matter of calculation but first of all a matter of sensibility, and we win others over to our point of view not by demonstrating the validity of our computations but by modifying their emotions and with this their understanding of the circumstances. Getting people to the negotiating table is only secondarily a matter of getting them to reason or even to be reasonable. It is, first of all, a matter of getting them to acknowledge or at least face the others' passions and points of view. (This is why the most tragic conflicts, such as those endemic in the Middle East, perpetuate themselves with a refusal to negotiate. It is not just lack of reason that makes such conflicts so intractable.) Reason and emotion together are essential to justice. A good heart alone, even combined with the best intentions, is not enough to make the world a better place to live. Feelings alone are obviously not enough for justice. Without knowledge and wisdom, a passion for justice is an empty passion, at best a kindly gesture toward humanity perhaps but no more.

An adequate sense of justice requires not only concern but also curiosity, a need to know about the state of the world and the plight of people outside of one's own limited domain. It is a familiar practical paradox—the "good" man or woman who is wholly devoted to his or her family and friends but oblivious to the rest of the world. But justice cannot be so limited, and it is against this too-cozy restricted picture of personal goodness that abstractions and theories offer a more global balance. Justice is neither personal in the too-limited sense nor is it abstract in the global sense, but it is rather a process of enlarged awareness that Peter Singer (following Lecky) has called "the expanding circle."[12] The inner rings of the circle consist of our natural feelings for our kin and our closest friends, but as the circle grows it comes to include acquaintances, neighbors, colleagues, countrymen, foreigners, and other species. What allows the circle to grow, according to Singer, is reason, but this is where I want to part company with his argument. Reason adds universal principles to the promptings of our biologically inherited feelings, but the danger is that reason will also leave those feelings behind. I want to argue that what allows the circle to expand is not reason (in the technical sense of calculation on the basis of abstract principles) but rather knowledge and understanding, in the particular sense of coming to appreciate the situations and the circumstances of other people and creatures. There is no line to be drawn between benevolence and justice, no place in our experience where affect and affection leave off and some new faculty called reason kicks in and takes over. Our emotions get more and more expansive and better educated and new perspectives join with the old to enlarge our world and embrace new populations in it.

David Hume, among many others, has argued that there are limits to how far our concern and benevolence toward others can reach, that the problem with any conception of justice based on personal feelings is the "distance" between us. This seems to me to be much overblown. It may be a fact that it is more difficult to feel compassion for a person whom we do not know and will never meet than for someone we know and already care about, but this problem of "distance" is much more often a matter of ignorance or hardheartedness than a function of our feelings. The problem of the homeless in this country, for example, is not one of distance, but the very opposite; it is a problem of proximity. The homeless are not unknown to us. We can and do get a personal picture of them on the streets and on television nightly and through books like Jonathan Kozol's moving *Rachel's Children*.[13] And they are not different but rather frighteningly like us, with much the same backgrounds, with much the same personal histories. They are not just, in some abstract sense, "fellow Americans." They came from similar families, with similar skills, similar aspirations, before a financial catastrophe, or a disastrous divorce, or a bout of mental illness, or skyrocketing rents, or the closing of an industrial plant ended their "normal" lives and dumped them onto the streets. What I want to argue is that our sympathy for them (and, one hopes, the resultant urgency to do something about the problem) is a natural reaction, and that this reaction—not the pursuit of some abstract system or policy (which may and certainly should follow as a means)—constitutes the heart of justice.

It is our hardheartedness, not our compassion, that is unnatural. The sameness of the homeless stirs our sympathies, but it also stimulates our defenses. The homeless man who speaks our language, who may have gone to the same school or, years before, rented an apartment in the same complex, terrifies us. "There but for the grace of God" is not just an abstract phrase of cosmic gratitude but a recognition of the real contingencies that threaten us all. And some of us build a defensive (and willfully uninformed) ideology: "It's their own fault"; "They should get a job" (many of the homeless already have one); "They should get off the bottle" (as if that were the universal explanation for wretchedness, rather than an easily affordable tranquilizer); "They should see somebody about their depression" (as if public mental health were so readily available, and as if being homeless were not itself a more than sufficient cause for depression). Rather than express sympathy for the homeless, we supply a context in which they are failures, or (even better) are on the streets by choice ("a life-style," in one of the more obscene suggestions of the decade). By intentionally misunderstanding and misappropriating the tragedy we may manage to "distance" the problem, but distance itself is not the problem, nor is numbness of feeling. The problem is that we let our beliefs—even our reason—get in the way of our feelings.

THE PATHOLOGY OF BELIEF

His fellow man can be killed with impunity underneath his window. He has merely to place his hands over his ears and argue with himself a little in order to prevent nature, which rebels within him, from identifying him with the man being assassinated. Savage man does not have this admirable talent, and for lack of wisdom and reason he is always seen thoughtlessly giving in to the first sentiment of humanity.
JEAN-JACQUES ROUSSEAU, DISCOURSE ON THE ORIGINS OF INEQUALITY

An intellectual without an ideology is defenseless.
IRVING KRISTOL

IN AN INNOCENT SENSE, of course, beliefs are essential to life, to emotion and to justice; one has to know about the world to live and feel in the world. Justice presupposes not just a good heart but a good amount of intelligence and knowledge, what Lorraine Code has called our "epistemic responsibility."[14] But there is another kind of belief that is not just personal knowledge of the world but a self-righteous, impersonal moral stance toward the world that parades as knowledge and blocks emotion—even as it generates outrage and indignation on its own behalf. This kind of belief—or ideology—is the enemy of justice, and this may have little to do with whether the beliefs in question are conservative, liberal, libertarian, Marxist, or anarchist in orientation. Indeed, I have often thought that one of the curious by-products of the evolution of the huge human cerebellum is our ability to distance ourselves from our lives and our emotions and falsify them in spectacular ways. Philosophy should provide edifi-

cation and concern, but it too often encourages escape through rationalization. Our beliefs should give us orientation and engagement,
not a rejection of life.[15]

A sense of justice requires intelligence as well as sensitivity, but
theories of justice may impose blinders as well as insight and argument. Those blinders are ideologies, which interpret ideas and information that ought to stimulate our concern in ways that turn them
into a righteous condemnation of this or that policy, government, or
system. Of course, justice on a large scale can come about only
through our involvement with policies, governments, and systems,
but to insist on this is not the same thing as saying that everyone
should have an ideology. In his book, *Quandaries and Virtues*, Edmund Pincoffs writes: "I will argue that the structures known as ethical theories are more threats to moral sanity and balance than
instruments for their attainment. . . . They restrict and warp moral
reflection." So too I want to argue that ideologies are not the pathway
to justice but its primary obstacle. Pincoffs adds, "An unjust person
could be an authority on the justice of social practices," and, indeed,
we are well aware that the most articulate ideologues are often those
with the most dangerous ax to grind.[16] The most sophisticated thinking about social policy and justice may be a refusal to feel compassion.
A friend and colleague who served in Cambodia in the sixties, told
me that, under his command, the soldiers who were not college educated, who were not versed in the wiles and ways of "reason," typically remained sensitive to and repelled by the war crimes that had
by then become a daily feature, if not a necessity, of the war. The
college-educated recruits and officers, on the other hand, were able
to rationalize these handily, cutting themselves off quite effectively
not only from guilt and shame but from humanity as such, their own
as well as that of the enemy they were fighting. Reason as rationalization seems inversely proportional to justice. The casual comments
that people make, as a consequence of their ideologies, ought to make
our blood run cold: This one claims that homosexuals and drug-users
deserve to get AIDS, that one insists that the poor and the needy are
just too lazy and too pampered by the government to get a job, this
one maintains that we should not send aid or food to Ethiopia until
they get rid of their Marxist government, that one defends the terror-

ist bombing of a domestic airliner on the grounds that most of the passengers were rich capitalists or that it was necessary for the terrorists to make the world take notice of their claims. Having an ideology does not make people more just, and it very often leads to shocking insensitivity, grotesque opinions, and some very real injustices.

The idea that a concern for justice requires some systematic thinking does not need defense from me. There are no simple solutions to the most glaring problems of justice, from crack-motivated crime in urban American streets to the dire poverty of hundreds of millions under governments sometimes sponsored by us. Hundreds of thousands if not many millions of words have been written demonstrating the complexities of this or that course of political action. What does require determined defense is the importance of the passions in the pursuit of justice, those personal emotions that make a theory of justice something more than just another set of abstract beliefs and arguments. The problem is well illustrated in a parenthetical aside by Robert Nozick, in a discussion of the rights of animals. Arguing against those who insist that animals have no rights, Nozick comments: "Animals count for something. . . . It is difficult to prove this. (It is also difficult to prove that people count for something!)"[17] Difficult indeed! But do people or animals need to be proved to "count for something"? Or is the entire project of philosophy and social theory gone awry when such a demand can even arise? Theory alone, no matter how well articulated, supported, or demonstrated, cannot give us even the beginnings of a sense of justice. We must begin with our emotional awareness that people (and animals) "count for something," before the apparatus of proof and demonstration can even begin. It is that emotional awareness, not the impetus of pure practical reason, that accounts for our sense of justice.

The problem with ideology is not its lack of intellectual rigor or even honesty, in the usual sense of the word. Ideologues are sometimes brilliant, and their passion (rarely acknowledged as such) moves them to provide elaborate detail and documentation. An ideology can be brilliantly developed even though it often lends itself to one-line sloganeering and the vulgar displays of ideological callousness that parade themselves as political opinions in this country. The problem is not that an ideology lacks intellectual rigor or even that it ignores the facts but rather that it blocks our proper emotional response. Ideology blocks compassionate feelings. We are far too used to hearing Marxists and other revolutionaries dismiss so many deaths as necessary or as coincidental to the overthrow of some hateful regime, conservatives who blame the poor for their plight and declare that "they get what they deserve," liberals who are so enamored of a system that they make themselves blind to the sufferings and injustices of people who have to live in it or pay for it.

It is not that ideology has nothing to do with feelings; ideology generates its own feelings, feelings of identification, especially pride, a sense of being in the right, and being threatened personally when one's beliefs are challenged. Indeed, much of the problem is that egos rather than issues are on the line. The last idea I would want to suggest is that feelings and beliefs are antagonistic to one another. Indeed, one might attack my account with a problem: aren't the emotions themselves determined by our beliefs and judgments? Yes, in fact, I would argue that emotions are ultimately a species of judgment. Moreover it is not as if any emotion is as good as any other. Our ethics is in part an ethics of emotion (resentment is nasty, love is beautiful); there are right and wrong emotions, and emotions can be right or wrong depending on the context and the conditions. When people are starving in Africa, jealous pride in the status of one's political beliefs is the wrong emotion. It is in the shadow of such unfeeling opinions and the actions and policies that follow from them that beliefs, especially political beliefs, become more and more suspect. Having the "right" beliefs may make it harder, rather than easier, to become a good and just person. Ideology, in the last analysis, may just be powerful feelings that refuse to see themselves as feelings.

We are much too inclined to think of justice nowadays exclusively in terms of theory, and we consequently measure our personal sense of justice by reference solely to beliefs. A businessman is considered to be just and fair by his friends and family because he believes in capitalism or the Democratic party or the ultimate resolution of justice in the hands of God. A young graduate student in sociology is considered just and fair by her friends (not her family) because she despises capitalism and "bourgeois" material comforts, and perhaps she even takes the occasional opportunity to attack these symbolically. But I want to argue that beliefs, and especially political beliefs, should not be equated with justice or with being a just person. What worries me is what I believe worried Plato, when he attacked the mere opinions of his sophist friends and acquaintances. The problem was not that such opinions might be false; in fact, it did not matter that an opinion might be correct. Truth and falsity were not the issue. The problem was rather that such opinions were second-hand, merely borrowed, the product of persuasion rather than thought. (Of course, Plato worried that the persuasive force might be passion rather than reason, but his central concern was that the opinions so derived were not, in an important sense, one's own.) In this sense, Plato argued, opinions were worthless even if, for all appearances, they seemed to be well thought out, supported by all sorts of reasons and arguments and ready with all sorts of replies to objections and counterexamples. So too Sextus Empiricus rejected "belief" as worthless, as "too intense," and as a falsification of life.[18] Needless to say, neither Plato nor the ancient Skeptics rejected opinion and belief in the ordinary practical sense, as guidelines for getting through daily life. But when it came to the grand arguments and theories about life and the cosmos, about justice in particular, the solidarity of opinion and belief interfered with rather than came to the aid of justice. Theories merely reflect personal prejudices, projected as objective and often insensitive truths about the world.

THE SOCIAL CONTRACT AND THE STATE OF NATURE

Outside of civil states, there is always a war of all against all.
THOMAS HOBBES

Man is born free, and everywhere he is in chains.
JEAN-JACQUES ROUSSEAU

ONE SUCH GRAND THEORY rules our thinking today. It provides the starting point for our thinking and the ground rules for our conceptions and discussions about justice. It has all the intellectual elegance that the smartest philosophers of modern times have contributed, and it has all of the appeal that our most deeply felt political opinions can provide. It is a theory that has become labyrinthine in its development but is almost childishly simple in its basic conception. It is the theory that has come to be known as the theory of "the social contract," and it encompasses not only a theory of justice but a theory of human nature and our basic emotions and motivation as well. In its most basic formulation, it is the view that justice—and the very existence of society as such—is created and justified by the fact that we all agree to its principles because they ultimately serve each of our best interests. In many versions of the theory, justice becomes a matter of reason whose purpose is to counter and control the unruly and usually selfish dictates of our natural passions. I want to argue that such theories rather reduce reason to the mere calculation of self-interest and ignore or even deny our emotional and essentially social nature.

The theory of the social contract comes down to us from the great social thinkers of the seventeenth and eighteenth centuries, especially Thomas Hobbes, John Locke, and Jean-Jacques Rousseau. It is the theory that justice is the product of a general agreement, a contract agreed to by each and every member of society. The great appeal of the theory is the idea that we are obliged to obey the rules of justice (and the governments that enforce them) because we have agreed to do so. It is our own word that sanctions the principles of fairness— together with the reasonable belief that these principles are in fact as fair to us as they are to others. It is as if we made a contract with the state, or more properly with each other, that we would live together according to certain rules, which are also—according to our best rational calculations—in our own interest as well. In return for our obedience to the rules, everyone else will obey them too (or be threatened and forced to do so). Just think of traffic rules alone to see how well this idea works as an account of both why there should be such general rules and how it is in our interest to obey them (most of the time) ourselves. So, too, in return for our agreement to be fair and support and participate in fair institututions—in particular the legal system but also the tax system, the market system, and the system of contracts and ownership—others will participate as well, to the advantage of all of us. We are willing to give up some part of our income to help those in need because we believe that, if we were in need, others would similarly help us. Such self-interested cooperation assures that society will be orderly and more or less peaceful, that property will be safe and secured and that our personal lives will be protected. Justice so conceived is the product of rational, mutual agreement, by means of which we all benefit, if not equally, at least far more than we would if left to our selfish, "natural" inclinations.

But what does this idea of an original agreement or contract presuppose? To begin with, there must have been individuals who could get together to make such an agreement, and presumably they did not already live together in any kind of organized or coherent society. They lived instead, according to the now-established mythology, in the "state of nature"—a primal, purely individual existence in which they all "naturally" served only their own interests, at whatever cost to whomever else they might run across in the pursuit of their needs and desires. Thus the theory presumes, first of all, a theory of human nature, according to which we are all essentially independent, autonomous creatures, capable of existing (whether well or badly) on our own. We are also selfish, or at least self-interested, creatures, more or less oblivious to the needs and interests of others and without enduring affections or attachments. But we are evidently very clever at figuring out what is good for us, and we are capable—according to the theory—of getting together and negotiating our personal and mutual interests and hammering out a contract that spells out the terms of our agreement and provides incentives and sanctions for our compliance. That is asking an awful lot from a first gathering of presumably primitive creatures who probably know very little about one another and certainly do not share even the beginnings of a language, much less the complicated legal concepts that are essential to contracts. Presocial humanity was both remarkably sophisticated and, it seems, only grudgingly cooperative. The state of nature is one of those grand ancient myths with which people have always proved to themselves both how clever we have always been and how much better off we are now.

Of course, there were prehistoric (more or less) human beings of one sort or another; that is not in question. But why should we think that they were, in effect, presocial proto-lawyers and statesmen who had little to do with one another but a keen sense of their own needs and interests? We do, of course, have an inspiring example of a society actually formed by virtue of such a contract, and that is our own. The "contract" is our Constitution. But, needless to say, it was not presocial savages who gathered together in Philadelphia two centuries ago. They were well-trained, highly skilled, and well-read lawyers and statesmen. (Some of their favorite reading was precisely the philosophical literature on the social contract.) And the society they "founded" was by no means society as such, society built up from the ground up, but a considerably improved version of the Western European (especially British) type of society that already existed in the colonies, in which property was already established, in which local laws against theft and murder and a thousand other crimes were already in place together with a system of punishment to enforce them. The social contract metaphor, on the other hand, presumes an outrageous pretension, that we can build society from scratch, and may have actually done so. The myth of the state of nature is an analysis of the raw ingredients we used to do this.

The idea of a state of nature is not, however, just a speculative historical question. This fascination with the idea of an "original" situation, before the founding of society, goes back to the ancients, to Protagoras and Plato and Lucretius, and it is still, in the most contemporary philosophers, a point of intense speculation and argument. The real inquiry is what *we* are like, beneath all of our social indoctrination and education, before the molding of our minds and personalities through socialization, culture, and language. What are we really like before we are molded into certain sorts of citizens by our cultures and taught to think about ourselves as we do through our educations, our science, our media and mythologies? In other words, what would life be like for us now if there were no society, if there were no mutual agreements between us to the effect that we should live together in peace and harmony and cooperate and be fair with one another? What would we now be like if we stripped off all of our cultural baggage, if we suspended all of our purely social ambitions having to do with careers and status, if we eliminated all of those clearly contrived desires that are produced in us by advertisers and status-seeking interpersonal rivalry, if we excluded all of those emotions that have to do with status and sociability, like envy and pride and vanity and romantic love? How would we act toward one another if we did not have the mutually agreed-upon strictures of justice, if society and the law did not instruct us to stay in our place and respect the rights of others?

Thomas Hobbes characterized human life in the "state of nature" as "solitary, poor, nasty, brutish and short." We are all basically selfish. Accordingly, if we are to live together we need something else, some sovereign authority that will force us to cooperate and compromise. The formation of society, according to Hobbes, is our escape from this insecure and unhappy "war of all against all." Society is formed by way of a "contract" agreed upon by all as a voluntary association of individuals who in their natural state would not tend to cooperate with each other but now do so for the sake of their mutual self interest.[19]

The portrait changes and sometimes becomes more flattering in the hands of other authors—we get more clever if not kinder in the state of nature—but it is essentially the same. The essence of the portrait is that before the formation of society through joint voluntary agreement we were independent individuals. What varies is the conception of our "natures" in the state of nature, and, accordingly, our reasons for agreeing to enter into society in the first place. Were we in fact (or should we think of ourselves in theory as being) as naturally selfish and mutually murderous as Hobbes made us out to be? Did we enter into society for our mutual protection and is that indeed our reason for staying there? Or were we, as Jean-Jacques Rousseau argued, rather benign and even compassionate creatures, even in the worst cases more or less indifferent to one another and not at all concerned to murder or steal (in part because there was no private property and therefore nothing to steal)? Are we, in fact, naturally good, as Rousseau suggested, and do we therefore live in society not for our mutual protection but for a more noble reason, to exercise our moral autonomy and express our goodness?[20]

The state of nature, on Rousseau's account, was quite a delightful place, in which natural man was happy and secure. Life may have been solitary but it was neither nasty nor brutal. Indeed, as we read Rousseau's account of the happy affluence and delightful independence we supposedly once enjoyed, the question that strikes us first and foremost is why we ever should have left or thought of leaving the state of nature for the artifices and civilized brutalities of society. According to Rousseau, it was only through a series of misfortunes of our own making (the development of agriculture and metallurgy, the declaration of private property, and our increasing interdependency) that we found ourselves in mutually dependent and oppressive groups, ruled by tyrants and dominated by the rich. It is in the context of such a society that we now find it necessary to reconsider what we call "society" in accordance with the radical and much more noble conception of "the social contract." For Rousseau, this was not an account of the actual formation of society but rather a wishful blueprint for an ideal society, a society of equals in which every citizen was again independent of every other, as he or she was in the state of nature, subject only to self-imposed laws. The importance of the social contract, then, is that through our agreement we are subject to just those laws and considerations that we ourselves have agreed to. Society and justice are not external impositions but our own critical choices and self-interests.

This pair of myths and metaphors—the "state of nature" and "the social contract"—dominates and has dominated the literature on justice since the seventeenth century, though such ideas have been around since ancient times. The appeal of the myth, whatever its other virtues or defects, is that it emphasizes an image of the individual's relationship to society and other people that we find particularly appealing—a relationship of mutual agreement and consent. Indeed, the idea that citizens necessarily participate in the formation and continuation of society has become so powerful that it no longer seems like an idea—much less a difficult and controversial idea—but rather a working definition of what it means for something to be a "society." The idea is that we are not trapped in society the way we are (for the moment) trapped on our planet, by virtue of being born there. We are, on this theory, all Americans or Britons or Frenchmen, Texans or Iowans or Californians by choice; we choose our governments, and we choose to be citizens and obey the law, by mutual agreement. But the reason we do so is not that we have any natural tie or affection for the others with whom we happen to share our world. We live in society because it is the rational thing to do. It is in our own best self-interest. And we believe in justice not because we care about other people but because we recognize that this too is rational and in our own best interest.

It is easy to see the appeal of such a theory, but it is also easy to see what nonsense it is and how false a portrait of our nature. We can and do make choices and mutual agreements, of course, but even in the most democratic societies our choices and agreements are grounded in our already shared social sensibilities. Of course, there are millions of people who, by choice or coercion, move from one culture to another, learning a new language and a new life, but this hardly proves the independence of individuals from society. The extreme choice of leaving the society in which one has grown up represents one of the most traumatic and unnatural ruptures in life. We are not and never have been naturally independent, and society has always been based, first of all, on the natural affections and affiliations in which we find ourselves with others. The idea that we could exist or have ever existed as purely autonomous creatures is at best an inspiring intellectual fraud.

Of course, virtually every author on the subject insists that there was in fact no such state of nature. (Rousseau boldly announces, "Let's begin by ignoring all the facts.") But these authors clearly do believe that, prehistory aside, we are independent, autonomous beings by nature, concerned primarily with calculating our own interests, living together only grudgingly. So, too, the authors who defend the idea of a social contract virtually never suggest that there was, in fact, such a historical agreement. But, then, it is not easy to understand what sort of binding force this fiction is supposed to have on us. If no one actually agreed to such a contract, is it a contract? If our ancestors did agree to such a contract are we bound by it? (In what sense are you bound by a contract or a promise made by your grandfather?) Do the suggestions that we *might* have made such a contract or *would* have made such a contract have the force of an actual contract? But if we are not really expected to make sense of the fiction that presocial creatures—presumably without a shared language or any established skills in negotiation, and in the absence of any legal framework—somehow got together in a sort of prehistoric caveman convention and hammered out the agreement upon which society as such (or any particular society) is formed, what is really at stake here? What does it mean to talk to individuals capable of bargaining and making the most sophisticated negotiations apart from their socialization and education in a particular kind of society? We can appreciate the importance of shared agreement and mutual concern in society, but why should we think that this is or should be the very nature of society as such? We can applaud society's individuality and autonomy, but do we have to pretend that these traits constitute human nature as such? We falsely ontologize our independence, and we falsify the very essence of our existence, which is not to be individuals with interests but to be social beings who define ourselves in terms of our attachments, affections, and social identities.

I think we should be extremely suspicious of all of those social thinkers who suggest that a theory of justice is an attempt to establish justice by creating society anew. Beginning with Plato's *Republic*, philosophers have developed theories of justice that try to replace their own society with another, better one, and the social contract is but the latest intellectual device for doing this. But the attempt to replace one's society suggests that the motivation behind these various theories of justice, however couched in the language of rationality, consists largely of such emotions as contempt and resentment. Could it even be that some of the quest is simple self-hatred, as in Jean-Jacques Rousseau's attempt to design a society that would no longer have room for people like himself? The theory of the social contract itself carries some heavy and often undeclared baggage in terms of a theory of human emotions. What does it say about us that we seek first and foremost to negotiate our own best advantage (or the advantage of those closest to us)? What does it say about us that the connections and attachments between us must be contractual rather than first of all felt? Of course, not surprisingly, Plato's imaginary city-state is not so far removed from the ancient Athens, and the imaginary societies that dominate social philosophy in America today resemble nothing so much as a more consistent, perhaps much-improved but in any case much more self-conscious form of democratic capitalism. Nevertheless, it does not take much critical imagination to realize how much the subject of justice has been distorted and overidealized by these philosophers. The very idea of founding a society (much less society as such) is so arrogant, so abstract and so distracting from the actual problems of justice and injustice that we should from the start be extremely suspicious of any theory of justice that starts by suggesting not a better but a different society or begins by pretending that society is unnatural and was formed by the rational agreement (for whatever reasons) of presocial individuals, as if we could, even in theory, momentarily retreat to that original position and renegotiate the basic terms under which we live.

It is against the twin mythology of a "state of nature," according to which we are all independent, autonomous beings, and a "social contract," according to which we are rational, mutually committed individuals, that my argument in this book is directed. My thesis is that it makes no sense to talk about human nature—whether as pure rationality or productivity and possessiveness—apart from those features that we cultivate and acquire in society, and at the same time that there is no need to bring in rationality as a corrective for an essentially selfish human nature. Our affiliations in society and with each other are not rational or a matter of self-interested calculation but a product of natural feelings and affections. It is selfishness and not society that is unnatural, and justice should not be conceived as a rational corrective to our natural human emotions.

JUSTICE, GREED, AND THE GOOD LIFE

ABSTRACT GREED

The great source of both miseries and disorders of human life seems to arise from overrating the difference between one permanent situation and another. Avarice overrates the difference between poverty and riches. . . .   ADAM SMITH

Greed is not a bad thing. You shouldn't feel guilty.

IVAN BOESKY

L AST YEAR, I ASKED my students, rather casually, how much money they thought that they could reasonably expect to be earning ten years from now. An economics major asked how she was supposed to know about ten years of inflation, so I assured them that 1989 dollars would do. A few thoughtful students confessed that, as they had no idea what they wanted to do for a career or a living yet, they could hardly estimate any expected income. But I told them that I was more interested in their expectations than I was in their career choices at the moment, and I asked for a few volunteers.

"Thirty-five thousand dollars," offered one student in the middle of class. The rest of the class, almost as one, chortled and guffawed.

"Too high or too low?" I asked, tongue in cheek, the answer being obvious.

"You can't even live on thirty-five thousand dollars a year," insisted one perturbed student, "and that's without a family."

"Well," I needled them, "how much would it take to live on?"

"A hundred grand," shouted a student at the back of the class, and almost everyone nodded or muttered in agreement.

"And do you think that you will make that much?" I asked.

"Sure," answered the same student, with more cockiness than confidence.

"How?" I asked

"Oh, I haven't the slightest idea," he answered, with a nervous giggle.

Everyone laughed.

"Well, I'm looking at a hundred and fifty, at least," volunteered a serious student by the windows. "I'm going to be a lawyer."

There were shouts of approval.

"I'd like to aim at a half-million," offered another student. There were claps and cheers.

"If you don't think positive, you'll never make it," he explained to the class.

"OK," I said, "I'm getting curious. I want everyone to write down their expected income for the year 1999, just on a slip of paper, and pass them to your left. Remember, I said *expected* income, not just a fantasy."

There was a moment of feverish tearing, a moment of sweaty silence, then a good deal of shuffling and an explosion of small conversation. I collected the ninety-some slips of paper.

This was the moment of truth. I read them out, one by one, pausing only a fraction of a second to raise my eyebrows or the inflection of my voice for those few figures that were near a million or over.

The average income of the class, projected for the year 1999 (in 1989 dollars) was over one hundred thousand dollars per student. If we did not include those students who saw themselves on "Lifestyles of the Rich and Famous," the average was still in the range of seventy-five to eighty thousand dollars per year.

"Does anyone know the median family income in the United States?" I asked.

"Isn't it about twenty-five thousand dollars?" asked one student.

"A bit less," I responded, "but that's close enough."

"And do all of you really believe that you can and will make three or four times (or more) the national average?" I asked. Their cockiness vanished. A few, the already-decided lawyers and M.B.A.'s, rightly responded that they were not exactly average. I agreed, but pushing them for their own estimations, the figures were so outlandish (a quarter-million and up) that I had to ask them how they thought that they would make so much money, when the salaries of most lawyers and executives (even most CEOs) were considerably less. Again, the cockiness vanished (these were serious students) and was replaced by a kind of confusion.

Switching gears, I asked them all, "Tell me, how will you spend all of this money?" And the first answers were as amusing as they were predictable.

"On nice clothes," one woman suggested, and three of the men simultaneously countered with "a fantastic sports car."

"Sexist responses," interjected one student on the left.

"Probably on my family," offered one young man in the front, and most of the class nodded their agreement.

I let the discussion go on for a while, as the students collectively debated potential budgets, projected family plans, calculated spending money and came to the conclusion, all things considered, that their expectations were not only unreasonable but unnecessary. The conversation took a dramatic turn.

"Actually, the people I know who are wealthy seem to have the most problems," one student volunteered. "Money seems to mean hassles as well as luxuries, and I'd rather not have the hassles."

"Yeah, look how miserable everyone is on "Dallas," one student interjected, and everyone laughed and chimed in.

"And "Dynasty."

"And "Falcon Crest."

"And my next door neighbors," whooped another.

"I think I'd much rather just do something I enjoyed and get by with lots of leisure time," said another, with contrasting seriousness.

"Money doesn't buy happiness," said another, solemn but embarrassed about the cliché.

"Yeah, where does all this pressure about money come from?" asked another.

"I guess that's really the question, isn't it?" I asked. I couldn't resist telling them how differently the class would have gone twenty years ago, when I had just begun teaching. "Your numbers would have provoked contempt," I suggested, "and the ideal of doing whatever you're best at and enjoy, and just getting by financially, would have been the consensus of the class."

"But that wasn't realistic either," protested one of the students, "and besides, that was then, this is now."

"And aren't all of those students rich Yuppies now?" challenged another student.

"You mean, like me?" I asked, hiding both my smile and my academic income. (It worked, because I got a general laugh.)

"But can we get back to that question—why money is so important?" requested one of the best students in the class. And we did.

I've often done that experiment, and I've gotten much the same discussion with almost every one of the recent classes. What still impresses me is not so much the enormous sums of money they all seem to think that they want and need to live on, but their utter naiveté about how to get it and their remarkable lack of sense about what to do with it. This isn't greed as I usually think of it, that gluttonous "take it all" philosophy that condones breaking one's trust or the law just to get more. There isn't that hunger to it, that sense of need. Indeed, there isn't even any real desire. It is rather, I think, *abstract greed*. Greed without lust. Greed without ambition. Greed instilled in these young minds not by desire but by their peers, by the media, and by the ill-advised or misguided lessons that their elders seek to impress upon them. Instead of teaching the virtue of justice, we are promoting as a virtue the self-defeating vice of greed. It is obvious that if these students actually wanted and expected such fantastic incomes, most of them would be doomed to a life of frustration and felt failure, even if, without that desire and those expectations, they might have been perfectly well off and quite happy. What we think and say that we want may be very different from what we do want and, most important, from what we need and ought to want for ourselves.

PLATO'S PROBLEM: SELF-INTEREST VS. JUSTICE

The egoist is, in the ancient and medieval world, always someone who has made a fundamental mistake about where his own good lies and someone who has thus and to that extent excluded himself from human relationships. ALASDAIR MACINTYRE, *AFTER VIRTUE*

Not getting everything that you want is an indispensable part of happiness. BERTRAND RUSSELL, *THE CONQUEST OF HAPPINESS*

IMAGINE THAT YOU CAME into possession of a magical ring, which had the remarkable property of rendering its owner invisible. You could slip into executive offices, professional football games, and private bedrooms with equal ease. You could just walk on and take that empty seat in first class to Tokyo or Tahiti. You could create mischief; you could commit murder. You could cause bureaucratic chaos, or just enough confusion to benefit yourself quite nicely, in your local tax office, for example. You could take whatever you want (assuming that, in your hands, it becomes invisible too). Or, if this isn't enough to suit your latent megalomania, imagine that the same ring gave you the power to travel through time. You could take a peek at the *Wall Street Journal* stock options report a month into the future. You could zoom into the past and kill off the boss who would later fire you or the teacher who would later flunk you, then zoom back before you are caught. Still not enough? What about a ring that can kill by telepathy? Just think of your target, say the magic words and—not a trace of foul play, just death by "natural causes." No risk to yourself. You don't even have to be there. You could be in Bermuda, or Paris, or at home in bed. The perfect alibi. The perfect crime. Of course, such power corrupts, but not you, or at least, not for a while. You would use your power sparingly, of course. And presumably in good taste. But, with cleverness and strategy, you could now get almost anything that you want and never get caught. Why would you worry about what's right, what's fair? Why should you worry about justice?

The imaginary bauble in question is the mythical Ring of Gyges.

Plato speculates on its use and abuse in *The Republic*.[1] The question confronting Socrates and us, Plato's readers, is whether we would have any need or desire to be just if we could get away with our injustices. As it is, one overwhelmingly good reason for obeying the principles of justice is the brutal fact that if we do not, then other people, perhaps the police, will surely make us pay. One can take an extra three pieces of chicken at the barbecue, but one should not expect to be invited again. One can embezzle funds at the office, but it is only a matter of time until one is found out and fired, or worse. One might fantasize about shooting one's competitors in business or on the L.A. freeways, but trying to do so will earn one a decade or two in prison. Indeed, one of the most important lessons we learn as children is that one rarely gets away with anything, much less with everything, and that misdeeds have unpleasant consequences. Crime sometimes pays, but, luckily, it usually does not. Or, in any case, we cannot allow ourselves to believe that it does. But, . . . what if it did?

This is Plato's problem, and it is the leading subject of one of the greatest books ever written. The protagonist of *The Republic* is Socrates, who is the champion of what was then the relatively new concept of *justice*. Greece had long been a warrior society (or rather, an antagonistic cluster of such societies), ruled and represented in history by those legendary heroes who fought the Trojan War and, more recently, fought among themselves with such ferocity. In such a warlike society, there was little room for the civil sense of justice as we know it, or as Plato was to defend it. Much less was there any sense of distributive justice and the very modern idea that the goods of society should be shared more or less equally. There was rule by the mighty, who had a keen sense of revenge along with an unshakable confidence in the unqualified legitimacy of their own desires. Greece was a tribal society that was organized around the skills and desires of those who were strongest because those skills and desires were essential to the survival of the tribe. In a phrase, might made right, though one could argue that Homeric Greece was a meritocracy in which making war was essential and those who won the wars deserved the spoils. Plato's problem was to show why the mighty should not do whatever they could do, why they should pay attention to justice and be just instead.

In Plato's Greece, the inequality of privileges and possessions among unequals was considered entirely normal and "natural"—and it is not irrelevant that both Plato and Aristotle were very much the spokesmen for the wealthy aristocrats of Athens. They argued for a new sense of justice, but they did not argue against their hierarchical society. Slavery was essential to the prosperity of a nontechnological but sophisticated agrarian society, and a justification for slavery was neither expected nor required. But the old Homeric notion of justice as vengeance was now called into question, and the idea that justice might involve destroying an entire family or even a city (for example, Troy) in return for a single offense was now considered barbaric. There was not as yet any sense that one had an obligation to share or sacrifice for those who were much worse off, but the idea that justice was something very different from "might makes right" was becoming very much a part of civilized life. It was Plato who would make it so.

The Republic was written around 380 B.C., about twenty years after Socrates' execution, 400 years after Homer, 800 years after the semi-factual events that Homer depicted. For Plato, and for Socrates, "what is justice?" was indeed the question, not only for the entire society but for each individual citizen. For Plato, justice is nothing less than "the good life" for all of us, the way we ought to live. For Socrates, justice was also worth dying for, and he gave his life not so much for his ideas (the fantasy philosophers have since entertained) but for the sake of justice, for the sake of the laws and for the good of his soul. It was not what we would think of as an "unselfish" sacrifice. Indeed, Socrates made it quite clear (in *Crito*) that his action was indeed quite "selfish," in that his soul was far more valuable to him than the few years of pleasure and influence he would have if he were to escape execution. (He was already 70.) Dying for the sake of the good life was not, for him, a contradiction or a paradox; death—the right kind of death—was an essential part of the good life. Dying for the sake of justice was not self-sacrifice but the ultimate self-fulfull-ment. But obviously Socrates had a much more elaborate conception of "self-interest" than the vulgar ambitions expressed by the owner of the Ring of Gyges.[2]

And yet, the idea of sacrificing one's life for justice (as opposed, for example, to sacrificing one's life for one's *polis*) was a view that appealed to very few Athenians, and no doubt it appeals to fewer of us. Even Plato, Socrates' prize student and the chief chronicler of his exploits and ideas, had serious doubts about the wisdom of such sacrifice, and when he had an opportunity to imitate his teacher he clearly said no, as did Aristotle after him (allegedly commenting that "Athens would not get a second chance to sin against philosophy.") This new concept of justice was not yet sufficient to persuade us to give up our lives for its sake. Indeed, was it powerful enough to make us give up anything that we really wanted, if, that is, we had the strength or cleverness to take it and get away with it? That is what the prospect of the Ring of Gyges, presented to Socrates by Glaucon in *The Republic*, is supposed to measure. Achilles and Agamemnon did not concern themselves with justice. They simply took what they wanted from life. So why should justice concern you, the new, more or less omnipotent owner of the Ring of Gyges?

The essential question is not the justification of justice as an abstract concept or as a desirable property of social institutions but the more personal concern: *What is justice to us and why should we be just?* Our modern way of thinking about this question defends justice by arguing that justice serves our collective interests. This is not Plato's view, but neither is it to be thought that he defends a sense of justice as self-sacrifice. What he suggests—and what I shall be arguing—is that a proper conception of justice requires a revised conception of one's self. Justice, according to the social contract conception, is an artifice of society. It is not a matter of personal inclination or virtue so much as it is a system of threats and rewards to which we agree for our mutual advantage. Justice, according to Plato, is first of all a personal virtue. The problem with the idea that justice is a kind of convention or a contract adopted by people for their mutual protection is that it fails us just when we need it most, that is, when there really is some monster of injustice against whom we want to defend ourselves. Against the owner of the Ring of Gyges, it will do no good to argue that "we will all be better off," for he or she is already better off and knows that there would be no advantage to obeying the terms of such a contact. And if justice is just another means of getting one's advantage, why should those who already have the advantage care or bother about it?

Underlying the idea of a social contract to protect us from one another is the uncritical and inadequate notion that we are all basically selfish and competitive. It is as if our selfish desires occur naturally, quite apart from ethics or society, but our sense of justice is not natural at all. Against this, Plato argues that justice cannot be just a social convention but must be found in the nature of the soul of the agent. This means that selfishness cannot be so simply opposed to justice, and justice must be understood in terms of what kind of people we are and should be. Justice does not depend on a contract or on anyone's sense of obligation. Indeed, the ancient Greeks did not even have our overly contractual notion of "obligation." It is simply not true that all of us are basically selfish creatures who need contractual obligations to keep us in line. Indeed, holding simultaneously to the antagonistic concepts of "selfishness" and "obligation" makes any adequate conception of justice impossible.[3]

Why should we suppose that we are all exclusively self-seeking? Except in certain usually well-defined circumstances—in a business deal or a sporting event, for instance—our lives are not competitive and our interests are neither antagonistic to nor out of step with the interests of our neighbors. We live not for our interests, our luxuries, our comforts, or even our needs, but rather to maintain an adequate conception of ourselves, our dignity, our proper place in society. We live not for ourselves but for our *selves*, to please our pride, our vanity, our self-esteem, our sense of honor and righteousness. But these emotional values, although putatively about the self, are all social and presuppose a life with and largely for other people. Dostoevsky gave us a character in his *Notes from Underground* who undermines all of his interests, even his health, just for the sake of spite, to prove that he is not a pawn of other people and their "rationality." Accordingly, Dostoevsky's character will suffer anything, so long as it represents his own free choice, his "most advantageous advantage"—his true self. So, too, what we all ultimately want is not our own advantage but rather something more precious, a sense of self and self-respect, which can be won only by rejecting the supposed tyranny of self-interest and understanding our essentially social nature.[4]

If you were the owner of the Ring of Gyges, wouldn't you take the opportunity to help a homeless person, to warn a friend of impending danger, to assassinate or harrass not some innocuous civilian who thwarted your ambitions but one of those monsters who wreaks havoc in the world and cruelly oppresses his or her subjects at home? Looking over the range of our daily actions, it is by no means clear that we always or even usually act exclusively for our own benefit, even though we do not often (knowingly) act against our own interests. But our interests for the most part include rather than oppose the concerns of other people and the interests of the larger communities in which we live. We dutifully obey the laws, help other people, share our time and sometimes even our money, and not because we seek some further reward or fear getting caught. Standing up and dying for the sake of justice may remain a rarity, but being just is not rare or accidental behavior for us, something nice to do when nothing else strikes us as particularly desirable. Being just and concerned about the well-being of others is as much a part of living well as satisfying our own desires. Justice is not selfish but it is essential part of the self.

PLATO'S SOLUTION: THE REPUBLIC

. . . asked by an anxious father, "How can I ensure that my son is a just man?" Xenophilus replied, "Make him the citizen of a well governed state."
DIOGENES LAERTIUS (QUOTED IN HEGEL, PHILOSOPHY & RIGHTS)

THE REPUBLIC IS DESIGNED to answer the question, what is justice? but it is not at all clear what the final definition of that critical concept turns out to be. What we would like is a set of instructions, some way of making evaluations and decisions. Plato does not give this to us, so many readers may be disappointed. But it is not Plato's aim to give us a decision procedure for bureaucrats; quite the contrary, his aim is to teach us that justice is a personal virtue and entails being a certain sort of person and having a certain conception of oneself. And as for substance, *The Republic* gives us not just a single analysis of justice but several, all of which Socrates rejects as perverse, confused, or far too limited. Why does he bother? Because it is Socrates' view that the true definition will emerge dialectically ("through conversation") from a consideration of all of the one-sided or wrongheaded answers now in circulation. Or perhaps we can read Plato as trying to tell us that there are many different conceptions of justice, appropriate and limited to different contexts, so that the heart of justice is not in the world but in our judgments. Or perhaps we should realize that the diversity of answers considered by Socrates and his interlocutors demonstrates not the stupidity of Socrates' fellow Athenians but rather the genuine conflict and confusion of various ancient and novel visions of the good life and the way the world works. In *The Republic*, in contrast to most modern works on justice, there is no theory of justice and no attempt to reduce justice to a few impersonal principles. Justice is nothing less than the very soul of the best individuals and the best communities.

The Republic is devoted to Socrates' defense of justice as a virtue that is desirable for its own sake and to his formulation of a blueprint for a society ruled by justice and by just men and women. (It should be noted that Plato's inclusion of women as guardians of the republic was a remarkably novel and precocious idea in a society that still considered women chattel.) The main theme is that justice as a virtue may be personal, but it is only a just society that produces just citizens. Plato realizes that while an extremely rare instance of the just man (notably Socrates) is possible even in an unjust society, the rest of us can only be expected to be just in a society that is itself just. And so *The Republic* turns from an account of justice in the individual to a plan for a just society, essentially an aristocratic republic. (The analogy between personal justice and the ideal society plays back and forth throughout *The Republic*. In general, there cannot be either without the other, despite the perfect virtue of Socrates in an imperfect society and although there would undoubtedly be some unjust individuals even in the perfect society.) What ties the analogy together is the quasi-musical notion of *harmony*. The ideal society has perfect harmony between its various parts just as the healthy individual enjoys perfect harmony between his or her various faculties, mind and body, reason, emotion, and desire.

The central feature of Plato's just society—and it is also the defining feature of modern society in Adam Smith's *Wealth of Nations*—is the division of labor: Everyone does what he or she can do best.[5] Thus justice turns on the notion of merit; what is essential is what people contribute to the society through their own special skills and talents. Of course, people are rewarded for their contributions to society, but it would be the greatest mistake to think that this means that they contribute *in order to* get rewarded. Citizens contribute because that's what they do and that's what they are, in order to improve society, and in order to exemplify themselves as citizens. The idea that they need some external bribes, or what we call incentives, already misses the point, though of course if society systematically deprived them of their rightful rewards such a perverse "you get what you pay me for" attitude could well become predominant. But the result of all of these skilled and specialized citizens working together is a maximally unified, efficient, healthy, and happy society (a point made again twenty centuries later by Adam Smith). In other words, the perfect city is the product of thousands of (imperfect) individuals, working together and enjoying the fruits of success appropriate to their roles and expectations. This is justice. So too, the just individual is a person in whom body and soul are in harmony, in whom desire is in accordance with reason so that, in effect, he or she has only desires that are appropriate to his or her place in the just society. If one is a "producer," a farmer or a tradesman, for example, then one is just and happy in the life of production. If one is a "warrior," one can enjoy the added luxuries afforded to those who protect and defend the city, and this difference in privilege is perfectly just. Finally, if one is a "guardian" (ultimately, even a philosopher-king) one has very special duties and privileges, including an intensive education in politics and philosophy, which Plato prescribes in considerable detail. (Philosophers have to understand the nature of justice if they are to know how to make it work.) The guardians, however, are subjected to severe restrictions, including the abolition of personal property and the familiar modes of family privacy. They share wives, and consequently children are raised communally, as new guardians. Whether or not we think such a system sounds fair, it should give us occasion in these days of millionaire senators to rethink what we mean by "public servants." What constitutes justice is a whole-hearted concern and engagement in society, the recognition that the pursuit of personal interests in the absence of a community in which those interests are defined, respected, and realized makes no sense whatsoever. For Plato, the essence of justice is belonging to a well-ordered and harmonious society and being the kind of person who makes possible such a society.

We should not be surprised that this image of a harmonious, prosperous, and happy society has inspired political leaders for so many centuries, but many elements of this hierarchical portrait of justice and the ideal society should repel and disgust us as well. What has no place in this portrait of justice, indeed is its enemy, is democracy, and the individual freedoms and choices that democracy both requires and makes possible. The unabashed acceptance of slavery as the economic presupposition of the republic should horrify us, and the idea that each of us is just and will be happy if only we accept without challenging our place in society should revolt us. Of course, *The Republic* is not entirely idealized fiction; it is, quite naturally, a good deal like Athens in the fourth century B.C., reflecting all of the political battles that Athenians had endured in the previous century or so. It is not a utopia, by any means, but an idealization of one strain of political thought that Socrates and Plato found particularly attractive. It is a vision that we, however, would and should find almost a paradigm of injustice. And yet, *The Republic* also offers us a vision of what justice is and must be. Whatever else it may be, justice involves the integrity and fulfillment of the individual and his or her contribution to society rather than, as we tend to think of it, an individual (namely oneself) getting what he or she wants or deserves. But whereas Plato has society wholly determine the role and the status of the individual, we insist that it is the well-being and rights of the individual that determine the nature of society. It is the individual who is the measure and standard of justice, but—and this is the critical point—this measure and standard is always embedded in society and unthinkable without it.

Plato suggests that, whether we are talking about the individual or society, justice is akin to health and happiness while injustice is like sickness and misery. Injustice is internal discord, which leaves society or the psyche weak and confused, at war with itself. This provides Plato with a solution to his problem, namely, how it is that justice must be considered desirable for its own sake. If justice is nothing less than the integrity and harmony of ourselves and our society, if we are "naturally" motivated to be just, then the denial of this harmony or the misfortune of living in a society that does not or cannot sustain it will inevitably not only make us miserable but also induce a kind of internal turmoil and conflict, *even if* we manage to do quite well for ourselves as individuals in such circumstances. Living in a just society certainly helps and encourages us to be just persons, not because society makes us just but because it gives us the opportunity to act out our natural impulses. Justice must be in the individual before it can be in society. And what external rewards or enticements does one require in order to pursue health and happiness?

What Plato means by justice is living the good life. To be sure, he was not concerned with many of the aspects of justice which very much concern us, such as the question of welfare for the poor and the debate over progressive taxation, and much of what he praises in his ideal society and disparages in democracy should offend us; but his basic idea, namely, that justice is not an abstract or isolated aspect of life but the very essence of living as a citizen in society, should be quite familiar and appealing to us. Socrates' insistence that being just and serving one's own interests are not distinct projects is his answer to the question, what is justice? Justice is living well and living right, which are indistinguishable. And why should we be just? Because not to be just is to be something less than a complete person or a full citizen, to be inwardly torn and conflicted and less than fully rational, to run a large risk of being miserable and untrue to one's own true nature. Perhaps this answer will not satisfy the probing of the new owner of the Ring of Gyges, who is already anxious to test the limits of these frightening new powers and, in that enthusiasm, gives justice a rather low priority. But Plato assures us, by the end of *The Republic*, that it is not merely a matter of justice being its own reward, for the just person will reap the rewards of society as well. Thinking things through, one will eventually throw away the Ring of Gyges (or perhaps just use it to do tricks on late night television) for the sole satisfaction of serving the public good.

Thus the ultimate argument of *The Republic* is that justice is good in itself but will also pay off in the long run. It must be admitted that Socrates (or Plato) never quite makes good on the guarantee of such a happy conclusion. But we might note that Socrates and Plato are not the only defenders of justice who have wanted to have their cake and eat it too, to defend the goodness of justice for its own sake, apart from any benefits for the just person, and then promise us those benefits after all. Over two thousand years later, the great German philosopher Immanuel Kant summarized one version of the entire Christian tradition in what he called "the summum bonum," the "highest good," in which virtue and happiness, justice and personal well-being, would be exactly matched. Evil would be repaid by punishment, good by reward. Of course, such justice is not to be found in this world, where innocent children are murdered by tyrants who thrive into their seventies, so Kant "proves" that justice will be rendered by God, in an immortal life quite apart from this one. Indeed, Kant even argues that it would be irrational to be virtuous and just if we did not believe in any such future justice. We are perfectly happy to pursue justice, even for its own sake and as its own reward, but we want to be assured that we are not going to suffer for it, or find ourselves at a disadvantage vis-à-vis those who are not so conscientious or fair-minded. That is how pervasive Plato's problem has proved to be, and in our modern secular society it has proved to be even more intractable than in Plato's day, when the concept of justice was still quite new. Is justice ultimately in one's own interest? That is what we want to know, but first we have to know more about ourselves, and what we really want out of life.

GREED RECONSIDERED

I don't do it for the money. I've got enough, much more than I'll ever need. I do it to do it.

DONALD TRUMP, *THE ART OF THE DEAL*

The rich man is satisfied with what he has.   THE TALMUD

WHAT PLATO MEANS BY justice is living the good life. But although the good life has certain material preconditions—adequate food, good health, political freedom—it is mainly a matter of living well with other people, living in a good society, and being loved and respected by friends and neighbors. Satisfying basic material needs is a perfectly acceptable, usually sociable and mutually beneficial set of activities, but it is hardly the proper goal or concern in life. What one's needs are depends upon one's place in society: a soldier needs a sword, a statesman an office. But trying to get more than one needs, more than one deserves, is an antisocial and self-defeating activity, damaging to one's reputation, one's honor and, consequently, to one's happiness. Greed is not good, even in a society that believes in the motivating power of greed. Greed is a kind of philosophical confusion, a misunderstanding of what one really wants—a secure sense of oneself and the respect of others. It is the ignorance or the absence of mutually agreed-upon standards of what counts and what is enough. It is that disastrous miscalculation, "If I only had another ten (fifty, five hundred) thousand dollars, then all my troubles would be solved." The good life presupposes but is not mainly a matter of material well-being. To be greedy is to miss that point and to humiliate oneself and harm others in the pursuit of much more than one needs or deserves.

I have always found it remarkable that, in attacking the pathology of greed, I sometimes find myself accused of denying human nature itself, or even worse, attacking capitalism, defending complacency, and undermining just that sense of ambition that "made this country great." This accusation reflects a misunderstanding of both capitalism and complacency—and it most certainly reflects a misreading of "human nature." I am attacking those unreasonable and unjust desires and expectations that make people not more productive but incurably unhappy, the kind that send people scrambling into careers that they don't really want and will never enjoy, side-tracking talents, interests, and concerns that might really make a difference even though they don't pay well. What is upsetting about abstract greed is just what is so innocent about it, that it has nothing to do with real wants, real needs or real expectations. Greed is not desire as such but the ultimately pointless (because endless and insatiable) desire for more. In *Key Largo*, the quasi-heroic character played by Bogart tells the hateful gangster played by Edward G. Robinson what he really wants: more. "More, yeah, more!" echoes Robinson, full of agreement but oblivious to the intended insult. Greed is desire without a goal, without the possibility of constraint or satisfaction. Because the greedy person is perennially frustrated, it is not easy for him to feel compassion for those who have less—after all, he is frustrated too—and *justice* becomes just another word to name what is wrong with the world. And finally, the frustration of greed leads to cynicism, and greedy success leads all too easily to the conclusion that there is no possibility of satisfaction anyway—so why worry about anyone else?

The idea of "wanting it all" has become socially acceptable, which would be just a bad joke if it weren't ruining so many lives. Justice begins with reasonable expectations for oneself, and getting rid of abstract greed should be one of its first aims. We don't need a theory or a plan for the redistribution of the world's goods so much as we need modesty and moderation, deep embarrassment about our wastefulness and thoughtlessness, awareness of how much damage we do not out of self-interest but through simple thoughtlessness or insensitivity. For most of us, the antithesis of justice is not so much injustice as greed. We are not cruel or heartless. We do not cheat or lie or steal. We just want and expect too much. Most of us do not live in conditions of scarcity, not even "moderate scarcity." We live a life of conspicuous consumption, lusting after novel but unnecessary commodities simply because they are heavily advertised and in fashion. But the problem is that such lust, because it is never satisfied (there is always something new), distracts us and erodes our ability to empathize with others. It leads us to exaggerate such emotions as envy and jealousy and it hinders such sentiments as generosity and compassion. And worst of all, after centuries as one of the seven deadly sins, greed has finally found its niche as a virtue in contemporary America, disguised as *ambition*—a word that is also offensive in almost every society except our own.

Greed need not involve personal gain as such. I listened with some disgust as the chairman of a department emotionally protested the fact that a member of his staff is teaching for another program while being paid with department money. Of course, it isn't his money or even his reputation as an administrator that is at stake, just the abstract idea of accumulation and status. It is bureaucratic, Weberian greed, depersonalized and institutionally rationalized, but it is greed nonetheless. Greed is a vice not confined to matters of money, nor is it (needless to say) unique to Americans. In a recent interview with Australian golfer Greg Norman, the message of greed came through unambiguously: "You've got to want; that's what it is. Golf is a matter of desire. . . . If you're happy making $300,000 a year, ('he said with a sneer') and don't care if you win a tournament or not, fine. I'm not happy with that. My desire, ever since I started playing this game, has been to be the best player in the world."[6] Greed is our obsession with success, our unlimited need to accumulate honors, credits, lovers, acclaim. It is not just the investment banker who "needs" another half-million that he can never spend. It is also the poet who cannot get enough honors and envies all other recipients, the entertainer who cannot get a large enough audience or enough applause (the character Jack Benny used to play). It is the scholar who cannot get enough recognition, the model who cannot get enough cover photos. Aristotelean excellence is one thing; insatiable ambition that blocks all sense of fairness and sensitivity is something quite different.

Indeed, our obsession with being "number one," not just good or even excellent, is one of the most visible symptoms of our national neurosis. And it is not just in economics and military power and sports; the *Guinness Book of World Records* attests to our fanaticism about being number one in everything, from telephone booth stuffing to hot potato handling. Not that such quests might not be amusing, but the fact that people spend their lives achieving them, and make their happiness dependent upon achieving something absurd and utterly unimportant contributes a great deal to our unhappiness. It is just another aspect of greed, just another indication that we have lost sight of meaningful standards of accomplishment and have replaced them with this fanatical notion of personal achievement. "I just want to be the best at something" is not just a formula for success; it is also a prescription for unhappiness.

It is often suggested and occasionally argued that capitalism is itself the source of greed, indeed, thrives on greed, encourages greed, even rationalizes greed as the best of all possible motives. (Those who argue thus usually quote Adam Smith on individual greed and "the invisible hand" as the engine of national prosperity.) But, as I have argued at length elsewhere, this notion betrays a deep misunderstanding of capitalism, which as much as any other economic or social system presupposes community and cooperation.[7] It is not incidental that Adam Smith preceded his *Wealth of Nations*—the supposed bible of capitalism—with his *Theory of the Moral Sentiments*, in which he argues that our community feelings and sympathies for our fellow citizens are as "natural" as our sense of self-interest.[8] Moreover, it is clear that there is just as much greed under socialism and communism even when it surfaces as the unlimited desire for honors, position, or influence rather than money and material luxuries.

I do not want to suggest that there is some fixed amount of greed in any economic or political system, much less that greed is part of human nature. Quite the contrary. I want to argue that greed is a very general problem for the question of justice because it is so *unnatural*. It has often been argued that greed is *unreasonable* rather than unnatural, but this assumes that there is already a predisposition to be reasoned away rather than the natural wisdom and moderation that is and ought to be cultivated into our motivation. John Locke, usually held up as the ultimate defender of natural property rights, also argued and with equal vehemence that our natural sense of possession is limited to what we can use and does not take away from or harm others. There are natural as well as social limits on how many close friends, lovers, developed talents, and devotions one can have, and nature has always quite handily thwarted those who would hoard with rotting, rusting, and other modes of natural obsolescence. Of course, painful experiences of deprivation might well make us cautious about having enough, but caution, too, is neither unwise nor unnatural. Even in desperation, enough is enough. But when it comes to the pursuit of wealth and fame, which are virtually inexhaustible, our natural sense of sufficiency is vulnerable to social pressure and fantasies. People say that there is no such thing as "too rich" or "too thin," but eliminating the now-much-diagnosed pathology of anorexia leaves only "too rich," and it should be diagnosed as pathology as well. The enemy of justice is not cruelty or even hardheartedness so much as greed and the corruption it produces, not primarily in governments and institutions but first of all in our individual characters. The problem with capitalist society is that it has lost sight (as Marx predicted it would) of exactly what *capital* means and what it is for. Greed is not essential to capitalism, but capitalism uncoupled from a keen personal sense of justice can easily lead to greed.

What fascinates me most about greed is not its lust but its abstraction. Greed is not need. It is not even intelligible as desire as such. Why is it that a man like Ivan Boesky, who already has a million dollars, not only wants more but is even willing to violate the mores of his community, breach the trust of his colleagues, break the law, and risk jail and lifelong humiliation—he is already a perennial example in business ethics books—for money that he could never possibly spend in any way except to earn more unspendable money? James K. Glassman has argued[9] that it is not so much greed that is fueling Wall Street today (greed has always been around) but rather intellectual stimulation, the power of ideas. It is the sheer joy of numbers, of "leveraging up" from a four-million-dollar cash investment to a seventy-two-million-dollar loan and who knows what kinds of profits, without ever asking about the company or the product, without actually running companies or producing things, without becoming personally involved with employees or customers. But this is also greed—not just monetary greed, of course, but greed of a more pervasive kind, a greed of the soul, a greed that insists "more!" not only materially but spiritually. It is that ancient hubris directed not against the gods nor even fate but against justice, for who could ever, whatever his or her virtues, claim to deserve so many millions.

Greed in America has a more tragic source, however, in the structural desperation and insecurity, even hysteria about the future that follows inevitably in a society that leaves so much undone when it comes to the most basic social issues. A recently widowed woman is seventy and healthy and on her own. How long will she live? Will she be able to take care of herself if (when) she becomes ill? One can never know, but one does know that one does not want to rely on the help of one's children, much less on the kindness of strangers or the social security system. One never knows how much one will need, and so one is driven to ever greater lengths of anxiety and desperation. Greed is not an inner need for the almighty dollar but the lack of social planning. How could an older person in America not be greedy? And how sensitive to justice can you be when you don't know whether you yourself may someday soon be eating dog food or sitting in front of a black and white television set in the communal lounge of a state-run "rest home?" And this particular terror is not just the province of the elderly. One sees it everywhere, in well-paid middle-age corporate executives who live with the fear that they may be "out-placed" (what a euphemism!) and never be able to find another job. One sees it even in middle-class students, who along with their anxiety about finding a career are already being force-fed with long-term anxieties as insurance companies invade college campuses, encouraging eighteen-year-olds to think ahead to retirement. How can one not be greedy when financial anxiety is the only established social plan that we have? Our sense of justice has become wholly contingent: "I'll be happy to take care of someone else just as soon as I've taken care of myself." Does that time ever come?

In times of felt desperation most of us could turn out to be basically selfish, to be obsessed with our own survival and not attuned to the problems of other people. But this tragic "state of nature" is not the context in which we talk about justice, and the remarkable thing is that even when circumstances are desperate, so many people in need turn first to help others, or share what little they've got, measuring their own misfortunes against the misfortunes of others and finding themselves better off.[10] Such familiar acts of charity and sacrifice alone ought to destroy that perennial philosophical suspicion that we are all "naturally" selfish, but philosophers and social theorists keep treating them as if they were the exception. What's worse, the same theorists keep treating "the human condition" as if it were essentially a desperate fight for survival. And selfishness is said to be not an unusual response to desperate circumstances but nothing less than "human nature."

THE MYTH OF SELFISHNESS

The least pain in our little finger gives us more concern and uneasiness, than the destruction of millions of our fellow beings.
WILLIAM HAZLITT (STOLEN AND DISTORTED FROM DAVID HUME)

THE CENTRAL PROBLEM, FROM Plato to the present, is what I call "the myth of selfishness." It is the false and unflattering idea that we are all basically, "naturally" selfish; generous and altruistic acts and feelings are the exception rather than the rule. It is an offensive theory, and untrue. Moreover, the idea that justice requires some form of selflessness and self-sacrifice provokes such a predictably antagonistic reaction that it is no wonder, especially in our individualistic and acquisitive society, that a philosophy should emerge that preaches just the opposite—that selfishness is acceptable or even virtuous. The most articulate but too often hyperbolic spokesman for this philosophy of self-assertion is the iconoclastic German philologist Friedrich Nietzche; the most widely read but vulgar spokeswoman is the popular Russian-American novelist Ayn Rand. The view is that selfishness is itself a virtue, assuming, that is, that one has an appropriately noble self (an enormous assumption). But many theorists who would not for a moment buy into this ethical version of egoism nevertheless defend or find themselves stuck with a psychological variant of it, namely, the view that all of our acts are basically selfish, whether we like it or not, and that we are therefore willing to be just only when it is in our own self-interest as well. (Corollary: an act that doesn't involve self-sacrifice can't really be justice.) But justice is not just an emotional concern for the well-being of others, and it is not always (or even usually) self-sacrifice. It is also, as Plato argued, a passionate concern for the goodness and well-being of one's self.

Much of the argument for the universality of selfishness turns on a double fallacy. First of all, people confuse acting intentionally—and thereby satisfying (or trying to satisfy) one's desires and intentions—with acting out of self-interest, that is, satisfying a certain restrictive set of desires and intentions. One gives to charity or helps a blind man cross the street; one has acted intentionally and satisfied the desire (trivially) to give to charity or to help the blind man. But in satisfying such desires one is not thereby acting out of self-interest. The second fallacy is essentially verbal and involves the unwarranted expansion of the derogatory term *selfishness* (which has built into it not only the suggestion of antagonistic and excessive competition but also the connotation of indifference or hostility to others' interests) to cover all self-interested actions, whether or not they are competitive, inconsiderate, or hostile. Talking about selfishness requires restricting the use of that term to its properly antagonistic setting and not expanding it to include all intentional or self-interested actions.

In ordinary usage, *selfishness* covers a lot of ground. It includes self-interest, self-centeredness, self-concern, self-absorption, lack of consideration for others, an excessively competitive spirit, not playing by the rules, being greedy or mean-spirited, or being just a jerk of a person. These are very different attributes. Self-interest becomes selfish only when it is overly self-absorbed, callous or indifferent to the interests or the rights of others, inattentive to limits or appropriateness, and oblivious to the standards of the circumstances. A man who gets a job in order to pay the rent is acting in self-interest, but he is surely not being selfish. A mother who protects her children against a child molester is acting in self-interest but is hardly selfish. Two friends who "use" one another as racketball partners are acting in self-interest but they are hardly being selfish. Indeed, anyone who runs through a detailed diary of his or her daily mental, physical, and social activities will find very few entries that could even plausibly be called selfish. In a month or even a year, most of us can remember our handful of selfish moments, with considerable embarrassment. On the other hand, if all we mean by *selfish* is "self-involved" then how could anything that we do or think not be selfish? But that, of course, is not what the myth tries to say about us.

We are not selfish creatures, and this is not because we are remarkably well-bred or well-behaved. It is because selfishness is, for most people, a rare exception in a life that is organized according to the implicit principle that one must fit into one's society and take as one's interests not just the limited benefits to a self narrowly defined but the well-being of those one lives with as well. In this sense, it is far more wrong to think that people are naturally selfish than it is to think that they are naturally good, a view that is too often viewed as laughably childish and dangerously unrealistic. But, of course, it is perhaps indefensible to think that people are "naturally" much of anything, and to portray the spectrum of human personalities and eccentricities with a palette limited to "selfish" and "good" is mere foolishness, like trying to paint a rainbow in only black and white.

Part of what confuses us about the myth of selfishness is the fact that the motives for our actions are often self-centered emotions. True, they define and protect the self, but they are not based on self-interest as such and may even run against it. An apt example is *spite*. Spite is well represented by the expression "cutting off your nose to spite your face." It is self-destructive. It destroys precisely the object desired and runs directly counter to self-interest. And yet, it clearly emanates from and expresses defense of the self. In spite, one defeats oneself, because doing so is more gratifying and far more conducive to a sense of self-sufficiency than being defeated by someone else. In spite, one acts for oneself but against one's self-interest. It is hard to say whether such an action is selfish or not, but, in any case, it shows that the category of "selfishness" is inadequate to characterize the variety of difficult or antisocial behaviors that may be obstacles to justice. Spite is an exemplary case, but if we look at the structures of jealousy, envy, resentment, indignation, and most other emotions, it will become clear that self-concerned emotional behavior is often on the side of justice rather than what is summarized as selfishness. Moral indignation, to take one obvious example, may be based on the self but is neither self-concerned nor self-interested, and it is certainly one of the main ingredients in any passion for justice. Compassion is, in part, a matter of empathy, of putting oneself in the other person's shoes, and thus presupposes both self-awareness and self-interest. Love is not just the admiration or worship of the beloved (a common but ancient misunderstanding); it is rather a sharing of selves, an enlarging of the self, and so is neither selfless nor selfish.[11] Anger and outrage presuppose some offense to the self but, again, we are not necessarily being selfish in feeling these emotions. The self is pervasive in most of our thoughts, feelings, and activities, but it does not follow that most of what we do is in any meaningful sense of the term "self-ish"—or at odds with our sense of justice.[12]

THE GOOD LIFE

'A living, or money,' Lee said excitedly. 'Money's easy to make if it's money you want. But with a few exceptions people don't want money. They want luxury and they want love and they want admiration.' JOHN STEINBECK, *EAST OF EDEN*

You can't ever get enough of what you didn't really want in the first place. SAM KEEN

WE HAVE ALREADY INSISTED that justice won't make much sense to us if it is not part and parcel of what we consider to be the good life. Sainthood is not our aspiration, and justice will not much appeal to us unless Socrates is right about justice being its own reward and inseparable from the good life as such. What this does not require, however, is the excessive assurance that Plato, Kant, and others have felt compelled to give us (and which we seem all too anxious to accept), namely, that the rewards of the good life are somehow guaranteed. Just as working hard can be an essential part of the Protestant ethic without being a guarantee of success, so too justice is an essential ingredient in our lives without guaranteeing happiness as well. This point may seem obvious, but hopes of a guarantee have produced a great many fallacious arguments in the history of social philosophy. Leaving aside the possibility of divine justice, it is painfully obvious that there will always be instances in which injustice prospers and justice fails. There will always be unearned tragedies. It is quite enough to show that justice and the good life are not antagonists, that for most of us, most of the time, justice is intrinsic to the good life and not at all at odds with it.

What is the good life? We can expect, of course, to find different conceptions of what it is to live well, not only moving across the globe from, say, Venezuela to Japan, or across the United States from New

York to Ames, Iowa, but even across the city or the block, or across the room. One person seeks nothing more than worldly success, while another values friendship most of all. An artist would give everything to produce that one masterpiece, while a research scholar would sacrifice all just to solve that one problem that has plagued her all of her life. These differences are not absolute, of course; artists and scholars still seek out friends, and they hope that their achievements will result in recognition and success as well. But their priorities are different, and given a choice between, say, unearned success and unacknowledged accomplishment, or between time-consuming philistine friendships and creative time alone, they will certainly choose the latter. This obvious fact—that different people have different goals and desires—has given rise to a number of misleading or outrageous positions and propositions. For instance, it has become a well-entrenched dictum of liberal philosophy that there can be no legislation—and not even much discussion—of ends (as opposed to means and procedures), as if everyone in the world might want something different out of life and there is no common good or goal.

The fact that we differ in our priorities, however, is too easily taken as proof that there is an infinite number of possible goals, that there are as many lifestyles as there are people, and that there is no accounting for tastes. Nietzsche, in his *Thus Spake Zarathustra*, argued that every virtue, every passion, and consequently every person is unique, an idea that we often repeat to ourselves when defending the legitimacy of individual differences. Some of our best current social philosophers, though quite opinionated, tasteful, and even snobbish in their own lives, insist on such openness in their social philosophy. Jeremy Bentham, expressing this liberal credo two centuries ago, insisted that "pushpin [a mindless game popular at the time] is as good as poetry."[13] The idea is that justice may provide the constraints for what we can pursue, but it doesn't tell us what to want or what to aim for. But this, I want to argue, is exactly wrong, and the whole philosophical division of "the right and the good" that goes with it has been a colossal mistake. Justice ("the right") does indeed contain the essential prescription for the good life, that no matter what particular goals or interests we may each pursue, it is our doing so (and learning to do so) in the context and community of our peers that makes our pursuits and activities meaningful. With very rare exceptions, the good life is a life with other people and the goal of the good life is to deserve their affection and respect as well as (consequently) one's own respect for oneself. The emphasis on our different interests and goals, one begins to suspect, is akin to not seeing the forest for the trees—a tired but nevertheless always useful metaphor. The trees, in this case, are the variety of goals that people in society pursue. The forest is the source of meaning for virtually all of those activities, no matter how well-defined, autonomous, or intrinsically important they may be. Even the satisfaction of our biological appetites is meaningful—except in the direst straits of deprivation—according to the social context. No matter how "personal" our goals, the aim of our every action is to satisfy a self that is part and parcel of society.

Why would we want success, except that success brings the respect of our neighbors and self-respect too? Why does anyone want power, if not to command the respect (or perhaps fear) of his or her fellow citizens? Even our appetites are, to a truly remarkable extent, governed and given meaning by their social contexts—we feast and dine as well as merely eat, our primary need for shelter is largely defined by "location, location, location," and "sleeping together" is, despite the pervasive Freudian "discharge" metaphors, a biological urge whose significance, quite obviously, lies not in our selfish urges but in our relations with other people. Beyond our rather minimal biological needs, we want material goods not so much because we need them but rather because of their social significance and the status they convey. Mary Douglas, in her book *The World of Goods*, asks the unorthodox question, why do we want goods?[14] Because, she answers, goods confer status. Because goods tell others who we are. Because goods can be shared, even if only in the degenerate mode of conspicuous consumption. Indeed, in many societies, material goods are significant mainly as gifts, not as possessions, and giving them away is what gives them (and you) significance. The idea of a consumer society, in which one wants to acquire and keep as much as one can for oneself, is an anthropological anomaly. Material goods are but one medium in the dynamic of human relationships. They are very rarely desired as goods-in-themselves and almost always desired as significations of status or respect or success, even if in the guise of "convenience," "economy," "efficiency," "comfort," or "luxury." Money and wealth, therefore, are nothing but means to a means to the good life, and justice should look elsewhere for its primary currency.

That currency, I keep urging, is fellowship and fellow feeling, belonging to a community (even as local eccentric or rebel) and being recognized and respected if not loved by others. To be sure, many goods save time and make life easier, but such efficiency is itself desirable only in a cultural context where the product of the activity in question is considered more important than the ritual or the process. Many goods provide physical comfort, but whether such comforts are desirable or permissible or enjoyable is dictated by society. Indeed, what possible explanation can one give concerning the desirability of expensive imported sports cars with top speeds approaching two hundred miles an hour in urban American traffic, where the top legal speed is fifty-five miles an hour and the actual driving speed may often average twenty to thirty miles an hour, with minute by minute slowdowns and stops? Granted, the fifteen minutes or an hour a month that one gets a chance to "let it out" on an open rural road may be exhilarating, and the stereo system may be fantastic, the design may be beautiful, and the roar of the engine (or even just the idea of it) may give the driver a sense of power—but is there really any accounting for such contemporary tastes except for the fact that such vehicles display social success to one's friends, colleagues, one or two enemies, and all of those thousands of passing strangers on the highway? Have we really become so obsessed with the acquisition of prestige goods that we forget what these goods actually mean?

"But," someone will surely object, "it isn't the ownership or possession of goods or success that people want. What they really want is experience, and experiences (that is, the right kind of experiences) constitute the good life." What is happiness, after all, but feeling good about life, having happy experiences? Indeed, isn't this almost trivial, certainly obvious? But the alternative is not a life without experience, or even a life filled with bad experiences. It is rather a better understanding of what we mean by "experience," and I would argue that what we call "meaningful experiences" are virtually always social. What constitutes the meaning of an experience? Is it really just our enjoyment of it, its entertainment value, its intrinsic excitement or enthusiasm? Is it plausible to suppose that what we feel is all-important and what we actually do is secondary, that the mark of the good life is strictly subjective and only contingently (and inconveniently) connected with our life with others—as some of our most popular myths would seem to suggest? Or is it rather the shared nature of experiences, the fact that we have them with (and not just "along with") other people that counts?

To test the popular idea that all we want are happy experiences, I invented (some two decades ago) a device which I called "The Happiness Box." It was based on a classic discovery, by Professor James Olds of Cornell University, that electrical stimulation of a certain part of the brain resulted in a joyful feeling of great well-being, which was so addicting that subjects (mainly rats) got so caught up in stimulating themselves (by pressing a little bar in their cages) that they literally starved and exhausted themselves to death. Well, I wouldn't subject my students to that, but in my refined version the stimulation was provided in a tank-like structure that also provided a complete life-support system. A person could volunteer to get in the box, with the assurance that he or she could also choose to get out of the box at any time too, and be provided with a continuous sense of joy and well-being along with the means to keep them alive and healthy. The catch, of course, was that, once in the box, no one ever would want to come out. An additional complication was the fact that, after several months one's body came to resemble a partially emptied waterbed, but as one would no longer have any sense of vanity this was of no importance. Indeed, given the virtually complete elimination of the usual dangers of life—car and airplane crashes and street-corner maniacs—one was likely to live in the box at least as long and certainly far more contentedly as one would otherwise.

I ask my students, would they get in the box? A few outspoken hedonists immediately volunteer, but most hesitate or say no. I ask why: Isn't this feeling of joy and well-being exactly what they have been telling me that they want out of life all semester? Why go through the hassles of school and bad jobs and who knows what else so that they just might, for a few moments, achieve what I am offering them with assurances right now? The answers are often limp but they all add up to the same: their conception of the good life is not, as they often claim, a mere matter of self-satisfaction and enjoyment at all, but a sense of being *significant*, of living a life with and for other people. The good life is living well, not merely feeling good or good about oneself.

In a more sophisticated version of the same apparatus, Robert Nozick suggested a device that would produce not just this general and all-pervasive sense of well-being but the concrete and detailed experience of an entire life as lived. More than a mere "happiness" box, one here gets to choose—in detail—all of the incidents and experiences of a lifetime, and experience these as if they were really happening. And this would include the experience (but only the experience) of relating with other happy and justly treated people. Nozick's results were similar to mine. He argued as my students do that the mere experience of accomplishment, love, and friendship will not do, that the doing is what counts. What Nozick does not argue—but, I think, he ought to—is that the resistance to getting into the box isn't so much the "doing" either but rather the being with and sharing with other people. But then Nozick's book, with its emphasis on personal rights and its harsh criticism of distributive justice, is hardly a treatise on compassion and sharing. It may not be clear to nonatheletes why there should be so much difference or any advantage between actually skiing down a steep slope and (safely) having the experience of doing so. But there is all the difference in the world between actually talking to or caressing another human being and simply "having the experience" of doing so, even if both people were to have it at the same time. Life has meaning in a world with other people. Justice—not just the idea or the illusion but our emotional engagement with others— is an essential part of life. Philosophers too often separate justice and the good life, distinguishing "the right" from "the good," giving the former priority and leaving the "ends" of human life so wide-open that one can only be left wondering why anyone would make so much fuss about justice.

By focusing on the goals people pursue and the luxuries and experiences they crave we strangely ignore the social context in which all such pursuits, luxuries, and experiences have value and meaning. Again, we miss the forest for the trees. When we survey the variety of goods and goals that human beings pursue in life, it is all too easy to conclude that there is no generalizing about or legislating the ends of human life. But what we ignore is the social context in which virtually all activity and enterprise take place. The good life is the communal life, though not necessarily (as this so often sounds) life in a small and exclusive community. In modern America, most of us are simultaneously members of several communities, one (or more) at work, another in the neighborhood, another composed of the people we play with or pursue our hobbies with. Community life may be life in a society of like-minded folks chosen from a potpourri of citizens with slight but significant differences in morals, talents, tastes, and preferences, but the character of a community may well lie in its diversity and complementarity rather than its like-mindedness. What is essential is that a person belongs, that he or she has a social self and is therefore capable of having an individual self, by way of differentiation from as well as identification with the others. Indeed, the need for a home as opposed to a mere shelter is already a social conception and a social value rather than a merely biological necessity or a personal comfort, and so too the larger need for a homeland—the spiritual shelter for an entire community. These are not luxuries but basic needs, and one cannot conceive of the good life or of justice without them.

There are exceptions, of course: the rare pioneer or woodsman who relishes unending solitude (though usually after disastrous or in any case unsatisfying social experiences), the saint who finds his salvation only in isolation. But it is not surprising that such pioneers, saints, and hermits often start talking, not really to themselves but to an imaginary audience, a projected community to substitute for the real one (however happy or unhappy) they left behind. And there is always the rebel and the urban misanthrope who surrounds him or herself with other rebels and misanthropes while "rejecting society." But he or she is no exception, and their antisocial society is no less a society for that. We are, as Aristotle said, social animals, and it is not just prudential nor is it a matter of dutiful obligation that we care about the well-being of our fellows as well as our own. Our selves, our desires and their satisfaction, are themselves communal and communally defined. Apart from mere survival, there could be no possible self-interest or self-satisfaction apart from community. Even our most personal charms and virtues—intelligence, good looks, generosity, and honesty—are taught by, constructed by, and meaningful only in a community that practices and recognizes such charms and virtues. Our most vulgar selfishness, even in the most pathological cases, is produced and encouraged by society, indeed often the very same society that suffers from that exploitation and abuse. And so we are seduced by greed and cherish the illusion that through acquisitive and competitive self-interest we are pursuing the good life. What we miss and are in danger of losing as a society is our awareness of the all-important social context of that pursuit, the fact that our successes and acquisitions make sense only in a community. We may like to think that we pursue the good life as individuals, but the fact is that we ultimately pursue it together—and the joint pursuit of the good life is justice.

INDIVIDUALISM AND THE PRIMACY OF COMMUNITY: A MIDDLE WAY

It seems to us that it is individualism, and not equality, as Tocqueville thought, that has marched inexorably through our history. We are concerned that this individualism may have grown cancerous—that it may be destroying those social integuments that Tocqueville saw as moderating its more destructive potentialities, that it may be threatening the survival of freedom itself.
ROBERT BELLAH ET AL., *HABITS OF THE HEART*

JUSTICE IS, FIRST OF all, a matter of individual virtues and feelings, but both justice and the individual are defined within community, and justice ultimately has to be the concern of the community. But this Platonic image of harmony between the individual and the community has been all but destroyed in contemporary thinking, and our views about justice tend to get split between the two ungainly metaphors of the isolated, naturally selfish or at any rate self-interested individual and the impersonal, abstract, impartial institution—the state, the law. What gets lost in the middle is the essential sense of ourselves as being members of concrete communities, living and working together with other people. What we get instead is an alienating portrait of ourselves as autonomous but ultimately lonely souls standing in uneasy relation to vast bureaucracies which in some sense operate only with our consent but, in our more immediate experience, confront us with their disinterested rules, regulations, and demands. In response to this alienating image, the concept of community has been brought back into discussions of justice, as we become increasingly aware of our very substantial personal loss and the consequences of our bad philosophy. Justice may be an individual virtue and a virtue of institutions as well, but both those individual and institutional virtues are primarily concerned with the good of the community.

A sense of justice is just this concern for community. It is not just that the community determines who we are and what sorts of people we will be; the community is also the object of our concerns, whether in our particular personal affections for other people or a more general sense of community spirit, patriotism, or humanitarianism. One might say that the aim of justice is indeed "general utility," as the utilitarians insist, but this does not mean the impersonal sum of the well-being of all individual citizens. Its significance is to be found not in an impartial, objective theory but in a certain kind of attitude, fellow feeling about one's place in the world with others. Justice is nothing if it is not concerned with "the greatest good for the greatest number," but without the merely calculative impersonality that this often implies, and not without the qualifications of "community spirit" and "individual rights" that the best utilitarians (e.g., John Stuart Mill) include in this famous formula. Individual happiness or "utility" just doesn't make sense without friendship and community, and justice is the pursuit of *shared* well-being. Having a sense of justice is not the same as pursuing self-interest, of course, but neither is a sense of justice indifferent to one's interests, for these more often than not are one and the same.

The community is the "subject" as well as the object of our concerns. Each of us is in some sense an embodiment of the community, the community condensed to the single perspective of a single individual. We have a shared outlook with shared values, one of which may well be the illusion of the importance and the uniqueness of the individual. We may move around the country or around the world, rebel

against our roots and "build a new life," but for most of us the attitudes and accent of our childhood go along with us, and like a crystal
in a chemical pool or a stranger in a strange land we seek out and
find others who are kindred spirits. Communal values also determine
the norms and expectations that define justice—or, more properly,
our sense of justice. It is not possible to have a community without
some sense of justice, some sense of what people can legitimately expect from and owe to one another, but neither is possible—however
attractive the abstract exploits of the philosophers may be—to have
a sense of justice without a (possibly implicit) community.[15] Justice has
too long remained the realm of those moralists who defend justice
"strictly on principle," without reference to the well-being of others
or the good of the community. I would argue that this is not a sense
of justice but rather self-righteousness. To this degree, at least, the
utilitarians have always been right in saying that justice and what is
vulgarly called utility go hand in hand. You cannot have a sense of
justice unless you care about the well-being of *particular* other people.
Mere abstractions won't do. We don't just live *in* communities; we
are communal creatures, and justice has to be understood in just these
terms. The individual is the creature of the community; communities
are not just collections of individuals.

And yet, the idea of community usually plays at best a secondary
role in the leading theories of justice being discussed today. I think
that a great deal of the problem is that so many philosophers and
social thinkers are concerned primarily with what the private, individual citizen can legitimately demand rather than who he or she is or
what he or she has to contribute and care about. Again, this does
not mean that justice is the same as self-sacrifice, but neither should
it be assumed that it is therefore self-interest. What is shifting here is
the very nature of *interest*—as well as the scope and nature of the self.
Our interests are not just in our selves, narrowly conceived, though
the standard theories wouldn't suggest this, we have as much interest
in giving as in getting, and the importance of gifts in the economic
structure of many societies—even our own—is again a reminder that
is important to my argument here. So many of our thoughts and our
theories are tied up with the notion of what we each deserve, and so

few of them are concerned with our responsibilities and our social affections and affiliations.

In the standard theories, we hear a great deal today about the importance of individual rights, but this is a notion that as often as not takes community as its antagonist rather than as its ground. We place an enormous emphasis on the comparative concept of equality, but this too takes the individual and his or her advantages and disadvantages as the primary unit of measurement and leaves little room for the natural inequalities that are part of the structure of almost all human groups from families to feudal dynasties. The idea of community has only marginal utility in utilitarian theories (which are collective rather than communal) and most accounts of "the public good" are strictly utilitarian (and thus collective) in nature. Indeed, the basic unit of almost all of the leading theories of justice, from Hobbes and Rousseau to Rawls and Nozick, is the isolated, autonomous individual. Society is secondary. But where in this picture do love and family come in? How about neighbors and friends and the notions of membership and citizenship? Indeed, how do such autonomous individuals form any relationships at all, except perhaps a business partnership or a political alliance? If we don't understand such essential human relationships, we certainly won't understand justice.

One cannot understand justice, in other words, unless one appreciates the primacy of human affections and affiliations, and this is why I keep coming back to the importance of the notion of community. But it is not to be thought that this renewed emphasis on community is either obvious or noncontroversial, for all too often the word serves only as an emblem for a kind of nostalgia, or as a euphemism for a dangerous sense of enforced group solidarity. One gets the uneasy sense that, under the attractive guise of *community* an arsenal of traditional weapons of oppression is being prepared: religious intolerance, the denial of individual dissent and difference, forced cooperation, and uncritical chauvinism. At best, the word appears to connote harmony and even sentimentality, while at worst it opens the door to totalitarianism and an attack on our most basic individual freedoms. Michael Walzer has recently complained that philosophical accounts of community have been "vague, mystical, or precious."[16] Indeed, the ideal of community and the implied warmth and security and protection from crime, conflict, and loneliness are too often presented as sentimental but vacuous symbols, in much the same way that the ideal of the individual is so often represented by an absurdly inflated image of the hero—the explorer or pioneer, if not Superman or Conan the Barbarian.

And so the illusion of the individual seems to be confronted with an equally illusory fantasy of harmonious togetherness, and as the long-standing debate between individual autonomy and community proceeds—in many ways the definitive social debate between medievalists and moderns—it becomes more and more apparent that both are empty abstractions, not flesh and blood descriptions of real people or their relationships. The truth, I want to argue, is that there are no individuals, there is no autonomy and no real freedom, outside of a social context. But neither is there any such entity as a community that is not first of all made up of flesh and blood, increasingly independent, and often obstinate individuals whose membership in that particular community is almost always contingent rather than essential. Justice is first of all a personal virtue with a concern for the community, but the essential unit of justice is neither the individual nor the community (much less the institution or the whole society). It is rather what we might clumsily call "affective unities," groups, however large or small, made up of people who care about one another and about their place in the social world they share.

The unusual emphasis on emotions and personal feelings in this book thus has another target besides the excessive intellectualization and abstraction of the notion of justice. It is the unreal and destructive dichotomy of the individual and the community, the phony ideal of the wholly autonomous man or woman and the potentially totalitarian image of a coherent, single-minded state. I want to reject the dual model, in other words, of Rousseau's "natural man" and "the general will," both fictional but polemically powerful and dangerous metaphors. What gets left out of both of them—an omission that Rousseau tried to hide with a merely borrowed sentiment of "sympathy"—are just those natural feelings of dependency and affection that Rousseau tried so desperately to deny. The isolated individual has no sense of justice (and, I would argue, no capacity to deliberate about justice either). On the other hand, a rigid and fixed community (like Plato's republic) may have a rigid sense of justice built into its rules and social strictures, but it is ipso facto incapable of tolerating or even understanding those individual freedoms and differences that we take to be essential to any adequate sense of justice. The locus of justice is neither the isolated individual nor the fixed and rigid community but the complex confluence of interrelated and mutually dependent individuals who move in and out of various relationships and communities. Our particular relationships and communities may be contingent and even transient but we are defined in terms of them.

What is right about radical individualism—the myth of the autonomous, independent individual—is the enormous respect it engenders for the individual citizen and his or her interests and decisions. What is wrong about it is its denial of the primacy of human relationships and its wrong-headed assumption that people will naturally pursue their own interests, which are only occasionally shared in some sort of tentative alliance. What is right about communitarianism is the insistence that we are not naturally individuals but are always, first of all, connected to other people with whom we share our world, our interests, and our sense of self. What is wrong about communitarianism is its archaic presumption of a stable, well-formed community in a world increasingly defined by mobility and transience. Furthermore, its emphasis on enduring institutions instead of on the people who participate in them loses just that central virtue of recognizing the primacy of personal relationships rather than impersonal principles. There is also the dangerous tendency to celebrate the idea of community indiscriminately, as if there can be no evaluation, comparison, and contrast of communities.[17] And communitarians seem to miss or misunderstand the very real fear that an individual might be "trapped" in his or her community. Against any theory of community, the now-standard and almost automatic counterexample is Nazi Germany, which is more than sufficient to provoke the most enthusiastic communitarian to admit that there are bad communities. But few communities are totalitarian death camps, and it would be a mistake to allow such examples to eclipse the essential insight that community, in some sense of the word, is the primary, basic unit of social life; individuality is created only within (certain) communities.[18]

And yet, the communitarian position makes me nervous. It is not just the nostalgia and unreality of the communitarian fantasies of community and the danger of the totalitarianism. It is the suggestion that we are wholly defined by forces external to ourselves, that our identities are wholly tied up with a community or a society from which we cannot escape. It is quite reasonable to say that we are born into society and are molded and educated in the shape of citizens of that (or some other) society, but we want to say—we feel that we have to say—that such shaping is only the starting point, that as we mature, we become ourselves, with our own personal preferences and personalities and choices. And there is always that essential existentialist point—that we can always and at least sometimes should say "no!" to our parents, our communities, even our nation. Communitarians are notoriously fuzzy about the sorts of community that should replace our radical individualism and what our allegiance to them ought to be. For those of us who have been brought up as "outsiders," however, the idea of such coherent, secure communities sounds more like a nightmare. We know about them and their much-touted "solidarity" all too well. Confronted with the promise of such communities, it is no wonder that we retreat to individualism.

The magical sound of "community" is too often an empty gong. I am struck by how often and how vigorously it is sounded by individuals like Jean-Jacques Rousseau who themselves never lived in one and were or are temperamentally unsuited for the very virtues they praise. B. F. Skinner, I am sure, never lived in a Walden II, and the renewed sense of community that is so heavily promoted today keeps looking to me more and more like the closed and tradition-defined context of an eighteenth-century New England small town. Have you ever visited such a town? If a rereading of Hawthorne's *Scarlet Letter* doesn't get to you, try taking an afternoon in Sturbridge Village in western Massachusetts, as I did recently, and let the claustrophobia and moral peevishness surround you for a few hours. Shared values? Assuredly. But at what cost? Security and the mutual attention and respect of your neighbors? Sure, but how much of that is gemütlichkeit and how much is straightforward fear and social coercion? Skinner lives in a New England town along with fellow communitarian Michael Sandel, but it is Cambridge and emphatically not Sturbridge.

Communitarian Robert Bellah lives in Berkeley, California—hardly a showcase of shared traditional values. The ideal of community sounds wonderful, until we start to fill in the details. Summer camp was great, but that kind of solidarity is something we grow beyond and not an ideal for philosophers. Community must be much more complicated than mere sharing of a tradition and values.

But where does this leave us? Radical individualism, for all of its attractiveness, is intellectually bankrupt and conceptually absurd, while communitarianism, the prominent alternative, is oppressive and unacceptable. Indeed, it is the very idea of communitarianism that forces so many people back to radical individualism, with its rather extreme demands in terms of individual rights and personal autonomy, and the familiar and powerful libertarian reaction to even the most modest suggestions of liberal social planning. So what I want to suggest here is a third way, a conception of justice and society in which individuality retains its central place but without the absurd ontology that so often goes with it, in which community retains its importance—and not just as the birth context and molder of men and women—in the ongoing identity and life of the individual. The idea is to locate the elements of social identity within the individual, not as "external" influences and constraints imposed upon the individual by society. It is to see the individual as in an important sense primary, but not the individual so often fantasized in classical liberalism, the individual who stands independent and separate from and even opposed to other people and society. The truth lies between communitarianism and radical individualism, in the emotional network that ties people together in groups both small and large but never escapes the individual altogether. It is in our personal feelings and affections, not in much-celebrated supposedly universal reason, that both our individual and our social identities are to be found. And justice, which is nothing if not a personal virtue and a wide-ranging set of personal concerns with and for others, must be found in our emotions too. Ultimately, what all this talk about the importance of community comes down to is caring about other people and recognizing that we are all in this world together.

JUSTICE AS A "NATURAL" FEELING

Before we can know what we are to do, we must know what we are.   PETER WEISS, *MARAT/SADE*

. . . during the time men live without a common power to keep them all in awe, they are in that condition which is called war, . . . and the life of man [is] solitary, poor, nasty, brutish, and short.   THOMAS HOBBES, *LEVIATHAN*

JUSTICE PRESUMES A PERSONAL concern for others. It is first of all a sense, not a rational or social construction, and I want to argue that this sense is, in an important sense, natural. What I want to get rid of, once and for all, is that demeaning bit of bad biology that tells us in so many words that we are all basically independent and selfish. To the contrary, we are, in our feelings and for the sake of our survival, mutually dependent and naturally social creatures. This is not to say that our natural dispositions are characterized by unabashed kindliness and generosity, but neither do they betray that essentially mean-spirited competition suggested by Hobbes and far too many contemporary writers. Nor is it to say that our sense of justice springs full-blown from the human heart; a sense of justice must be shaped and cultivated by education. But justice is not (as suggested, for example, by David Hume) an "artificial" virtue—as opposed to our "natural" virtue of sympathy for others in need.[1] According to Hume and many recent theorists, human society invents justice to protect person and property only because we do not have enough sympathy and benevolence. If we were all naturally kind and caring, this argument says, there would be no need for justice.

According to the many variations of this familiar theory, justice is an invention of human society, an "artificial virtue." What is natural, by contrast, is self-interest, and if there are also some signs of sympathy and pity, these are unfortunately too weak to count for very much. There is no justice prior to society, for justice is a product of reason, not any kind of natural sentiment. And once we have established justice—in theory through a general agreement or social contract and in practice through the application of that agreement—there is no need for the moral sentiments except in the confines of our personal life (a mother should care for her children and an employer should have some sympathy for his employees). Justice is too serious a business—involving the structure of society itself—to be trusted to mere emotion. Thus the kindly natural sentiments are sent to the margins of society and the rational artifice of justice takes center position. And we are all taught to be grateful that we live under a government of laws, not men, and not in the "state of nature" like savage beasts.

In this chapter, I want to raise some deep suspicions against these familiar presumptions. First and foremost, I want to cast serious doubt on the familiar idea that we are all naturally selfish. Insofar as we can talk about "human nature" at all, it is clear that fellow feeling and benevolence are at least as much a part of our natural personalities as self-interest, and in any case what counts as self-interest depends almost entirely on the social circumstances in which we find ourselves. In a cooperative, close-knit society, self-interest will dictate cooperation and, one hopes, the enjoyment of the company of one's fellows. Indeed, even in the rough-and-tumble competition of American business there is a much neglected but nevertheless essential underpinning of cooperation and shared values. I think that Rousseau was right when he complained that we tend to emphasize the worst characteristics of people in our own society and project then back onto "nature." But neither should we place all of our emphasis on the kindly sentiments—on compassion, care, and sympathy. There is, to be sure, a lot more goodness (rather than cleverness) than the philosophers have often allowed, but a keen sense of justice does not arise from and cannot depend on the kindly sentiments alone. We are "naturally"

vulnerable, easily made jealous, readily offended or outraged. We
have natural attachments and affinities, and natural antipathies to
people that threaten or harm us. We naturally look after our own self-
preservation, of course, but what this means is very different from self-
interest (much less selfishness) and, like all of our "natural" passions,
depends upon context and culture for its cultivation and its
significance.

What is natural about us? To be sure, we are not born with a sense
of natural rights or universal equality or conceptions of reward and
punishment. These we learn, in various ways, as we grow up in one
society or another. Nor are virtually any of our passions "born into"
us in the strong sense advocated by traditional theorists of human
nature. But what is natural in us is our sense of being-with-others,
not just in affection and dependency but in that our sense of ourselves
and our interests is, from start to finish, tied up with other people.
What is natural in us, I want to argue, is neither self-interest nor
global benevolence but reciprocity. In some circumstances, of course,
reciprocity will require mutual distrust and antisocial defensiveness,
but, at our best, what we reciprocate is altruism, a keen awareness of
the interests of others who indicate similar concern for us. In case of
continuous or repeated encounters with others—in other words, in
most typical social situations—the variety of strategies and attitudes
that may emerge is enormously complicated. ("I did it because he did
it to me after I had already stopped doing it to him after he did it to
me" . . . and so on.) Reciprocity already presupposes not just awareness of others but a sense of shared context and consequences. At the
most basic level, this natural reciprocity is our mutual recognition of
each other as persons and interlocking self-identities.

It has been said, and not without reason, that nothing about us is
natural (except, of course, our bodies); that is, that there is no human
nature. For example, one of my favorite philosophers, Jean-Paul Sartre, long argued that we are whatever we make of ourselves, that there
is nothing that determines us, just a world that we confront and create through our choices and actions. But this is, I fear, just an extension of the same old mistakes, the sharp and implausible separation
of nature and humanity (Sartre hated nature) and the equally implausible division of a human being into two metaphysically distinct and

probably incompatible aspects—body and consciousness. We are, however, creatures of nature, and we have natural as well as unnatural inclinations, natural as well as unnatural fears and desires, natural as well as unnatural ways of approaching the world. (Fear of heights is a natural fear; fear of flying is not.) It is true that society shapes and molds us and that as we mature we make decisions through which we shape ourselves. But even Sartre argues a rather vehement version of the thesis that our selves are created in collusion with (or as "being-for") others, and though he rejects both the notions of inner self and human nature he retains (despite himself) a conception of the human condition as inescapably social. Accordingly, I want to reject the sharp distinction between the natural and the social and argue that what is most natural about us is the social. I want to show that justice is much more a part of us than those idealistic rational constructions—and the sometimes cynical view of "human nature" that underlies those constructions—would suggest.

JUSTICE IN NATURE

In the jungle, there is no justice.
H. RIDER HAGGARD, *KING SOLOMON'S MINES*

The beginnings of justice, as of prudence, moderation, bravery—
in short, of all that we designate as the Socratic virtues, are
animal . . . *it is not improper to describe the entire phenomenon*
of morality as animal.   NIETZSCHE, *DAYBREAK*

THOMAS HOBBES INSISTED THAT there was no justice in nature. In one sense, he was certainly right. A large stone falls and crushes a small stone; none of us is so sentimental as to think that this is unfair. A volcanic eruption destroys a forest; a monsoon ravages an uninhabited tropical island. "So it goes," remarks the character in a Kurt Vonnegut novel. Whether these are works of God or manifestations of forces of nature is not much our concern. We might watch in awe or fascination (preferably from some safe distance), but the question of justice is not raised. Indeed, there is no justice in nature, unless perhaps one takes the all-accepting view of Alexander Pope that "whatever is, is right."

But, of course, it was not stones, volcanoes, and monsoons that Hobbes had in mind. He was referring to people, or whatever creatures immediately preceded people, in the so-called "state of nature," humanity before it was socialized and civilized, humanity not yet fully human. His thesis was that there is nothing in either nature or human nature that makes us just, except for the conventions and laws of society. In nature, as opposed to society, there is only unceasing competition and brutality, "red in tooth and claw." But I want to argue that this is an inadequate vision of nature as well as an inaccurate view of human nature. Ever since the Greeks and before (for instance, in much of the Old Testament), "nature"—and in particular the notion of the "bestial"—has gotten a raw deal. If, as Rousseau charges, we err by projecting back onto nature vices that have only been cultivated by society so, too, I would argue, we flatter ourselves by supposing that such virtues as a sense of justice are unique to us and wholly foreign to nature. And so, before we go back and look at Hobbes's controversial thesis that men and women in the state of nature had no conception of justice, let's first go back to nonhuman nature and ask ourselves whether it is all that clear that in nature there is no justice. Is it true that justice (and therefore injustice) is an exclusively human characteristic? And is it true that justice is a purely artificial virtue, formulated by mutual agreement rather than in some sense a part of our natural outlook on the world?

For example, my dogs Fritz and Lou are one year-old twins (male and female) and though dimly domesticated are as natural as can be.[2] Since they were two months old, they have consistently displayed behavior that can only reasonably be identified as hopeful, jealous, envious, and resentful (as well as amply affectionate and playful, needless to say). I pet Lou, and Fritz comes trotting over at a desperate clip. I offer Fritz a Cheezit; he crinkles his nose and turns away disdainfully. But then when I offer one to Lou, who chomps down with evident delight, Fritz predictably demands one too. By now, they are used to getting treats at the same time and if I give Fritz two beef scraps in a row, Lou's ears flap forward, her eyebrows go up, and she utters a soft warning growl. Once I got the flu and we missed their evening walk. There was no doubt that two (if not three) creatures felt cheated. (A chair leg paid the price, in retaliation.) I can imagine a tedious behaviorist saying something about "reinforcement schedules" here, but to those of us who haven't had our common sense destroyed by any of the more vicious ideologies of the social sciences, it seems obvious that some basic repertoire of legitimate expectations, demands, and cooperative and competitive emotions is already at work here.

Perhaps I would be stretching it to say that Fritz and Lou have a vision of a world in which I love them equally, treat them similarly and follow a (more or less) regular routine of walks, runs, rides, treats, and feedings, and that they thus have a sense of justice, but it seems to me that such talk is not absurd. What is missing, perhaps, is any demonstrable sense of offense that *the other* is being cheated, and this to be sure is part and parcel of our own sense of justice. Between the two of them (and me), there is a good amount of rivalry and me tooishness, but when they are among other dogs, they display the utmost concern and protectiveness of each other. And, of course, they know full well what is their territory and what is not, and its markings (though invisible and unsmellable to me) are as clear and distinct as any Cartesian idea. Between themselves (and with some other dogs) they clearly feel compassion as well as competition, and though they may not have a sense of fairness they seem to display a keen sense of injustice, at least regarding themselves. I imagine cruelly waving a sirloin in front of their noses before I slap it onto my plate. I am sure there are those who would dismiss their desperate looks and ensuing whimpers as nothing but "behavior," but I assure you that such people will never be invited to my house for dinner.

Is it fair that the female black widow spider consumes her mate after intercourse? Is it fair that a large crocodile, if it is hungry and no other food is conveniently available, will attack and devour his smaller companion who is sunning himself on the same bank of the river? Is it fair that your cat captures, tortures, and kills a young mouse just for the sport of it? Why are we so moved watching one of those familiar PBS nature documentaries, when the wolf just misses the fawn, or the lioness tackles and kills the baby antelope? Despite the inevitable unctuous voiceover narration, "That's the way it is in nature," "It's the law of the jungle: eat or be eaten," we do not take nature's tragedies as just "the way it is." And I would insist that this is not just maudlin projection, mere sentimentality, and "anthropomorphizing." We are sharing, not just projecting, a primitive sense of compassion and justice. True, animals do not share our trans-species sympathies, elaborate theories, and unreasonable biological expectations, and neither the wolf nor the lion feels the least bit guilty about its eating habits. But this does not warrant the glib assumption that they have no strong feelings about how the world ought to be or that they have no legitimate (which does not mean, "by virtue of the law") expectations. It is true that there is a violence in nature that we have unsuccessfully strained to eliminate from our "civilized" societies. It does not follow that nature is nothing but violent, or that all sentimentality and fond feelings are simply our own projection.

On the other hand, it is too easy to move from the natural violence of tooth and claw to the conclusion that we too are by nature part of that Darwinian panorama, except for the conventions of society and the rational control cultivated by society. But this seems wrong on at least two counts: First of all, it presumes a view of human nature that is as dubious as it is unflattering. I have already argued at length that we are not—contra Hobbes—naturally violent and selfish creatures who abstain from attacking one another only because of legal restraint and awe for the power of the state. Second, it accepts a vision of nature that is equally unflattering (though it is more flattering to us), as if the brute fact that many animals kill and eat other animals were enough to prove that nature is little but relentless butchery. With respect to the first point, it is important to remind ourselves that it is not with the conventions of society and the rather recent arrival of rationality that we have learned about justice and how to get along with one another, but, rather, justice has been a part of our makeup (and the makeup of nature) all along. As Peter Singer insists, in his book on the biological basis of ethics (*The Expanding Circle*), "Human beings are social animals [and] we were social before we were human."[3] We lived together, cooperated with each other, and refrained from harming each other long before there were laws, governments, and political philosophers.

On the second point, it should be enough to point out that most

of the most vicious carnivores are also social animals and live in amiable social groups. Lions live in prides, wolves in packs, and violence
among them is rare. Not only cubs but adults play, tease, fondle, and
caress. Only a jaded Darwinian or a hunter looking for an excuse
could fail to see how much in nature is innocent vitality, beauty, and
fun. My colleague Charles Hartshorne has long argued that it makes
at least as much sense to say that birds sing in praise of God as it does
to insist that they do so only in answer to the brutally competitive
"territorial imperative," and only a behaviorist killjoy would deny
how much obvious affection and mutual enjoyment there is in nature
(though not, perhaps, between mating spiders). Nature is not a "jungle"—in the sense in which that term is so often used (with reference
to Wall Street and inner-city high schools, for instance). And are we
really any more just than a puma who tackles an elderly buck when
her cubs are hungry because we have *other* people raise chickens and
calves in utter deprivation and discomfort in order to kill them so
that we can enjoy their disguised flesh with a special vermouth sauce?
Violence is not opposed to justice, but hypocrisy is.

I want to argue that justice had its origins long before human reason invented its rules and started passing laws, and certainly long
before human philosophers made up the myth of a social contract
whereby all of us (or our ancestors) agreed to be social and civilized
because that was the rational thing to do. But half of that myth—the
"state of nature" part—was aimed at saying something interesting and
useful about human nature, about the way we are before our indoctrination and cultivation into a particular society. That attempt to say
something about human nature—and nature in general—has been
dropped from the philosophy curriculum. It is as if there is nothing
interesting to say about our natures—as opposed, notably, to our social structures and our ability to carry out purely rational deliberations. I want to go back to those old questions about human nature
in order to undermine this standard philosophical picture and argue
that justice is a *natural* feeling, in a crucial, often denied sense.

When I talk about human nature, I do not mean something fixed
and rigid, determined entirely by our genes and impervious to cultivation and personal choice. The mistake of those older theories (and
many current ones) was to make too much of the distinction between

"nature" and "culture" (which anthropologists tell us is itself one of the most interesting marks of different cultures) and to wrongly assume that whatever was natural about us would be instinctual, virtually a reflex action, or at any rate invariable and thoughtless behavior. It was also assumed (indeed, the phrase "human nature" invited this assumption) that whatever would count as part of our essential nature would have to be unique to us. That assumption, of course, begs a great many questions, since it is precisely what we share with nature that is at issue.

Whatever else we may be, we are first of all biological creatures, bodily beings and part of nature, developing in accordance with its laws. As Mary Midgley says, "We are not just rather like animals: we *are* animals."[4] One need not deny our intelligence, our flexibility, or even our "free will" in order to recognize that everything that we do is constrained, first of all, by the limited and perhaps peculiar compositions of our own bodies and brains. It may be, as Sartre and some existentialists (including myself) have argued, that no matter what facts about ourselves may confront us there is always that distinctly human perogative of saying "no!", of distancing oneself, of resisting one's own basic nature—though often at great cost. There must be no underestimating of the importance of reflection in human freedom, but the facts about us and what we find ourselves wanting and needing are often not themselves of our own choosing. We can distance ourselves from our feelings, and we can and do conscientiously cultivate our feelings, but these abilities do not undermine the claim that our most basic feelings are part and parcel of our biology. No matter how great our freedom (and it is difficult to overestimate it), we are ultimately biological creatures pursuing ends that we have inherited, in part, from the hundreds of generations that preceded us.

Human beings are social animals, but this is to say not just that we live in groups but also that we are formed and defined in and by groups, and that our needs and interests are for the most part shared needs and interests. We may be animals and therefore part of nature, but we are also members of societies that bring us up in their cultures and teach us to speak a certain language and see the world in a certain way. Justice is (in part) an outlook that we learn in a particular society and, though there may be biological foundations for all such learning (for example, our sense of dependency on the group and our concern for its well-being and the well-being of our fellow members) it is quite clear that our particular sense of justice depends upon our particular upbringing, our particular group and culture and—in pluralistic, heterogenous socities such as our own—the complex and sometimes hostile .interactions between families, groups, and cultures. It is thus foolish to deny that there are many conceptions of justice and injustice, but it is just as foolish to deny that there are certain underlying traits that make us not only human but naturally social and sociable. What we need to find is a more subtle analysis of what is "natural" to us than the alternatives of mindless instinct and thoroughly rational learned behavior. What we think, feel, and learn has a biological basis far more substantial than the all-but-trivial "potential" to be taught the requisite concepts and ideas. What is natural about us is our need for one another. Justice is not just a purely rational idea, and we care about justice not because it is rational to do so but because that is the kind of creatures we are.

IS JUSTICE AN INSTINCT? A LOOK AT HUMAN NATURE

Confining myself to the first and most simple operations of the human soul, I think I can distinguish in it two principles prior to reason; one of them interests us deeply in our own preservation and welfare, the other inspires us with a natural aversion to seeing any other being, but especially any being like ourselves, suffer or perish.
JEAN-JACQUES ROUSSEAU, *DISCOURSE ON THE ORIGINS OF INEQUALITY*

. . . ethical philosophers intuit the deontological canons of morality by consulting the emotive centers of their own hypothalmic-limbic systems.   E.O. WILSON, *SOCIOBIOLOGY*

IS OUR SENSE OF justice in some sense "natural," an essential aspect of the "human condition" or perhaps even a biological instinct? Or is it rather a matter of learning, a product of a certain sort of upbringing in a certain sort of society, perhaps even a matter of local social convention? The answer, of course, is both. But such questions have been eclipsed in most of the recent literature, for in their quest for the rational basis of justice philosophical theorists have all but ignored the real-life origins of justice. But it is not just the excessive rationalization of justice that is responsible for this neglect of the origins and nature of our feelings for justice. It is also a general resistance to talking about such enormous and woolly notions as *human nature* and a general suspicion of such concepts as *instinct* in the discussion of human behavior. It is widely believed that virtually no human activities can be explained by reference to such a "primitive" psychological notion (although it is presumed with equal arrogance and lack of argument that virtually all nonhuman animal behavior can be so explained). Virtually every human action, it is argued (or assumed), is a product of our intelligence and flexibility—even our most stupid, unthinking, and habitual actions. A few "mindless" counterexamples—yanking one's finger away from the flame, throwing out one's arm before one hits the ground in a fall—are simply mentioned in passing as rare contrasts to the normal, intentional pattern of human response. Human behavior, on this generalized account, is "rational" through and through, however flawed (and irrational) that behavior might be. In one sense, this assessment seems absolutely correct: we are now beyond the arbitrary division of the mind (and the brain) into isolated faculties, and it is no doubt true that the intelligent, conceptual, cerebral features of human consciousness (and subconsciousness) pervade virtually every aspect of our thought and behavior, even the most "mindless." But the equally commanding converse of that observation is that more "primitive" mental processes not only underlie but partly determine even the most sophisticated acts of intelligence and reason. We do not have fewer instincts than other creatures, but we have woven ours into a much more complicated psychological tapestry of culture, language, and self-reflection.

The arguments against instinct in human behavior (and biological or sociobiological determinism in general) almost always suffer from a too-limited or too-technical or simply too-demeaning notion of *instinct*. Some philosophers seem to think that an instinct is akin to a reflex response (the finger from the flame or the suddenly extended arm that stops a fall), literally mindless (actually brainless, since the neural arc is completed in the lower part of the central nervous system). But this would eliminate all human action from the realm of instinct (such reflexes would not properly be called "actions") and almost all animal behavior, too. A bird's ability to build a particular kind of nest is instinctual, but it clearly is not reflexive in that primitive sense. Indeed, birds show remarkable ingenuity in their use of materials (e.g., strips of discarded McDonald's packaging) to realize their "preprogrammed" blueprints, and while one would be more than surprised if a finch built an eagle's nest, the variability and adaptability in the finch's nest building behavior is at least as remarkable as the uniformity of finch architecture. So too, a female worker bee's ability to follow her coworker's instructions to find flowers is instinctual, but it is by no means so simple as a "hard-wired" model would suggest. It may be possible (as one leading entymologist has suggested) to actually build a "bee computer," but computers, too, need software as well as hardware and at least a modicum of information provided as data. But the variability of the bee's data and the complexity of its communication should shut up our glib talk about "lower animals" and instinct, and the fact that bee behavior tends to be rather stereotyped (e.g., when defending the hive against intruders) does not by any means rule out the possibility that a defending worker is to some degree conscious of what she is doing and that that consciousness might be viewed as—dare I say it?—a primitive and instinctual sense of justice. It is the well-being of the queen and the hive that counts, at whatever cost to oneself.

Technically, the word "instinct" is used in biology to describe animal behavior that is strictly unlearned, stereotyped, and inflexible, so much so that the behavior continues even in the most absurdly inappropriate circumstances. The most common examples are those insects which carry through with a programmed sequence of behavior even when the point of that behavior has been obliterated. The female digger wasp, for example, carries food (a dead insect) to the lip of her burrow, enters the burrow to check on her larvae, comes back up to drag in the food. If an observer moves the food even a slight amount, the wasp checks the burrow again before attempting to take in the food. This mildly sadistic process can be repeated any number of times, and the wasp will, every time, check the burrow once again. (But then again, doesn't this sound like nervous parents everywhere?) With amusement and no small feeling of superiority, we watch such ridiculous behavior as an obvious contrast to our own. (Human instances of such pointless repetition are considered pathological and presumed to have some unconscious intelligence and intentionality.) But it is a mistake to think that such inflexible behavior is all that there is to instinct. The term designates genetically inherited behavioral tendencies and by no means must these be "hard-wired" in such a way that allows no flexibility or adaptiveness. The word "tendencies" here must be treated with great caution; it can easily become trivial. (Some sociobiologists have so trivialized the Aristotelean concept of "potential"—meaning only that something could happen under some conditions, vacuously explaining virtually any behavior whatever). It is true that instinct is not learned, but it does not follow that it must be mindless or that it is opposed to (rather than basic to) learning and what is passed on by a culture. Indeed, there is obviously something right about the assumption made by those anthropologists who speculate about "human nature" whenever they find similar patterns of thinking and behavior in every people they study, for example, some sort of incest taboo and some sense of the transcendent or superhuman. The fact that these allegedly universal features of human life can be explained rationally does not mean that they are not first of all instinctual, and the fact that religion, in particular, can become one of the most intellectually sophisticated human activities does not eliminate the possibility that there is some "prompting in the human soul" which is not merely the result of acculturation or language.[5] There can be little doubt that human mating behavior has underlying (and barely hidden) instinctual promptings and patterns. We can be fully aware of our instincts, pursue them with intelligent strategies, and embellish them with the most sophisticated symbols of our culture. We can also cloak them, counter them, and develop powerful systems of prohibition and sublimation, turning natural desire into cultivated disgust, for example. What is critical is that we do not view instinct as utterly stupid, inflexible, atavistic behavior. Indeed, I would suggest that we would do much better to view instinct as the genetically inherited wisdom of the species.

Is justice an instinct? What would this mean? Philosophers today don't like to talk about instincts at all, and justice is discussed only in the hyper-rational language of strategies of maximization and rights. Obviously, such strategies and concepts are not inborn or in any sense "natural" (except, trivially, for the fact that they are the product of our natural intellectual capacities). But we too easily suppose that what counts as justice must be found in the satisfaction of certain purely rational standards (e.g., that everyone should be treated the same or that everyone should get what they deserve) rather than in the satisfaction of certain prerational urges or demands. Of course, there is no reason to suppose that our rational standards will disagree with our prerational urges; indeed, there is every reason to suppose that the former will articulate and express the latter. It follows that the realm of reason, in which the instincts have so often been denied, may actually be a good place to start looking for them. Could it be, for example, the recognition of other people *as people*, not necessarily as equals but as others to be attended to in a certain way, as we would like to be attended to ourselves, is not so much the highest principle of rationality as a basic prompting of species self-recognition, the same as we find not only in the "higher" mammals but in even the most primitive creatures? Could it be that the idea of desert is not, at base, the product of reason or (as Alasdair MacIntyre argues) of tradition but some much more basic sense of propriety and merit, founded, originally, in primitive family and tribal deference and mutual dependency on special skills and the rewards that reinforce them?[6] Could it be that the central sense of "balance" or "fit," which is so central to our conception of retributive justice, is not so much a principle of practical reason as it is a natural pattern of perception, an essential demand that we impose on the world? Needless to say, we should not expect to find such "principles" operating in some inarticulate and perhaps even subconscious way, for that would be to make once again Rousseau's much-cited mistake of projecting back onto nature what is properly to be found only in people in civilized society. But neither can we or should we dismiss the idea that prerational promptings underly the various principles through which we give an account of our sense of justice. What we will have to look for is some demonstrable sense of a "natural" concern for others which is not simply self-interested (but not disinterested either) and which displays all of the variability and plasticity that is so evident in our social theories and practices.

Almost a century ago, Nietzsche, Freud, and William James all suggested (in very different ways) that our most basic social sentiments were indeed based on instinct. Today, the place to start our investigation of the indisputable linkage between social behavior and biology is in the discipline named "sociobiology." Its recent origins can be traced to a monumental book published in 1975—*Sociobiology: The New Synthesis*, by Edward O. Wilson of Harvard University.[7] Unfortunately, that discipline has often and sometimes rightly been accused of intellectual irresponsibility, not only because of the political objections to *possible* applications of the theory to touchy social issues but also because of Wilson and his colleagues themselves, who have made outrageous and obviously polemical comments regarding the scope of their craft. Against his colleague John Rawls, working just across campus, Wilson suggests that ethics (and the question of justice in particular) should be taken "out of the hands of the philosophers." The specter of biological determinism combined with the suggestion that culture and education could not significantly change our behavior provoked an explosion of outrage. But the basic premise of sociobiology—that biology to some extent determines our characters and our cultures—seems to me undeniable. Before we are thinking, self-analytic, rebellious creatures, we are first of all social creatures who have distinctive feelings for each other and predetermined tendencies for how we behave in groups. And what sociobiology has given us is a way to understand what sort of thing our biologically grounded, "natural" sense of justice might be.

THE SOCIOBIOLOGY OF ALTRUISM

Scientists and humanists should consider together the possibility that the time has come for ethics to be removed temporarily from the hands of the philosophers and biologized. . . . While few will disagree that justice as fairness is an ideal state for disembodied spirits, the conception is in no way explanatory or predictive with reference to human beings.   EDWARD WILSON, SOCIOBIOLOGY

AGAINST THE MISTAKEN VIEW that human beings (and all other living creatures) are essentially selfish and primarily interested in their own survival, biology teaches us the very opposite, that human beings, like all creatures, are essentially "species beings." Against the ancient wrong-headed view that animal behavior is essentially selfish, the fundamental category for contemporary sociobiologists is "altruism." This is a term that has often been abused and distorted in various writings on ethics (e.g., by Ayn Rand, who turns the contrast between selfishness and altruism into the distinction between noble self-preservation and pointless self-sacrifice). To be sure, there is something of a logical gap between the rather sophisticated intentions that go into the altruism of human philanthropy and the unthinking reactions that enter into a doe's panic-stricken efforts to hide her fawn from the wolf who approaches the clearing, but the first point to make is their similarity. Both the philanthropist and the doe are making a sacrifice (how large or life-threatening isn't yet the issue), and the same question raises its head, whether in biology or moral philosophy: what could possibly motivate an individual to make such a sacrifice? But the question is based on the obviously fraudulent presupposition that every individual strives first and foremost for its own interests and survival. Hobbes marked this off as the one natural right that no state or power could abridge, and even Rousseau took individual self-preservation to be the preeminent natural sentiment. Moral philosophers have long struggled against the presumption that every human action—moral or not—is ultimately motivated by self-interest, and evolutionists used to take it as a matter of course that the struggle for individual survival and self-preservation is the first principle of biology. But moral philosophers have come to the conclusion, in various ways, that not all motivation is self-interested and that moral motivation, in particular, is not and perhaps must not be self-interested. Evolutionary biologists have similarly come to the conclusion that the struggle for survival and self-preservation, even if primary, does not take place on the level of the individual organism. The harder question is, at what level does it take place? And how can this be under-stood as the basis of altruism? Is altruism, once understood, the basic biological sense of justice we are seeking?

For many years, it was believed that the level of self-preservation was the species. That would indeed explain why the doe risks her life to save her fawn—as her means for preserving the species—but the explanation is not convincing. Is there any sense in which the doe can be said to be aware of her species? And is it plausible to suggest that she is aware of her fawn primarily as a representative of the spe-cies? It seems much more plausible to suppose that she risks her life because the fawn is her own. But, then the question becomes, Why should she care whether the fawn was hers or not? What does she owe to her fawn? (Or as one wit recently put it, What has posterity ever done for us?) Why does she not save herself and have another one? Of course, such thinking is too cynical for any creature except a human being, but the point is critical: why do creatures care about their young? One popular answer is that they care, not about their young as such, but about the survival of their genes, and genetic sur-vival depends upon one's offspring. But again, the answer is not wholly convincing. Why should the doe care about the survival of her genes? Does she in any sense know that she has genes? It is obvi-ous that her genes make her care about her young as a means of assuring the survival of her genes, but is this the motive for her behav-ior? And, in any case, this is hardly selfishness or self-interest; and as an animal's sense of its own group or even species expands, we can expect that this expanded sense of self-preservation will develop as well.

In pursuing any such line of inquiry we are forced to recognize the disparity between two very different and hard-to-connect levels of analysis, genetic theory on the one hand and what we might call the animal's "phenomenology" on the other, in other words, what the animal knows, believes, perceives, desires, and otherwise experiences. To pretend that the latter has no dependence on the former is an error, but to deny the significance or existence of the latter is also an error. Genes determine perceptions and attitudes just as assuredly as they determine physical and physiological features, though subject to far more extensive modification. And so at least two equally difficult questions arise here: What is the nature of those genetic features whose function is to preserve the genes themselves? And what kinds of experiences and goals guide the animal to act in such a way as to maximize the chances of the genes' survival? (How does the altruistic creature perceive others of its kind and, in particular, its own off-spring?) But what do we mean, in both questions, by "the genes"? A "gene" here is obviously not an individual strip of DNA but rather a *type* of gene, which may be instantiated by any number of similar strips of DNA. (Thus *genotype.*) A very specific set of genes is unique to the doe herself. She shares a very large subset of genes with her fawn, a somewhat smaller subset with her various relatives, a smaller subset yet with other members of her species, another with all hooved animals, another with most mammals, most vertebrates, and so on. Which are the genes that are to be preserved? The doe's genes are not equivalent to the genes of the species, and her urge to preserve her offspring should not be confused with a desire to preserve the species. Of course, the species will not survive if no members of the species survive, but this is very different from shifting the locus of survival from the individual to the species to the individual gene. What is clear is that animals act altruistically (at least where their own offspring are concerned) and that such behavior is neither narrowly self-interested nor "rational" but instinctual. What is not clear is the scope of altruism, whether we are naturally disposed just to care for our immediate kin, or for others of our kind, or for something that is concrete but also invisible and extremely abstract, our genes or genotype.

While the theory of evolution in some general outline is now virtually taken for granted by most people who have no theological ax to grind, the details of the theory of natural selection have undergone enormous changes since the days of Darwin. To begin with, Darwin, writing several decades before Gregor Mendel carried out his famous experiments with peas, did not know about the gene. Consequently, he could not specify the mechanism for the transmission of the traits that he described, so the "level" or "unit" for natural selection was not yet an obvious problem. With the discovery of the gene by Mendel in the 1860s, the vague and general thesis that the survival of the species was the result of natural selection became the much more focused exploration of the mechanisms of mutation and adaptiveness.

One result of this research was the curious thesis, defended by Richard Dawkins in his appropriately titled book, *The Selfish Gene*, that the basis of natural selection is the gene, so that the gene becomes the focus for survival.[8] Individuals, groups and species alike exist, so to speak, for the sake of continuing the gene. It is somewhat like the old joke that human beings are an invention of water to get itself carried from one place to another. Organisms and their offspring are vehicles to carry genes from one generation to another. Our altruism is nothing less than our basic role as servants of biology, having little to do with family or fellow-feeling but with the blind unconscious impulse to salvage and transport our genes. (Schopenhauer's pessimistic view of life as nothing but the pointless will to more life sits well with much modern biology.)

There is a tendency in the popular literature (to which Dawkins's title but not his thesis lends itself) to go one step further and anthropomorphize the gene, as if the gene itself were "selfish" and actually tries to arrange matters to assure its survival. But such purposive (or "teleological") thinking is just what the modern theory of natural selection is intended to rule out (which is why it is often so starkly juxtaposed with the straightforwardly teleological notion of "creationism"). Natural selection is a matter of chance, not design. If an organism or its offspring is well adapted to the environment (a risky matter if there are sudden changes—a dwindling of the food supply, a change in the climate, local pollution, overpopulation, or the arrival of some new predator, for example), then those genes will survive. If an organism or its offspring are ill adapted to a new environment, those individuals, perhaps an entire group or species, will die out, and the genes they carry will die out with them. But the gene is not just a passive passenger, of course. If the gene should reduce the chances of survival of the organism or its offspring who carry it, either because the gene has mutated or because the traits it produces are maladaptive in a new environment, then it becomes the mechanism of its own demise. On the other hand, mutations that make an organism adaptive to new conditions that would have been fatal (the mutation of antibiotic-resistant bacteria is an obvious example), then the gene obviously enhances the likelihood of its survival along with that of the organism that carries it and its offspring. Altruism, then, would have to be accounted for in terms of an evolutionary mechanism that in-creases rather than decreases the chances for our survival.

Within the frame of this established picture, however, the phe-nomenon of altruism raises a special set of problems. Altruism is the tendency of an individual to help others in the same group or species, to risk and even sacrifice its life for the sake of others. But suppose that an individual is among the first in its group or species to acquire an "altruism gene." It helps others but is not helped in return. It risks its life for others but cannot expect to be saved by those it has risked its life for. It is pretty clear that such an individual has little chance of surviving for very long, and therefore its new altruism gene has little chance of surviving. (In more prosaic human terms, nice guys finish last—or rather, they don't tend to finish at all.) Of course, if the entire group or species were to mutate at once, so that every indi-vidual had an altruism gene, then the intragroup cooperation would very likely increase the chances of everyone's survival and therefore of the gene's survival. But even then, we all know from experience what happens if there should be another mutation, in a few individ-uals, who went back to the philosophy of looking out for number one. The trusting innocence of the others would allow the mutants to have inordinate successes, reproduce frequently and, consequently, spread their genes throughout the group once again. So the hard question becomes, how can altruistic genes appear in a group without being wiped out? In a philosophical perspective, this amounts to the question: why wasn't Hobbes right? Why aren't we all naturally selfish and our lives solitary, nasty, brutish, and short, except that we all find that organized society serves our selfish interests and, once estab-lished, the authority of that society threatens us with punishment if we act too freely on our naturally selfish impulses? How could a caring and compassionate creature survive, unless all of the other creatures simultaneously became caring and compassionate too?

Charles Darwin wondered how the few "offspring of sympathetic and benevolent parents" could fare against the larger number of chil-dren of "selfish and treacherous parents belonging to the same tribe," and how "the bravest men, who freely risked their lives for others" and would therefore "perish in larger numbers" could live to pass on their genes to larger rather than ever smaller numbers of children.[9] A partial answer, of course, is that altruism within a group is an obvious advantage, sometimes even a necessary condition, for the survival of the group against an external threat. But the life of most animals, most of the time, is lived within the group. Status and survival are determined by the group. Reproductive ability—including especially acceptance as a mate—is an intragroup concern. The advantage of altruism and cooperation in the face of an external threat cannot therefore account for altruism. Altruism, to be favored by natural selection, would have to be advantageous within the group as well. This is obviously the case with humans, for whom the threat of an external threat that is not itself man-made is virtually extinct (except, perhaps, for a few deadly viruses). Accordingly, Darwin tried to explain intragroup altruism not by reference to heredity but rather in terms of human reason and group praise and blame—in other words, in terms of ethics. But this was not only to abandon his own proto-sociobiological mode of explanation (which he was prone to do regarding human evolution); it also tended to presuppose just those features of society he was seeking to explain, namely, why we should care about praise or blame from others, and why reason should have developed in the fashion that it has. Is the explanation, in fact, individual self-interest?

It is clear that purely selfish behavior—behavior that tends to give one's own survival top priority—is an evolutionary dead end. But pure altruism, giving one's all for the species or (in more "New Age" terms), giving oneself over for humanity or for the sake of the Earth itself, is also evolutionary suicide. If justice were nothing more than mutual compassion, it is not likely that those who were born with a significant sense of justice would survive in this competitive world. Thus I want to argue that justice is not just altruism but involves both care and compassion and those very "negative," especially defensive, emotions such as anger, envy, jealousy, and vengeance. The nasty edge of justice, as well as its sense of mutual concern, has made it evolutionarily successful and essential to society. People aren't naturally selfish but they aren't naturally selfless either. "Pure reason," if there were such a thing, would be a mechanism for personal extinction rather than a means to survival. There is something to the wisdom of that old Talmudic scholar who said, "If I am not for myself, who is for me?"[10] Altruism, as we have come to understand it, is an essential piece of the puzzle of human nature but it is certainly not the answer. The truth (as so often) lies between pure selfishness and pure altruism, and the evident locus of altruism and cooperation is, to employ two overly sociological rather than biological terms, the family and the tribe and, eventually, by extension, the whole of humanity and life on earth.

It is possible to have something of one's genotype survive without having children, of course. If one's siblings have children, those children also carry many of one's genes. One will therefore have altruistic and even self-sacrificial feelings towards one's siblings and their children. So too with cousins, uncles, aunts, although the percentage of one's genotype carried on (and thus the chances of one's genetic survival) diminishes as kinship becomes further removed. Of course, the human desire for continuity—which we pretentiously call "immortality"—has become much more imaginative than this, and whether or not genetics determines our desire for continuity (along with religion and philosophy), the preservation of our genes (as opposed to our souls or our creations) is just one part of the picture. In his *Symposium*, Plato has Socrates give but limited praise to "vulgar" biological immortality while he offers extravagant praise to the sort of immortality achieved by Homer, "for who would not prefer such glorious children as these [*The Iliad* and *The Odyssey*]?" And many religions, both before and since Plato, have intellectually rather than biologically evolved a variety of visions of immortality, most of them, interestingly enough, falling into the categories of extended selfishness (purely individual salvation) or cosmic selflessness ("the One," Nirvana, etc.). The one ancient religion that seems to tune its visions of immortality to modern biological wisdom is Judaism: what survives of an individual is his or her influence, memories, and genes. There is no immortal soul, but neither does one melt anonymously into the vast indifference of the universe. We are neither basically selfish nor unthinkingly and self-destructively altruistic. What we care about begins close to home and close to our genes, but in modern Judaism, at least, what we end up caring about is an open question.

THE EXPANDING CIRCLE AND THE RISE
OF RECIPROCAL ALTRUISM

When a person (or an animal) increases the fitness of another at the expense of his own fitness, he can be said to have performed an act of altruism. Self-sacrifice for the benefit of offspring is altruism in the conventional sense but not in the strict genetic sense, because individual fitness is measured by the number of surviving offspring. But self-sacrifice on behalf of second cousins is true altruism at both levels; and when directed at total strangers such abnegating behavior is so surprising (that is 'noble') as to demand some sort of theoretical explanation.   E.O. WILSON, SOCIOBIOLOGY

ALTRUISM, THE BIOLOGICAL IMPULSE to care for "one's own," gives us the opening wedge in the age-old but nevertheless perverse and mistaken theory that people (and animals) are basically selfish. But this is surely inadequate, one might object, for no one would say that people are just if they care only for their own children, and in terms of self-interest, it can be argued that we have only "expanded the circle" slightly—to use the metaphor that Singer borrows from W.E.H. Lecky—from individual selfishness to a selfishness that includes oneself and "one's own."[11] But our opening wedge (to mix the metaphors) now opens the way to a further expansion, to include friends and extended family and, eventually, communities, even total strangers whom one recognizes as "kin" just by virtue of their being human or intelligently sentient. (It is hard to overestimate the significance of such moving political terms as *fraternité*, *sisterhood*, and *the family of man*.) Altruism is not selfish, but it is certainly not selfless either, and if we are to understand justice we cannot take the "pure" phenomenon of self-sacrifice as our model. The doe saves her fawn because it is, in some sense, part of her, but so too we care about justice because humanity is, in the relevant sense, part of us. Moreover, I already argued that altruism is not by itself sufficient (though it certainly is necessary) to account for our natural promptings of justice. An understanding of altruism as contextual and contingent is also needed. In simple nonscientific language, we tend to be nice to other people because they are nice to us. Altruism, in other words, is not just concerned with how we perceive and treat other people. It is, first of all, concerned with relationships. We have the natural propensity for altruism, but whether or not that propensity is exercised usually depends on whether or not it is or will be reciprocated. Caring for one's own young is thus not the model for justice; it is only the opening of the argument. The origins of justice lie not in altruism as such but in reciprocal altruism, our natural tendency to help and care for each other, but, when necessary, to punish one another as well.

How does the circle expand, from strict kinship relations to more distant relations to community to all humanity and beyond? I think that Rousseau (and many other philosophers) had it right when they pointed to resemblance as the key to sympathy; we feel closest to those who are (or seem to be) most like us. In terms of evolutionary biology, that means shared genes, but in terms of a larger biology that includes all the phenomena of perception and intelligence, resemblance is recognized in everything from a familiar smell to an abstract principle of human equality. We may owe our first allegiance to our blood kin, but we learn early to recognize that we have much in common with our neighbors, our heroes, our pets, even our gods. Familiarity breeds reciprocity (whether or not it sometimes breeds contempt), and the circle expands as we learn to recognize and bring out the similarities we share with all of our countrymen and women and many of the beasts that we live with. Reason no doubt can play a role in this growing awareness, but its primary ingredients are perception, sympathy, and reciprocity. The expanding circle does not require a leap of reason but rather an open mind and (a bit of folk biology) a receptive heart.

Kinship may be genetic but we know very little of our genes. (The fact that we want to know whose genes we share is an intellectual and cultural overlay, not a natural inclination.) What we do recognize is proximity and familiarity, and our sense of kin is defined first of all not by our knowledge of genetics but by our being raised together and sharing a life. When two siblings long separated are reunited, they are, not surprisingly, a bit shocked and considerably confused. For most of us now, in a mobile, rapidly changing urban society, "proximity and familiarity" describes friends and colleagues as well as (or rather than) family, and with television and inexpensive jet travel, the circle of our phenomenological kin is enormous indeed, because we recognize how many features we share with millions of people around the globe. Whether or not we want to join Lecky (and Singer) in enlarging the circle to include " a nation, a coalition of nations, then all humanity, and finally, . . . the animal world," the point stands that the altruism identified by the sociobiologists in every parent's concern for his or her offspring is by no means limited to actual genetic kinship. As the world becomes more proximate and familiar to us, our mutual concern will expand as well. The danger, of course, is that sibling rivalry (and contempt bred by familiarity) will nurture not the altruistic aspects of justice but rather its defensiveness and antipathies. But the first move is expanding the circle and moving beyond the myth of natural selfishness.

If the circle is to be expanded, I would want to argue that it must be first of all through just this sense of kinship and shared humanity (and animals too). I want to be very cautious about joining Peter Singer in the invocation of *reason* as the means of building on our natural impulses. The danger is that reason, instead of building on our natural impulses, may instead undermine them. If the basis of justice is personal feeling for those we care about, there is a very real danger that, in overenlarging the circle to include everyone and everything or in turning from the personal to the impersonality of reason, we will lose precisely that dimension of the personal that produces justice in the first place. But I want to be equally cautious about premature enthusiasm for those universal feelings of love, called agape, which have been defended by some of the great (and not-so-great) religions of the world. There is the very familiar danger that such feelings, however noble their object or intent, will degenerate into a diffuse and ultimately pointless sentimentality, or worse, that form of hypocrisy that (it is often said of such "lovers of humanity" as Rousseau and Marx) adores the species but deplores almost every individual member of it. The natural sensibility that is at issue here is nothing so lofty as love or even universal care but rather a kind of kinship or fellow feeling, which may well produce much caring and many kindnesses but will also provoke rivalry and competition. The basic biological sense we seek, in other words, is not so much a particular attitude or emotion as it is a sense of belonging, the social sense as such.

That social sense can best be summed up in the realm of genetics and evolutionary biology as the phenomenon that Darwin described and has since been named "reciprocal altruism." Reciprocity is extremely important in all intelligent social life, for it provides the quid pro quo or tit for tat which is the basis of every ethical system larger than the family (though it is obviously central to dealings within the family as well) and which is the foundation metaphor of justice. (It is worth noting that much of ethics and current theories of justice dismiss such tit-for-tat dealings as sufficiently personal [or insufficiently impersonal] and sufficiently self-interested [or insufficiently disinterested] to be irrelevant or at least inadequate.) But reciprocity presupposes an enormous leap in genetic development, not just in terms of intelligence as such but in terms of the capacity to devise interpersonal strategy. One can have enormous intelligence (as do idiots savants) but shockingly little of that interpersonal sense that is required for even the simplest strategic exchange. And it is not necessarily thinking or negotiating that is essential here. Successful traders and businessmen often claim (truthfully) that they don't so much think about what they are doing as "just feel" or "just know" what to do. So, too, animals display a remarkable array of strategic behaviors—mother birds pretend to have broken wings to lead predators away from the nest, monkeys fool one another by uttering misleading cries—and we feel no need to postulate Pentagon-like tactical mentality behind their behavior. In such cases, even Darwin himself seems to have erred in giving too much credit here to the role of reason and not enough to heredity, but to attribute strategic skill to heredity is not to relegate it to merely automatic behavior. Good game players usually describe their own skill in nonintellectual terms. A good billiards or pool player simply "sees" the shot, she doesn't calculate it. A good poker player doesn't sit skimming a mathematical odds book on the one hand and a psychology of facial expressions text on the other. Of course, one must (to some extent) acquire such skills but it doesn't follow that such skills are not also (or may not alternatively be) genetically based or that the general capacity for strategic behavior—the tit-for-tat attitude as such—may not be so based.

Reciprocal altruism, in summary, is the readiness of an individual (or a group) to aid another individual (or group), with the expectation that it will be helped in return. The usual but by no means most dramatic example is that of mutual grooming among apes and monkeys. (Cats, by contrast, do not seem to have this ability or these expectations. Mother cats groom their kittens and occasionally one another. All cats, of course, groom themselves, but there seems to be little evidence of reciprocity.) Monkey A grooms monkey B with the expectation that he will be groomed in turn. But the key to reciprocal altruism is not just this hopeful expectation. It is the reaction when the expectation is not fulfilled. It is a reaction of resentment, a reaction of hostility, perhaps even a reaction of vengeance. Here again is the old cynical question: what if one monkey finds that he can get groomed by everyone else without doing any grooming in return? And what if others perceive his strategy and follow it? The answer is that there can be no altruism (except in isolated cases) unless there is also a keen sense and expectation of punishment. The strategically selfish monkey must "learn his lesson." He suddenly finds himself without groomers, and perhaps he is even snubbed or exiled from the group. If failure to fulfill the terms of reciprocity were not punished, there would be an obvious advantage (one familiar to us in large, impersonal urban societies) to being a cheater or a dead-beat, to taking without giving. Punishment is both deterrence and reform, but it is also retribution, not in an abstract sense determined by law but in the most gut-level sense imaginable. We feel the need to punish wrongdoers because doing so is the precondition of any successful scheme of mutual cooperation. That knowledge is built right into our genes, and it manifests itself in some of our most powerful motives and emotions. It follows that any adequate discussion of our natural propensities and sense of justice must include not only the "nice" feelings of kinship and altruism but their necessarily "nasty" correlates.

The example of mutual grooming may seem unimportant and unessential to the life (as opposed to the comfort) of the animals, but part of my point here is to emphasize the essentially social (as opposed to survival) instincts and inclinations of animals. And how many of our activities, from "common courtesies" to getting along at the office or "bucking for promotion" are just so many variations on mutual grooming? ("You scratch my back, I'll scratch yours.") Sometimes, however, the success of reciprocal altruism can be a matter of life or death. Birds and antelopes acting as scouts, for example, often risk their own lives warning their respective flocks and herds of impending attack. It is expected that others will do the same in return. When a group of zebras is attacked by lions, some zebras will risk their lives fighting off the attackers. If enough zebras fight, a victory is likely; if only a few fight, the outcome is sure to be disastrous for them. Again, it is expected that others will do the same in return. Animals acting in concert can be very effective in warding off predators who could easily kill an isolated member. Animals in groups who practice "every beast for itself," on the other hand, have to have a very high rate of reproduction for the group to survive, because many will fall to predators. Especially in life and death matters, reciprocal altruism requires harsh punishment for those who fail to reciprocate. The bird or beast who does not warn the group when danger approaches will be ignored or abandoned. The zebra who hides from a fight and allows his fellows to be killed must be taught that the risk in battling lions is less than the certainty of being punished by the group. This may sound overly rational and calculating, but the fact is that it goes on in nature all the time, without either reason or calculation. The genetic mechanisms are obviously complicated, but the results are quite clear. Reciprocal altruism, including the demand for punishment, gives an obvious genetic advantage to those in the group who comply and condemns those who do not. It thus becomes a powerful force for group cohesion as well as an advantage in competition with other groups. It also explains the need for hostility and punishment within otherwise amiable groups and shows that justice cannot ignore the role of the negative emotions, not as obstacles to justice but as some of its driving forces.

TIT FOR TAT AND THE EVOLUTION OF COOPERATION

Oh what a tangled web we weave, when first we practice to
deceive. SIR WALTER SCOTT, MARMION

ONE DOMINANT METAPHOR IN recent evolutionary theory is the game, which does not, of course, suggest that the animals that are fighting for their survival are having fun. But it is a metaphor that has the virtue of embracing both competition and cooperation within a framework in which the integrity of the group is presupposed. In this, it is both slightly similar to and dramatically different from that "state of nature" model that defines so many theories of justice from Hobbes and Rousseau to Rawls. It is similar in that it imagines a group of individuals (or subgroups) competing for ends but willing to cooperate to achieve them; it is quite different in that there is no illusion of group formation: the integrity of the group and an enormous amount of mutual agreement has to be presupposed before the game analogy can take hold. Furthermore, the ultimate aim of the game, as opposed to the various ends and interests of the creatures in the mythical state of nature, is the game itself, in other words, the continuation and stability of the group. Here again, one is tempted to use the terms "altruism" and "selfishness" in order to force a false distinction between individual self-interests and dedication to the group, but the two are intimately intertwined both in nature and in human society, and it is only the rare example of human eccentricity and rebellion (taken as the very definition of human nature by French existentialists and American screenwriters) that underscores the possible frictions between them. So we have to be careful here. Playing games presumes pursuing goals, and one might say "different goals" (I want it to turn out so that I win; you want it to turn out that you win). Playing games often involves competition, but this competition is always framed by mutual cooperation and profound shared interests. Reciprocal altruism is well explained by the game analogy because the very term is otherwise misleading, "reciprocal" suggesting two fully independent individuals and "altruism" suggesting a high degree of generosity or selflessness.

One problem with the game analogy is the fact that we so often tend to think of games in terms of one particular type, the so-called zero-sum game. A zero-sum game is distinguished by its utter competitiveness. One person (or team) wins, the other loses. Or, if there are several players, the sum total of all winnings and losings is zero. (For example, five poker players might end an evening with holdings of [+ 8], [break-even], [− 5], [− 5], [+ 2].) Even here, of course, the overriding interests of group integrity are obvious even if not center stage: people play poker for shared enjoyment or mutual distraction; it is only the occasional "big game" or a player's getting in over his head that allows the zero-sum character of the game to eclipse the shared objective. Team sports presuppose tremendous amounts of group cooperation and coordination as well as competition. In fact almost all games pay off for all participants quite apart from the inner logic of winning and losing. In practice, the zero-sum game is something of a myth, and it is only in theory that most of our favorite games are zero-sum games.

Most of the interactive games that we actually play, however, are not even in theory zero-sum. The indirect or vicarious benefits not only of participating in but also of observing most social activities are too often ignored or dismissed as minimal. Playing baseball or football provides (not only "should provide") much more benefit than winning the game. Watching baseball or football may provide even more, though the formal game theorist may have a hard time explaining this (unless, of course, the spectator holds a bet on the outcome.) Political writers often note with disgust how much of democratic politics is determined by the vicarious thrills of watching a scandal unfold and a candidate undo himself. The truth is that the emotional benefits of such a spectacle may far outweigh the grey expectations of so-called political reality. Just being part of a group activity confers benefits (at various levels of abstraction) that the activity itself might not suggest at all. The best example I know is office meetings, whether in a corporation, a political group, or an academic department. Everyone complains that they are a waste of time. (Complaining seems to be one of the regular rituals regarding meetings.) Everyone agrees that "so many meetings are useless." But the fact is that, even if very little or nothing is accomplished *in* the meeting, the real payoff is the mutual confirmation of group membership (even if it is expressed in mutual bickering, insults, or contempt). Meetings solidify group solidarity, even if they display or bring out divergence and disagreement. So too, most social activities, including "just lying around in the sun" as well as more rigorous, goal-oriented joint enterprises, fulfill the function of increasing the integrity of the group.

I mentioned at the beginning of this section that the game model differs from traditional "state of nature" thinking in that there is no illusion of group formation. Quite the contrary, the integrity of the group and a great deal of mutual understanding and, even more important, familiarity, must be presupposed. One problem with a great many explanations of social behavior, and this is particularly true of game theoretical explanations, is that they suggest if they do not presume a "one-shot deal," an isolated confrontation or conflict that (apart from the agreed-upon rules of the game) has no context, no background, and no continuity. Our dramatic image is: two champions from opposite sides of the globe facing one another for the final showdown, two teams from outer space facing each other for the one and only time, two professional poker players meeting in a small Western saloon for the big game. But the truth is that almost all of our activities, including those that are quite clearly designated as games, depend upon a familiar context in which the game is played, and the most ruthless competition has its rigid restrictions and established limits. (The "jungle" metaphor in business is particularly revealing in this light.) Two teams who play each other in football have very likely played one another before and will play one another many times again. Poker groups are much more often than not the same bunch of guys who meet regularly, perhaps in the same den or kitchen, perhaps even for years or decades. Almost all of our social activities presuppose a social background in which we feel reasonably comfortable and confident about what is going on. Most of our competitions—no matter how novel and how exciting they may seem at the time—are of necessity routine. (It may be the first time you've competed at Wimbledon, but your participation is possible only because thousands have competed in the same place before.) Most of our activities are repetitive, long-standing campaigns rather than final showdowns. Most of our games are repetitive or very long and protracted. That gives the game model a very different place in our thinking about justice.

Perhaps the best example of this broadened consideration is the game model that has attracted so much attention in economics as well as in social and political philosophy. It is called "the prisoner's dilemma," and it is distinguished by the fact that although it is not a zero-sum game it is harshly competitive. The standard example (which gives the game its name) is this: two suspected criminals are arrested and separated for interrogation. The prosecutor approaches each suspect separately and offers him a deal: "If you confess (and your colleague does not), you'll get a light sentence. If you do not confess (and your colleague does), we'll hit you with the maximum sentence." It is evident that if neither confesses, there will be no case (and no sentences). If both confess, they will both go to jail, though with shortened sentences for their cooperation. Each suspect thinks: "If I stick by my pal and keep my mouth shut and he does the same, we'll both walk out of here. But then, suppose he confesses, (the dirty fink!): I'll be here until I'm middle-aged and he'll be home watching television. But if I confess, the worst that can happen to me is a shortened sentence, and maybe (if he keeps quiet, the poor sap!) I'll pretty soon just walk outa' here."

The dilemma is obvious, and the model has been applied to any number of human social situations from economic bargaining to nuclear deterrence and the problems of global pollution. ("If I let my car's catalytic converter burn out I'll increase my speed and gas mileage and I won't make the city's air pollution that much worse; but if everyone lets the catalytic converter burn out, then we'll all choke to death.") In such cases, the distinction between one's own selfish interests and the larger interests of the group (or the species) seems to make some sense, but it does not follow that the response to such a dilemma must be the demonstration that it is ultimately in one's rational interest to go along with the group (in this case, to repair one's catalytic converter). Typically, such demonstrations presuppose that it is rational to pursue one's own individual interests, but the very nature of the dilemma thus thwarts those calculations that would demonstrate one's personal advantage. Besides, what kind of degenerate notion of "rationality" is this, couched purely in terms of self-interest? The most common alternative, the attempt to break out of the prisoner's dilemma altogether and talk only of duties and obligations, takes rationality too far in the opposite direction, away from any personal considerations. Thus the Kantian reply, "What if everyone were to do that?" But, of course, the presumption is that everyone won't. This, however, is just the move we have been fighting all along, with particular respect to "justice." It is true that cooperation will ultimately benefit everyone and that a person has certain obligations, but the selfish, cynical freeloader knows nevertheless that he can get away with not cooperating and be none the worse off for it. The proper answer to such collective prisoners' dilemmas is that one ought to join in with the group neither out of self-interest nor out of duty but because we are all in this together. Among other things, not to cooperate is to be a lousy human being. It is selfishness that is unnatural in such cases, not cooperation.

One might try to base this argument on rational calculation of one sort or another, but it should be clear that what we are talking about is not essentially reflective or even reasonable. It is an inherently felt sense of group membership and participation. It applies to our animal examples (warning the group, fighting predators) as well as to human interaction, and though we might be loath to talk about strategic calculation on the part of birds, antelopes, and zebras, the phenomenon of reciprocal altruism is itself sufficient evidence that something like this strategic decision has already been made by nature, that is, proved to be advantageous in natural selection. But here, too, to talk about advantage is to miss the point. Whether or not cooperation is advantageous, that is not the reason why these animals behave as they do. They don't figure out, "I ought to do this because it will be good for the group." They simply know, "This is to be done." So, too, with us: for all of the game-theoretical and strategic talk about justice, the basic element is our natural tendency—not based on calculation or entirely on cultivation—to do what ought to be done. The "prisoner's dilemma" (like most game-theoretical dilemmas) is a deviant case.

We may on occasion be pitted against one another—more likely than not by some sadistic or conniving human being rather than by nature—but that is not our usual situation.

There are (at least) two things wrong with the prisoner's dilemma, in addition to the unflattering suggestion that the model of our thinking is the self-serving calculations of a desperate criminal (or irresponsible citizen). The first is that the standard example ignores whatever relation and mutual affection (including contempt and resentment as well as fondness and friendship) exists between the two suspects. The calculation is virtually always expressed (as seems to be the social scientific wont) purely in terms of the mathematics of the various outcomes (the length of the sentences) and probability that the other *as a rational agent* will confess. The example ignores the possibility that the two men might know each other very well (and that both might know, for example, that one of them has an almost hysterical dread of prison while the other has been used to serving time since his early experience with reform school). It ignores the comparative likelihood of each particular person's confessing under pressure—which is what both prisoners will most likely dwell upon in their own deliberations, not the abstract rationality of utility functions and probabilities. And what about such questions as: Does one want to get even with the other? Does one want to protect the other? Is one of them furious because he knew all along the caper wouldn't come off and now wants to say, in effect, "I told you so"? Game theorists like not to be bothered with such "merely subjective" concerns, which interfere with the pure rationality of the decision. But, the elegance of theory and the thrill of theorizing aside—once one subtracts such "subjective" elements from the case one no longer has an example.

The second problem with the example is partially a derivative of the first, and it is the point we began by making. The case presumes a one-shot deal, a one-time decision rather than an ongoing relationship which is filled with deals and decisions. Of course, there are such incidents in our lives; occasionally they turn out to be fatal. But most of our dealings with other people are not one-shot games involving purely rational agents but repetitive activities in the context of long-standing relationships. A fly-by-night business may depend on the oddities of one-time operations, but most enterprises strive for and presuppose a long-standing relationship with the customer (as Tom Peters argues in the bestselling *In Search of Excellence*).[12] A chimp may on occasion find himself confronting a total stranger in the woods, but he will spend most of his time dealing with other chimps whom he has known all of his life. A group of zebra may at some time find themselves facing an attack by an animal the likes of which they have never seen before (a group of touring French schoolchildren, misbehaving on the savanna), but most of their lives they will spend facing the same predators, possibly even the same group of predators or exactly the same lion. And what happens in the long-term situation is very different from what happens in the one-shot case. In a long-term situation—even when it is a matter of life and death, of predator and prey—an arrangement is worked out, an accommodation (which is not yet to say, a "social contract"). So the question for humans too becomes not, "What is the rational strategy in this particular situation?" but rather, "What should we/I do given that such and such has been going on for so long and in the past he/she/they have done such and such and in the future we will face similar situations in which I wish that he/she/they would do such and such?" Reciprocal altruism, in particular, presupposes such repetitive and longstanding arrangements, for on a one-shot basis, reciprocity is always over-simplified and altruism is virtually always a less than optimal strategy. A businessman acts not just in terms of the current bargaining situation but in the light of the other person's reputation and past dealings and his own hopes and expectations for future arrangements. A bird or beast acts "for the moment" perhaps (as so often we do) but that moment is pregnant with the future and full of the past.

The problem of strategies for repeated games has been the subject of much recent work in game theory, although, again, one might complain about the very restricted view of rationality that enters into these calculations. Nevertheless, the results of recent research are enlightening, particularly with reference to prisoner's dilemma–type games. In a book enticingly entitled *The Evolution of Cooperation*,[13] Kenneth Axelrod tackles the problem of strategy for repeated games of this sort: what would be the optimum strategy for the two aforementioned criminals who faced prosection not just once but any number of times? (In fact, of course, prosecutors might have such a strategy, as might public defenders, but few criminals would have so many chances to establish a strategy with the justice system.) But this is just the ongoing situation of almost every businessman and, closer to home, every married couple or pair of siblings. If the other person cheated you or lied to you last time (if your partner in crime confessed), how should you behave this time? If the other person played it straight with you last time (if your partner kept his mouth shut), should you play it straight this time? Over a long period of time, there are numerous sequences of possible actions, but in terms of strategies, a few prime possibilities present themselves: play it straight until the other cheats and then you cheat all the time, too; play it straight no matter what the other does; start out cheating and don't stop no matter what the other does, for example.

What Axelrod found (using computers to run through the outcomes of all possible strategies) was that the optimum strategy, charmingly entitled "tit for tat", is to play it straight until the other cheats, then cheat once but go back to playing it straight so long as the other does. If the other keeps cheating, he thereby cheats himself. If you refuse to cheat, of course, you become the sucker to his continuing successes. This may seem self-evident, but that only shows how steeped we are (whether by heredity or experience) in reciprocal altruism, for that is exactly what this strategy is. Pure selfishness is self-defeating, but so is pure altruism. What does work is the presumption of cooperation coupled with the threat of punishment, even, in extreme desperation, the threat of mutually self-destructive punishment. In real life, of course, the games are many and complex, with many different "players": and transactions over long periods of time—even lifetimes. But our instinctual sense of tit for tat, or reciprocal altruism, is the mechanism that lies behind them, and our sense of social belonging, that basic sense that we really do matter to one another and, even in the most hostile circumstances, cannot ultimately do without one another, is its presupposition. In political philosophy, this hardnosed strategy for mutual cooperation, and not the abstract ideal of a perfect universe of rational beings is the basis of justice.

THE LEADER OF THE PACK: JUSTICE IN THE REAL STATE OF NATURE

While a society of equals—whether baboons or jackdaws, lions or men—is a natural impossibility, a just society is a realizable goal. Since the animal, unlike the human being, is seldom tempted by the pursuit of the impossible, his societies are seldom denied the realizable.   ROBERT ARDREY, THE SOCIAL CONTRACT

WE HAVE TO GET away from thinking about justice as something distinctively human and opposed to the "bestial" in us. Our sense of justice is continuous with and not imposed on nature, and it has often been pointed out that animals show more sense in matters of justice and mutual well-being than we do. It is ironic that our most popular metaphors about social disorder refer to "the law of the jungle" and "acting like animals" when in fact the jungle and the animal kingdom show little of the sociopathology that plagues us in modern, urban human societies. On the other hand, both cynics and conservatives compare us, with mixed relish and disgust, with those most efficient and sociable of all creatures—the ants. (It is not merely incidental that Edward Wilson, the father of sociobiology, spent the first several decades of his career studying ants.) But the comparison is ill-chosen, and not just because an ant colony is so offensive to our sense of freedom and individuality. Ants cooperate but they hardly reciprocate, and while their behavior is clearly altruistic it would be difficult to justify the thesis that it is so out of any consciousness of desert or mutual expectation. And yet, we shouldn't forget that justice for Plato lies in the harmonious working together of the various members of society, each of whom knows his or her place. Justice is not reciprocity but undisturbed harmony. Ants certainly recognize one another and display all the earmarks of fellow feeling (greeting one another, total cooperation, joint hostility to strangers). All the ant colony lacks, on Plato's account, would seem to be a few philosophers to properly reflect on their happy situation. But what is missing is not only freedom but reciprocal response, a sense of individual strategy, and a memory of past encounters rather than just a program for mutual recognition. Surely any adequate conception of justice must take full account of the importance of social harmony and efficiency, but harmony and efficiency alone are clearly not enough for justice. As much as some people might admire the efficiency or the savagery of ants, ants make poor candidates for a natural model of justice.

The problem, however, is that social philosophers, when talking about "subhuman" animals, treat them more or less all like ants, as beastly automatons programmed to cooperate without any intelligence or consciousness at all. Now I am an intellectual agnostic on the question of ant and insect feelings (though I personally find it hard if not impossible not to believe in them), but it is clear that such agnosticism is not plausible with most mammals (except, that is, insofar as one is willing to accept the ridiculous position that we do not know the feelings of our fellow humans either). So instead of generalizing about justice in our fellow creatures, I would like to take a look at a couple of close mammalian relatives who would be denied thoughts and feelings only by the most fanatic of behaviorists: the wolf and the chimpanzee. The chimpanzee is an obvious choice: in purely biological terms, the human is closer to the chimpanzee than the chimpanzee is to the gorilla. The wolf is not so obvious a choice, except for its reputation as a social animal (too often betrayed by the more dramatic lore of the "lone wolf"). My aim is to get us to think about human justice in terms that are continuous with the rest of the animal kingdom rather than unique to humans—thus emphasizing our natural feelings instead of our overblown rhetoric of justice. What we call justice differs only in complexity and not in kind from reciprocal response patterns in other intelligent animals. Personally, I would rather talk about dogs, my own in particular, and regale you with further stories about their games and rituals, their pet peeves, their sensitivity, their occasional generosity, their touching sense of mutual dependency, their frequent fights caused by jealousy or envy and, occasionally, resentment. But the charge of sentimentality would be inescapable, while with wolves I am forced to rely on much more objective research.

Wolves as predators are ideal examples of "the highest degree of cooperation and coordinated movement"[14] (Wilson, *Sociobiology*, p. 246). The entire wolf pack is an ideal study of reciprocal altruism, in which not only joint ventures but friendships, animosities, and ongoing feuds are in evidence. Wolves form pair bonds with distinctive sexual roles, allowing for the raising of large litters, and families together form packs, allowing them to attack and kill much larger prey than themselves. The rules and roles of the pack are firmly established, but certainly not by hard-wired instinct or automatic behavior. In the field, wolves engage in remarkably well-coordinated strategic action, for example, some lying in ambush while others drive a herd of caribou towards them (Kelsall, 1968).[15] Within the pack, wolves are also highly adaptable and find—or make—their place. Like humans, they are instinctually social but not instinctually bound to any particular role or status, although their individual features (male or female, powerful or sickly) have much to do with their ambitions and their success. Within the bounds of their instincts and within the pack, wolves prove themselves and test and develop their skills, most of which concern the pack's mobility, need for food, and constant struggle against the elements. It has been noted that the existence of wolves is extremely similar to that of early human hunter-gatherers. Their social behavior is set by their nomadic circumstances as well as by their biology. These circumstances establish necessities and, consequently, a sense of duty. (How did modern philosophers ever get the idea that duty is defined by moral principles?) Mothers have duties to their pups; scouts have specific duties to the pack during their watch. Wolves' pack and family roles make it appropriate to talk about individual wolves in straightforward ethical terms. If we shy away from such terms as *duty* and *obligation*, we should ask why philosophers and animal behaviorists have made us feel compelled to do so and whether any other terms as accurately reflect pack life or our own social life. So, too, we can talk with clear and unambiguous sense about *virtues*. Some wolves are very dependable, others are less so. One or two make good leaders, others do not. Some females make excellent mothers; occasionally, and for a variety of reasons, one is an utter failure. All in all, there should be no objection to our talking about what Mark Murphy calls "the good wolf," not according to *our* evaluations (according to too many northwestern ranchers, the only good wolf is a dead wolf) but in terms of its own context and role in society.[16]

So, too, I think that we can talk of *fairness* here. Some wolves are fair, a few are not. Some arrangements are fair (from the wolf's own perspective); some are not. Wolves have a keen sense of how things ought to be among them. Much of this sense of propriety is, no doubt, mainly a matter of contingency and habit (as it is with us), but there is no reason to deny without evidence that some of it is inborn too. But whether learned or innate, justice is just this sense of what ought to be, not in some bone-in-the-sky ideal theoretical sense but in the tangible everyday situations in which the members of the pack find themselves. Wolves pay close attention to one another's needs and to the needs of the group in general. They follow a fairly strict meritocracy, balanced by considerations of need and respect for each other's "possessions," usually a piece of meat. What they lack is the ideological squabbling that leads otherwise intelligent and sensitive human beings to insist on just one of these ingredients of justice and ignore or deny the others.

The members of a wolf pack are individuals. They have particular qualities, roles, and personalities. They recognize each other according to their differences and behave quite specifically to one another, nuzzling, growling, snapping, playing. One could make the point that all wolves are equal in that they are all worthy of recognition as members of the pack. But it is even more obvious that all wolves are neither created nor treated as equal in another sense. Dominance relations are central to the organization of the pack. Dominance is expressed in priority of access to food, favored resting places and, especially, in mating.[17] (Wilson, p. 247; Mech, 1970). Wolf packs are hierarchies. There is almost always an alpha wolf at the top and an omega (the "trailing" wolf, the wolf that travels far behind the rest of the pack) at the bottom. Every wolf has his or her place in the pack. The alpha wolf is the leader, "the lord and master of the pack"[18] (Wilson, ibid.) the animal that coordinates the movement of the pack and leads the chase. Other wolves defer to him in ritualized ceremonies. And yet any overgrown, particularly ferocious wolf could in fact force the pack into submissive positions, so it is not fear that defines the alpha position, nor is it status alone, nor does the position necessarily depend upon the male wolf's virtues. Some studies have shown that the lower-ranking wolves are the best hunters and often make the most kills. (This is but one of many more analogs to Plato's hierarchical republic that could be pointed out here. The common claim that

Plato held an anti-natural view of justice, in opposition to Aristotle's "naturalistic" view, should certainly be reconsidered in light of these animal analogies.) Justice is a matter of rank and of knowing one's place and duties within the pack. Outside the pack, of course, the concept does not apply—but then, neither does it apply for us, until we expand our sense of our own "pack" to include people of other groups, other nations, other worlds.

Rank among wolves is both learned and "natural." It is in the establishment of deference and leadership patterns, as well as in mating behavior, that reciprocal altruism is most in evidence. Rank is established early in life with seemingly innocent puppy play-fighting and reinforced throughout life in frequent confrontations, most of which consist of no more actual hostility than a growl and a submissive gesture. Occasionally there is a serious challenge to the leadership, and at some point there will be a change. But despite the central importance of the alpha male (the pack may fall apart without him), the role of every wolf is in some sense essential, and nothing would be more detrimental to the pack than a breakdown of cooperation because of internal squabbles. Wolves don't think in terms of winners and losers, so the sort of political envy that defines a Cassius or a Cataline is unknown to them. Every wolf knows his or her place, with or without a fight to prove it. Why should the fact that we humans do not "know our places" but are always trying to "get ahead" mean that we, not they, have "ethics" and a need for justice? The difference isn't having a sense of justice but our apparently unique ability to create situations and societies in which that sense of justice is thoroughly thwarted.

Because wolves cooperate as a group and sort themselves into ranks and roles to provide organization and coordination, considerations of fairness become particularly important. Rank determines priority of access to food, among other things, and it is obvious that access to food is, for wolves, one of the primary "social goods"—but it is by no means the only one. Wolves also need acceptance by the pack and "self-esteem." None of this would make any sense, however, if wolf life were dog-eat-dog, or if all eating were a form of feeding frenzy. Access to food is not a matter of "might makes right" but an established order of priorities. Rank establishes priority, but not exclusively. Sharing is in fact the norm, and generosity is common. Perhaps it would be stretching it to say that every wolf has a built-in sense of every other wolf's "right" to his or her food, but every member of the pack has a clear ownership zone (about a foot and a half from the mouth) in which a piece of food will not be disputed by any other wolf, no matter what his or her rank. Food within that zone "belongs" to that wolf. When a small animal is killed by a lower-ranking wolf, he or she will be virtually immune from encroachment on its "property" by a higher-ranking alpha or beta. But what is most significant here is that the existence of ownership does not preclude but rather makes possible generosity. There can be no generosity if there is no security in ownership, but where there is such security, acts of generosity are distinctive (to the wolves themselves as well as human observers) and cannot simply be dismissed as the result of implicit threats or force.

Here again the phenomenon of reciprocal altruism comes into focus. A wolf who is generous can expect generosity in turn. A wolf who violates another's ownership zone can expect to be punished, perhaps ferociously, by others. Wolves will engage in a form of generous behavior called "mutual submission," whereby one wolf will solicit food from another and the "have" wolf will regurgitate food for the "have-not" wolf to eat. One might also talk about fairness with reference to physical aggressiveness. It is obvious that violence within the pack would endanger the survival of the pack and ultimately of the species itself. In fact, fighting rarely occurs within the pack. Domination and submission are not based on physical force as such but rather on displays of threat and deference. Two rivals will display to each other until one loses face and withdraws. The dominant or alpha wolf may assert its status by using its jaws to pin the subordinate to the ground—but its jaws do not close. Ritual goes hand in hand (paw in paw) with respect; no one in the pack suffers physical injury, except in the rare cases of rivalry over mates or dominance status[19] (Fox, 1971, p. 20). So long as rank order is observed and respected, there is little hostility or aggression. Social mobility is a dangerous luxury among wolves and not necessarily essential to justice, but this does not mean that wolves can't be individuals and ought to be viewed, as we (probably wrongly) view ants, as creatures devoid of social sense and without any sense of possible conflict between their own interests and the demands of justice.

JUSTICE FOR BONZO: SOME PRIMATE CONCEPTS OF FAIRNESS

Competition occurs everywhere in nature, but competition within
a species is almost never for material resources.

V.C. WYNNE-EDWARDS, ANIMAL DISPERSION

BEFORE PHILOSOPHERS START TO write about imaginary prehistoric humans in the "state of nature," they ought to spend some time watching chimpanzees—or at least a few old Tarzan movies. Some conservatives may bristle at the suggestion that they are only once or twice removed from the great apes, but chimps actually practice the kind of community most conservatives can only talk about. They occupy a "persistent and reasonably well-defined home range over a period of years."[20] (Wilson, op cit, p. 268) Every chimp is public-spirited. Respect for authority is taken for granted. Every chimp has his or her place in the troop, and the roles of both male and female are distinctively tied to their biology. Even so, every chimp is a distinct individual with a distinctive personality and a distinctive contribution to make to the group. The group, though it may stay together for generations with little migration in or out, is "a loose consocialization of about 30–80 individuals" (Wilson, ibid.), an ideal community according to much utopian and actual urban planning from Saint Thomas More to Skinner's Walden II.

A dominance hierarchy exists in chimpanzee groups as well as in wolf packs, but it is not quite like the stereotype (most often observed in the neurotic environment of the zoo) of the overbearing male who monopolizes the food and the females and is resented by all of the other males. The alpha chimp sits atop the linear "pecking order" with no really noticeable advantage over the other chimpanzees. Alpha males don't really lead the group. They need not have any special skills or talents and they need not be particularly good hunters. In fact, they don't actually *do* much of anything, like many a monarch and political muckety-muck in human society. The alpha position, in other words, is one of status rather than function. In terms of human justice, it is a matter of vanity rather than merit. Accordingly, Jane Goodall insists that the position of alpha male confers nothing but "a psychological advantage."[21] Instead of brute force, most alphas get their positions through ambition, persistence, intelligence, and skill in forming coalitions and alignments with other chimpanzees. The alpha male may be an intelligent, active chimp (Goodall's "Mike") or a brutish, thug-like creature (Goodall's "Humphrey"). Mike held alpha rank for a substantial amount of time by distinguishing himself by running through the group rolling cans from Goodall's campsite ahead of him. He lost the rank when Humphrey rose up and beat him senseless, but such displays of violence are rare and usually unnecessary.

The much-celebrated charms of Tarzan's "Cheetah" notwithstanding, chimpanzees can be ferocious. Physical aggressiveness among group members is sharply curtailed; the contest for alpha male is usually one of wits and not of brawn. Although dominance interactions are frequent, they are typically subtle threat displays, and fighting rarely breaks out among group members. Confrontations like that between Humphrey and Mike are uncommon: intragroup struggles are not advantageous to anyone and extremely disturbing to the group. A good threat display, without need of physical force, establishes and reconfirms the order within the group. Indeed, as even the most casual observer recognizes, the primary mode of interaction between most chimps—including adults—is *play*. The marked displays of status that establish the hierarchy are closely akin and similar in style if not form to the playful gestures of the young. Our images of animal life in the wild are strangely perverted by the idea that everything is a "struggle for survival" (in the infinitely repeated phrase of television "nature" documentaries). But the truth is that play is at least as much a part of nature as the Darwinian struggle. It is play that provides the vehicle for our sense of reciprocity and altruism. And it is central to our concept of justice as well. It is not just that we think that everyone ought to get some fun out of life (it is worth noting that "fun" is a term untranslatable into many languages, e.g., Japanese). Our conception of justice as fairness typically hinges on game metaphors and game analogies, which is why social philosophers so often turn to game theory as a workshop for their theories of justice. A sense of justice, however essential and serious, is not the wholly somber concern that we often make it out to be. In a society of potentially vicious individuals, play, not the social contract or the power of the state, is most effective at keeping order. (In that sense, football really is more important than politics.)

The playful gestures of the young function as a harmless form of intragroup competition and, over time, establish the group hierarchy. But we too easily forget what an incredibly sophisticated form of activity play is. It is not just "behavior" but behavior that requires both self-awareness and a keen sense of the other's intentions and well-being. One acts as if he or she is attacking but must at the same time clearly communicate the fact that it is only play. Play, in other words, is a form of what Gregory Bateson called "metacommunication" (communication about the meaning of other acts of communication).[22] Very young chimps (like puppies) do not have the power to hurt one another seriously, so it is not as if they have to have this sophisticated awareness from the first. But as one bites and the other yowls, the lesson that biting hurts gets learned, and by adulthood, the dangerous gestures that one chimp makes toward another are much modified and communicated in a much more complex way. These adult games, like infantile play, are carefully contained, but now by the self-awareness and social awareness of the participants. In both adult and infantile play, an awareness of one's own status and intentions is essential— a particularly remarkable bit of consciousness (and especially troubling to those who insist, whether for species-chauvinist or methodological reasons, that all animal behavior must be understood without reference to consciousness). Play among apes and monkeys (as among wolf pups and puppies) is devoted largely to mock aggression, chasing, and harmless fighting. Chimps and other apes and monkeys invite play with a "play-face," typically mouth open, teeth covered, perhaps a series of hoots. (Wilson compares this to the "relaxed grin of human beings." "A man who taps a friend on the arm or punches him lightly on the chest is unlikely to receive a hostile response if he remembers to grin broadly at the same time."[23])

Among chimpanzees, as in wolf packs, there is a keen sense of fairness and propriety. When a chimpanzee (or a group of chimpanzees) makes a kill, the hunter or hunters give out a cry that indicates there is fresh meat. One can imagine a troop of hungry chimps and a veritable free-for-all as the meat (a highly coveted chimpanzee food) is torn to pieces and devoured. But this is not what happens. In chimp society, the hunters themselves have priority, and the other animals surround them and the kill in what Goodall calls a "sharing cluster." The animals that were not involved in the kill do not grab for or make off with the meat; regardless of their relative statuses in the hierarchy, they will beg for some of the food. Their success or failure will depend on a variety of factors, such as the amount of meat involved, the amount the possessor has already consumed, and the relative age, rank, and relationship of the individuals. Some males are more generous, some more tolerant, some more aggressive. Those who beg may reach out and touch the meat, often glancing at the face of the possessor as they do so, as though to gauge his mood—or they hold out a hand, palm up, toward him, or reach to his mouth for the morsel he is chewing.[24]

In fact, most of the chimpanzees will get a piece of the kill, but the explanation is not so much pure generosity or simple altruism as it is, again, reciprocal altruism. Next time, one may not be the hunter and, someday, one's hunting days will be over. Generosity is insurance, which is not to deny that it is also generosity. (Once again, the glib distinction between self-interest and altruism finds little application in everyday life.) And yet, a chimp may choose not to give up part of the kill to a particular individual for any number of reasons. There is nothing automatic about it. Perhaps one of the begging chimps had been stingy in the past. As with humans, some chimps just don't like each other. Reciprocal altruism and personal affections together create a complex tapestry of feeding arrangements, with the possibility, at least, that some unpopular chimps may well go hungry. One might argue that such calculated and whimsical sharing is hardly an example of distributive justice, but that objection seems to assume just what we are questioning, that a conception of justice presupposes an unrealistic ideal of equality and an inappropriate emphasis on the objectivity and impersonality of distributive decisions. On the other hand, could one argue that the chimp who makes the kill has a "right" to keep as much of the meat as he wants and to decide as he likes who should get the other pieces? Does the notion of a *right* make sense here? Is this how the chimps see it? (The mere notion of *expectation* seems quite inadequate.) These questions are certainly complicated, rather than answered, by the fact that although meat is highly coveted it is almost always shared. Plant food, which makes up the majority of the chimpanzee diet, is not shared, except between mother and child. Where ordinary food is concerned, chimpanzees keep what they gather and distribution is not an issue. It is, perhaps, not nearly so complex as the distribution of food and favors in even the most "primitive" tribal society, but a sense of fair distribution seems to me to deserve the name *justice*, whether or not it involves a theory or a concept of justice as such.

One can draw a number of conclusions about justice in nature from these cursory observations of wolves and chimps. Some of them would be controversial and polemical, for example, the idea that hierarchies are natural and philosophers should just learn to live with them instead of pursuing an impossible ideal of equality. But what should strike us about both wolves and chimps that is not nearly so controversial is their intelligence, their distinctive personalities, their remarkable (and sometimes ingenious) playfulness, their sociability and social organization. They are not, as Descartes infamously suggested, mere automata programmed to perform actions that happen to be marvelously coordinated. These are creative, intelligent, imaginative individuals who live and live well together and adapt and adjust to the most minute changes in their social environment. Instinct plays an enormous role, of course; instinct establishes the sense of sociability in the first place, and instinct no doubt establishes the basic patterns of social perception and thus sets the social agenda. Nevertheless, social living itself is a dynamic interplay of individual power and personalities. Social consciousness doesn't mean the lack of individuality or personality, but it does mean that our ill-considered dichotomy between self-interest and altruism (whether in the hands of a social theorist or a sociobiologist) makes little sense and explains even less. The group is primary, and "the individual" and even "self-interest" make sense only within the group. This isn't fascism; it is basic biology. The individual wolf or chimp, excluded from its pack or troop, is a monster, a pathetic if also dangerous creature who is not to be taken as exemplary but as pathological. So too, an individual human being, excluded from society and considered in isolation, as in the "state of nature," is not "natural man" or the true individual but a monster, a pathetic being without an identity, without a personality, without a future, without a past, without an existence. A human being is human only by virtue of his or her social membership, and it is the nature of that membership to care about others, to respond to them as appropriate under the given circumstances, to be kind and helpful when possible, defensive and punitive when necessary. That is justice, in the state of nature as well as in the most sophisticated and civilized society. The circumstances and the terms of reciprocity vary greatly between different human cultures, but we should not be misled into thinking that justice is nothing but a cultural artifact without a proper foundation in nature.

THE SOCIAL CONTRACT AND "THE STATE OF NATURE" RECONSIDERED

The just society, as I see it, is one in which sufficient order protects members, whatever their diverse endowments, and sufficient disorder provides every individual with full opportunity to develop his genetic endowment, whatever that may be. It is this balance of order and disorder, varying in rigor according to environmental hazard, that I think of as the social contract.

ROBERT ARDREY, THE SOCIAL CONTRACT

THE PROMINENT FOUNDATION OF so many current theories of justice—the so-called "social contract" and the contrasting "state of nature"—should be reconsidered within the context of this biological picture. It is all well and good to insist that this picture is merely hypothetical and in fact a thought-experiment to bring to light the rationality of certain social arrangements. But the fact is that certain deep assumptions are being made about justice and about human nature before that thought experiment even begins. One need not accept the hard determinist's view of the world and insist that what we are by nature determines what we must be in order to recognize that we are by nature certain sorts of creatures. We are, like wolves and chimps, products not just of our genes but of the conditions in which we find ourselves, which are, first and foremost, social conditions. That is where the state of nature theorists go so wrong; there is no individual in the state of nature, no war of all against all except in a few paranoid or polemical minds and in the self-justifying rhetoric of some Wall Street hostile takeover moguls. It is not just the fact of our sociability that is in question here; it is our natural constitution as social animals, in which reason may play a major role, but only because it becomes instrumental in the management of the increasing complications of our natural reciprocity.

The idea of mutual agreement between autonomous, rational individuals is so simple and so appealing that it sometimes seems almost impossible for us to think of a palatable alternative view. Do we not enjoy the fruits of that agreement and sometimes quite consciously abstain from antisocial or even violent actions just because we value the peace and the sense of community and security that we know depend on everyone's resisting certain obvious uges and ignoring certain dangerous desires? But why do we think that this is strictly a matter of reason and mutual agreement rather than a rationalization of a more basic sense of mutual cooperation and dependency? Do we not in fact think of society and especially of government, in terms of mutual consent and mutual benefit? Do we not insist, not just for ourselves but as a matter of universal political principle, that the state should serve and listen to its people just as its people should serve and—with critical caution—obey the state? But even on the most superficial anthropological, biological, or historical examination, does this mean that society was formed by the coming together of already independent and autonomous fully formed human beings—or is it an idealized way of saying that societies and governments have evolved over the centuries by way of a natural process of mutual adjustment and mutual suspicion? (Robert Nozick suggests, in place of social contract theory, that states emerge out of such an evolutionary process as mutual protection associations.)[25] We never were, never could have been, and never wanted to be the independent, autonomous creatures that Jean-Jacques Rousseau, expressing his own paranoia, fantasized about. We never were the selfish, nasty, brutal beings that Thomas Hobbes posited. We never were and never could be the purely rational beings that John Rawls envisions. We are not in any sense the independent and self-interested creatures that smart philosophy and bad biology make us out to be. It is true that we are often suspicious of governments and rightly distrustful of the state in any form, but it is ultimately self-defeating if not self-destructive to be distrustful of society per se, even if in any particular case it makes perfectly good sense to be reflective and reform-minded about the character of one's own group or culture. We are social creatures, and the illusion of the self against society is no more than one of the dominant but very peculiar rules of reciprocal altruism in a society that has grown much too large and complex to have any simple rules.

From the earliest transitional, quasi-human beings, *Australopithecus* and onward, we have been social animals with social instincts, born into and living in already established groups. We would certainly not have survived otherwise. A group of cooperating men can kill a saber-toothed tiger which could easily kill any of them individually. Our attachments to and dependency on not only our parents but our peers and our neighbors precede by hundreds of thousands of years (or more) our willingness to engage in negotiations and make explicit agreements. Our compassion and affection for one another, however threatened by mutual distrust, envy, and jealousy, and our sense of sociability and mutual cooperation, however threatened by ambition and deviousness, have a far more solid and unshakable basis than a possibly nonbinding rational agreement. Our so-called autonomy and individuality are not natural endowments at all but, quite the contrary, characteristics learned and cultivated in a particular kind of society, as are our rationality and our ability to negotiate contracts and other agreements with other people. Hobbesian greed and selfishness are not so much aspects of "human nature" as they are learned and cultivated social vices. (Rousseau was quite right when he diagnosed the Hobbesian "state of nature" as in fact a pathological projection of a certain sort of society, ascribing to nature the vices of Hobbes's own society.) If only Rousseau had followed through with his own observation and not himself ascribed so much to "natural man" that could only have been given him by society. It is true that we are naturally benign, as Rousseau so happily argued, but we are so not because we are indifferent to our fellow creatures but because we are already beholden to them and responsive to their behavior. Our "natural goodness" is nothing but reciprocal altruism in circumstances of plenty and in the absence of the more vicious status-games of the world Rousseau rightly so despised.

We are bound by our biology, our culture, our circumstances, and our characters. It is no argument against freedom and autonomy to say, against so much of recent philosophy and ideology, that freedom and autonomy have their limits. Nor is it an argument or excuse for excessive government to insist that society is prior to individual rights. The Greeks had it right: to live a good life, live in a good society. The idea that the good life is something prior to and opposed to society as such is a bit of insanity that only the anonymity and agoraphobia of modern urban society could inspire.

JUSTICE IN CONTEXT, CULTURE, AND CONFLICT

To breed an animal *with the right to make promises*—is not
this the paradoxical task that nature has set itself in the
case of man?   NIETZSCHE, *ON THE GENEALOGY OF MORALS.*

LET ME SUPPOSE THAT the reader is willing to accept,
perhaps with reservations, my thesis that justice is first of
all a natural sentiment, an inborn sense of our connectedness with
others and our shared interests and concerns. But how, a critical
reader will want to know, does this explain our actual experience of
justice, which more often than not involves conflicts rather than cooperation and almost always involves some particular context rather
than any generalized feelings about other people? And doesn't the
sense of justice vary enormously from culture to culture—indeed,
don't some cultures lack any sense of what we would call "justice"
entirely? I have been talking (though cautiously) about "a" or even
"our" sense of justice, but isn't the very heart of the problem of justice
the fact that we so often disagree about what is just? Some people
(including some theorists) insist that justice is essentially refusing to
harm others unnecessarily and paying attention to their needs. Others insist that justice is essentially respecting people's rights or protecting their property. Some insist that justice is essentially recognizing
that all of us are basically equal. Others insist that justice is essentially
giving people what they deserve (whether reward or punishment).

And so on. How does a "natural" sense of justice explain all of these differences of feeling and opinion? How do we know which of these conflicting views, if any, is right? And, given the profound disagreements between them, how can any of them be "natural"?

It is the virtue of reciprocal altruism that it can explain both our natural sense of justice and our enormous flexibility and variability. Reciprocal altruism "teaches" us that we are fellow creatures and that we should, with strategic variations, return like for like, with a certain natural bias toward altruism. But altruism so considered is contingent on and part of self-interest, not opposed to it, and what we call "selfishness" is not so much natural as a natural response to a situation in society where reciprocity means not altruism but mutual self-defense. A society that praises competition and the free market in all matters will thus tend to encourage or even necessitate an unnatural focus on self-interest, but there should be no mistaking this artificial cultural set-up for "human nature." Justice, considered in such circumstances, will inevitably focus on such matters as the fairness of the competition and the rights of the "winners." On the one side, there will be those who urge a "level playing field" and display a concern for the equality of the competitors. On the other, there will be a powerful, defensive emphasis on the "rights" of those who are most advantaged, whether or not they in any sense "deserved" the fruits of their victory and whether or not it was, in fact, a fair contest. Beneath both arguments there will be a nagging concern for those who seem not to be able to play the game at all, who don't seem to move according to the rules of the market or merit. Here is where our peculiar debates about justice begin, but it is by no means true that all or even most cultures think (as we do) in terms of justice. David Miller, in his book *Social Justice*, speculates about why there is virtually no emphasis on what we call "justice" in primitive societies but only in market societies such as ours.[1] In primitive societies, he tells us, everything depends upon concrete social relationships in small close-knit groups. Person-to-person relationships are most important and family members are far more important than strangers. These emotionally charged relationships, as opposed to the emotional neutrality one finds and expects to find between partners in an economic exchange, involve face-to-face feelings rather than contractual agreements. As Miller puts it: "Primitive men will often feel a responsibility for the welfare of the other, to whom they are bound by ties of kinship, past obligation, and so forth; again, this contrasts with the indifference which is characteristic of interpersonal relationships in market societies."[2] Our sense of justice, in other words, is a product of our own peculiar culture, a culture defined by an enormous amount of anonymity, one-time encounters, casual acquaintances, and a remarkably single-minded obsession with contracts and economics at the expense of personal relationships. In such circumstances, altruism is for the most part confined to family, friends, and occasional acts of charity, and reduced to mere courtesy and civility. Reciprocity comes to mean little more than fair payment for what one has to sell and legally imposed punishment for those who break the law.

This is not the place to discuss the huge array of fascinating cultural differences where justice is concerned or the peculiarities of our own conceptions of justice, but I am concerned to make the much more general point that our sense of justice is always context- and culture-bound and is cultivated from a natural sense of fellow feeling in different ways because we find ourselves participating in different social practices and activities.[3] Accordingly, what counts as altruism— outright generosity, or gift-giving by way of increasing one's own status, or playing fair, or simply giving an opponent the benefit of the doubt—will vary enormously too. To be altruistic in the wrong way can be unjust as well as inappropriate. And what reciprocity means again depends on the rules and practices of the activity, whether it is intrinsically competitive or cooperative, whether there are established measures of value, and what conflicting demands and expectations may come into play. What justice requires, accordingly, is not just some general sense of justice but a cultivated, practiced sense of *judgment*, learned through experience and participation. But judgment as I want to understand it is as akin to emotion and feeling as it is to reason (it is therefore often misidentified as "intuition"). And judgment is not at all a simple, straightforward matter (though it often seems so at the time) but a complex synthesis of many factors and considerations. Fellow feeling may be natural and universal, but the particular ideas we have about justice often differ and conflict. These disagreements, I would argue, are not matters of nature but of context and culture and the inevitable result of conflict and competition in a world in which "equality" has become an almost unintelligible abstraction. But we rationalize these conflicts and our inevitable inequalities and incommensurabilities into ideologies, turning conflicts of interest that might well be negotiated and tragedies that might well be corrected into belligerent disputes about justice or injustice. What I want to examine in this chapter—though not as closely as the topic deserves—is the nature of our differing conceptions of justice and the reason why questions of justice so often turn into conflict.

As I have argued, our natural sense of fellow feeling and our practice of reciprocal altruism contradict the all-too-familiar view that people are "naturally" selfish and nonsocial. But the exact nature of one's sense of justice, to be only slightly paradoxical, isn't "natural" at all. Different societies live in different conditions (urban, rural; affluence, want; a history of chaos, an established constitutional government), and accordingly they have different values, different senses of what is just and what is not. The problem, of course, is that we are a pluralistic society, and even within our society (or even in our own neighborhoods) we do not all live in a single set of cultural or environmental conditions. (Indeed, the identity of this "we" is in itself extremely problematic.) There are circumstances of communal desperation in which justice can hardly mean anything other than sharing more or less equally or according to need. There are circumstances of affluence in which questions of need and equality are all but irrelevant. There are circumstances of chaos in which questions of guilt, innocence, and punishment tend to absorb all of our concerns for justice, and there are all sorts of circumstances, depending on the subcultural context, in which various traditions determine justice quite apart from any concerns of need or merit. In some contexts, the ideal of impartial, reasoned judgment will provide a paradigm of justice; in others it will not. In fact, the very idea of impartiality will be offensive and entirely contrary to justice. In some societies and circumstances, what each person gets is of paramount importance; in others, what a person gives is much more significant, the "getting" being something of a side issue and, in some societies, an actual embarrassment. To understand "our" sense of justice, then, it is necessary to get specific culturally and to see under what basic conditions our natural sense of fellow feeling is honed and cultivated into what we call (and argue about as) "justice."

If one tries to subsume all of these differences under a single theory or criterion, one is bound to become disappointed or dogmatic. It does not follow, however, that all is chaos or irrationality or "relativism." It seems so only if one thinks of justice in just those terms that I have been attacking, as an overarching rational structure that ought to be imposed on all particular contexts and conditions. From that point of view, virtually every concern for justice is indeed riddled with conflict and contradictions. But justice and our sense of what is just actually operate in exactly the opposite direction, not from the top down but rather from the bottom up, beginning with the particular contexts and activities in which our natural sense of fellow feeling is cultivated and articulated into particular social norms. In such contexts, there is rarely any serious conflict of overarching principles; the various considerations are not so much opposed positions but rather the criss-crossed social structures out of which we cultivate a specific sense of justice and a keen sense of judgment. Let me illustrate what I mean with a concrete example.

WHAT IS JUST?

. . . a classic case of injustice . . . [on the use of the rotation system for World Series umpires]

BOSTON GLOBE, OCTOBER 16, 1988

I'M TEACHING A CLASS of thirty bright, competitive honors students. My problem is, how to grade them? A lot depends on it, and they never let me forget that—their future in the field or, at least, the likelihood of their taking any more courses, their prospects for graduate school and a career, whether they are able to stay in school or hold on to their fellowships and maintain their good relations with their parents. In one case the possibility of getting a new sports car is at stake, and for all of them it is a matter of their sense of honor or competitive pride among their peers and their individual sense of self-esteem. (Not to mention the reputation of the course and its instructor and the integrity of "the system.") So, I know what I have to decide: what is the fairest way of assigning grades at the end of the term? The rules are set: I cannot make up my own grading system or substitute some wordy evaluation for the single symbol (A, B, C, D, F) that is required. I cannot use the grades to mean something other than what they have long been taken to mean (A = excellent, F = utterly unsatisfactory, and so on). I cannot avoid the responsibility, and I cannot take advantage of it by requiring or requesting (or even hinting) that a student should "do me a favor" in exchange for a better grade. The institution (that is, not just this particular university but a much larger, less well-defined institution called "higher education in America") has established the context of justice in this case. I am not in any "original position" or "state of nature." (Indeed, even if I were to start my own private school this would not, could not be the case.)

On what basis should I grade my students? Socrates at one point defined justice as giving each one his or her due. This is what one might call a formal characterization of justice. In less flattering terms, that means that it really doesn't tell us anything at all. We already know that, to be fair, we ought to give each student precisely what he or she deserves—his or her "due"—but how do we figure out what each one deserves? So, too, Aristotle gives us a formal characterization of justice which, simply stated, says "treat like cases alike and different cases differently."[4] That is, if I use written tests as the sole basis for grading the course, two students who each get scores of 84 both deserve B grades, or neither does. If I add in consideration of class participation for one student I must do so for the other as well, and assuming that they perform similarly in class, their grades should still be the same. But notice again that this formal characterization, while setting a guideline for all further deliberations, doesn't really tell us anything very helpful about how we should decide about grades. "Treat like cases alike" is one way of insisting that we should "be fair," but consistency isn't everything in justice. Flunking both students with their 84 scores (in the upper third of the class) may be consistent but it isn't fair. And "treat like cases alike" doesn't yet tell us how to recognize when two cases are alike, or what particular characteristics are relevant for the purpose of this "likeness." A black student and an Oriental student are different, but it would be clearly unjust to grade them differently for that reason. Formal characterizations of justice—"give each student his or her due" and "treat like cases alike, different cases differently"—don't give us an adequate standard (much less an adequate theory) of justice.

The obvious answer would seem to be: a student's grade depends on his or her performance in the course. But how is this to be measured? By how much they talk in class? (What if he or she is shy?) By how fast they can think on exams? (What if they are "brooders," who come up with a well-wrought answer only after lots of time?) We all know that "objective" exams test the test and the tester more than they test the student. Research papers display time and effort but not often creativity; creative papers occasionally display ingenuity but more often immaturity. Should a student get a good grade by virtue of the fact that he or she seems to be paying attention in class (appropriate noddings of the head, appreciative laughter at the right time)? Should a student be rewarded just for being "bright"? Should such a student be punished if he or she doesn't work up to potential (no matter that the work is the best in the class anyway)? Should a student's social status or "clout" be of any consideration? (Does the daughter of the chairman of the board of regents deserve special consideration?) What about those students who "need" an A (as they so desperately tell you) in order to get into medical school or law school, or to stay in school, or just to please their parents? Should our considerations be tailored to each individual student or should we, as a matter of principle, treat each and every student the same? If some students cheat, should others be rewarded for *not* cheating? If the teacher just happens to like a student, should that enter into the equation? Should paying attention to such personal concerns be considered unfair? Or does the teacher like a student precisely because he or she is a good student? Indeed, don't we usually base our evaluations on such feelings, perhaps supported (but occasionally in spite of) "objective" confirmation through examinations and papers? But it's not "just a feeling": it's the accumulation of fair judgment and experience, against which we see mere "calculation" of grades as offensive, impersonal, and sometimes the mark of a bad teacher.

I always take this question to the students themselves, and their answers are predictably charming, self-serving, and confused. The last time I did it, they didn't even know, at first, what was being asked of them. They had never been asked for their opinion before, and they were sure that it must be some kind of trick. Accordingly, the initial responses were mostly smart-ass, as expected. One student immediately suggested that they be allowed to grade themselves. This was generally applauded but not taken very seriously. I countered with the suggestion that they grade one another. There was a moment's nervous shuffle followed by the embarrassed realization that they distrusted each other far more than they distrusted me. The ball was back in my court. "So how can I grade you fairly?" I repeated.

The key to fairness, they generally agreed, was to treat everyone the same, to ignore my personal feelings and the differences between them and treat them all as equals. They brought up the familiar arguments against the validity of tests, the unfairness of giving better grades to those who have the temerity to talk in class, the impossibility of any adequate system of measurement. And so they fell back on the demand that I treat them all fairly, that is, in just the same way.

I agreed with all of this, and offered to give them each a C in the course. There was a general commotion and much booing and hissing. In a fit of sly generosity, I amended my offer and gave each of them an A. There was the predictable cheering, clapping, stomping, and whistling of boisterous approval. But this reaction slowly gave way to silence. One student, one of the best, raised her hand and objected demurely that all A's wasn't fair either. "That means that those of us who really did work hard—well, it's as if our grade doesn't mean anything." The point took hold: good students suffer when grades are inflated.

"But the not-so-good students benefit a lot," commented one not-so-good student, noting that there are a lot more of them than there are true A students.

"The greatest good for the greatest number," chortled his friend.

"But that renders all grades meaningless," objected the same good student, "and it reduces the incentive for all students to work and learn."

"You mean to say that you work only for the grade," replied the not-so-good but obviously bright student, his voice dripping with sarcasm.

"Of course not," snapped the good student, flushed with embarrassment. "But you can't really separate the work from the expected reward."

"Of course you can," was the expected response. "Besides, since you already know you have the A, you can work hard with peace of mind as well."

The conversation was getting off the track, as such conversations almost always do. I tried to put it back on.

"Suppose I don't give you all the same grade but rather different grades. How can I do that fairly? How am I treating you equally?"

"By applying the same standard to all of us," the chorus answered.

"But is that fair?" I asked. I offered them the example of two hypothetical students (not at all dissimilar to several pairs of students in the room). The first is extremely bright, grew up in an academic family, went to a first-rate high school, and has already had several courses in the same subject. Needless to say, he finds even the most technical material of this course quite easy and does superbly on the exams. But he's also bored, takes little initiative, often disrupts the class with irrelevant comments and, in general, seems to be learning (or contributing) nothing. The other student is not so bright and is the first in his family ever to finish high school and go to college. The quality of his prior education is modest at best, and he has had none of the preliminary courses which would give him an edge in this class. And yet he works his butt off preparing for class, spends hours in the library catching up on his background and doing auxiliary reading, spends time after class and in every office hour making sure that he understands the material, and asks the most sincere, clarity-inducing, and sometimes provocative questions in class. His performance on exams is still somewhat modest, as you might expect, but the sheer amount of his learning and the improvement of his skills has been spectacular. "Now," I asked, "would it be fair to apply the same standards to both of them?"

There was some fussing around with the possibility of a single guideline, such as "performance," that would work for both students, but it always came out ambiguous. One student suggested a disjunctive standard, so that every student is graded *either* on effort or results, but that too seemed inadequate. There emerged a general consensus that, while both effort and results could be graded by some standard, the choice between standards made the grading procedure look subjective.

"You could apply the 'hard work' standard to the bright student and the 'results' standard to the hard-working student and shoot them both down," observed one student.

"Right," added another, "and that means you could apply just about any standard that you wanted to any student—'tall' as a standard for short students, 'attractive' as a standard for ugly students, 'black skin' as a standard for white students; we'd all flunk."

Nervous laughter. I followed through; "Does the fact that there is more than one standard at work mean that I could in fact add and apply any standard I choose? Could I grade students by the color of their skin, for instance?"

Everyone insisted that I could not do so, but they were at a loss for an argument. "Skin color is irrelevant!" shouted one. "So why isn't 'hard work' irrelevant too?" answered another. "How about being a fun person in class?" volunteered still another, "That seems to be relevant enough." "How about being fun in bed!?" snortled the same smart-ass student who had initially suggested that they all get A's. Predictable laughs, a few equally predictable huffs of indignation (divided, for the most part, along gender lines).

"You seem to think," I interrupted the gaiety, "that if there is no single standard, then anything goes, everything is arbitrary. But why should a single standard be right, if we've already seen that any one standard neglects or cheats at least some students? And why should the multiplication of standards and the need for judgment in applying them mean that anything goes?"

"But it doesn't seem to be very precise," remarked the brightest student, "and it would be awfully dangerous if you had a teacher you couldn't trust."

I took the implicit compliment in stride, and said, rudely, "I guess that's just the risk you have to take. But let's not jump to the conclusion that evaluation is an 'anything goes' procedure and that one is always at the mercy of the neuroses of the evaluator. There may be multiple standards, and there may be a few sadistic teachers, but the whole business is defined and circumscribed by the enterprise itself, namely, education. So even if there is no single standard, there is a domain of relevant standards: hard work and correct answers are obviously relevant and central. Paying close attention and participating in class are relevant but perhaps not quite so central, at least in this class; being charming is rather borderline, I would say, while skin color and attractiveness are certainly out of the domain."

"But isn't it arbitrary which of those standards you apply?" pursued the brightest student.

"There isn't a standard about how to apply the standards, if that's what you mean, but you would all be quite clear and in general agreement about any case where I didn't apply them fairly, or if I applied some irrelevant standard." ("Good in bed isn't ever irrelevant!" chimed in the smart-ass student.)

"Then how come we disagree with our grades?" asked the student who had suggested "tall" as a grading standard for short students. (He was nearly six feet tall.)

"Because what you want isn't always what you deserve," I answered quickly, "and self-interest rather obviously clouds one's sense of fairness."

"How about *your* self-interest?" interrupted a student who had been silent so far.

"My only interest is that you all do as well as possible," I lied. "But that brings up an especially difficult question that you all know too well. What about *need?* Is that part of the domain? Every term I have students who "need" an A to get into medical school or law school or graduate school. Another student "needs" a B just to stay in the program, while still another "needs" to pass this course or his parents will take away his Corvette. Should that be relevant?"

"Only in *my* case," answered a student off in the corner, making the point better than I could have done myself. The other students laughed.

"I had an Iranian student last year who would have been sent back to Teheran if I didn't give him a B. His life was in danger. What should I have done?"

"What *did* you do?" asked several students in near-unison.

"He turned out to be a very good student. I gave him an A," I replied. "But what if he had been, beyond argument, a C student?"

There were mumbles of concern. "Well, that's a special case," answered three or four students at once.

"Then why aren't we all 'special cases'?" asked the student in the corner. "All of our lives are ultimately affected by our grades."

"Yeah, it seems unfair to use any general standards to grade us," volunteered the same student who had suggested A's all around, and a few fellow dissenters argued that each student ought to be treated as a unique individual.

It seemed that we were back to square one. I pointed out that, however desirable this might be, it would mean in effect eliminating the grading system and replacing it with a perhaps exhaustive description of the situation of each student. An excellent idea, perhaps, but this was not what was demanded of us. One radical student reminded me of my own existential teachings: I could refuse to give grades, and simply take the consequences. I turned it around by reminding the class that they were the ones who would probably take the consequences, and the radical suggestion died a quiet, embarrassed death. Some complained that the competitiveness interfered with their education, and they suggested that it could be minimized by eliminating grades. But now, I pointed out, they weren't talking about the fairness of the grading system but rather the whole educational context and the purpose of higher education. Inevitably, one of the brighter students insisted, "Well, why don't we talk about that?"

And, of course, we did. Because what makes this common case so manageable is the fact that it is embedded in a context, the institution of "higher education" in this country, in which certain goals and not others define the enterprise. There may be considerable debate about whether college is supposed to give students information or teach them social skills or prepare them for careers or just make them more literate and sensitive human beings, but this knot of lofty intentions can be sharply distinguished from a great many alternative aims that are not even candidates for debate and so are irrelevant to our concerns here about justice. Of course, there are extraordinary circumstances, in wartime or moments of urgency, in which these values may well be trumped by more global concerns of justice, but under almost all circumstances we respect the intrinsic value of education. It is in that context that practiced judgment gives rise to a seemingly spontaneous sense of justice, and no substitution of an overarching rational scheme or "objective" grading system for such personal concern and judgment would do justice to the context or have anything but a deleterious effect on the individual students and teachers involved and the institution as a whole. No matter how rational our policies, they depend upon—they do not replace—experienced personal judgments prompted by feelings of caring, compassion, and concern for the integrity of our shared enterprise—whatever it might be.

THE DIMENSIONS OF JUSTICE

I want to raise the discussion of justice to a new level of
abstraction.   JOHN RAWLS, *A THEORY OF JUSTICE*

"Blimey, this redistribution of wealth is trickier than I thought."
"DENNIS MOORE" (JOHN CLEESE, *MONTY PYTHON'S FLYING CIRCUS*)

WE KNOW WHAT JUSTICE means in the specific context of the classroom because we are part of a tradition and understand the purposes of education and grading, because we have a long, shared history in which these activities are meaningful and important. In the context of the classroom, we know what is fair and what is not. In a word the main consideration is merit—giving each student what he or she deserves. Test-taking ability, hard work, and intelligence are relevant to the evaluation but hair and skin color and family fortunes are not. But even there, we see that there is room for considerable disagreement. Should hard work be rewarded regardless of actual performance? Should brilliance be rewarded even if it is effortless? Should the tests themselves be tested and perhaps viewed with suspicion? There is no easy answer to these questions, and they are properly left up to the teacher for his or her personal but also professional judgment. (Aren't these almost always the same?) Judgments regarding justice are almost always like this, not applications of an abstract for-

mula to concrete cases but rather a closely considered and felt engagement with the situation and the people involved in it, in which
conflicting criteria and concerns are sorted and sometimes singled out.

There are dimensions to justice, and their appropriateness depends
on the context at hand. The more specific and well-defined the context, the more confident and spontaneous our judgments. It is not so
much that the situation is simple; rather, experience has already di-
gested and synthesized the various competing concerns and considerations. In most established games, for example, the limits of fair play
have become virtually second nature for any seasoned player. In the
realm of the law, the accumulation of precedents serves much the
same purpose, so that daily conflicts in law are almost always well-
defined and clearly embedded in a framework in which a myriad of
considerations have already become codified. (Supreme Court and
World Court decisions, by contrast, concern those that are not so
well-defined or clearly embedded.) But the reason we have judges,
magistrates, and referees and not merely personal computers on the
bench and on the sidelines is that justice requires sensitivity and experienced judgment and not merely the mechanical grinding out of an
already established decision procedure.

One of our most prominent social thinkers, Michael Walzer, has
introduced the concept of a "sphere of justice" as a way of insisting
that there are no overarching principles of justice, only particular contexts in which various sorts of concerns come into play.[5] There is
justice in the courts, justice at the office, justice in the marketplace,
justice in school, justice in the family, justice in the working of the
bureaucracy, but no Justice as such. Obviously, I am very much in
sympathy with this idea, except that the metaphor of a "sphere"
makes the various realms of justice sound much too singular and self-
enclosed. What makes justice so difficult and so seemingly impervious
to theoretical analysis is not just the distinctive contexts in which
differing conceptions of justice apply; it is also the fact that, in even
the best-defined of these contexts, various dimensions of justice overlap and compete with one another. Different dimensions come into
conflict, and even in our straightforward classroom example, we find
divergent and contradictory conceptions of justice operating in the
same circumstances at the same time.

There is no neat classification of these various dimensions of justice, but two of the most basic considerations are certainly merit and equality.[6] In the classroom, we consider a student's motivation, effort, and accomplishment, and we ask whether he or she deserves our attention or support. In terms of merit, everyone is ostensibly different, and it is almost impossible to imagine what it would be for everyone—even in the most routine tasks—to have equal abilities, to be equally productive and make equal contributions. But, on the other hand, there is a sense in which everyone is the same, in the most innocent and uncritical sense: we are all human beings. We all have feelings. We all have needs, interests, fears, and affections. Peter Singer and others have plausibly suggested that the most defensible notion of equality is expressed not in terms of abilities or advantages (in which we are clearly unequal) but rather in terms of our needs and interests.[7] The argument is that everyone's needs and interests—no matter what they are—should be taken equally seriously. In this sense, it is our sameness and not our differences that are in question, and one person's interests and concerns are of equal weight to anyone else's interests and concerns. Indeed, it is not at all clear why we should draw the line here at human beings, and in fact many people treat at least some animals (notably their own pets) as full equals in this sense. Particularly successful and creative people may deserve a rich reward by virtue of their merit, but even a "dumb" animal deserves the minimal respect of not being teased or tortured or killed for no reason at all. This is not a question of merit, and from the standpoint of universal equality much too much of our zoology is tied up with the category of "beneficial to man [sic]."

The distinction between equality and merit provides the central conflict in our considerations of justice. On the one hand, there is a sense in which we quite properly think of all sensitive, intelligent creatures (not just human beings) as having similar basic needs and interests and deserving a certain basic respect. On the other hand, we have a keen sense of every person's and even of each creature's uniqueness in the world, their differences in desirability, skill, talent, and ability, the differences in their contribution to the world, their different virtues and vices, their contributions to good and evil and, consequently, their different worth; and we feel that they should be respected and rewarded (or punished) according to these differences. (Of course we can and should apply equal standards in the evaluation of merit, but this is very different from treating people's needs and interests equally.) It is easy to see how the two conflict. If we treat people equally, we are forced to ignore or deny the differences between them, but as soon as we start to pay attention to individual achievement we necessarily leave equality behind and discriminate against those who, perhaps because of no fault of their own, lack talent or background or intelligence, or perhaps even the health or strength to serve society in any useful way.

The idea that justice has dimensions—that it is not a single measure—is not at all new, but we resist the idea that these various dimensions cannot be reduced to one, or weighed and balanced in a single grand formula that will suffice in every circumstance. In addition to equality and merit there are literally dozens of other considerations, all of which, again, find themselves at home in certain contexts and not in others. For instance, there are questions of special needs, the plight of sick and disadvantaged people for whom merely equal treatment is insufficient. There is the notion of entitlement—what a person has a right to, quite apart from questions of equality, merit, or need. The most straightforward example of such a right is the result of an explicit contract: you promised me that you would pay me fifty dollars to paint your fence; I completed the job and now I have a right to the money. So, too, those social and legal guarantees that we call "civil rights" are the result of a promise of sorts made by the society as a whole. Much more abstract, but clearly central to our thinking about justice are "human rights," which may or may not be spelled out explicitly but nevertheless override the customs and even the laws of any particular society or culture and these, clearly, do not depend on any contract, explicit or otherwise. We cannot even conceive of justice today without the notion of such rights, despite the fact that they played little role in social thinking until just a few centuries ago. Freedom of political speech, for instance, is one of those bedrock human rights which has nothing to do with any particular government promise or state charter and is utterly central to our thinking about justice, but which would have been incomprehensible throughout most of history. But even freedom of speech, we are constantly reminded by the news, is a right embedded in a context which qualifies and occasionally contradicts it. There are no absolute rights, not even human rights.

Somewhat more controversial, but also central to our society, is the sense that one has a right to hold onto whatever legally acquired wealth and material goods one already possesses. One has this right even if he or she already has much more than anyone else, whether or not he or she needs it, and whether or not he or she in any sense deserves it. Indeed, one may have a right to money that one does not earn in any sense, and "unearned" income plays an important role in our debates about justice. One may have a right to money through inheritance, for example, and one of the major controversies about justice is how we can justify the cascade of wealth falling from generation to generation, carrying with it enormous amounts of power and privilege, increasing with the years without regard to any personal virtue or productive activity whatever. The notion of rights is often held up as the hallmark of egalitarianism, but this emphasis on property rights runs directly counter to the idea of equality. So, too, merit is opposed to equality (assuming the people's talents and achievements are not equal) and one cannot wholly support one without violating the other. Despite our popular emphasis on rights, equality, and merit, it is important to appreciate just how inegalitarian our sense of justice is. We may believe that everyone is, in some abstract sense (and not just before the law) equal; but we also believe that people need, deserve, and have a right to unequal portions of the rewards of the world.

A very different dimension of justice enters into our considerations with an extraordinary institution that we call "the *market*"—that disorganized system of bargaining that defines not only capitalism but much of our sense of fairness as well. To listen to many of the most vocal defenders of the free market, of course, one might think that the market is just a measure of merit, because hard work, efficiency, and inventiveness will almost always win in the competition for dollars and the respect and admiration that comes with success. Sometimes, of course, merit and the market cooperate entirely, and the illusion of their total compatibility is fostered by stories about the young, bright, hard-working entrepreneur who invents a product of enormous value and becomes wealthy as his or her reward. But other inventors of equally valuable products, who worked equally hard with similar inspiration, have reaped only a nominal honorarium for their efforts, or nothing at all, because some conglomerate snatched up the patent and made its fortune through marketing. True, the original inventors may have been incompetent as businessmen and could never have marketed their products so successfully. But the scenario nevertheless strikes us as a gross injustice, and we have to recognize that market-thinking ultimately values something distinct from either equality or merit. Men make millions with ideas and products of no merit at all, and the most precious fruits of our civilization often find themselves without market value—at least during the life of their creators.[8]

One consideration that cannot be left out of any discussion of justice is "the public good." Indeed, we have already defined a sense of justice as, in part, concern for the well-being of the whole community. Not surprisingly, egalitarians argue that a society of equals tends to be less torn by envy and strife, and defenders of merit argue that encouraging people to do their best will guarantee a better society for all. Defenders of the unregulated free market almost always base their defense on the (historically contingent) claim that freedom in the market all but inevitably produces prosperity for all. Indeed, without this defense, our belief in the desirability of a market economy would be shaky indeed, the entrepreneurial "freedom" of a small number of wealthy individuals notwithstanding. But the public good is not always best served by either equality or merit or the market, and in a few notorious cases the good of a whole society depends on the grossest injustice against one or more of its members. The ancient rituals of human sacrifice made this point quite explicitly, and our modern system of celebrities and scapegoats may well work in much the same way. We can hardly talk about justice without taking into account the good of all, but this cannot by itself be the single key to justice either.

There are other dimensions of justice (some of them will be mentioned in the next section) but for now it is more important to shift our attention back to the perspective from which this argument takes place. An emphasis on dimensions of or criteria for justice tends to eclipse the theme of my entire enterprise, which is to highlight our sense of reciprocity and fellow feeling with the people with whom we share our world. Justice is too often defined in terms of one or the other of these dimensions; I want to insist that the sense of justice is rather that cultivated sense of judgment in which these dimensions are weighed according to context and concern. Justice, in every case, is the overall concern for how people (always including oneself) fit together in society, and the choice of criteria or dimensions is subservient to that concern. In our current (I would say "obscene") debates about the plight of the homeless or the rights of maniacs to own military assault weapons, we hear a great deal about rights and merit and even need, detached from any sense of engagement or compassion which would make sense of those discussions. And so my point here is not just to show how complicated justice really is but rather to get away from the interminable debates about the priority of rights versus merit versus equality and so on and get back to the one concern that underlies them all.

The notion of "dimensions of justice" is not an easy idea for us to accept, for it means not just that our sense of justice is complex but that it is riddled with contradictions and conflicts. We almost all agree that equal respect for people as human beings is in some sense imperative, but when it gets down to most particular cases it is not at all clear what that is supposed to mean. We all tend to agree that people should get what they deserve, but once this formula is taken out of its merely formal mode and applied to real people who differ in all sorts of ways in terms of talents, ambitions, conscientiousness, accomplishments, and contributions, we are not at all agreed as to how these different considerations are to be weighed against each other or against needs, or how much we should simply leave these difficult decisions up to the impersonality of "the market," where the skill of marketing suddenly takes top priority and the needy, who have nothing to sell, get systematically screwed. (The Nobel prize in economics usually goes to the scholar who can hide this obvious fact under the econometrics of a formal theory.)

Still in the glow of Plato's promise, we think of justice as a singular ideal, a unified concept which, once understood, will provide us with a nifty decision-making procedure that can be applied even-handedly and wholly fairly by even the biggest nitwit of a judge or magistrate or, better, by a computer. The fact is rather that there is no such ideal and no such procedure is possible. What we call "justice" is the correction of particular injustices that can be determined because they happen to fall neatly along one or another of these various dimensions. Someone is starving, he should be given food. Someone invents a new kind of mousetrap; he should be given credit and benefit from it. Someone paid for a new television set and it was never delivered; he should get his TV set. Sally was promised a bonus if she finished the report by October 18th and she did; so she should be paid. Someone stole your money; it should be returned and the thief punished. Someone won the state lottery; he should be paid his winnings.

But when these dimensions intersect and two injustices confront each other with opposite resolutions, justice is not a simple decision procedure but a matter of negotiation or, if necessary, fighting it out. (The national motto of Chile is By Reason or by Force.) Which, of course, is just the "solution" that all of those single-minded theories of justice have sought so hard to avoid. When I talk about a "sense of justice," accordingly, it should not be thought that I mean some singular emotion or sensibility that can be applied in each and every social situation. Our sense of justice, too, is a complex and often conflicting set of feelings that vary with context and involve sophisticated forms of judgment. (That complexity and context-sensitivity is what we properly call "intuition.") Our sense of judgment is not simply an application of a clearly defined, already established and internalized set of rational principles of justice, for there is no singular set of principles and no singular sense of justice.

"SIMPLE JUSTICE"

Justice is getting what one deserves; what could be simpler?
JOHN HOSPERS, *HUMAN CONDUCT*

IT WOULD HELP TO see how the various dimensions of justice enter into even the most seemingly straightforward and "simple" deliberations and often conflict with one another. In the pages that follow, I want to consider another everyday issue of justice in which most of us are involved, one way or another, the distribution of "merit" money for the work we have done. Imagine yourself in the position of a supervisor of two employees, with a fixed amount of bonus money to distribute between them. (Let's just say, for convenience, $1,000.) What are the considerations, the dimensions of justice, that you have to take into account?

There seems to be almost universal agreement on at least three points, ever since Plato:

(1) The first is that justice is not merely a matter of "might makes right." Strength and power may be essential to defending justice, but they do not constitute justice. The fact that one of your employees has threatened to beat the stuffings out of you if she doesn't get a big bonus is not an argument on her behalf.

(2) The second point is that *irrelevant* considerations should not enter into our deliberations. For example, the fact that one employee is a woman and the other a man, or that one is Chicano and the other Chinese, are irrelevant to the question how much of a bonus each should receive. But, of course, the question "what is relevant?" can be just as hard to answer as the question "what is just?"—in fact, it is pretty much the same question. Is the fact that one works harder a relevant consideration? (Probably not in a high-pressure business where only results count.) How about the fact that one is smarter than the other? Or the fact that one has been with the company five times as long? The fact that one is charming while the other is a perpetual grump and slob? The fact that one is heavily in debt? And, perhaps hardest of all, the fact that you like one better than the other? To treat your employees differently for no reason is obviously unfair, but to treat them differently for the wrong reason is also unfair, and so is treating them similarly without regard for relevant differences.

(3) The most obvious way to reconcile the demand for equal treatment with attention to differences is to insist on equal standards. That is, whatever we decide is relevant to the evaluation in question, we should use the same criterion for both employees. But, as in our decision concerning what is relevant, the hard part is deciding whether the two cases are similar enough to warrant the use of the same standard. If one employee carries out routine tasks in which

conscientious hard work is the primary concern while the other is a problem solver such that the only concern is the right answer, no matter how much (or little) time it takes, it is far from obvious that it is fair to evaluate them in the same way. Just as two students, one a hard-working novice, the other experienced and routinely insightful, require different considerations, so too, different people in different jobs—and sometimes in the same job—require different standards of evaluation to be fair.

What sort of standards are available and required for a fair evaluation? In what follows I want to suggest a baker's dozen or so of them, and that is by no means an exhaustive list:

equality: ignore all differences, give them $500 each, split down the middle. (The illusion is that such even splits provoke no resentment and require no justification.)

desert (results): who has actually produced more? (Of course, deciding how to measure production is already half the concern.)

desert (effort): who has worked harder? As any fair-minded employer knows quite well, results are important but they do not always reflect true merit. Charlotte may get the credit for a discovery whose groundwork was ninety-five percent completed by Carol.

ability: how much promise a person shows. How long does one have to be "promising" before only results count? Is it really fair to reward promise as such?

need: does the fact that one has two sick children and another child in college while the other is single with a substantial trust fund enter into our deliberations at all? Does justice on the job always have to be job-related?

market value: could one of them get another job with higher pay? Better pay what it takes to keep 'em.

rights: are there any outstanding agreements or legitimate expectations that already commit you to paying a certain bonus to either of them? Can one have a right to a "bonus"?

the public good ("utility"): what would have the best effects for the most people, for the rest of the employees, for the company, for the larger community?

duties and responsibilities: how much of a burden are we compensating them for? Why does a CEO make so much more than his or her hard-working employees? Is any of this a psychological question? How much is a matter of tradition?

risk and uncertainty: we pay more for a dangerous job, whether or not it requires more skill and whether or not it involves a greater contribution than a safe job. We reward investors who put their money at risk, quite apart from any question of any time and effort they may expend and any skills they may have. Marx was surely wrong in insisting that the fruits of an enterprise belong solely to those who do the physical labor. (Of course, *how much* of a return on risk is justified is a matter of serious debate.)

seniority: how long has a person been with the company? Does this in itself give him or her special status, apart from skill and accomplishment?

loyalty: not the same as seniority (though seniority may be a sign of loyalty). The concept of loyalty has been deemphasized recently, as more and more young executives "fast track" and jump from company to company, as more and more companies fire their older rather than more recent employees (often just months before benefit packages kick in). But this, I suggest, is a symptom of a much deeper problem, namely, our tendency to see ourselves as individual contractors rather than as participant members in our jobs and institutions as well as in society as a whole.

moral virtue: in addition to all of the above, we sometimes reward people for simple trustworthiness or honesty, even when this does not necessarily benefit the company (as loyalty does). Congeniality is often included in this category, but so too are the more dubious considerations of personal affection. Are such personal considerations fair? Is virtue itself a personal consideration?

tradition: finally, no institution exists in a historical vacuum, and surely it is relevant to people's expectations that bonus money has in the past always been distributed a certain way, whether strictly egalitarian or always unequal (say $750:$250), and then in favor of the older employee or the newer one, the one who works harder or the one who produces more, the needier of the two or the more demonstrably virtuous. One can buck tradition, of course, but not without some special justification. Corporate cultures have their own inertia, as any executive knows who has too quickly tried to change one.

There are other considerations, even in this simplified domestic case of justice. But the point has been to show that, even in the simplest cases, justice is not simple. It requires judgment, not a decision procedure, and it involves a broad range of considerations. Trying to divide the $1,000 bonus fairly between our two employees, we try to apply some sort of fair and consistent standards and take into account their very different contributions (and, perhaps, very different *kinds* of contributions) to the company. One tries to strike a balance between these various considerations, and most of the time our judgment is fair and reasonable. But the point is that there is no possible formula, and consequently no possible theory, that will tell us how to judge such cases. Justice is contextual, and it virtually always involves conflicting considerations, different dimensions of justice, any one of which, may involve internal contradictions and conflicts.

Of course, we might use the bonus to send a message—to warn, to reward, to punish, to praise—and we might also use it to correct a previous inequity or to admit some prior mistake of our own. But the point is not that justice is a kind of stew with lots of different ingredients and spices, much less an incomprehensible clash of contradictory claims and demands. An employer who agonized too much over the distribution of a thousand dollars of bonus money would not be virtuously conscientious or philosophical but incompetent and indecisive. The fact is that the various dimensions of justice fall into order rather readily, not because of a theory of justice (which most often seriously distorts such decisions) but because of practice and participation in the context and the institution in question. Thus our acquired as well as our natural sense of justice is critical, and only in special cases— often called tragedies—do two or more dimensions of justice clash or contradict one another in such a serious and unusual way that we are forced to rely on extraordinary deliberations and negotiations. The familiar appeals to incommensurability, inconsistency, and undecidability in political theory are more often than not rejections of the wisdom of our pretheoretical sense of judgment, if not sophistries in defense of some possibly vicious ideology.

The most oft-repeated image of justice is its impersonal stance, represented by the blindfolded statue that remains detached and unfeeling and perceives no personal identities or differences except those dictated by the concerns and principles of justice. I want to argue that there is no such impersonal stance, no unique concerns or principles of justice, and that the most essential dimension of justice is the very opposite: perceptive and sensitive judgment based on compassion and feeling for particular people.

RICH MAN, POOR MAN: TRADITION, MERIT, AND THE MARKET

The law, in its majestic equality, forbids the rich as well as the poor to sleep under bridges, to beg in the streets, and to steal bread.   ANATOLE FRANCE, *LE LYS ROUGE*

ONE CONCERN HAS COME to dominate discussions of justice in the modern world: the blatant abyss between the rich and the poor. Egalitarians, not surprisingly, see the problem as one of gross inequality, while some defenders of merit argue (indefensibly) that some people deserve to be wealthy while the rest have yet to prove themselves. Many people, without ideology, simply accept the inequity as a matter of fate or luck (easy to do if you are on the side of the fortunate). Only the most callous are indifferent to the worldwide tragedy of desperate human need, but too much of the discussion and debate about justice in recent years has had as its primary purpose the denial of that need, or the dismissal of any obligation on our part to do anything about it, or the rationalization of the growing gap between the affluent and the miserable. And so between the impossible demand that the wealth of the world be distributed equally and the various attempts to defend or rationalize the status quo, the rich get richer and the poor get poorer. Where is our sense of justice? It has to be something more than either a demand for the impossible and a defense of indifference. But is the gap between the rich and the poor the injustice in question? Or is it the indifferent and merely abstract attitudes of the rich themselves? I want to argue the latter, that inequality is not as such injustice. The real injustice is indifference, but it is a form of indifference that has several dimensions, a long history, and deep roots.

Plato argued in *The Republic* and Aristotle in his *Nicomachean Ethics* that justice and the good life are so inextricably bound together that one cannot live well without being just. But Plato and Aristotle were aristocrats (or, at least, lived with and taught the sons of aristocrats); they took gross inequality to be perfectly natural and not at all unjust. They accepted slavery as a necessary condition of civilized society. So, for them, the compatibility of justice with gross discrepancies between the rich and the very poor, the coexistence of aristocracy and slavery, was not a problem. But we believe—and we start all of our deliberations about justice with the view—that "all men [sic] are created equal." It is not fair that some should be so wealthy while others, perhaps only a couple of blocks away, do not even have a roof over their heads or enough to eat. So how can we continue to enjoy a standard of living several hundred times that of most people in the world, many of whom are starving, and still think of ourselves as just? How can we reconcile our desire for justice with the embarrassing fact that we ourselves seem to be the beneficiaries of injustice? In response to this nagging question, some defend our more or less absolute right to keep what we've got, while others struggle with the hard questions of redistribution—ways and reasons to convince (or force) the rich to share with the poor.

What complicates and even undermines the question is our brilliant but peculiar economic system, the so-called free-market economy. It is, in a sentence, an economy in which every individual does what he or she wants, buys and sells what he or she can (including his or her own time and skills), invests his or her time or money in chosen enterprises (including state lotteries as well as businesses and artistic endeavors), and either reaps the reward or endures the loss. One consequence of the market system has been a great disparity of incomes, depending in part on the skills and cleverness of different individuals but also on such contingencies as fortunate timing, lucky guesses and, especially, that first but ultimate gamble: when and where and in what circumstances one is born. But the compensating thought—now virtually the credo of American secular religion—is that good fortune, through luck or talent, might come to anyone, at any time, no matter who they are or what their present situation. Thus the most glaring injustice of the free-market economy is held up as its most benign feature. Accordingly, nothing in our society has proved to be quite as devastating as the growing realization that the credo of "social mobility" is, for many people, a cruel illusion. Prosperity comes for the most part to the already prosperous. Poverty sticks with the poor.

In almost any other culture, this would be obvious and not at all a cause for concern. Plato and Aristotle took the economic distributions of their world—insofar as they thought about such matters at all—pretty much for granted. People were born into and almost always stayed in (whether or not they ever felt trapped) a certain way of life. The son of a soldier would almost certainly want to be and become a soldier. The daughter of an aristocratic mother would almost certainly want to become an aristocratic mother. Being rich or being poor simply went along with one's inherited role in life: statesmen and generals were wealthy and lived in luxury while cobblers lived modestly. One had to be satisfied with one's lot in life, if one did well and was treated well, because one was living exactly as he or she ought to. But we do not believe—we resolutely refuse to believe—that people (in general) should be so locked into place by the contingencies of their birth. We believe in social mobility and free choice, so that a person can (and is encouraged to) entertain even the wildest ambitions, endure the greatest psychological hardships, abandon and perhaps alienate all of his or her family and childhood friends in order to gain a "better" position in life. It is a matter of the greatest concern to us, therefore, that this social mobility seems to be systematically closed off to a vast army of the underclass, for this is not just a matter of injustice but a symptom of hypocrisy. To be sure, this system (or lack of one) has fostered ingenuity, inventiveness, and entrepreneurship, and with them prosperity on a scale unimaginable in more closed societies. But given that the premise and the promise of capitalism has always been *general* prosperity and not just the prosperity of the lucky few, the gap between the rich and the poor has special implications for us that it would not have for most other societies.

Part of the problem is that we are so abysmally educated about the nature and presuppositions of our own economic system and, just as important, the alternatives to it. Business students are taught the workings of the stock market and the basics of corporate finance but

very little about the perennial problem of unemployment or the problems of distributive justice. They hear a lot about supply and demand
and costs and benefits but very little if anything about values. We all
are taught that the only alternative to capitalism (an archaic concept)
is something terrible called socialism (another archaic term), which
makes freedom of choice impossible and prosperity unlikely. But beyond these parodies—there are some terrible market economies and
some happy and prosperous "planned" economies—capitalism and socialism have much in common, and Plato and Aristotle, for instance,
would be disgusted with both of them. Both systems are too narrowly
economic and seem to place the importance of material well-being
above all other social values. Poverty is seen as a problem not because
people are sick or suffering or deprived but just because of the inequality as such. Indeed, the very idea of happy, self-satisfied poor people
is enough to disturb both liberals and conservatives, the former because in theory such people ought to be suffering, the latter because
they ought to be goaded into doing some "honest work." And both
capitalism and socialism preach radical change in the social system for
the sake of distributive justice—the former to spur innovation and
freedom for the market, the latter to enforce material equality and
eliminate the contingencies of fate and the market. In both cases (despite the rhetoric) traditional values are sure to suffer.

In most socialist societies, our ancient Greek philosophers would
no doubt be horrified by the upheaval in traditional relationships and
values—even if there were no gulags or "reeducation" centers—and
they would have utter contempt for the lack of inspiration and excellence, no matter what the theories of social solidarity might proclaim.
In our free-market society, they would be similarly horrified at the
philosophical cost (in addition to the obvious psychological costs of
anxiety and insecurity) of the emphasis on market values. Almost
everything, including our time and our labor, even our loyalties and
in many cases our love, has a price and is for sale. Any unifying sense
of social significance and cohesion is lost. What counts is what something (including one's time and effort) is "worth." Whether or not
capitalism has increased the discrepancies between rich and poor and
whether or not it has raised or lowered the "absolute" standard of
living for the poor—both of these claims are the source of perpetual

debate—the free-market system has wreaked havoc on traditional institutions and values.

And that is what Plato and Aristotle would find missing from modern society: what we (not they) would call *tradition*. Tradition is not, of course, an economic system, but this is just the point. There is very little justice to be found, they would argue, in any economy as such. Justice applies only to whole persons, not to emaciated *homo economicus*, and to whole communities, not the one-dimensional, merely transitory community of the market. This sense of personal virtue and social cohesion would be first and foremost for them, and if the tradition that holds together society includes an enormous gap between rich and poor (or even slavery), the tradition is nevertheless to be maintained and respected. If Plato and Aristotle would not be bothered by the difference between rich and poor, that is not because they lacked compassion; and generosity would be high on the list of virtues for both of them. But the idea of radical social change, with the elimination of poverty as its primary and perhaps only aim, would strike them as just as crazy as a market system that placed no restrictions on behavior and supplied no independent sense of values and worth. No doubt they would be amazed that we can do without slavery, and they would probably see technology as a somewhat vulgar but admittedly efficient substitute. But most of all, they would be confused by all the fuss about social justice and the distribution of wealth. What, they would wonder, is the issue here? People have what they have because of their position in society. What people earn and what they are expected to have is determined by tradition. How much more sensible than this mad scramble, in which twenty-year-olds (and even forty- and fifty-year-olds!) wrack their brains about what they are going to do with their lives.

Tradition is a defense of material distribution that one hardly ever hears mentioned these days, in part because it is not an economic theory as such (how does "a happy family life" or "a devout religious community" fit onto a scale of mean family income?), in part because it is (like "socialism") so systematically misunderstood and demeaned by its critics. "Tradition is nothing but a defense of the *status quo*," argue even the least radical critics. "It allows no room for free enterprise," argue the defenders of the market. But both of these charges are wrong, I want to argue, and our sense of economics—even for the most unabashed defenders of the free market—is profoundly qualified by and embedded in a larger social sensibility, in which tradition is the primary ingredient. This is not to say, of course, that there is no qualitative difference between traditions, that some are not better than others where justice is concerned or that tradition alone can be used to defend any established practice. But it is a dimension of justice that is of great importance in discussions of distributive or social justice in particular, just because noneconomic social considerations are so often ignored.

Tradition, of course, can be used and is used as a defense of leaving things the way they are, but in a society that has as its whole history a tradition of immigration, innovation, and change, such a defense is a limp rhetorical gesture at best. It is their sense of tradition, not their commitment to the free market, that requires most conservatives to attack the profitable businesses of pornography and prostitution (to name but two). A sense of tradition, more than any abstract theory of rights or a much more concrete fear of violence and social upheaval, explains the hesitation of liberal John Rawls to pursue the more radical policies that his sense of equality so clearly entails. Tradition does, of course, put a brake on social change, and in any society that begins with inequality it virtually guarantees the continuation of inequality. But is economic inequality, in itself, such a terrible thing? Or is it only so glaring because we place so much undue emphasis on economic values alone? Does the free market system in fact depend only or even primarily on matters of supply and demand—or are there always more profound social factors that define and limit the market?

To ask this question is to answer it. Except for the highly artificial (but also very elaborately structured and regulated) institutions of electronic bidding and transfer, what we call the market is still (as it was in ancient Athens) a place where *people* meet, who have not only common or complementary interests but also a set of shared values, including the promarket values of wanting a good deal and readiness to negotiate but also, as Alasdair MacIntyre keeps repeating, some larger if unarticulated sense of "the good" and a whole host of traditions governing the way things are done.[9] (If you've tried to shop in another country, you become keenly aware of how many such expectations you—and the salesperson—have.) Tradition holds markets in place and makes them possible. Tradition teaches people to accept losses without becoming violent, like the pistol-packing loser in an Old West poker game. (Why should we take this for granted?) Tradition tells us that some things are not for sale (although the list seems to be dwindling every year). And tradition, not just inertia, not the market, and not some conspiracy of the wealthy, keeps most of the wealthy well-off and most of the poor impoverished.

But to defend tradition is not to defend the status quo, much less to insist that the poor stay poor and the rich get richer. It is rather to make the larger point that economic inequality is part of the fabric of a way of life and that one cannot and should not highlight that one set of threads while ignoring all of the other social values that are just as or more essential to happiness and the good life. To defend the importance of tradition is not to say that there should be no free market, that there should be no change, that there should be no systematic attempt to change economic distributions. Indeed, liberalism itself is a tradition, as Alasdair MacIntyre argues in his book, *Whose Justice? Which Virtue?*[10] So is the free market, which is not, as ahistorical economists seem to put it, a spontaneous mechanism of the moment. To defend tradition is ultimately to put a premium on the notion of social solidarity, on shared enterprises and a shared sense of history—even different histories. It is to suppose—as I am arguing throughout this book—that the good life is essentially a social life with coherent and enduring relationships with other people, precisely not the sort of relationships that one finds in the market.

The most important single ingredient in our sense of tradition, the one which is indispensable for our sense of justice, is merit—the idea that people deserve compensation, rewards, and punishments. It is often assumed without argument or analysis that the free-market system recognizes and rewards merit, while socialist systems do not. Both assumptions are wrong. The free market certainly does depend on some sense of comparative market worth, but this has to do with supply and demand and not merit as such. We all have our favorite example of some celebrity, wheeler-dealer, or entrepreneur, without talent or taste, who has been handsomely, even obscenely, rewarded for appealing to the most vulgar or greedy audiences or markets. Even the most faithful customers may express (or try to hide) their embarrassment, but the demand is there; and for the market, demand is what counts. The market may reward merit but does not do so dependably, and it punishes poor marketing more severely than lack of merit. A smart socialist society, on the other hand, will certainly make sure that excellence is rewarded and mediocrity punished, although how this jibes with the insistence on equality is something of a problem. But this is a problem in our society too, of course: how do we reward people for their virtues without at the same time admitting that some people are, at least in some context or other, *better* than others? And worse yet, how do we keep from getting carried away by the absurd idea that a person who makes more money in the market— whether it was luck or skill or reward for some actual contribution to society—is better than everyone else? Although we'd like to think that merit is at least sometimes rewarded we cannot depend upon the market to do so.

Among the worst misunderstandings of the idea of tradition is the mistaken charge that tradition allows no recognition for individual merit; it only recognizes people for their social positions, not for what they do. But the truth is just the opposite, that without a tradition, without an established set of practices and a sense of worth and quality, there can be no merit, for there is no basis upon which to make any such judgment.[11] The degenerate sense of "aristocracy"—which we all learned to scorn in terms of the incompetent fops of pre-Revolutionary France—is not at all the concept defended by Plato and Aristotle, which meant, simply, "rule by the best." What counts as "best"? Do we really have to ask? A tradition is an established set of standards and values, according to which people are expected to do their best (at whatever it is they are supposed to do), and each practice (including government administration) has its own established criteria. For Plato and Aristotle, it was obvious that people should be rewarded for what they did and not just because of their social position. But one would not be doing that sort of thing—or doing it so well—if one did not occupy that social position with all of its benefits and training. The question of distribution, accordingly, was at most a minor issue.

For us, of course, it is *the* issue. We want to say that people should be paid and rewarded according to their merits, but we are all too

painfully aware that appearances often sell better than actual performance, that some people can get rich on the basis of no merit at all
(they've inherited a trust fund and a good commodities broker), and
that people who have worked hard all their lives are out on the streets
because their skills have just been displaced by the market. In response to such hard-luck stories John Rawls finds it necessary to fly
against merit as such in his *Theory of Justice*, on the grounds that all
of our skills and talents and even our motivation is ultimately a matter
of luck and out of our hands.[12] But this is overshooting the target and
sacrificing a good chunk of justice (and our intuitions about justice)
along with it. It is true that we should not place so much faith in the
market where justice is concerned, but it does not follow that we
should reject our sense of merit and worth as well. It may sometimes
be unclear just *who* is in a position to judge our worth, but it does
not follow either that we should leave it up to the market (as Friedrich
von Hayek has long argued) or that we should (or can) give it up
altogether, as Rawls suggests.

Now it is not my aim here to defend the idea of aristocracy or to
suggest that we drop the question of distribution (and redistribution)
from our deliberations about justice. But I do want to point out a set
of conflicts and contradictions that our free market rhetoric often
glosses over, and I want to set up a contrast against which our conceptions of justice can be judged, something different from the usual
crude contrast with the worst oppressive and most inefficient socialist
dictatorships. When wealth is singled out as a source of separate concern—separated from honor and happiness and standing in the family
and the community—the free market breeds philosophical stupidity
(and cupidity) as well as prosperity, and a truncated conception of
both justice and the good life. When people assume that they deserve
what they've got and fallaciously conclude that whoever doesn't have
anything hasn't earned it, deserved pride becomes wanton cruelty,
and any sense of justice has been jettisoned. It is not always true that
those who are wealthy deserve to be wealthy, and it is almost never
true that those who are poor deserve to be poor.

Only since Adam Smith has economics been conceived as a separate realm of human life. But Smith himself did not believe for a
moment that economics is the most important part of life or that

the pursuit of profits and the values determined by the market were anywhere near so important as those basic moral sentiments and mutual affections that made life worthwhile. Karl Marx gave us the wrong idea (though he did not seem to ever accept it in his own life) when he argued that economics is the "base" that determines the "superstructure" of our lives. The truth is rather that our ideas and our ethics determine our economics, our demands, and our expectations, and Marx himself railed against the pervasiveness of materialism (not as a metaphysics but as a lifestyle) in modern society. Accordingly, we should be extremely suspicious when conservatives argue that economic freedoms are the most basic and the precondition of all other freedoms and when liberals write as if an equitable distribution of income would allow everyone to achieve his or her full potential in life. The good life is not and has never been securely tied to income or weath, and it has often rightly been said (but too rarely by economists and social philosophers) that our attention to wealth is itself the biggest obstacle to living well and to justice. Economic values are not the primary concerns of justice, and our sense of justice cannot be so easily quantified. The existence of wealth and poverty in modern society betrays a pathology that does not lie in either capitalism or inequality as such but rather in the values that give wealth priority over community and create poverty as a consequence.

BASIC NEEDS, BASIC RIGHTS

How selfish soever man may be supposed, there are evidently some principles in his nature, which interest him in the fortune of others, and render their happiness necessary to him, though he derives nothing from it except the pleasure of seeing it. Of this kind is pity or compassion, the emotion which we feel for the misery of others.   ADAM SMITH *(THEORY OF THE MORAL SENTIMENTS* I, I, i)

AGAINST THIS DISCUSSION OF tradition and against the celebrated if sometimes conflicting notions of merit and the market, it is essential that we cut through some obscene rationalizations and sophisticated philosophical subterfuges and lay down a "floor" for our discussion. Whatever the virtues of the free market, whatever the importance of merit and considerations of desert for justice, whatever tradition may dictate and whatever suspicions one may have about the nature or origins of rights in general, a discussion of justice depends on the recognition of certain basic needs, and with them, what has recently evolved as a concept of basic rights. Without this, there can be no sense of justice, no matter how judicious one may be.

Basic needs are those whose objects are absolutely necessary—or at least, necessary in all but the most exceptional cases—for human subsistence. It is true that some saints and heroes have continued to flourish even when they were starving or bleeding to death, and that some great artists (Degas, Monet) managed to paint masterworks when nearly blind, but for most of us a bout of the flu or a migraine headache is enough to temporarily halt our pursuit of the good life. Basic needs involve things that are minimally necessary to keep a person alive and healthy, including, most obviously, food, adequate clothing and shelter, clean air, and uncontaminated drinking water. Freedom from pain is perhaps the most basic of needs, and other psychological needs, such as the need for nurturing as an infant, the need for encouragement as a child, the need for respect as an adult, are also basic. Psychologists and behavioral biologists have long argued that the need to be cuddled in infancy and the need of all "social animals" from bees and ants to wolves and primates to take their place in the social system must be high on our list of biological as well as social motives and necessities. The satisfaction of such needs allows a person to be human, and we quite rightly point out that depriving a person of food, a home, or a place in society, or subjecting a person to pain or humiliation, renders him or her something less than wholly human (but not, I insist, "an animal"—the usual metaphor for deprivation and the consequent hostility).

So far, I presume, there can be little argument. People have natural needs, and these are real enough quite apart from whatever learned and manufactured "needs" people may acquire as part of a specific social culture or community. As individuals, we are particularly frail and vulnerable creatures, and though Rousseau can fantasize about hearty and independent individuals surviving quite happily alone in a land of plenty and we can all pick our favorite (probably fictional) examples of the Robinson Crusoe type who does quite well for himself, the truth is that most of us survive (whether or not we *could* survive otherwise) only as dependent members of a social order that provides us with supermarkets and ready-made jobs, water and sewage systems, and a variety of possible social arrangements.

The notion of need becomes controversial when needs become relative to culture and when they are converted into rights, which make demands on other people. We would like to have a notion of need that is absolute, based upon the general physiological similarities of all human beings and the observation that there are certain amounts of deprivation and suffering which make life intolerable. Thus Robert MacNamara, as head of the World Bank, declared a war against "absolute poverty," the abject misery found in so many third world countries and, though to a much lesser extent, in our own country as well. But MacNamara's conception ran into fierce opposition, politically motivated of course, but philosophical in its argumentation. The notion of "absolute need" ignored the great differences in needs between different people and different cultures. A neurotic, wealthy American may prefer to starve rather than eat canned vegetables, while peasants and poor people of many "primitive" cultures have demonstrated that they can thrive on a diet of grass and insects. A diabetic or a heart patient needs expensive daily medical care to survive, but this "need" is relative to the level of available medical technology. Americans are considered poor if they don't have a car or a refrigerator, while members of some other cultures are considered extremely wealthy if they have a radio, a hut, or perhaps a large collection of banana leaves. So, the argument goes, needs are relative. There are no basic needs as such, but only needs relative to culture and personal circumstances.

People and societies do differ, of course, and not only their acquired needs but the needs that they consider to be basic differ as well. But to say that there is no single line to be drawn is not to say that there are no lines to be drawn, and however much one wants to relativize the concept of basic needs (and I think that one can honestly relativize it only so much), the idea that there is some degree of deprivation and suffering that is intolerable for almost everyone seems to me to be beyond argument. And with this recognition comes the awareness that the inequalities in wealth and material goods that distinguish us from one another are not all of the same kind. Some people are not just worse off but intolerably worse off. And with this recognition—questions of merit and the "magic of the market" aside—comes (or ought to come) that sense of deep compassion that we feel (or ought to feel) for our suffering fellow creatures. Basic needs may not be the subject with which our argumentation about justice begins, but I want to argue that it should be where all arguments end. A starving child is not merely a topic or an illustration for an ideological argument.

It is tempting to supply a concept of duty or obligation here, and perhaps a concept of rights to justify or explain our feelings. I don't think that this is really necessary. Why should we have to justify our feelings of compassion? Why do they need the support that moral philosophy seems to think that it alone can provide? There are states of misery that are beyond the bounds of our competitive enterprises and more basic than our ordinary sense of morality, merit, or propriety. But what we really do not need, and should attack as inhuman, are those arguments that attempt to cloud the obvious, to block our recognition of others' dire needs and the feeling of compassion that follows. It is true that basic needs are relative and not absolute in the sense of a single, universal measure of misery. But it is also true that they are absolute in the sense that they are concerns which no amount of argument should lead us to ignore, which are so compelling that they require special recognition and attention. Many people have tried, but real human misery cannot be reasoned around or rationalized, whether by appeal to "the will of God" or by reference to some overarching theory of justice.

There is no mystery in the notion of need, and little room for the suspicion that the notion has been manufactured by moralists or philosophers. There are, of course, manufactured and purely artificial needs, created by advertisers and peer pressures, the products of culture alone and not biology. Moreover, the line between culture and biology is often unclear (e.g., what every society regards as "healthy food," the technology an advanced society requires to maintain its basic needs in the face of increasing complexity). But there are undeniable needs, and there are states of misery that are beyond the

bounds of cultural determination, irrelevant to our competitive enterprises, and more basic than our ordinary senses of morality, merit,
and propriety. It is the recognition of and sensitivity to these basic
needs that forms the foundation of our sense of justice, and without
this sensitivity, no system of equality, fairness, or merit would be just.
But sensitivity has always seemed a thin foundation for the edifice of
justice, and those who recognize the importance of basic needs have
always insisted that some stronger source and sanction is needed.
Thus the Old Testament prophets attacked poverty not in the name
of compassion but in the name of the Lord, and more modern moralists insist on some concept of duty or obligation to back up, to justify,
or to explain our feelings. But duties pertain to the doer, not to the
victim, and modern morality and philosophy has seen very clearly
that there is all the difference in the world between dictating to others
that those in need ought to be helped and giving a voice to the poor
with which they themselves can *demand* to be helped, not as a matter
of charity but as a matter of *right.*

Rights are the ultimate defense of feelings, the backstop behind
compassion and indignation, a fallback position for the obtuse and
insensitive. We cannot imagine a sense or a system of justice that does
not include a conception of rights, including both such basic rights
as the right to food, a decent place to live, and freedom from torture,
and such nonbasic but nevertheless essential rights as the right to free
speech and freedom of religion. The concept of basic rights puts in
the hands of the needy a powerful weapon that does not depend on
the good will or compassion of others. But the concept of basic rights,
unlike the concept of basic needs, does not just refer to our basic
biology but already has built into it a complex system of moral claims.
It is not clear, in other words, where rights (as opposed to needs)
come from. Thus our founding fathers fudged the issue by making the
existence of rights "self-evident" and attributing their source to God,
and even the most enthusiastic and articulate authors on the subject
today (e.g., Ronald Dworkin in his *Taking Rights Seriously* and Robert
Nozick in *Anarchy, State and Utopia*) are notoriously silent on the
question of the origin of rights. Dworkin so much as admits that the
existence of rights cannot be demonstrated (p. 81) and Nozick simply
begins his book by saying, "people have rights."[14] Not surprisingly,

their critics complain that the notion of rights simply appears "out of thin air." Furthering our suspicion is the observation that the supposedly "self-evident" language of rights did not appear on the political scene until modern times[15] (MacIntyre, p. 67) and motivating that suspicion is the incredible abuse to which rights-talk has recently been subjected. People declare that they have "rights" to virtually anything that they want to do. They have the right to be offensive; they have the right to say whatever they please. Potential mass murderers have the right to buy semi-automatic rifles on impulse, and pornographers defend their practices by appealing to the Constitutional protections for freedom of speech. And so rights go on the defensive in philosophy. Instead of appearing "out of thin air" they need a "ground." Against the notion of rights, Jeremy Bentham called them "nonsense on stilts." More recently Alasdair Macintyre has compared the belief in rights to the belief in witches (p. 67), and Elizabeth Wolgast has cautiously suggested that we jettison the notion of rights in favor of a stronger conception of duties.[16] (Thus, for example, we should stop talking about "patients' rights" and insist more on physicians' duties and responsibilities.) But rights-talk serves an essential purpose in our conception of justice, and re-emphasizing utility or duties will not serve the same ends. I confess to being suspicious of all talk of rights, but I cannot even conceive of justice without them. The "ground" of rights, however, cannot be the thin air of theories. It has to be in our feelings, our most basic feelings of inviolability and violation. To talk of basic rights is to recognize the urgency of basic needs. To be sure, the one does not follow from the other, but what further justification does a compassionate person need to compose a sense of duty and obligation to the needy?

The abuses of rights-talk tend to discredit rights-talk as such, and one too readily concludes that the very concept is suspect, since there doesn't seem to be a way of "drawing the line" between uses and abuses (the Supreme Court's efforts to define "pornography" is a good example). So, too, the fact that rights often seem to differ with the laws and customs of different countries is used to throw doubt on the concept itself, as if any such concept that is not universal and necessary for all people cannot or should not have such central status for any of them. But all of these arguments are unsound and unfortunate.

It is true that distinguishing rights, like any other moral notion, takes good judgment and does not readily admit of a mechanical decision procedure (the insight behind the Justice's crack on obscenity, "I know it when I see it."). But it does not follow that the concept is illegitimate. And though rights may differ from place to place (Americans have the right to make fun of their political leaders, citizens of many countries do not) it does not follow that rights are thereby illusory. As so often in this book, we see again that it is the unreasonable demand for a clear and absolute ideal that leads us to neglect or deny the perfectly reasonable if contextual and not always clear values that are essential to any society and any sense of justice. And, with regard to at least one set of rights—what we are calling basic rights—their universality and necessity are not in question. Rights may be relative in the sense that they cannot be absolutely justified, but they are absolute insofar as they correlate with basic needs, and we are hardly human if we fail to recognize them.

Against all of those attempts to separate justice from need, and in a half bow toward those who insist that justice must begin with rights, my thesis here is that our sense of justice requires the recognition of basic needs and therefore basic rights—intrinsically legitimate demands that are binding on anyone who is able to help. They thereby give rise to certain duties. But a number of very different concerns are hidden in this seemingly simple equation, so there is often a dispute where simple sensitivity would seem to be called for. It is one thing, for instance, to respect a person's right not to be tortured. To respect that right, one refrains from torturing him, and since presumably one does not have any such urge to begin with, the demand is hardly oppressive. If we have an enormous surplus of food and others are starving, there does not seem to be much of a question about what should be done, even if "the market" must be protected from the abuse of our generosity. But when the costs become prohibitive, the arguments become more vigorous. Decent health is certainly a basic need, but what does it mean to say that everyone has a right to medical care? Treatment for any illness, at any cost, no matter what the patient's condition and identity? (Should we take "heroic" measures to save an ailing ninety-year-old? Should we spend many millions learning how to cure a rare disease when hundreds of thousands

of children are being threatened by a disease long conquered just because there is no money for vaccinations?) Similarly, we can agree
that a child has a basic right to a decent education in our society,
but who has the correlative duty to provide it? The parents? The
community? The state? If a person is homeless and starving and needs
shelter and food (two basic needs, indeed), we may feel comfortable
with the idea that he or she has a right to such things, but who has
the duty to provide them? These are real moral and political problems
and it is not my purpose to suggest solutions to them here. But what
I want to block is the backward logic that infers from the difficulty of
such questions the illegitimacy of the process and the undesirability
of doing anything directly to solve such problems (e.g., suggesting
that "the market" will eventually take care of it). There is a point
where politics stops, and economics too. There is a point where debate should be considered not the mark of rationality but the symptom (if not the cause) of insensitivity and barbarousness. What are
inhuman are those arguments that attempt to cloud the obvious, to
block our recognition of others' dire needs and the feeling of compassion that follows. It is true that basic needs are relative and not absolute in the sense of a single, universal measure of misery. But it is also
true that they are 'absolute' in the sense that they are concerns which
no amount of argument should lead us to ignore, which are so compelling that they require special recognition and attention. It has long
been tried, but real human misery cannot be reasoned around or rationalized, whether by appeal to "the will of God" or by reference to
some overarching theory of justice.

JUSTICE IN AN UNJUST WORLD

Life is not fair, and it is a good thing for most of us that it is not.
OSCAR WILDE

THE CONFLICT BETWEEN THE various dimensions of justice and between the opposed interests that they represent inspires
ideologies and theories of justice that are intended to settle the matter
(according to one's own preferences and priorities) once and for all.

The notion of a social contract—like most other theories of justice—is an attempt to impose an order, the rudiments if not the structure of rationality, on society. The idea is that one dominant dimension of justice, the "right" one, will guarantee justice. But the overwhelming, awful fact that confronts anyone interested in justice is the undeniable, inescapable, and ultimately all but intolerable unjustness of the world. No matter how cavalier one's views on fate and the inevitable inequality of people, the circumstances in which many children are born are nothing less than appalling. No matter how fervently one believes in merit, or the "magic of the market," the enormous rewards that accrue to outright crooks, frauds, and gangsters and the inhuman poverty and suffering in even the most successful societies should make the most gung-ho free marketeer weep. No matter how conservative one's opinions or how settled on the status quo, the amount of continuing theft and coercion in the world and the number of fortunes built on theft and coercion are more than enough to shake if not shatter one's convictions. And then, of course, there are the liberals and radicals who begin with the observation and the firm opinion that the world as it is is just plain horrible, filled with massive injustice and unnecessary suffering, and then propose and perhaps even promise a whole new, better world in place of this one. Needless to say, the inevitable disappointment only increases our despair and our sense of resignation.

This opposition between the world as it is and the world as it should be has inspired some of our greatest philosophers, starting with Plato, but it is that sense of the "otherwordly" that makes our studies of justice seem so remote, so implausible, so utopian and convinces so many people—not usually philosophers—that there is no justice. There is an abyss between the world as it is and what we conceive and expect by way of justice. It is not a pretty or an inspiring picture. Perhaps its best characterization was drawn by Albert Camus back in the early days of the Second World War. He described what was then popularly called "the human condition" as a hopeless confrontation between rational man, with his futile expectations of justice, and an irrational or at least indifferent universe. He called that confrontation, and the feeling in which one recognized it, "the Absurd":

What, then, is that incalculable feeling that deprives the mind of the sleep necessary to life? A world that can be explained even with bad reasons is a familiar world. But, on the other hand, in a universe suddenly divested of illusions and lights, man feels an alien, a stranger. His exile is without remedy since he is deprived of the memory of a lost home or the hope of a promised land. (*The Myth of Sisyphus*)

In his popular novel, *L'Etranger* (the stranger), Camus suggests a more Stoical, accepting version of the same image: Just before his execution, Meursault (the stranger) declares, "I opened my heart to the benign indifference of the universe." But "benign indifference" is an attitude that few of us are willing to tolerate. Certainly Camus himself cannot tolerate it. His life work, one might well suggest, represents an attempt to come to terms with this opposition between our rational expectations and demands for justice and the realistic disappointment about the way the world is and, even more upsetting, the way we are.[17]

There is a hunger behind the philosophical quest for a theory of justice. The point of developing such a theory of justice is not primarily to give us understanding; it is rather to give us edification, a direction, a blueprint for the good society. It is to give us hope. Or, in despair or self-interest (occasionally both together), it is one more attempt to rationalize the way the world is, to defend the status quo, even at the cost of such brutal revelations as "everyone deserves what they get" and "there's ultimately a reason for everything."[18] We all want a just world, or at least we think that we do. At the very least, we want justice to be done when it is to our advantage, and we would rather that it be done when it is not to our disadvantage. But the great frustration for those who hold even so limited a desire for justice is the abyss between what justice demands and the way the world really is. The world is not fair. It isn't even an approximation of justice, and much of what we do in the name of justice only makes it worse. Our theories are attempts to give direction to a world that seems directionless, sense to a world that sometimes seems senseless. Almost inevitably, they are ill-fitting if not so loose that they have nothing to hang on to. Or else they are attempts to come to grips with the world as it is, as in Alexander Pope's glib "whatever is, is right," Hegel's (often misunderstood) claim that "the real is rational," and Nietzsche's dramatic slogan, *Amor fati* (the love of fate, taking whatever comes, even with a kind of joy). Rarely is a philosopher today so vulgar, but the business of rationalization (of inequality in incomes, of our luxurious lives in a world of misery) is still big business for philosophy.

We defend our belief in a "just world" because we cannot stand the idea that, whatever our misfortunes, there is no justice. Philosophers think bigger, but the motivation and intent are the same. They rationalize reality, they try to reform it, occasionally they try to radicalize it. But they too often want not just an explanation or a cure for this or that outrage but a grand scheme in which everything fits and makes sense and all outrages can be corrected or prevented. The more seriously one takes this attempt the more one is bound to be disappointed. The theories remain abstract to avoid this awful letdown: there is no escaping the conclusion that life is unfair, and there is no escaping the sense of responsibility that we have to change it, not wholesale but bit by bit, a tiny piece at a time, not (except rhetorically) in pursuit of justice but against injustice where we find it, in our own little spheres of justice and, when we can, in the unfathomable world at large.

This is not to give up on justice. It is to relocate it. It is to accept, as so many theorists apparently cannot bring themselves to do, the phenomenon of moral luck as an essential part of justice, not its primary obstacle. But it is also to give up our gloating, our confused and self-serving sense that somehow we are entitled to our advantages or that we deserve them. None of us made it on our own. We were born with the right genes, our intelligence, our talents, our basically healthy bodies, the acceptable skin color for where we live. However much we like to applaud the "self-made man" (now woman too), none of us makes ourselves. We ride free on the benefits we received from birth, or by luck along the way. We benefit from the happy circumstances of the society in which we live. What is required for justice is thus not another theory that will make us feel more self-righteous and secure in our advantages, but neither are we expected to adopt a theory that would make us give up the life we are living. We don't have to give up on justice to realize that the ideals of equality and merit will never be realized. The ideal of justice as such is not only unattainable but unintelligible.[19] (For a good argument on this score, see Elizabeth Wolgast, *A Grammar of Justice*.)

Nevertheless, there is much to be done. The charming thing about ideal worlds populated by merely imaginary beings is that they don't have to start with our problems or our personalities and, if sufficiently abstract or sketchy, they don't even have to worry about the laws of logic. And the common sense of the concretely compassionate citizen is no match for the brilliant abstractions of the philosopher. Every sensible proponent of justice is, ultimately, in the position of Plato's favorite target, a bright young fellow named Thrasymachus who was overwhelmed by Plato's superior intellect and abstract idealism. But justice is not an unrealized ideal, floating above the real world and discoverable by human reason. It is not that there is no justice but rather that we are looking for it in the wrong place. Justice is to be found, if it is to be found anywhere, in us, in our sense that there are wrongs in the world to be righted. You don't need an all-embracing sense of justice to recognize the presence of injustice, often right in front of your nose. Justice is not an ideal state or theory but a matter of personal sensibility, a set of emotions that engage us with the world and make us care—as reason alone with all of its brilliant arguments (even if we could agree on them) cannot. I sometimes think that justice is like love, in that it is the loving that is most important, not the being loved—and certainly not just theorizing or talking about love. So, too, it is one's active sense of justice that is essential, not the realization of justice (which is often impossible) and certainly not the theorizing and talking about justice. Justice is that vital sense of engagement in the world in which the dimensions of justice coalesce in judgments based not on rational formula or theory but on experience and emotion. That may not seem like enough, but it is, perhaps fortunately, all that we've got.

JUSTICE AND THE MORAL SENTIMENTS

No virtue is more esteemed than justice, and no vice more detested than injustice; nor are there any qualities, which go farther to the fixing of character, either as amiable or odious. Now justice is a moral virtue, merely because it has that tendency to the good of mankind; and, indeed, is nothing but an artificial invention to that purpose. . . .

The whole scheme, however, of law and justice is advantageous to the society; and 'twas with a view to this advantage, that men, by their voluntary conventions, establish'd it. . . . Once established, it is naturally attended with a strong sentiment of morals.
DAVID HUME, *TREATISE*

M Y THESIS IN THIS book is that a sense of justice is first of all a matter of emotions, to be cultivated from our natural inclinations of fellow feeling and molded into a durable state of character. Justice is not primarily a matter of abstract principle, not a theoretical construction, not a postulated ideal state against which the real world should be (unfavorably) contrasted. But we have so far said very little about the emotions that make up this sense of justice, and, more generally, we have said very little about how the nature of the emotions makes this intimate connection between emotion and justice plausible. If an emotion were no more than a physiological disturbance or a rush of feeling, for example, as many theorists and much of our vernacular conversation suggests, then our so-called sense of justice would be little more than an itch or a minor convulsion, something like the queasy feeling in the pit of the stomach that some people identify as the source or symptom of their moral sensitivity. But though this feeling may occasionally serve as a sign that one's moral alarm system has been triggered, it hardly suffices as an analysis of or basis for justice. And yet I want to argue that the sense of justice is primarily, not secondarily or symptomatically, emotional. Our sense of justice begins, most generally, with *caring*—about ourselves and our place in the world, about those whom we love or feel akin to, about the way of the world and the fate of the sentient creatures in it. Without caring, there can be no justice. Why else would justice *matter* to us? Justice begins with our emotional engagement in the world, not in philosophical detachment or in any merely hypothetical situation.

Needless to say, this account of justice and, more generally, of morality, is very much at odds with the reigning tradition of ethical thought today. That tradition is best represented by if not also derived from the singularly brilliant philosophy of Immanuel Kant, perhaps the most important philosopher of modern times. Today, that tradition is well represented by John Rawls at Harvard and his much-discussed theory of justice. It is a tradition that virtually dismisses all emotions—including compassion and sympathy—from serious moral consideration.[1] Justice and morality, according to this tradition, are matters of practical reason, best viewed from a disinterested, dispassionate, and ideally detached vantage point. According to the tradition, emotions are too variable, too capricious, too personal and particular, too irrational to be proper ingredients in moral thinking. Justice and morality, by contrast, involve enduring principles, universal in scope, impartial and impersonal in application. I obviously think that this traditional way of thinking about morality is not only wrong-headed but dangerous, but I want to spend my time here not attacking the tradition so much as elaborating and defending a new version of an alternative view of morality and justice, a view that is sometimes called "moral sentiment theory."

"Moral sentiment theory"—this not entirely adequate label is usually used to refer to the moral philosophies that emerged from Scotland, in particular, about two to three centuries ago. The leading and best known proponents of this theory were David Hume and Adam

Smith (who also wrote the bible of capitalism, *The Wealth of Nations*.) They both defended the centrality of the "natural" sentiment of *sympathy* in morals. But they also distinguished between sympathy and justice, which Hume, in particular, declared not to be "natural" at all, and their sense of the scope of the moral sentiments was, I want to argue, much too restricted. Morality is indeed a matter of the passions, not reason alone, but it is a cauldron of sometimes violent as well as benign passions. Emotion is not opposed to reason, and to insist on separating our feelings from our most fundamental ideas is already to rip apart our subject matter so that it will never be comprehensible. Our sense of justice is not opposed to sympathy but presupposes it. A sense of justice is an extremely complex amalgam of many conflicting passions, in which such emotions as sympathy (but perhaps not sympathy as such) are crucial ingredients.

Moral sentiment theory begins with the view that the basis of morality is to be found in our natural disposition to have certain emotions. This does not mean that morality is not, above all, a matter of doing the right thing. Ultimately, it is action that we care about, not motives and feelings. But it is clear that we don't think of ourselves or others as moral if the right thing gets done for the wrong reasons, and we don't praise an apparently just action that turns out to be motivated by greed or malice. This general observation has led many generations of moralists, from Aristotle to Kant to John Rawls, to conclude that morality and justice have at least as much to do with the motives and intentions behind the action as with the actual action and its consequences. Thus the insight that morality and justice require the right reasons becomes the over-intellectualized proposition that our reasons for acting must themselves be the product of *reason* (a natural pun and the source of much mischief in philosophy). This proposition in turn supports the intellectualist demand that our reasons consist of general (if not "a priori") principles rather than any personal inclinations or feelings. But surely a good reason for helping another person in need, for example, is "I felt sorry for him." Indeed, one is hard put to think of another reason that is so convincing.

And yet, reading through the philosophy of the past two centuries, the ordinary reader would be shocked to find that "I felt sorry for him" is all but ignored, if not simply dismissed, as a basis for morality or justice. A good reason is supposed to be the product of reason, which is typically understood as a rather sophisticated process of dispassionate deduction of particular acts from a set of rational, impersonal principles. The good person, the just person, thus becomes something of a private bureaucrat, in effect looking up the right rules and applying them impartially to a particular case. The seemingly natural response, "because I felt sorry for him," has no place. Indeed, it is a sign that the moral bureaucrat is not really doing his or her job. To an appeal to compassion, the hard-headed moralist might well respond with the familiar epithet "bleeding heart," and there would be no mistaking his or her contempt for such a simple-minded response to the complicated questions of morality and justice.

What is missing from the usual analyses and theories of justice is a sense of the priority of sympathy and compassion. This, certainly, is part of the thesis I want to defend here. But if the emotions that give rise to or constitute our sense of justice were limited to the kindly sentiments, the analysis would surely be inadequate and incomplete. What about vengeance, and what about the keen sense of injustice we feel in our own case through such emotions as envy, jealousy, and resentment? What about moral indignation? What about guilt and shame? The kindly sentiments represented by compassion and sympathy could not by themselves possibly explain the enormous range or the profound depth of the many sometimes violent passions that constitute our sense of justice. We need a far richer set of moral emotions than the traditional moral sentiment theories of sympathy can provide. Our sense of justice is not simply a kindly sense of sympathy and compassion but a cauldron of sometimes competing passions, all of which have as their basis an almost visceral sense of what the world should be like, not by way of some grand philosophical blueprint but rather by way of specific expectations and demands. Our sense of justice begins not with a principle but with a feeling, "this is unfair!" Or it may begin with a keen awareness of someone else's suffering. It could begin with a disturbing sense that things are out of order, that some pain or punishment is undeserved, that an expected reward has been ignored, that someone has much more than someone else, for no apparent reason. The sense of justice often begins with a sense of deprivation, a bit of senseless pain or in self-defense, which can turn into a sense of revenge. It can begin with a simple sense of "mine!" which becomes a sense of possessiveness that turns into jealousy. But in all of these cases, what is primary is *caring*, that is, the fact that things *matter* to us. Without emotional engagement—whether sympathetic, defensive, or hostile—there can be no sense of justice.

The divorce of ethics from emotion, of reason from passion, and of justice from benevolence has turned ethics and the theory of justice into a set of detached, impersonal speculations and purely rational arguments about what people and society *should* be like, ignoring for the most part what they actually *are* like or, worse, assuming the worst about them—that people are naturally selfish and mutually destructive. But the point of our argument so far has been to make the modest and, one would think, obvious point that people aren't so selfish, much less "naturally." They are, if anything, naturally sociable and social beings; sociability and reason are as much a part of human nature as so-called self-interest. But at least since Kant, ethics in general has been saddled with the unfortunate antagonism between "pure practical reason" and "the Moral Law" on the one hand and the mere "inclinations," which are "without moral worth" no matter how benevolent, on the other. Our sense of justice, accordingly, has been distorted and pushed to the side of pure reason, while our generous impulses and ill-defined "intuitions" have, at most, been given dubious recognition as evidence for our rational principles.

The idea of some basic opposition in the soul between divine reason and all-too-human if not beastly emotion goes back to ancient times, of course, and as we pointed out earlier, the idea that such passions as vengefulness, mercy, forgiveness, and compassion are unrelated to or even opposed to justice, has a long theological, philosophical, and political history. The result is that justice has become something abstract, formal, official, even inhuman, and personal sentiments have been reduced to "mere" personal sentiments, which are not to be allowed to interfere with the properly dispassionate and impartial workings of reason or the state. My aim in this book is to reintroduce those lost but essential ingredients in justice. I want to mend the split between the supposedly antagonistic Platonic parts of the soul (which are not nearly so antagonistic in Plato at all) and reintegrate our thoughts and our feelings about justice. "Justice" should not be opposed to compassion and benevolence, and it cannot be understood or practiced without these kind feelings. Of course, one can go through the motions, acting on principle or a narrow sense of duty, but one still has to ask where such principles and duties come from, and we will be wary of overly cool if not cold, "dispassionate" behavior. To be sure, we are perfectly satisfied when the faceless bureaucrat in the government office satisfactorily settles our complaint, but we can abstract the action from the agent only because we have already dismissed the agent as no more than an instrument, who could readily be replaced by a computer. We evaluate a real person's behavior as just or unjust on the basis of particular motives and actions along with his or her general character, and among the crucial ingredients in that amalgam of motives, actions, and character are the moral sentiments and what we might more generally call moral sensibilities. No matter how efficient or even fair a society, there can be no justice without such moral sensibility.

A HISTORY OF THE MORAL SENTIMENTS

Were there no such moral sense and sense of honour in our constitution, were we as entirely selfish as some refiners allege, human life would be quite different from what we feel every day, a joyless, loveless, cold, sullen state of cunning and suspicion.
FRANCIS HUTCHESON, *A SYSTEM OF MORAL PHILOSOPHY*

THE THEORY OF THE moral sentiments, in a broad sense, goes back to Aristotle, although he did not so sharply separate the emotions that prompted action from the action itself and from rational considerations that preceded it. But he did recognize that the right emotions were as essential to right action and insisted that a just man was moved by just feelings as well as just thoughts. Augustine and many other Christian thinkers placed a special premium on the emotions, not just faith and love but on all of those sentiments which defined the various virtues (and, of course, those deadly passions which constituted the worst vices). But moral sentiment theory really comes of age in the eighteenth century, in Scotland, with the idea of

an "innate moral sense" discussed in the works of the Earl of Shaftesbury and developed by Francis Hutcheson.[2] Hutcheson did more
than just recognize the importance of feeling in the appreciation of
values; he developed a detailed taxonomy and account of these feelings and their relation to different kinds of value. David Hume picked
up Hutcheson's theory and converted it into a genuine theory of
moral sentiments. Adam Smith in turn picked up the foundations of
the theory from his friend Hume and worked them out in his too-
neglected book, The Theory of the Moral Sentiments (1759). But just
as moral sentiment theory was making considerable headway in the
illumination of the moral emotions and their place in considerations
of justice and ethics more generally, the theory encountered a nearly
fatal obstacle in Germany, in the philosophy of Immanuel Kant.

With Kant, philiosphical thinking about values became singularly
obsessed with "reason" and rational principles and abusive of the passions. That particular phase of philosopher-king type ethics may be
for the most part less than two centuries old, but it has done enormous damage. Kant argued fervently against reliance on the "inclinations" in moral matters, insisting instead that all evaluations of
"moral worth" should rely on obedience to principles and practical
reason rather than on having the right feelings or displaying a proper
character. He wrote, for instance, "The appeal to the principle of
moral feeling is superficial, since men who cannot think believe that
they will be helped out by feeling, even when the question is solely
one of universal laws. They do so even though feelings naturally differ
from one to another by an infinity of degrees, so that feelings are not
capable of providing a uniform measure of good and evil."[3] Kant defines current thinking about justice to a remarkable extent, though
he himself did not discuss justice as such at any significant length.
But, even in his own times, Kant was recognized as a philosophical
extremist, and he was surrounded by thinkers who found his rationalism excessive. His harsh antisentimentalism was in part a reaction to
the work of the eighteenth-century Scottish moralists, and he was
answered, in German, in kind, and almost immediately, by the cranky
but always perceptive Arthur Schopenhauer.[4] No matter how bitterly
pessimistic Schopenhauer may have been about life in general, he hit
the Kantian nail right on the head when he pointed out that Kant's

theory of morality had in fact left out the very basis of morals—namely, the sentiment of compassion. Unfortunately, philosophy tended to follow Kant rather than Schopenhauer, and moral sentiment theory was mostly neglected until this century, and then it revived in Germany rather than in English-speaking philosophy. Max Scheler published his *Nature of Sympathy* in 1912 (not in English translation until 1954),[5] but it was almost entirely ignored by moral and social theorists in the English-speaking world. And when Anglo-American philosophy once again picked up the linkage between ethics and emotion in a much-maligned theory called "emotivism," it was only to *dismiss* ethics along with emotion, for what could be more frivolous and less worthy of serious discussion than mere sentiment?[6]

Traditionally, moral sentiment theory is concerned with one emotion above all others, the emotion of *sympathy*. There is considerable confusion about the meaning of this term, however, both in the writings of the moral sentiment theorists and in our own conversations. Technically, sympathy (literally "feeling with," like "com-passion") is the sharing of feeling, or, as a disposition, the ability to share the feelings of others. This is the way Adam Smith uses the term, and it provides for him a way of defending the thesis that people are not essentially selfish but are essentially social creatures with emotional bonds between them. But sympathy is often used not in this sense of "shared feeling" but rather as a synonym for benevolence, a wishing well toward others, sympathy *for* others. This is the way that Hume often uses the term, and for him, too, it is a way of denying the Hobbesian portrait of humanity as essentially selfish. But it is obvious that there is considerable room for misunderstanding here, and what Hume and Adam Smith call "sympathy" seems inconsistent, or at best something of a grab-bag of mixed kindly feelings. It is one thing to say that one is upset and has kindly feelings towards a fellow creature in pain. It is something quite different to say that one actually *shares* those feelings, and something else again—a much weaker claim—to say that one appreciates or understands the plight of another. In fact, *sympathy* is sometimes used to refer to mere understanding, without any supposition of shared feeling whatever. It is often confused with *empathy*, which is also defined as "identification with" another, "putting oneself in the other's shoes" and vicariously experiencing his or her emotions. And both Hume and Smith often talk about sympathy as if it were no more than a generalized sense of altruism, a concern for others with no benefit to oneself, or a sense of fellow feeling and camaraderie, as opposed to the usual Hobbesian picture of individual selfishness.

Insofar as sympathy involves actually *sharing* feelings, it is clear that the suffering one shares with the sufferer is, for the most part, pretty limp stuff and not nearly adequate to motivate ethical behavior. I may in fact feel slightly ill because you have just broken your leg in three places, but it would be absurd to compare my feelings to yours. Indeed, it almost seems absurd to talk at all about "sharing" feelings in such cases. I may feel upset to hear that you have just lost your grandfather, have been called for a general audit by the IRS, or have been fired from your job because of a general "downsizing." But the fact that I too have negative feelings (sadness, fear, indignation) *because* of you and even *for* you hardly adds up to a sufficient measure of emotion to be called "shared feelings." Of course, if indeed we share the situation, if it is *our* grandfather who died, *our* partnership that is to be audited, or *both* of us who are to be fired, it is perfectly plausible to say that we share the appropriate feelings. But this would not be the usual case of "sympathy." The usual case is that I have a fairly mild sense of pathos caused by and about your rather awful suffering, and it makes little sense to compare the two much less to talk about them as "shared." For this reason Smith, in particular, suggests that a sense of justice is needed to supplement sympathy, which by itself is not nearly powerful enough to counter the inevitably self-serving motives of most people. Justice, for Smith, is an internalized sense of fair play, and justice, not sympathy, provides the main pillar that supports the whole society. Justice, unlike sympathy, is a passion with a determined content, albeit a negative one; justice is the sense that one should not cause harm to one's neighbor.[7] Sympathy and justice, together with a sense of benevolence, provide Smith with a portrait of human nature in his *Theory of the Moral Sentiments* that is very different from the usual Hobbesian interpretations of his later work, *The Wealth of Nations*, in which self-styled neo-Smithians insist (wrongly) that the wheels of capitalism are moved by individual greed alone.[8] Sympathy, according to Smith, is fellow feeling, feeling not so much *for* as *with* one's fellows. Our sense of justice moves us to avoid harming one another, and between the two, the Hobbesian picture of human life as "a war of all against all" and as "nasty, brutish, and short" gets replaced by the much more flattering portrait of a society of citizens who care about and naturally avoid harming one another.

Hume's theory of sympathy and justice is somewhat different from Smith's, and to make matters more difficult it is clear that he changed his mind between the writing of his early masterpiece, *A Treatise of Human Nature* (1738), and his later *Inquiry Concerning the Principles of Morals* (1751). In the early work, Hume treats sympathy rather casually, commenting that it is usually a weak emotion compared with most of the motives of self-interest. In the later work, Hume defends sympathy as a universal sentiment that is sufficiently powerful to overcome self-interest in a great many cases. Sympathy is not so much "feeling with" as it is a form of benevolence, a feeling for one's fellow citizens and a concern for their well-being. For Hume as for Smith, however, sympathy is too often countered and overwhelmed by selfishness and, for this reason, a sense of justice is required. But whereas Smith takes the sense of justice to be a somewhat natural revulsion at harming one's fellows, Hume takes justice to be an artificial virtue that is constructed by reason for our mutual well-being. It is an advantageous conventional scheme rather than a natural sentiment as such. Thus for Hume, not for Smith, sympathy is a genuine moral sentiment and justice is not. Even so, Hume admitted that justice was so beneficial that it became inseparably associated with the moral sentiments, for what could be more basic to these sentiments than our sense of the general good for everyone, "a feeling for the happiness of mankind and a resentment of their misery."[9]

Hume does not go so far as to say that justice itself is a matter of sentiment, but he insists that the moral sentiments in general and sympathy for others in particular are so essential to morals that there can be no ethics without them. Both authors are dead set against the Hobbesian view that people are motivated only by their own selfish interests, and both advocate the importance of distinctive, natural "social passions." Indeed, the core of their argument is, in Smith's terms, that "nature, when she formed man for society, endowed him with an original desire to please, and an original aversion to offend his brethren." Moreover, "nature endowed him not only with a desire for being approved of, but with a desire of being what ought to be approved of, or of being what he himself approves of in other men." It is not just sympathy but a whole complex of mutually perceiving and reciprocal passions that tie us together. Thus it does not take too much tinkering with Scottish moral sentiment theory to incorporate justice along with sympathy under its auspices and take the whole as a welcome alternative to both the "man is essentially selfish" thesis and the overly intellectualist view of Kant and most current justice theorists.

Adam Smith does not pursue a systematic theory of the moral sentiments, but Hume does, and in his general theory he not only emphasizes the importance of the emotions in ethics but also uses a very different way of understanding the emotions. And yet, he remains caught in traditional models and prejudices. Hume's oft-quoted comment in the *Treatise* that "reason is and ought to be the slave of the passions," displays both his radical defense of the importance of the emotions and the traditional tendency to see reason and the emotions as antagonists. That was indeed a bold and an extreme statement, so powerful and memorable because it was such a devastating rejection of traditional rationalism. (Such statements, in turn, provoked Kant's extremes in his defense of reason against the emotions.) I find Hume's statement to be problematic because it reinforces rather than challenges the unfortunate separation of reason and emotion. But when we look at the details of Hume's theory, we can appreciate that he himself saw beyond this antagonism. Among Hume's many virtues were the insightfulness and thoroughness with which he developed a general view of the emotions which undercut that traditional "reason versus passion" antagonism. The primary virtue of moral sentiment theory, however, is its view that we are essentially and "naturally" social creatures with fellow feeling and concern for others as well as and as part of our own interests and ambitions in life.

THE PROBLEMS WITH PASSION: WHAT'S WRONG WITH EMOTIONS AS JUSTICE?

Love out of inclination cannot be commanded; but kindness done from duty—although no inclination impels us, and even although natural and unconquerable disinclination stands in our way—is practical, and not pathological love, residing in the will and not of melting compassion.

IMMANUEL KANT, *GROUND FOR THE METAPHYSICIS OF MORALS*

WHY SHOULDN'T EMOTIONS BE central to justice? Why should they be excluded from consideration? Plato and Aristotle, neither of them enemies of reason or defenders of unbridled passion, nevertheless thought that the right emotions were necessary to good character and virtue and, in particular, to that all-important sense of justice. Christian philosophers from St. Paul and St. Augustine to Aquinas, Luther, and Kierkegaard have emphasized the importance of the virtuous passions, notably, love, faith, hope, and generosity. David Hume and Adam Smith made an impressive case for the centrality of sympathy and benevolence. In our everyday ethical judgments, we certainly value warmth and generosity and distrust cold, calculated self-interest. So why has ethics, with its long tradition of a rich appreciation of the (right) emotions, recently turned its back on the passions, not so much arguing against them as simply dismissing them?

The theory of the moral sentiments is very much opposed to that long tradition in which emotions are considered to be mere feelings, pleasant or unpleasant sensations that are the direct consequences of certain specifiable physiological changes (a flushed face, a pounding heart, a queasiness in the stomach, a lifting or falling sensation in one's breast). If emotions amounted to no more than this, then it would indeed be hard to see why they should have any more relevance to morality and justice than should a headache or a bout of nausea.[10] But if a passion is something more, a kind of perception (as Hutcheson suggested) or some more elaborate set of ideas and judgments about the world (as Hume argued), this would certainly explain the connection with morality and justice. A feeling of moral indignation, for example, is not just a physiological commotion but a way of engaging with the world both personally and morally.

This primarily physiological view of emotions goes all the way back to the ancients and depends on the obvious observation that virtually every strong emotion is accompanied by, if not composed of, a set of distinctive physiological disturbances, which cause in us feelings of a certain kind. Thus the medieval physiologists talked about the various "humors" of the body which were responsible for this or that emotion, and Descartes, more abstractly, discussed emotions as a function of "animal spirits" that went coursing through our bodies, causing the various emotions. More recently, William James set the stage for much of contemporary psychology and philosophy with his theory that emotions are, essentially, a set of sensations caused by visceral disturbances.[11] But even Descartes and James found themselves forced to talk not only about the physiology of our bodily innards but also about the context of emotions. It may be obvious that a strong emotion has some physiological aspect, but it is just as obvious that almost every emotion is *about* something, perhaps an unpleasant or offensive situation, perhaps a recent accomplishment.[12] An emotion might be caused by an immediate disturbance, or it might be triggered by a memory of something that happened long ago; but a physiological disturbance in the absence of any such cause or context is not an emotion at all. Emotions are about the world and not just physiological disturbances. (Indeed, it is worth asking whether an emotion must involve any physiological disturbance at all; surely there are long-lasting, calm emotions—Hume suggests the sense of justice as a primary example—which may have no noticable physiological or sensational components.) An emotion is a way of seeing and engaging in the world, and our sense of justice is just such an emotion (or, rather, a complex set of emotions).

It is largely because of the crude physiological view of emotion and the apparent abyss between mere emotion and articulate, intelligent reason that professional philosophers and legal thinkers, who are trained in and earn their bread and butter with rationality, reject emotion as the proper domain of justice and morals. But even when the crude physiological view is set aside, emotions do not emerge in a more favorable light. Justice, we are told, must be a matter of reason; emotions just aren't suitable. Here are eight Kantian arguments that the emotions have no proper role in justice:

(1) *Emotions are ineffable.* Of course, the problem is that this argument remains pretty much untried—if not ineffable—itself. The truth is that philosophers and other social thinkers have spent nearly three thousand years developing a vocabulary and a set of methods for describing and analyzing institutions and arguments. They've left the description and analysis of the emotions to the poets. Not surprisingly, it is largely a metaphorical, nonliteral, and literary language that we have inherited. Even most psychologists avoid talking about emotions and "affect," as much as possible, staying with the more easily statable and testable hypotheses of learning theory and the like. But it is nonsense to say that we cannot describe or analyze our emotions; we do it all of the time, and we make some pretty accurate predictions about other people's behavior (as well as our own) on a basis that is all but closed to those who think that behavior can be scientifically predicted only on the basis of environmental conditions and previous patterns of behavior. Emotions aren't ineffable; theoreticians just think and talk too little about them and in effect render them ineffable by virtue of the fact that they think they are. Could it be that we have trouble talking about our sense of justice not because there is nothing to say but rather because the language of justice has been exclusively appropriated for theory rather than feelings?

(2) *Emotions are too personal.* Which may be taken, on the one hand, as a confession of modesty, or embarrassment, but on the other, as a bias that has too long ruled philosophical ethics. The idea that all proper thinking should be "objective" and impersonal, detached and distanced should by now be recognized for what it is—a form of pathology, not a method. Much has been written about how the rise of the scientific method in the seventeenth century had disastrous effects not only on religion but on ethics and our conceptions of ourselves, distancing us from ourselves and getting us to see ourselves in all sorts of inhuman ways, notably, in various machine metaphors and atomistic images. Today, it is obvious how calculating reason fits so well into our current favorite machine metaphor—the computer. But emotions don't fit nearly so well, which leads one to think, not

that emotions are inappropriate to hard thinking but, to the contrary, it is our emotions, not our reason, that makes us human. Emotions are indeed personal, but so, I am arguing, must be justice.

(3) *Emotions can't be judged: we just have them.* But, of course, we do frequently judge emotions as wise or foolish, warranted or unwarranted, reasonable or unreasonable. Adam Smith pointed out in considerable detail that the very nature of an emotion such as sympathy is that it is bound to a particular context and is always to be evaluated (and sometimes altered) on the basis of the context. A person who feels cheated has grounds for that feeling and those grounds can be evaluated—by himself or by someone else. Feelings aren't just "facts" about our psyches; they are evaluative judgments that can be discussed, debated, developed and further argued, just like the reasons and arguments that are advanced concerning more abstract and purely impersonal topics. Our arguments about justice typically become so impassioned not because we lose track of the argument but rather because emotion ultimately *is* the argument, and disagreements about what is just or fair much more often involve differences in feeling than mere differences of opinion. Someone who holds a false opinion is just wrong, but someone who fails to feel an appropriate sense of justice or injustice is an inadequate or possibly even an evil person.

(4) *Emotions are subjective.* True, but what is wrong with subjectivity? It is so often assumed, without argument, that to be subjective is to be beyond argument and beyond reason, but of course, this simply isn't so. *Subjectivity* means having an irreducible relation to a particular subject, but that doesn't mean that the subject in question is incapable of following or presenting an argument or being persuaded by rational considerations.[13] There may be no disputing of tastes, if it is the choice between vanilla and chocolate ice cream, or between a good sour mash bourbon and a single malt scotch, but there are certainly grounds for discussion and dispute if the choice is between the appropriateness of vengeance or forgiveness, rage or shame, resentment or humility. Subjectivity may not be the end of an argument about justice, but as even Kant recognized, it is always the beginning. Without some emotional involvement in a situation (if only vicarious), we are not more "objective"; rather, we find the situation simply irrelevant. Objectivity depends on a prior subjectivity. Objectivity

presupposes some subjective orientation, some framework within which anything matters. Objectively speaking, the universe is not even unjust. It is rather, as Camus precipitously proclaimed, "indifferent." It has nothing to do with justice at all.

(5) *Emotions are irrational.* Some are. Most are not. It is certainly not true that emotions per se are irrational (or worse, nonrational—not even intelligent enough to be stupid or foolish). Getting angry for the right reasons may be the height of rationality, while not getting angry when one has good reason makes one, as Aristotle says, a dolt. A sense of justice is itself the basis for most of what we consider rationality in social matters; rationality in the much-celebrated sense of constructing a system of principles on a groundwork devoid of emotion is in fact the very opposite, a form of insanity that psychiatrists usually refer to (in schizophrenics, for example) as dissociation. To put it only a bit paradoxically, it is rational to feel certain emotions at certain times and irrational not to. Emotions themselves are not irrational but rather essential to rationality.

(6) *Emotions are capricious.* This was Kant's favorite argument against them, the idea being that emotions are unpredictable, dependent on our moods and changes in the weather, while reason is eternal and unchangeable, no matter what the circumstances.[14] Certain emotions—sympathy, for example—might prevail in one society but not in another. Now it seems to me, though I won't push this here, that reason itself (we're not just talking about the laws of mathematics) is also variable from time to time and from culture to culture, and that—through the convenient and often self-deceptive instrument of rationalization—reason is quite adjustable to particular circumstances and prejudices. More important, and more interesting, is that this famous complaint about emotions simply ignores—rather than comes to grips with—the Humean thesis it is attacking, namely, that such sentiments as sympathy are in fact natural and universal. They may, accordingly, still be contingent in the sense that they depend on the happenstance of human genetic, social, and psychological make-up, but so long as one doesn't start with the unreasonable demand that any principle worthy of the name "reason" must in fact be eternally and universally true and applicable to whatever weird creatures on whatever unimaginable planets, the matter-of-fact universality of benign human senti-

mentality would seem to be sufficient. This is not to say, of course, that we wouldn't all like to see a good deal more of it. Indeed, Hume himself offers the hypothesis that the only reason we need justice at all is because of the relative scarcity of benevolence and good will among men and women.

The familiar charge that emotions are capricious and undependable ought to be juxtaposed with another, equally familiar complaint—that emotions are stubborn and obsessive and, quite the contrary of capricious, tend to stay long after they are wanted or appropriate. Any adult over the age of thirty (twenty?) knows the pain that comes with love that won't go away even though the relationship that was its home has disintegrated or exploded. We all know the agony of an urge to vengeance that won't diminish even after revenge has become impossible or inappropriate. But despite the pain and occasional foolishness, I would want to argue that this intractability of emotion is in fact one of its great virtues. Love is an important emotion in our lives just because, once established, it tends to stick in there, through thick and thin. Its obsessiveness is its dependability and the locus of its significance. If one could just love for an hour or a day or two, the emotion would be meaningless (whether or not it would still be "fun"). If vengeance were a passing impulse rather than an obsession through which people defined their lives, it is hard to see what would be so important or necessary about a criminal justice system—questions of deterrence and rehabilitation (rather than punishment) aside. What makes the sense of justice so essential to us is precisely the fact that it does not go away, and the more it is stimulated, the more entrenched in our minds and our social relations it becomes. The grand theories produced by reason, on the other hand, take considerable effort to keep in mind, even while we are lecturing or being lectured to about them, and after the lecture they are shelved along with our notebooks. Our sense of justice, on the other hand, is alive and alert all the time.[15]

(7) *Emotions concern only the particular, not the universal.* One of the more specialized arguments, but one which has carried great weight from the Platonic dialogues to the neo-Kantian ethics of John Rawls, is the idea that ethics and rationality are about universal categories, not particular people or situations. An ethical principle has the form

"always do such and such, regardless of the particular circumstances." But our emotions are always situated. One loves a particular person. Or one loves a great many particular persons. And if one loves humanity or humankind (that is, really loves people as opposed to the abstract category alone—as is often said of those two brilliant misanthropes Rousseau and Marx) one loves (or would be capable of loving) each and every human being. (The Christian virtue of agape is thus ambiguous, between the love of humanity and the love of each and every member of humanity, but I have no doubt that the proper interpretation is the latter and not only the former.) But on the strange conception of ethics that comes down to us from Plato, only the universal ("the Good") really counts. Particular affections do not. Indeed, they should be resisted, fought against in favor of the universal.

The extremely perverse consequences of this traditional obsession can best be seen in a much-discussed counterexample to utilitarian ethics. Indeed, it is such an obvious objection that John Stuart Mill tried to anticipate it in his classic defense of the theory.[16] Utilitarianism, as a rational theory, demands that "each person counts as one and only as one."[17] It is overall balance of pleasure and pain that counts, not personal preferences or affections. (As usual, this substitution of a universal principle for the particular sentiments of care and benevolence is supposed to make the theory rational.) If one can save fifteen people instead of four, for example, utilitarianism dictates that you should save the fifteen. Two rowboats are sinking into the dark lagoon right before your horrified eyes. You have the time and means to save only one of them. The first contains fifteen strangers. The second contains your spouse and three children. Utilitarianism insists, on the basis of universal principles, that you save the fifteen. Common sense and any sense of humanity dictate that you save your family. Obedience to universal principles, when personal affections ought to take primacy, is the height of injustice, not its paradigm.[18]

(8) *Emotions are irrelevant to ethics because they cannot be commanded.* One of Kant's most infamous arguments in ethics is that "the love that is commanded [in the Scriptures] can only be the love of duty, of Practical Reason, and not *pathological* love, that of melting compassion." What he is arguing, essentially, is that one cannot command an emotion, and so ethics cannot involve the emotions. It is an often

repeated argument. For example, Nietzsche similarly says that it is absurd for Christian ethics and psychology to command that we love our neighbors. But here it seems to me that Christianity is right and Kant and Nietzsche wrong, that it does make perfectly good sense to "command" an emotion and hold people responsible for their emotions. Indeed, that is how we learn many emotions. ("James, you ought to love your little sister.") Whether or not one can simply "do" an emotion, one certainly can reflect about it, criticize and, in doing so, alter it, reinforce it, undermine it. One can cultivate emotions, for example, by putting oneself in certain situations. (A good way to cultivate a keen sense of distributive justice is to sit down and talk with poor people. A good way to avoid developing such a sense is to stay in one's neighborhood and write paranoid articles about the rising crime rate and the lazy bums who are eating up our taxes in welfare.) Whether or not it makes sense to simply say "have a sense of justice" or "get indignant," there is no doubt that we do hold each other responsible for our emotions and we do tell each other, even if indirectly, which emotions to have and which to avoid. Both individually and as a culture, we *cultivate* our emotions, which is, perhaps, not quite the same as simply commanding them, but it does mean taking responsibility for them and making them our own. The question, then, is which emotions should we cultivate—the emotions of compassion and fellow feeling, or the emotions of defensive acquisitiveness? It is first of all, in our emotions, not in our theories, that our sense of justice is formed.

A COGNITIVE THEORY OF EMOTION

I'll be judge, I'll be jury, said cunning old fury.
LEWIS CARROLL, ALICE IN WONDERLAND

EMOTIONS ALWAYS SEEM TO cause trouble. In real life, of course: a burst of angry indignation spoils the Friday night dinner party, falling in love at the wrong time and with the wrong person wrecks a marriage and a career. But emotions also cause trouble for those who would like to have a nice, neat computer-like model of the human mind, the human mind as rationality personified, if as yet unperfected. And then emotions break in, like unwanted guests, demanding attention, imposing their own agenda, clouding or eclipsing reason and threatening to take over. Plato accepted emotion as one of the lower parts of the soul, so long, that is, as it could be kept in control by reason. Hume reversed the traditional dominance-submission model when he insisted that reason is and ought to be the slave of the passions, but he too found emotions an odd ingredient in his Newtonian model of mind and could never quite figure out whether they were simple impressions of pleasure and pain or much more profound ideas that embodied their own rationality. Since ancient times, philosophical and psychological theories of the mind have been uncomfortable trying to accommodate the emotions. What I would like to suggest here is that emotions should not be so sharply distinguished from the "cool" facilities of reason, that the emotions themselves are primarily cognitive in nature—which is not in the least to deny them their passion.

First of all, we have to get rid of the idea that feelings are primitive, unlearned, unintelligent and disruptive of our otherwise quite rational and reasonable lives. The fact is that emotions—which are very different sorts of "feelings" than a cold shiver down one's back or a headache—are often insightful rather than merely stupid, cultivated rather than simply suffered, and essential to the good life, even to rationality, rather than disruptive of life and reason. It is generally thought and has often been argued that emotions are primarily physiological phenomena, the results of "visceral disturbances" or some higher level commotion (or deficiency) in the hypothalamus and limbic system, the "lower" (even "reptilian") centers of the central nervous system. But such arguments almost always commit an elementary fallacy: Even if certain physiological states or events must cause or accompany emotion, it does not follow that those states or events are all that there is to emotion, that emotions *are* merely physiological phenomena. I have argued at length elsewhere that emotions also involve the highest centers of the brain and the mind, our faculties of judgment and intellect. Our emotions have their own intelligence, not a detached or selfless intelligence, to be sure, but an intelligence that engages us in the world and makes us care about ourselves and others and our shared place in the world. Emotions are central components of the life of the mind, not just disruptive or peripheral or "lower" parts of the soul. The meaning of life, to summarize an answer to the biggest question of philosophy in a word, is to be found in our emotions. So too are our sense of justice and our most basic judgments about the fairness (and unfairness) of the world.

Along with the mistaken idea that emotions are stupid goes the idea that when emotions conflict the problems they present are non-negotiable, unreasonable, and insoluble. Emotions can be overcome and controlled, it is argued, but they can't be reasoned with, improved, or cultivated. I want to argue that, to the contrary, emotions have their own logic, their own rationality. They have strategies, and they are open to argument and cultivation. Indeed, one might well argue that it is so-called reason and its paradoxical problems that have become stupid, stubborn, entrenched, insoluble, and nonnegotiable. The most brilliant theories of justice, for example, all seem to end in contradiction or become self-devouring, caught up in defending themselves against every conceivable counterargument and all but indifferent to the world they supposedly describe. Given this intellectual cul de sac, we might well achieve more mutural understanding with our emotions. While the intellect prides itself on its detachment, the passions are always engaged. They are projections into the world, not retreats from it—which is not to say that an emotion can't become self-absorbed, but when it is, it is the world of the emotion that is self-absorbed, not just the emotion. Our feelings of justice, unlike our theories, are already engaged and involved in a world they not only describe but *live in.*

Part of the problem in our misunderstanding of emotions is in the metaphors we use. It seems so obvious, for example, that emotions are "in" us, but what is this "inner" realm that we so confidently refer to, and how do such "inner" activities ever make contact with the world "outside" of us? With this problem in mind, many philosophers, drawing on a concept developed by the nineteenth-century empirical philosopher-psychologist Franz Brentano, insist on talking about the "intentionality" of emotion, the fact that every emotion is of necessity *about* something. An emotion is never merely self-contained: it always refers to something else, to the person one loves, to the situation one finds so embarrassing, to the comment one found so offensive. The feeling of injustice, for example, is not just an inner storm, an explosion of feeling and physiology that just happens to be causally connected to getting cheated or being passed over. The feeling is *about* getting cheated or being passed over, and if there were no such perceived injustice there would be no such emotion. (This is not to say, of course, that one can never *wrongly* feel cheated; but one cannot feel cheated without believing or perceiving oneself to have been cheated.)

So too, we recognize that emotions tend to be spontaneous, but this is too easily taken to mean that they simply appear, quite apart from our own volition, as if they have nothing to do with us except by way of afflicting us with their insanity. But the truth is that we often cultivate our emotions, sometimes quite consciously. When one falls in love, one tries to think about one's newly beloved at every opportunity. One studies his or her picture, rehearses conversations, fantasizes about the future. So too, one gets angry by working oneself up to it, carrying on an internal monologue, that is, in all of its accusatory and critical aspects, very much like a prosecuting attorney making a case. ("I'll be judge, I'll be jury" wrote Lewis Carroll.) Emotions are more like unthinking actions than they are afflictions. Although our syntax has trouble with this, emotions are done by us, not given to us or inflicted upon us. This is not to say that we are completely free to choose any emotion we wish, irrespective of the circumstances, our emotional habits and characters, and our physiological "weather" at the time. We talk too much of isolated, individual feelings when we ought to make more of what Lord Keynes called "habits of feeling" and deTocqueville "habits of the heart," not episodes of emotion but character and personality. What we call the spontaneity of emotion is more often than not the unthinking expression of an emotional habit that we have perhaps been cultivating for months, years, or even decades.

One cannot simply decide, for example, to adopt the cosmic resignation of a Stoic at the scene of gross injustice; such attitudes take years if not a lifetime of practice and cultivation. One cannot simply decide to have an intense passion for justice, after years of calculated and cultivated selfishness and greed (though one can obviously make a decision to start trying to cultivate such a passion). And I do not doubt or deny that such varied physical influences as the time of day, the state of our health, the chemicals in our bloodstream, the ions in the air, and the phase of the moon propel us toward certain emotions and delimit our emotional capacities in certain ways, but none of this, again, is to reduce our emotions to merely passive physiological reactions. (Such circumstances affect our intelligence too, as every student studying for an exam knows full well; but we rarely hear theorists insist that cleverness or insight or argumentative ability is merely a reaction to environmental and bodily circumstances.) Our emotions are not only very much our own; we are our emotions. However we might apologize or make excuses afterward ("I'm so sorry, I don't know what got into me"; "I couldn't help myself: I was furious"), we really know that what we said in the fit of anger was much closer to what we actually believe than all of those months or years of polite, considerate conversation. The burst of anger may have been spontaneous and even unexpected, but the increasing anger so suddenly expressed was itself the long-protected product of careful cultivation.

Emotions, I have argued at length elsewhere, are primarily forms of judgment, ways of experiencing and engaging in the world.[19] They are conceptual structures, casting others and ourselves in dramatic scenarios in which things matter. It is true that emotional experience can and should be contrasted (but not too much) with those "objective" and disinterested attitudes that we try (never with complete success) to adopt when we are doing science or just observing a situation, but the difference is not that the former are stupid and inevitably distorted and out of control while the latter are intelligent, accurate representations of "how things really are." Emotions lend a keenness to our perception and sometimes to our judgment that is not available to the disinterested, and, where most matters human are concerned, a readiness for insight and understanding that the most brilliant social scientist may not be able to approximate. It is through our emotions, not through our considered abstract judgments, that our lives, our selves, and other people (as well as everything else) have value to us. A friend or neighbor, a lover or a sibling means something to us not because he or she falls into some objective category but because we care, because we perceive, think of and treat that person through our emotions. We judge that they are important to us, close to us, not indirectly, by way of a syllogism or sociological analysis ("he's my brother, so I should think of him as such-and-such") but directly, through what we misleadingly call our "feelings." But it is not just that in our emotions we recognize our relationships; it is through our emotions that we constitute them. Thus the German phenomenologist Max Scheler defended the idea that emotions are "genuine cognitive acts," and Jean-Paul Sartre characterized the emotions by the dramatic phrase, "magical transformations of the world."[20] The idea is that we put our world together and give it meaning through our emotions, not at our whim, of course, and not as isolated individuals. But through the emotions that we share as intelligent mammals and learn together we set up the scenarios that we live in, including our keen emotional sense of justice and injustice.

The idea that emotions are judgments is a powerful weapon in the attack against those old, destructive dichotomies, active and passive, voluntary and involuntary, rational and irrational. We make emotional judgments, but (usually) the facts and values of a situation are so obvious and unavoidable that it is as if the answer were indeed simply given to us. We cultivate our emotions and the judgments we make, which is to say that we are in part responsible for them but not to insist (on what is absurd) that we are therefore free to make them as we will, regardless of circumstances. And although some of our emotions are certainly irrational, others provide us with paradigms of rationality. Otherwise, how are we to make sense of the fact that one can fall in love with the "right" as opposed to the "wrong" person, that one can get "insanely" but also justifiably jealous, that our anger is sometimes warranted and at other times unwarranted, that we are sometimes entitled to our sense of indignation or injustice and other times not at all? It is often said that the problem with emotions and acting on the basis of emotion is that emotions can't be argued with and can't be evaluated. (The pop-therapy nonsense which defends all emotions on the grounds that "an emotion just is; it isn't good or bad" is just the other side of the same stupidity.) The truth is that every emotion already contains within itself a wealth of evaluations (the simplest case: fear as the judgment that something is dangerous and one ought to get away from it—quick!), and such evaluations are always themselves open to evaluation. Indeed, the evaluation of our evaluations may even be part of the emotion itself (getting embarrassed about being embarrassed, getting angry at oneself for getting angry).

One of the most fascinating but least investigated aspects of emotions is the fact that we reflect on them, and, through reflection, change them, often significantly. This obvious fact is neglected because of the blinding assumption that emotions, as primitive physiological reactions, must be quite separate from our reflection about them. (And indeed, many of our more abstract theories of emotion— like Freudian psychoanalysis, to name only the most prominent—do have the actual effect of separating us from our own feelings, so that we look at them as if from a great distance.) But as evaluative judgments, our emotions are readily prone to evaluation in return ("Intellectually, I know that it's OK, but emotionally, I feel that it's wrong"). But an evaluation of an evaluation (by the same person) tends to change the evaluation. I can't long feel prejudiced against someone when at the same time I am horsewhipping myself internally for having such feelings. And this isn't just to say that I don't give myself a chance to act on that prejudice; I undercut my ability to feel it as well. Here is a more protracted example:

I'm at a new neighborhood shop, in a great rush. The salesman is amiably chatting with the customer before me, and I get extremely irritated. I would be furious, but I think, "This is a new shop; this is exactly what this person ought to be doing. I'm the one whose haste is out of place." And so I do not get furious, I just remain impatient, which I try to hide. After a moment or two, I start enjoying the conversation, as I think, "Isn't it nice to live in a city where people still treat each other so nicely." I'm not suppressing my emotion; I have *transformed* it through reflection. How often we can and should do this with envy, resentment, jealousy (which is not to say that these emotions are always or even usually bad or inappropriate) is one of the questions that I want to tackle in this book. But I think of a recent case of an intelligent, seemingly sensitive white honors student at Texas, evidently on the defensive in his own academic career, who wrote a ghastly article on some recent advertisements for the United Negro College Fund, belittling their claims and efforts on behalf of needy blacks. It seemed clear to me and quite a few angry readers and letter writers that defensiveness and envy had overpowered the student's better sentiments. A modicum of reflection (which one hopes transpired as soon as those angry letters started to arrive) undercuts that envy, not just judging it from above as unwarranted and misplaced but actually entering into the envy itself and converting it to commiseration combined, presumably, with a bit of embarrassment and regret. But to dismiss or attack such a case as simply the conflict between unfair, stupid emotion and fair-minded, intelligent reason seems to me to miss the point that it is one's emotional outlook itself that is expanded and corrected. As Hume and Nietzsche both argued, what we call reason is often a matter of emotion versus emotion, not emotion versus something else, and the cure for a bad emotion is the cultivation of the right ones.

The cultivation of emotion through reflection develops a life of its own, not just in the realm of psychological theory but also (and more fundamentally) in our ordinary talk, in our everyday myths and metaphors about emotion. The language of justice shapes and structures our feelings for justice, not just our theories of justice but our own stories, casual comments, and everyday arguments. On the other hand, the wrong way of talking, the wrong metaphors, can corrupt, undermine, and even destroy our sense of justice. For example, the distinction between reason and emotion, with the concerns of justice exclusively on the side of reason, teaches us to dismiss or belittle our gut reactions and appeal to impersonal argument and the theories of the philosopher-kings. It thus supports rationalization and discourages empathy, bolstered by such familiar political labels as "hardheaded" (good) and "bleeding heart" (bad). But such misunderstandings pervade our emotion talk, and we too often substitute a more mechanical metaphor for one designating intelligence and insight. To think about emotions as uneducable, to think of emotions as weakness, this is already to make the cultivation of emotion haphazard at best, or worse, vicious.

It has always fascinated me how entrenched certain impersonal and destructive metaphors have become in our thinking, especially what I call the "hydraulic" metaphor of emotions—the idea of the emotions as fluid forces, pushing their way up through the psyche, accumulating, and eventually bursting through. Think, for example, of all of the images we use for anger—"bottling it up," "letting it out," "bursting," "exploding," "channeling it," and "redirecting it"—which make the human mind sound very much like a plumbing system. (It should be obvious that our ordinary way of talking is not opposed to but rather influential in the great psychological theories of emotion.) Anthropologists have catalogued some fascinating differences in other societies, for example, in Tahiti, where the source of emotions is said to be the stomach. What is similarly fascinating (and halfway to the proposition that different cultures have different emotions, even different *basic* emotions) is the extent to which emotions do and do not get *talked about*. The Tahitians talk a great deal about anger but very rarely feel it. We talk a great deal about romantic love, in fact so much that our actual experiences of it seem pitiful by contrast. In his discussion of Tahitian psychological language, Robert Levi (*The Tahitians*) introduces the idea of *hypercognation*.[21] An emotion is hypercognated when we talk about it all of the time. (It is *hypocognated* when we talk about it rarely, especially in contrast with the frequency with which we actually have that emotion.) An interesting question: is our sense of justice becoming hypocognated in our current society? Are we worrying less about justice and, consequently, acknowledging our feelings about it less too? Our myths and stories now seem to be more cautionary tales than expressions of indignation and outrage. But if we don't cultivate our sense of justice by talking and caring about it, how should we cultivate it at all? Or will that sense become, by default, nothing but individual defensiveness?

CARE AND COMPASSION

It was Midge Decter who declared that 'compassion' is a term she cannot abide. The pages of The Public Interest *are full of articles by young . . . technocrats who may well be able to abide the emotion but who insist that it would cost too much.*

NORMAN BIRNBAUM, THE NATION, 23 APRIL 1988.

WITHOUT CARE AND COMPASSION, there can be no justice. That is the theme of this book. Care is perhaps the most general of all emotions. In a broad sense, to have any emotion already presupposes that one cares, that one is engaged, that one has interests, that one "takes something personally." Care thus embraces the hostile and vindictive emotions as well as the considerate and kindly sentiments. We should not forget, in our rush to sensitivity, that care (*die Sorge*) is introduced in Goethe's *Faust* as a burden, not as a blessing, and it is because we care about someone or something that we become possessive, defensive, and vengeful as well as nurturing and supportive. Caring is not an unmixed benefit, and to think of care as only a kindly, nurturing affection is to get less than half of the story. Most of the violence as well as the kindness in the world begins with care.

Compassion is a much more specific emotion than care, and so it may be much easier to define and examine as a critical ingredient in justice. Of course, compassion too is related to other feelings, notably pity and sympathy. Empathy, we should note, is not so much an emotion of this class as it is a techique or a strategy for sharing and understanding emotions, an effort to put oneself in the other's place. The most obvious specifying feature of compassion ("suffering with") is that the object of one's concern is somehow in pain. One does not feel compassion for a friend who has just won the local lottery (except, of course, in a very unusual set of circumstances). One might well feel compassion for a friend who is getting divorced, but it would be inappropriate, at least, to feel compassion for a friend who was getting married. (Again, one makes exceptions for the unusual and unfortunate instance.) It is often suggested that (as the prefix might suggest) that in compassion one *suffers with* the other, but one need not actually feel his or her pain for oneself; indeed, compassion suggests that one somehow stands safely above the misery of the other, thus holding on to the luxury of commiseration. A student who has just flunked his exams does not feel compassion toward a fellow-student who has also flunked his exams. They just feel miserable together. It is the student who has passed her exams with flying colors who is in a position to feel compassion for the other two, though the giddiness of her own success may make it difficult to do so. Compassion, this ability to feel for those less fortunate than oneself, is the cornerstone passion of our sense of justice.

Care encompasses almost all emotions, inasmuch as one must care about the world in order to feel anything else about it. We can restrict our characterization of care, however, to include just a certain set of "positive" feelings about another being (or any number of other beings), feelings whereby one wishes them well and is moved to act (where possible) on their behalf. But note that being moved is not the same as acting, and we often care for or about someone whose fate is quite out of our hands (caring about what happens to a soldier on duty in Vietnam; caring what happens to one's five-year-old child as he starts his first day at kindergarten). Such positive feelings about a person are no guarantee of continued "niceness"; caring always sets up the possibility of ingratitude and betrayal, and though the limits of tolerance may sometimes be stretched remarkably (notably between parents and their young children) the possibility of negative reaction is always there. Indeed, one might hypothesize that the more intensive the care and the more the limits of tolerance are stretched, the more violent the reaction will be should those limits be violated.

Of course, for some parents, those limits might be reached by a simple act of disobedience or a particularly cantankerous Saturday morning. For others, it may take a wholesale, humiliating act of rejection, the sort that Arthur Miller and Sam Shepard, and of course Shakespeare, portray in some of their writings. But Regan and Goneril are not your average daughters, and Lear is not your average father, and the elasticity of mutual care and affection is in most families never broken (between parents and children, that is). Furthermore, caring about anyone or anything sets up a zone of dangers and threats which promote aggressive defensiveness and hostility. One would not long think that a father loved his little son if he made no effort to save him from the abuse of a stranger, or if he harbored no ill feelings towards such an abusive stranger. To care is also to be prepared to fight, and against the sweet image of women caring for the world the way mothers have always cared for their children should be juxtaposed the not-so-sweet image of a mother defending her children against the dangers and offensiveness of the outside world. Some campers and backpackers know that there is nothing more vicious or dangerous in nature than a female protecting her young. Care breeds violence.

In its narrower, kinder sense, care is restricted to the gentle, affectionate sentiments and their appropriate activities. Motherly love, for example, is almost always held up as a paradigm of caring in this sense. To care for someone is to be concerned about them, but note that this is an expression that is interestingly ambiguous between an activity (which may or may not involve any particular emotions) and a set of feelings (which may or may not be expressed in any particular actions). As a special feeling of affectionate concern, with or without a sense of responsibility, care characterizes our emotional relationship with most of our friends and loved ones, but it would be hard to extend it in this sense to include other people in general. Milton Mayeroff has defined "to care for another person" as "to help him grow and actualize himself."[22] It is clear that such a notion of caring has to be somewhat discriminate and well-aimed. While a good teacher may truly care for twenty, thirty and in rare cases even a hundred students, beyond that—as in saying that a school principal "cares for" (as opposed to a more abstract "cares about") all three thousand of her charges—we have to admit that we are losing that intimate sense of caring as personal concern and moving to a quite different general sense of responsibility. Caring in the specific sense is irreducibly personal, and while it is undoubtedly a virtue (I deny that it is a peculiarly feminine virtue) one could easily argue that it does not as such have the scope to be a moral, that is, general sentiment. (It is worth noting that Adam Smith refuses to recognize love as a virtue for precisely the same reason, because it is irretrievably particular and incapable of generalization.)

Even while celebrating care and putting it at the very heart of justice, I have insisted that we should not and ultimately cannot take caring to be an unqualified blessing, much less as another saintly ideal which few mortals (and no men) could ever hope to achieve. But designating care as essentially "selfless" does just this, for virtually everything that we care about *engages* rather than abandons the self. This idealization of care violates the obvious facts of justice—that justice (and not necessarily the rational *principles* of justice) sometimes requires emotions and actions that do not fit the idealized "care" program at all, and (a related point) that to care about something may be to take a negative as well as a positive stand. To care about hunger is to be *against* it and to care about revenge (a critical aspect of justice) is surely not to have the benign, nurturing feelings that are exclusively discussed as "care." Care idealized as affection becomes just as much of a problem as the abstract and idealized rational principles it was meant to replace. And even the positive, nurturing sense of care is not all sweetness and sentimentality. Along with care goes responsibility. Consequently, care causes guilt. Care causes anxiety and anguish. Care can be a burden. Caring for someone prompts feelings of jealousy and, if that someone is intentionally injured, a desire for revenge. Every hunter, hiker, and female-cat owner knows that one of the most vicious and dangerous creatures in nature is a mother whose young are threatened. So too with caring humans. A good (liberal feminist) friend once told me that she had not only come to accept the idea of a death penalty but realized that she would readily kill with her own hands any creep who tried to injure her children. Care, if it is care at all, has its hostile, even violent, consequences. Nell Noddings identifies caring as "the ethics of the mother," as if this indicated only a sweet, selfless joy, devoid of competitiveness and violence.[23] But she holds a strangely one-dimensional image of the experience of motherhood. To be sure, most mothers I know have those moments of quiet rapture that Noddings describes as "joy," usually when the baby is nursing or asleep. (She contrasts this feeling with the "anguish" of much male philosophy.) But to think of quiet joy as the essence of caring even in motherhood (how does a mother feel when the infant has been screaming three hours and it's after three in the morning?), much less as the essence of caring for and about other adults, is to render the concept of care not ethically central but ethically useless.

Caring has been much celebrated in philosophy lately as an alternative to justice and as a weapon against male philosophers and social theorists. It is not clear that caring can handle this burden. Caring in the general sense requires nothing less than an overall treatment of all of the emotions, from anger to vengeance as well as love and compassion. This is not what the caring theorists have in mind. Caring in the specific sense of "caring for," as a matter of responsibility (e.g., taking care of a sick relative, attending to the education of one's students), falls much more under the traditional moral categories of "duty" and "obligation" than the caring theorists would like, whether or not we insist (and why should we?) on understanding such duties and obligations in terms of abstract moral principles. The kind of caring that is so much in the news is rather the specific, affectionate "caring for" that is more a matter of emotion than duty, though one should not overly oppose the two. In her admirable book-length analysis, *Caring*, Nell Noddings provides a complex characterization of caring in this sense in terms of burdens and concerns, desires and inclinations, regard for another's interests. We should note that though caring is defined as mainly a matter of emotion, it is not therefore devoid of or cut off from action. Indeed, much of the time, caring requires action, or at least the desire to act, for the sake of the other person. But not always; action is not always possible. And the lover who watches his love sail into the horizon or the parents who watch their child drive off to college do not care less because there is nothing (then and there) that they can do to show their caring. But can such caring replace or account for our sense of justice? I think that its role is surprisingly limited, although I have argued that without caring one could not have or develop a sense of justice, no matter how many principles one defended. Caring for something and someone is the seed from which the sense of justice grows.

It is this emotional sense, of course, that is intended in the current celebration of the ethics of caring as an alternative to the overly cold and dispassionate ethics of justice. But, since I am defending something very much like this approach in this book, I think that it is only appropriate to express some misgivings about the degree of combativeness and one-dimensional analysis that characterize this new ethics of caring. Not surprisingly, the paradigm offered for caring is motherly love, as opposed, one supposes, to the stern and detached authority of the distant father. But caring even in the specific sense demands the inclusion of the violent, defensive emotions as well as the virtues of unalloyed affection. Caring is important to ethics, even essential, but let's not fool ourselves about its true nature and consequences. There is good reason why Buddhism emphasizes *not* caring as essential to peace and enlightenment. Caring is a considerable virtue: perhaps it is even the first virtue. But affectionate feeling alone is not enough to explain or take the place of justice.

Compassion, on the other hand, is an emotion with much larger scope. One need not be intimately acquainted with a person or a creature in any sense in order to feel compassion for him, her, or it. One can feel compassion for millions of people at once, and one can feel compassion for complete strangers. On the other hand, one cannot be completely ignorant of them. I have often wondered about the fact that fictional murder doesn't seem to move us when we don't know anything about the person. In Agatha Christie's novels, for example, and in the play *Arsenic and Old Lace*, when characters are dispatched whom we have never (or only very briefly) met, their murder is much more of a puzzle to be solved than a tragedy to be lamented. I am not convinced that it is the fictional status of these characters that explains our lack of compassion for them. Compassion is a more specific and, accordingly, more complex emotion than caring. Indeed, it might be said not to be an emotion at all, but rather a mode of having emotion—"feeling with" another person. Compassion is intimately linked with sympathy, understanding, pity, benevolence, fellow feeling, and friendship. It is also associated with tenderness and kindness and identified with caring. Discussions of compassion, like sympathy, suffer from considerable confusion concerning the idea of "shared" emotion. But we don't need this strong sense of "feeling with" in order to make good, solid sense out of compassion.

Compassion is, perhaps, not so much "feeling with" as "feeling for" someone who is suffering. This does not mean, as some of the early moral sentiment theorists seemed to argue, that we have to actually feel the same or share the suffering, albeit with somewhat diminished intensity. Hume, for example, suggests that sympathy and compassion are identified by such shared feelings, so that when a friend is suffering from a gouty toe or a migraine headache, for example, we feel at least a twinge of the same. If a friend is going through a nasty divorce, we relive (in shadow form) a similar experience of our own. But however such a picture may appeal to our sense of camaraderie, it is not an adequate portrait of compassion. One can have compassion for a friend in pain without having any semblance, no matter how faint, of his or her affliction. I am reminded of a friend in graduate school who, though fully compassionate with friends who had headaches, confessed that he had never had one and could not imagine what one would be like. (So too, I had a teacher who had never suffered from insomnia and could not imagine it, until jet lag after a trip from the Far East temporarily treated him to an experience that most of his friends had enjoyed for decades.) One might suggest that this supposed "feeling with" is nothing more than an instance of the old saying, "misery loves company," but this would seem to confuse the (usually false) supposition that a friend in pain wants you to be in pain too with the Humean claim that your own compassion with a friend in pain means that you feel the pain as well. Indeed, one need feel nothing of the sort (though one will, of necessity, feel something, namely compassion). To have compassion is to be concerned, to wish fervently that the suffering would cease, and to want (perhaps desperately) to do what will bring this end about.

It makes good sense, but it can be deeply misleading, to say that compassion, pity and sympathy are "feelings." They are indeed aspects of consciousness and not actions or activities, but they are also engagements in the world, instances of involving if not identifying oneself with the circumstances and sufferings of other beings. Compassion and its kin are above all else motives: they move us to act (whether or not it is evident what we should do). They are not simply self-enclosed sensations like a headache or a gouty toe that focus our attention within ourselves and distract us from the world. Compassion and its kindred emotions focus our attention on the world, on the person or creature who is suffering. Compassion, pity, and sympathy are feelings, but they are not "mere" feelings. Moreover, they are not dispositions to instantiate a theory or a principle of justice. This is, to put it politely, backwards. One may be moved to accept a theory or a principle of justice on the basis of strong feelings of compassion which the principle or theory seems to address. The feeling of compassion may be elegantly articulate, as in some of the best socially conscious poetry and journalistic prose, but it can also be dumb and only felt. Indeed, I have no reservations about ascribing compassion to nontalking animals and very young children, although they may often be confused or have no way of knowing exactly what is going on (what the victim is suffering from). What I do not want to allow is for compassion (and related emotions) to be either dismissed as "mere feelings" or to be coopted by an overly intellectualistic account such that they become nothing more than applied abstract beliefs. To say that they are feelings makes them vulnerable to the first danger but clearly saves them from the second. But so long as we keep in mind a healthy cognitive picture of the passions we should not feel tempted to minimize the significance of our feelings.

In his now well-known essay, titled "Compassion," Lawrence Blum provides us with a very general but quite adequate sense of compassion as felt concern for another who is in some serious or grave conditions.[24] Compassion is not appropriate, for example, for a driver who merely suffers some inconvenience on the way to visit a friend. Compassion can be complex: one can still feel compassion for a blind man who has managed to get a rewarding job, marry well, and be happy, whereas pity, for instance, would be inappropriate. Blum analyzes compassion as an emotion (or an emotional attitude), as a moral phenomenon with particular moral value. He too is anxious to provide an alternative to the overbearing "Kantian" interpretation of morality, and (a bit like Kant), he argues that the feeling of compassion is "good in itself," a virtue even in the absence of beneficent action. "That compassion is often appropriate when there is a little or no scope for the subject's disposition to beneficence shows that compassion's sole significance does not lie in its role as motive to beneficence. . . . The compassionate person's expression of concern and shared sorrow can be valuable to the sufferer for its own sake, independently of its instrumental value in improving his condition."[25] Blum also points out that compassion should not be thought of as a Kantian "inclination," for being compassionate is quite distinct from "doing what one is in the mood to do or feels like doing." Indeed "compassionate acts often involve acting very much contrary to one's moods and inclinations. Compassion is fundamentally other-regarding rather than self-regarding: its affective status in no way detracts from this."[26]

This is an extremely important point, first because it rightly rejects the tendency to treat all acts based on emotions (and the emotions themselves) as "self-interested" in an ethically damning sense, and second because it is important to recognize that the moral sentiments have a moral significance that is independent of (though not entirely separated from) the actions to which they typically give rise. If a person frequently expressed compassion but never demonstrated willingness to help, we would eventually reject his or her claims to be compassionate; but it would be a serious misunderstanding of the virtue of the moral sentiments to insist that a person *only* feels compassion when he or she acts of volunteers to help. In his *Nicomachean Ethics*, Aristotle points out the independent virtue of *eunoia*—wishing another well but not putting oneself out on his or her account, but of course this is not to be praised to the *exclusion* of helping others. The first virtue of our moral feelings is that we have them, that they represent a certain way of engaging with the world. Their secondary virtue is that they sometimes prompt kindly and considerate actions and make the world more just, but the cynical critics of "do-gooders" are correct in pointing out that a world in which everyone acted on their compassionate impulses would very likely be almost as much a mess (certainly no more than that) as it is now.

It may seem odd or even masochistic to insist that pain in itself can be a virtue, but in compassion we can see how this may be so. An executive who is forced to fire someone, a military commander who has to order men to their death may well feel and ought to feel distress because, while doing their duties, they also feel compassion. At such times, it is good to feel bad, and to avoid the pain is, in some sense, immoral. Thus when the executive pleads that "it's just a business decision" or the commander insists that "it's nothing personal" we can recognize in their detachment a kind of moral bad faith. So much for the "wisdom" that says that "you shouldn't take it personally." Taking it personally is what converts an immoral or at any rate distasteful action into a moral one. (Which is not to say that any immoral act can be made moral if only one feels guilty or compassionate enough about it. The rapist who feels sorry for his victims is not much—if any—better than his purely hostile or cold-blooded colleague.) But it is in this sense, at least, that the "negative" and painful emotions are essential to a sense of justice. One certainly has no such sense if one does not feel guilty about being unjust or does not feel ashamed about betraying a trust. Thus Aristotle, with some discomfort, insists that shame is one of the virtues, not because it is good to be ashamed but because it is wicked not to feel shame when one ought to.[27] Painful emotions in such circumstances are good and desirable, and only an utterly amoral hedonist would deny their virtue.

In the general sense, one can have compassion only if one cares, but care here refers to concern rather than affection as such. One can have compassion for someone who is suffering even though, in the specific sense, one does not care for him. One may even despise him. But to have compassion is, nevertheless, to have some concern for the other's good. (It need not be a primary sense; one can have compassion for one's losing rival without in any sense wishing that he would win.) But what counts as "concern" here is not entirely clear. Blum rightly points out that one can take genuine interest in relieving someone's suffering as a professional challenge. This is not compassion. What compassion requires (care does not) is some "imaginative reconstruction" of the other's condition. This is not "sharing feelings," much less confusing "his for yours," which Blum identifies (with reference to Max Scheler) as a pathological condition.[28] One need not have ever actually experienced such suffering, much less such suffering to the same degree. But one must in some sense be able to imagine sufficiently similar circumstances and experiences and to a certain extent "dwell" on them. One need not (as in the "sharing" analysis of sympathy and compassion) have the same feelings as the other, in either kind or degree, but one must feel some degree of distress. So, the other may be in physical pain, but to feel compassionate one need not feel some dim echo of physical pain. (Indeed, it is extremely hard to imagine oneself in pain—as opposed to imagining *that* one were in pain—even when confronting another who is in pain.) And if the other feels humiliated or depressed one need not feel humiliated or depressed oneself. But if one does not feel some form of distress, one is not compassionate. And if (through "imaginative reconstruction") one feels distress only about the possibility that one might, someday, oneself be in similar pain, this hardly counts as compassion either.

One of the more disturbing features of the popular social philosophy of our time is the pervasive, confident contempt for "do-gooders." What could possibly be wrong with a kind emotion and the actions that go along with it, whose only aim is to help other people? The problem is that compassion, by itself, is often ill-informed, even stupid, vaguely directed and self-serving (though it pretends to be the very opposite). Thus while compassion typically prompts kindly action or a search for ways of helping where none was evident before, it also often prompts precipitous action, or makes more difficult the sort of cold, professional behavior that may be necessary (e.g., in a medical emergency). Blum points out that compassion may make worse an already hopeless situation and may hurt its recipients by concentrating too much on their plight. It can be "misguided, grounded in a superficial understanding of the situation."[29] Indeed, we all can think of examples where being too caught up in a tragedy makes us less rather than more capable of coping with it, and other examples where a superficial understanding of someone else's plight has led us to intrude where we were not welcome or intervene where we were not competent.

But this admission does not give too much to the cynical critics. The limitations of compassion hardly undermine its virtue or the overall utility of compassionate actions. Blum rightly concludes that "because compassion involves an active and objective interest in another's welfare, it is characteristically a spur to deeper understanding than rationality alone could ensure. A person who is compassionate by character is in principle committed to as rational and as intelligent a course of action as possible." Compassion without intelligence is no virtue, and intelligence without compassion is not justice. My aim in this book is to put the passions back where they belong, as the core of our sense of morality and justice. But it is not my thesis—it is the very opposite of my thesis—that the passions should be opposed or starkly distinguished from reason. The significance of compassion is that it forms the core of our sense of justice and provides rationality with a heart.

SENTIMENT AND SENTIMENTALITY (EMOTIONAL KITSCH)

A sentimentalist is simply one who desires to have the luxury of an emotion without paying for it."   OSCAR WILDE, *DE PROFUNDIS*

IT IS PERHAPS BECAUSE of the exclusive and overly saccharine emphasis on care and compassion that the sentiments have had such a bad time in Anglo-American moral and social philosophy. The "moral sentiment" theorists—Hume and Adam Smith in particular—are now studied only because of their many other virtues. Their celebration of sympathy has (until very recently) all but disappeared from the philosophical scene. Kant did away with "melting compassion" as an ingredient in ethics once and for all in a single sarcastic comment, and the other "inclinations" did not fare much better. It should not be surprising, therefore, that sentimentality has had an even worse time of it and is not only excluded from most discussions of ethics but, when it is discussed at all, it is condemned as an ethical defect. Indeed, sentimentality is roundly condemned not only in moral matters but in the arts as well, where it has earned the special name, *kitsch*. To call an artwork sentimental or kitschy is to say that it is very bad art—if, indeed, it deserves recognition as art at all—and to cast suspicion on both its creator and its appreciative audience. To call someone a "sentimentalist" in ethics is to dismiss both the person and his or her views from serious consideration, adding, perhaps a disdainful chortle and an implicit accusation of terminal silliness. But isn't my sense of justice here, whatever else it may be, just such an example of sentimentality? Am I not, when it comes right down to it, just a sentimentalist?

It is worth noting that the offensive epithet *sentimentalist* has not always been a term of abuse: just two hundred years ago, when Schiller referred to himself and his poetry as "sentimental" (as opposed to Goethe's "naive" style), he had in mind fineness and intelligence of feeling, not saccharine sweetness and the manipulation of mawkish emotions.[30] But in 1823, Robert Southey dismissed Rousseau as a writer who "addressed himself to the sentimental classes, persons of ardent and morbid sensibility, who believe themselves to be composed of finer elements than the gross multitude."[31] The charge of elitism is worth noting, for it was soon to be reversed: a sentimentalist would have distinctly inferior feelings. If Rousseau's audience was objectionable early in the century because it believed itself to have finer feelings, the object of Oscar Wilde's scorn, the young Lord Alfred Douglas, was attacked for his fraudulent and contemptible passions.

By the end of the century, "sentimentalist" was clearly a term of ridicule and abuse.

It is not surprising—although this simple correlation seems to have escaped most writers on the subject—that "sentimentality" went into decline about the same time that sentiment lost its status in moral philosophy. The key figure in this philosophical transformation, of course, is Immanuel Kant; in fact, Kant's unprecedented attack on sentimentalism was at least in part a (visceral?) reaction not only against the philosophical moral sentiment theorists (whom he at least admired) but also against the flood of popular women writers in Europe and America who were then turning out thousands of widely read potboilers and romances which did indeed equate virtue and goodness with sentimentality. Sentimentalism in philosophy became the fallacy of appealing to emotion instead of argument (a fallacy now defined in almost every textbook). To be accused of sentimentalism meant, as we have seen so often, that one had an unhealthy preference for heart-felt feeling over hard-headed reason. Sentimentalism more generally became a matter of moral bad taste, a weakness for easy emotion in place of the hard facts and ambiguities of human social life.

I do not intend to ignore the hard facts and ambiguities of human social life, but it is part of my thesis here that there is nothing essentially wrong with sentimentality (though of course there are pathological excesses and inappropriate objects, here as in all moral enterprises). On the contrary, sentimentality is essential to ethics, and the real worry is rather morality and theories of justice devoid of feeling. I do not want to argue that sentimentality (or the emotions in general) are good in themselves, but neither is sentimentality—as is so often charged—merely emotion for its own sake. Whether sentimentality is appropriate depends upon the object and nature of the emotion in question, the character of the "sentimentalist," and the overall social context.

Oscar Wilde argued that the feelings which constitute sentimentality are "in some important way unearned, being had on the cheap, come by too easily . . . to be sentimental is to be shallow." But while I am not sure what it would be for a sense of compassion to be "earned" (as opposed to proved in action), I am not at all convinced that being naturally compassionate is any kind of vice. And as for "shallowness," I have long believed (along with Mark Twain) that the most profound insights invariably lie on the surface, and that justice will get far more mileage out of surface sensitivity than it will from the "deep" abstractions of most moral theory. So, too, Michael Tanner has recently argued that sentimentality "doesn't lead anywhere."[32] Sentimental people, he argues, "avoid following up their responses with *appropriate* actions, or if they do follow them up appropriately, it is adventitious." If this objection could be sustained, much of what we are arguing in this book would be fatuous. But it seems to me that sentimentality need not be so unflatteringly defined and that the "appropriate" actions might be modest indeed—even so simple as firing off a letter or two to one's congressman or dropping a check in the mail. It is sometimes said (with some aesthetic confusion, I think) that the problem with sentimentality is that it is manipulative and indeed it often is. But whether this is offensive or not surely depends upon the context and the campaign being waged. The manipulative sentimentality of a novel such as *Uncle Tom's Cabin* turned a morally flawed country around when it became a best-seller back in the mid-nineteenth century. And we often subject ourselves voluntarily and knowingly to emotional manipulation—by going to see such films as *Terms of Endearment* and (to inspire a more brutal set of emotions) *Jaws*—and the fact that we sometimes complain afterward that such films are manipulative strikes me as a curious bit of self-protection that cries out for analysis. I would suggest, as a start, that we find ourselves embarrassed by our own sentimentality, quite apart from any judgment we might make about the quality or subtlety of the movie in question, and we are somewhat frightened by the power of our own emotions—whether sympathy or horror. Sentimentality is not nearly so ineffective as its critics suggest, and its manipulative function is a virtue insofar as its aim is virtuous. Indeed, being deeply moved by some specific (even if fictional) sentimentality would seem to be a much more reliable prod to action than a well-rationalized set of moral imperatives.

The most common charge against sentimentality is that it involves false emotion; but what is it for an emotion to be false? One suggestive argument is that sentimentality is objectionable because it deals only with vicarious and not real emotions. But it seems to me (though I won't argue this here) that vicarious emotions are real emotions.[33] If what makes them vicarious is their being at least one pace removed from the situation that provokes them, they are in that respect no different from compassion in general (as analyzed in the preceding section). Whether or not an event or a scene is fictitious is irrelevant, for the sake of the more spectator-like emotions—sympathy and compassion in particular. (The difference between fiction-inspired horror and real-life terror, on the other hand, is a more formidable case to explain.) But to be moved by another person's or creature's suffering which is not also your own is precisely what the moral sentiments are all about, and fiction can be viewed as the exercise of our emotional facilities. If this is sentimentality then surely we need much more of it in morals and social philosophy—not that there isn't enough suffering in real life, of course, but we do prefer to hone our affective skills in more measured doses. Only when a person starts denying real suffering and retreating to fiction—as if by way of inoculation rather than exercise—does sentimentality become pathological. (The usual example is Rudolf Hess, who wept at a romantic opera produced by the inmates he would soon murder.)

Another argument is that sentimentality is "false" because it is *distorting*. Mary Midgley, for instance, argues that "the central offence lies in self-deception, in distorting reality to get a pretext for indulging in *any* feeling." Sentimentality centers around the "flight from, and contempt for, real people."[34] So too, Mark Jefferson argues that "sentimentality involves attachment to a distorted series of beliefs."[35] But the reply to this objection is, first of all, that all emotions are "distorting." Anger looks only at the offense and fails to take account of the good humor of its antagonist, jealousy is aware only of the threat and not of the wit and charms of the rival, love celebrates the virtues and not the vices of the beloved, envy seeks only the coveted object and remains indifferent to questions of general utility and the fairness of the desired redistribution. But why call this "distortion" rather than "focus" or "concern"? And what is the alternative—omniscience? Always attending to everything that one knows or remembers about a subject? (Reviewing the history of Denmark as well as the literature on stepchild relations before one allows oneself to be moved by *Hamlet?*) Never having a "nice" thought without a "nasty" one as well? What is wrong with sentimentality is not its distortion of reality for the sake of emotion, for all emotions construct a perspective of reality that is specifically suited to their concerns.

What becomes more and more evident, as one pursues the objections to sentimentality and removes from consideration those concerns that are appropriate to art and aesthetics rather than ethics, is that the real objection to sentimentality (and kitsch in art too) is the rejection (or fear) of a certain kind of emotion or sentiment, variously designated as "cloying sweetness" or "sugary stickiness." The charge of sentimentality is almost always aimed at a common human sentiment—our shared horror at the death of a child, for example. What is wrong with such shared sentiment, predictable and unimaginative as it may be? It is true that such matters, especially if presently baldly, unambiguously, "perfectly" are virtually guaranteed to arouse emotion, and they therefore provide a facile vehicle for second- or third-rate painters, novelists, and moralists. But if such incidents are clichéd, it is just because they are so common and a matter of virtually universal concern, and the fact that such commonality may make for bad art and uncomfortable sermons should not be used to encourage our embarrassment at experiencing these quite natural sentiments ourselves. I am convinced that the ultimate target of the stylish attack on sentimentality is not emotion as such (angry indignation and bitter resentment have never gone out of style in Western intellectual life) but the "sweet" sentiments that are so easily provoked and so embarrassing to the hard-headed. It is true that such sentiments distort reality. But why should the idealization and optimistic editing of these sentiments provoke indignation? Is hard thinking really all that preferable to soft sentimentality? And what, exactly, are we supposed to be thinking about if not about things that so move us that we cannot get them out of our minds?

What I am suggesting is that the attack on sentimentality is wrong-headed and possibly worse, a matter of self-deception or serious bad faith. (These charges, of course, are the same ones that the critics level at sentimentality.) The attack on sentimentality is, I am convinced, at bottom an attack on the kindly emotions as such, and sometimes an attack on philosphical innocence as well. Allowing oneself to become teary-eyed about the tragic death of an impossibly idealized Little Nell while reading Dickens does not "make us unable to deal with the real world" as Midgley suggests but rather activates our sensitivity to actual tragedies.[36] The vision of our "emotional economy" according to which we have only so much sympathy to "spend" seems to me to be a particularly ill-considered and corrupting metaphor. It is true that a single trauma can exhaust our emotional resources, but it is unlikely that reading about Little Nell will do that to us. Indeed, that is precisely the virtue of sentimentality, that it stimulates and exercises our sympathies without straining or exhausting them. So considered sentimentality is not an emotional vice but a virtue, and what is so often condemned as sentimentality is nothing other than the exercise of our moral sentiments and our sense of justice.

THE CULTIVATION OF JUSTICE AND THE "NEGATIVE" EMOTIONS

*. . . examine the lives of the best people and ask yourself . . .
whether misfortune and external resistance, some kinds of hatred, jealousy, stubbornness, mistrust, hardness, avarice and violence do not belong among the favorable conditions without which
any great growth even of virtue is scarcely possible.*

NIETZSCHE, *THE GAY SCIENCE* (I, 19)

NO ONE, NOT EVEN a saint, can have a sense of justice without the capacity for anger and outrage, even the ability to hate. Indeed, one might well argue that justice is impossible without hatred, or at least without the hatred of evil and outrage at the sight of injustice. The heart of justice may be compassion for others, but its origins and its passion are to be found in the more violent, even hostile emotions. Mercy, grace, and forgiveness may (with qualification) be important civil and religious virtues, but they presuppose, rather than merely oppose, such vehement emotions as vengeance. Our sense of justice may dream about and aim at peace and universal contentment, but it is also bound to give due weight to our competitiveness, our acquisitiveness, and our "rights." The attack on sentimentality is, I have suggested, part and parcel of the general discomfort with emotion and personal feelings. But it is also aimed at the saccharine nature of many appeals to sentiment, and the charge also holds against much of moral sentiment theory itself, which sweetens and overemphasizes the kindly sentiments (and the kindest side of the kindly sentiments) and so ignores much of what makes up our moral and interpersonal life. The idea that "love will conquer all" has always been either naive or hypocritical. It is not love alone that makes the world go around but a whole cauldron of passions. Sympathy and compassion are indeed essential for our sense of justice, but they are part of a whole society of passions and sentiments, or what Max Scheler nicely called "a democracy of the emotions." Sympathy, compassion, and benevolence are not all-powerful in us, as Hume and Smith both noted with modest despair, but neither are we oppressed by the tyranny of selfishness and mutually hostile emotions that Hobbesians so fear. Our sense of justice is not just the product of New Age sentiments but a dynamic engagement in a world which we ourselves know to be often offensive and unfair, in which we see others similarly and even more oppressed or deprived, a world we accordingly resent and act to change. Spite is just as much an expression of that sense of justice as charity, although, to be sure, there are many reasons (having to do with fairness and prudence as well as civility, character, and social utility) for preferring the one to the other.

My overall argument is that justice is a complex set of passions to be cultivated, not an abstract set of principles to be formulated, mastered, and imposed upon society. Justice begins with compassion and caring, not principles or opinions, but it also involves, right from the start, such "negative" emotions as envy, jealousy, indignation, anger, and resentment, a keen sense of having being personally cheated or neglected, and the desire to get even. Our sense of justice is cultivated from these "negative" emotions. I would not say that a person who has not suffered some pain or injustice cannot feel compassion, but there is a fairly straightforward sense in which such a person does not yet know what pain or injustice are. The usual emphasis on "empathy" rightly signifies this important linkage between one's own experience and coming to understand and "feel for" the experience of another. But the critical point is that we learn about justice and injustice not as mere spectators ("ideal" and "impartial" or otherwise) but by being engaged in the world. (Rousseau's idea that we are "naturally" compassionate doesn't seem to explain this critical connection, and John Rawls's vision of persons as rational decision-makers makes

our engagement, at best, once-removed, as if we were impartial spectators of our own engagements.) So we learn about justice by being
cheated or treated unfairly as inferiors, by being punished when we
expect to be rewarded, by having something that we think is indisputably ours taken away from us, by being hurt—and, in some primal
(hardly rational yet) sense, wanting to get even. Our celebrated notion of rights, which many theorists take to be the key to justice,
is first of all that almost visceral sense of inviolability, the absolute
unacceptability of certain intrusions, interferences, offenses. That is
why rights are trump for us, but it is not the having of the right that
explains the inviolability; it is the sense of inviolability that accounts
for the ascription of rights. Of course all of this must, necessarily, take
place in a social context, in which what is happening to us also happens to others and there is a (more or less) established set of conventions and expectations. But justice is not something we learn about
merely by observing, much less through thinking alone. Our knowledge of justice begins with our experience of our own place in the
world; our sense of justice is first of all our emotional response to a
world that does not always meet up with our expectations and demands. Our sense of justice, in other words, has its origins in such
emotions as resentment, jealousy, outrage, and revenge as well as in
care and compassion.

Resentment, jealousy, outrage, revenge—this is not the usual list
of "moral sentiments," to be sure, but my point is that we can only
understand justice if we ourselves are wholly engaged in society, victims and undeserving beneficiaries rather than judges sitting on high.
Of course the kindly sentiments are essential to ethics and justice,
but they, too, are as often as not emotions felt at a (safe) distance,
"sentiments" and not passions, commiserations and not engagements.
The benevolent sentiments are only a small and not very representative piece of our emotional portrait, and even the most benign sentiments have their complications, their dark side. One cannot love
without feeling in some sense protective, without caring, and with
caring comes defensiveness and, if one's beloved is harmed, indignation and a desire for revenge. So too one can hardly feel compassion
without wanting to do something to change the world, to end the
suffering, but every compassionate act is thereby a revolutionary act

as well and requires resentment of the way the world is, a big Sartrian "no!" to the way things are. One cannot care about the homeless in America without being outraged at the governments that ignore them. One cannot care about fairness without getting furious and even vengeful at those who break the rules and corrupt the practice. Even so simple and conservative a gesture as giving to charity challenges the way the world is. To pretend that one can be compassionate and fair-minded without at the same time giving outrage and even hatred their due is to eviscerate the moral sentiments and with them our sense of justice.

It is worth noting (with some sense of irony) that sympathy and the other undeniably positive passions are often not only neglected but actually denied by cynics who wouldn't think of denying the existence of the antipathetic passons—envy and resentment in particular. Nietzsche, to take but one obvious example, heaps scorn and skepticism on all of the Christian accounts of love and pity, but he never for a second pauses to doubt the existence or the sincerity of resentment. But could one be resentful without at least the capacity to be sympathetic? Can one be jealous if he or she knows nothing of affection? Why do we so readily suspect and even deny the sympathetic passions when we are so ready to diagnose the antipathetic passions? These emotions—sympathetic and antipathetic—go hand in hand; one cannot have one without the other. One cannot have attachments without the possibility of loss, and one cannot suffer a loss without first having enjoyed (however briefly or even vicariously) attachments. One cannot care without opening oneself up to disappointment and betrayal, but neither can one be disappointed or betrayed if one has never opened oneself up to caring. One cannot have pride without the possibility of shame, and one cannot be shamed if one has no pride. The positive and the negative passions travel together. They are both real, even when it is socially expedient to fake the former rather than the latter. (In university life, I often suspect that it is the other way around.) But a life without the potential for envy, anger, resentment, even spite is very likely a life without love, without care, even without dignity.[1]

The first part of my argument has been that, whatever one's "principles" of justice, they are utterly meaningless without the fundamental human sense of caring and compassion and the ability to understand and feel for the well-being of other human beings and other creatures who may be very far away and personally quite unknown to us. But the final part of my argument is that the usual set of sympathetic or altruistic passions is too limited, at best half the story of the moral sentiments. The antipathetic emotions are as essential as the sympathetic passions. Envy and jealousy have as much to do with the origins and development of justice as pity and compassion. There is nothing "negative" about indignation and outrage in the face of injustice, and there is very little that is "positive" in the love of an evil cause or person. To be sure, our first reactions to disappointment and hurt are rarely just or fair, or even rational, but only when we are hurt or slighted, cheated or offended do we begin to develop a sense of justice.

THE PRIMACY OF INJUSTICE AND ITS PASSIONS

The violation of justice is injury. . . . it is, therefore, the proper
object of resentment, and of punishment, which is the natural
consequence of resentment.
ADAM SMITH, *THE THEORY OF THE MORAL SENTIMENTS*

IT IS TOO EASILY assumed that a fully developed sense of justice, because it is such a noble virtue (even the chief of the virtues), must be derived only from equally noble (though perhaps more primitive) emotions. I think that this is wrong. My argument is that the sense of justice emerges as a generalization and, eventually, a rationalization of a personal sense of *injustice*.[2] There are rare examples, perhaps, of saintly, noble, or richly privileged creatures who never suffered an injustice but received the full-blown idea of justice from exemplary parents or from peers or out of the blue, but they are, unfortunately, rare indeed. The Buddha is sometimes presented as such an example, but it worth noting that Jesus is not. Indeed, it is quite significant that the very heart of the Christian religion turns on the idea of a grave injustice being done to God Himself. The very idea that someone else "died for our sins" signifies a dramatic moment of injustice, whether or not it was also an act of divine self-sacrifice. We get a sense of injustice by suffering injustice. And we cultivate our sense of justice only by integrating and empathizing our various experiences of injustice into a (more or less) coherent set of social sympathies and antipathies in which we ourselves play an active and not merely spectatorial role.

Our sense of injustice is not a general sense of outrage—that comes later and already involves a number of grand generalizations. In fact, such passions as outrage and indignation are often secondary emotions of justice, not because they are inessential or unimportant but because they follow (though often fast) on the heels of some more primary emotion like resentment. First we sense ourselves cheated; then we react with indignation. Outrage and indignation are our proper reactions to injustices; resentment is that sense of injustice as such. Resentment, and its kindred emotions, are, first of all, forms of perception, spontaneous evaluations of the world and how we (and others) are being treated in it. Resentment, like envy, typically begins with some perceived inequity. "He got more than I did!" But resentment is not just a matter of differences or inequality; there are many differences and inequalities that we accept as a matter of course. Many of them are expected and, on reflection, seen to be deserved. Some of them are unexpected and nevertheless "just the way things are." Resentment depends on a very special kind of evaluative perception, a complex set of social expectations in which judgment plays a crucial role. The idea that our sense of injustice already includes at its very core judgments and evaluations of what is right and proper thus undercuts the traditional division between rational reflection and merely emotional reaction, and the critical question becomes how we learn to make such judgments and perceive such inequities. Why are some (in fact most) differences between us acceptable and not matters of injustice at all? Or, better, why are any differences between us judged to be unjust, rather than just "the way things are"?

The first part of the answer is, certainly, the perception, the noticing, of the difference itself, not just as a difference but as an inequality. This alone, of course, is not enough. The perception already presupposes an evaluation, a judgment that this is a difference that makes a difference, that one person is advantaged and the other disadvantaged. But much more must be involved. It must be judged that the person who has the advantage does not *deserve* that advantage. Thus we see that the ingredients of what are often presented as part of a theory of justice must already be presupposed as an aspect of our pretheoretical and prereflective emotions and judgments. (The importance of reflection and theory is that these allow us to correct—and not just rationalize—our emotions and judgments.) But important inequalities, even if undeserved, do not in themselves signify injustice. What must be added is blame. Herein appears one of the major asymmetries between justice and injustice, and one of the main reasons too why injustice must be primary in our thinking and feeling: justice obtains, but injustices are done.[3] The world itself cannot be unjust. Nor is it reasonable, from this point of view, to say that "life isn't fair," for life as such doesn't *do* anything for us or to us.[4] Our sense of injustice depends upon a sense of blame, and a person who cannot blame (because he or she lacks the concept or, more likely, does not have the self-esteem to self-righteously recognize the transgressions of others) will not have a sense of injustice either. (Can he or she have a sense of justice? Only in the abstract, as a political or theological hope, not as a guide to action.)

But to insist that our sense of injustice presupposes a sense of blame is still too simple, for the blame in question is only sometimes to be aimed at an individual. Much more prevalent are complex social actions, even the structuring of a whole society, which wrongly hurt or deprive people but for which no individual or definite group of individuals can be blamed. Some of these social actions—the ones we should worry about the most (because they seem so unlike actions at all)—are collective acts of omission, the failure of a great many people to come to the aid of those in need, even when they themselves are (in any number of senses) the indirect beneficiaries of the inequities in question. In general, what counts as an inequity, what gets noticed as an unjust difference, almost always depends on the society and the social situation. In themselves differences in reward based on differences in ability are neither unjust nor unfair. Differences in physical strength and prowess are bound to be critical in a manual labor–intensive or a warrior society,[5] and there is nothing unjust about celebrating and rewarding those who abound in these virtues. On the other hand, differences in physical attractiveness are bound to be important in a society in which too many people have no essential social role and appearance rather than performance is valued. In such societies, vanity rather than virtue is what counts, as Rousseau would no doubt put it, and a pervasive awareness of injustice is bound to be the rule rather than the exception.

Rousseau tells us, in his *Discourse on the Origins of Inequality*, that differences in nature are real but of no importance. It is society that makes them so. Being tall or strong or smart or blonde is not, as such, any reason for distinguishing one person from another. But when fashion dictates that it is better to be this or that, then considerable inequalities emerge. Children learn early on that it is better to be smart than dumb, smiling rather than sullen, nice rather than mean, attractive rather than plain, and they expect to be rewarded (and punished) accordingly. Their treatment by their elders and by their peers quickly and continuously confirms these expectations. And, indeed, if there were no countervailing messages (e.g., that beauty is only skin deep, that "toughness" is good, and, more generally, that all people are created equal) our sense of injustice would be limited to breaches of these expectations. But given the cross-currents and contradictions in our expectations, not to mention the predictable inconsistencies in our behavior and in contrasting social contexts, our sense of injustice involves an extremely complicated sense of differences and deserts, depending on the context and the appropriate forms of judgment and evaluation.

But, of course, only the most unfortunate child first learns his or her sense of injustice in such complex and contradictory circumstances. (R. D. Laing and Gregory Bateson have suggested—in very different ways—that schizophrenia is, at least in part, a child's appropriately extreme adjustment to such circumstances.)[6] Most of us, reared in a more or less coherent family setting, grow up with a reasonably unified set of demands and restrictions, according to which we are rewarded or punished with an underlying foundation of security and affection. It has been suggested that our sense of justice begins with that sense of stability and well-being, but one doesn't begin with a sense of justice but rather with a set of expectations which, sooner or later, are bound to be violated. One child gets less than the others;

he or she notices. An expectation has been violated. The "why?" question may or may not arise (that probably comes later). For now it is just a howl of precocious indignation. Indeed (as all parents will attest) it does not matter whether the amount in question is deficient in fact or only in appearance. It is not, first of all, a matter of reason. Excessive expectations breed an excessive sense of injustice (and inhibited expectations can breed a deficient sense of injustice). But the appropriateness of our sense of injustice is not yet in question. This immediate sense of injustice is primary; a well-developed sense of justice comes much later, and only after a good deal of experience of injustice to oneself and others.

Injustice is first of all this sense of personal slight, or to put it differently, no violation of principle is claimed, no broad-based comparison or contrast is made except that limited to the context (and perhaps some similar or related context) at hand. We do not first have a theory that informs us that such and such a situation is inherently unjust. We rather have an expectation that gets thwarted, not just as a matter of frustration (as Robert Gordon has recently argued, in his *Structure of Emotion*) but together with a sense—no matter how primitive or ill-founded—of blame.[7] A child gets less than he or she expects, perhaps on the basis of a promise, perhaps on the basis of observation of what the other children have gotten. (Does the notion of a "reasonable expectation" even fit in here?) Let us suppose that it is a family practice to serve the elder first, then the siblings in descending order. One evening there is a slight deviation and the eldest is indignant, feels cheated. Does the explanation, the illness of the younger brother, make any difference? That depends: has the older brother ever been ill himself? Can he thus be appealed to? Empathy is taught before justice, as its prerequisite, but its basis is the personal experience of slight. ("How would you like it if your sister did that to you?" "Don't you remember how bad you felt?") This is, obviously, how parents teach justice and fairness. "How would you like it if he did that to you?" It is not surprising tht a bright child first hears such a question as a trick. He or she knows that something is being "pulled." So, too, expectations of punishment are taught in terms of the breaking of rules, and one expects to be punished—and that others too will be punished—accordingly. When the punishment does not come, the idea of "getting away with it" arises, which is not, of course, a simple negation of justice but—as imitation is to admiration and hypocrisy to morality—the recognition that injustice can be turned to one's personal advantage. (It is from here that Plato's Glaucon—not Thrasymachus—takes his cue.) Parents teach their children a sense of injustice, in other words, not just in their consistency but in their lapses and inconsistencies as well. What parents do not do (except for a small number of academics with unusually neurotic children) is to teach justice and fairness as a set of principles. The offenses and expectations that give rise to a primal sense of injustice are purely local; they are not generalized, and often they are not even generalizable. Three children are used to a certain routine at dinner time. A cousin comes to visit and there is confusion. There is no established expectation regarding an extra child. Does he or she deserve special treatment, first serving or an extra helping? This is where we learn about "spheres of justice," when the established sphere is disrupted and we learn the limits of our expectations. But what we learn about first is injustice, and so too we must learn to circumscribe the sphere. Do the routines refer to one's family alone, the whole community, the country, or the world? (The greatest shock of injustice for many children comes with the birth of a new sibling, or for only children, the moment they step outside the family, as the sphere they have gotten used to suddenly expands.)

Justice may consist of generalities, but injustice—even if widespread—is always localized. It may not follow, as Michael Walzer argues, that there is no need or justification for some larger projection or rationalization.[8] Indeed, one might well argue that it is exceedingly difficult not to so project and rationalize, especially when one has learned and mastered a language in which such generalization and rationalization is virtually a matter of grammar. For us, at any rate, such intellectual activities virtually always follow a perceived injustice, even if clumsily and (as is almost always the case) ethnocentrically, but we should not confuse our theories of justice with the keen sense of injustice that underlies them. Japan and most "primitive" cultures have a keen sense of injustice based on their own social structures or hierarchies, but few of them have any principles or procedures of the Rawlsian variety. I have often wondered how much of John Rawls's labyrinthine argument in *A Theory of Justice* comes down to little more than an exquisitely tight intellectual defense of his (never quite stated) sense of outrage at the living conditions of the poor in Cambridge, Massachusetts. Or how much of Robert Nozick's *Anarchy, State and Utopia* could ultimately be pinned down to his sense of personal pride in his hard-earned rise from Brooklyn to Harvard ("I earned this; you can't take it away from me"). But from these two examples it is evident how varied and opposed our sense of ethical outrage can be, depending on perspective and personal experience. Thus we should not expect this sense to be singular or unified, without ambiguity, conflicts, and contradictions. Why in the world should we suppose that all of those contextually bound bits and pieces of experience and our moral education should fit together in one coherent, harmonious whole? Before we can even attempt to formulate an all-embracing theory of justice, we have to have some sense of justice, but to get that we need a generalized sense of injustice, and that depends on those personal experiences of injustice and the antipathetic emotions of injustice—envy, jealousy, resentment, and the urge to revenge.

Which of the antipathetic emotions are responsible for that sense of injustice from which our sense of justice gets cultivated? Through which feelings is the sense of injustice disclosed? Well, to begin with, all of those emotions of moral disgust and condemnation—loathing, contempt, scorn, disgust, disdain, dislike, hatred, and the like—disclose to us the occasional awfulness of the world. It is not a well-thought-out evaluation, ready with reasons. It is more a visceral response, as to a foul taste or a bad smell. Nietzsche used to say that he did ethics first of all with his nose, to detect the odors of decay and hypocrisy.[9] What disgusts or offends us is as important to morality and justice as what pleases us or warms the cockles of our hearts. The moral sentiment theorists just plain had it wrong when they placed sympathy in such a distinguished position and all but ignored our feelings of moral repulsion and disgust. What is most impressive about the list of antipathetic emotions, however, is its length. It is an interesting and perhaps revealing question: why do we have so many more names of emotions (and accordingly so many more emotions) for negative and hostile feelings for others than we do terms of affection? (And why have so many philosophers obsessed about the meaning of the word *good* when so many of our moral feelings and judgments rather consist of a sneer or a snarl?) It is always worth noting that other languages have vocabularies for the antipathetic emotions which include at least the recognition of emotions we omit. My favorite example is the German *Schadenfreude*, delight in another's suffering. The sometimes subtle distinctions between such feelings as scorn, loathing, and contempt (and being "beneath contempt"!) need not occupy us here. The point is that one cannot understand our sense of justice without appreciating the force and importance (as well as the warrant) of the antipathetic passions.

Most evident among these, of course, are the straightforwardly moral emotions of outrage and offense, anger and indignation, although these are (as we already noted) often based on reaction to or reflection on injustice rather than constitutive of our sense of injustice itself. Anger and outrage are, at their very core, emotions that accuse someone (on occasion, and with a mix of metaphor, some*thing*) of an offense. One should distinguish anger from mere irritation and peevishness (even when these are rather violent) just because those emotions do not have that essential quality of indictment. They are rather expressions of annoyance, whether general or particular— though in the latter case, with repetition, irritation can become real anger. Indignation goes one step further. The offense in anger and outrage may yet be purely personal—an insult or a slight—but the offense involved in indignation breaches some larger practice or principle. It is, in other words, not just a personal offense but something more. (We sometimes refer to this emotion as *moral* indignation to make this point clear.) Anger and outrage do not have to have self-interest or a personal slight as their object, but it is necessary to take the offense personally, to identify in some sense with the offended person or party. Aristotle tells us that anger takes as its occasion a significant offense to oneself or one's friends. I think that we can safely expand that to include any offense to a person or persons with whom we can empathize. I get indignant about the Marcos's treatment of Philippine citizens, and I do not have to know even one Philippine citizen to do so. Moral indignation, on the other hand, is always about an issue that is larger than personal self-interest, though, to be only slightly paradoxical, one must take even the most impersonal principle personally if one is to get indignant about its breach.

There are also emotions of entitlement—possessiveness and deprivation—which get prompted mainly in their breach or violation, in envy, jealousy, resentment, bitterness, and spite, for example. These emotions are often (but by no means always) accompanied by anger, occasionally by indignation, and they too often eclipse compassion and dignity, for all too obvious reasons. Deprivation, loss, and fear of loss are central to these emotions, but notice that all of these presuppose some initial sense of belonging or ownership. Pride is a possessive emotion just as much as envy is. So, one has to admit, is vanity, although the difference between the object of vanity and the object of pride is itself an important ethical insight into the nature of our sense of justice. (Pride, so long as it is not "false," is deserved: vanity, even if it is warranted, is not.)[10] In our legal-minded society, we tend to think of ownership and possession in terms of deeds and property rights, but the proper sense of ownership or "mineness" goes much deeper than that. It is common to communal-property societies as well as private-property societies, and it is clearly present in most animals by way of the much-vaunted "territorial imperative." John Locke had it half right when he spelled out the importance of property as entirely natural, once one had "mixed one's labor" with it. (He was half wrong insofar as he leapt to the conclusion that this sense of property was already a "right" and prior to the attachments and conventions of society.)

Envy is a sense of deprivation (whether or not of something deserved) whereas jealousy is (in part) a fear of losing something one already in some sense possesses.[11] (A man can be jealous of the rival who is very successfully flirting with his wife, but he can only be envious of the handsome politician who has a romance with a glamorous starlet whom he has never met.) Obvious, when we are talking about people as the "objects" of such emotions (already an awkward phrase) the sense of "possession" that is in question gets quite tricky and complicated, not like the crude sense of ownership at all. And it is not just the legality of marriage that conveys this sense of possession (or possessiveness) between husband and wife and vice versa; it also applies to friendships and even cooperative enterprises at the office, so that it makes perfectly good sense for someone to feel angry or jealous or betrayed when a member of his "team" is pulled away for another (perhaps competing) project. The language of rights is often introduced as a front for these emotions, which are central to any culture which believes in "private property" and perhaps essential in any society that has a sense of merit. But even animals have most of these emotions, whether or not it makes sense to speak of their having rights, and even the seemingly clear meaning of the word *ownership* (seemingly clear because we have so thoroughly defined this term for legal purposes) is not in fact at all clear. In what sense does one "own" a tree, a dog, or for that matter a husband, a wife, a child, an employee? In what sense does one own something that one never uses, or whose use is out of one's control? Emotions such as envy and jealousy surface in societies that have no comparable legal sense of ownership (indeed, one might argue that the legal apparatus would obviate the need for such emotions if ownership were defined more precisely). They have much to do with distributive justice, and it is not surprising that whole ideologies tend to turn on the proper place of such emotions (envy as a desirable goad to hard work and productivity, envy as an insidious obstacle to an ethic of hard work and personal advancement, envy as a good reason for eliminating competitiveness and differences in status). Of particular importance here is the emotion resentment, but to this we shall soon devote an entire section. (Spite is an interesting but perverse case, of special interest to justice because of its extremity—"if I can't have it no one will"—but I see no reason to dwell on it here.)[12]

Emotions ascribe responsibility, which is utterly essential to our sense of injustice. We do not first ascribe responsibility and then respond emotionally. The emotion itself ascribes responsibility; it immediately recognizes (or simply presumes) that a harm or hurt has a cause. (Indeed, we typically presume that someone or something is the cause of our pain prior to any investigation or evidence. An elderly dog, feeling an arthritic pain in its thigh, will instinctively snap or growl at a presumed culprit even before it turns its head. After buying a ticket the theater-goer miscounts his change and immediately turns back to the booth to make an accusation.) Injustice, in other words, is not just getting the short end; it also requires that someone be to blame. Anger, indignation, outrage, vengeance are all emotions that ascribe responsibility (in the form of blame), but then so do gratitude, admiration, and emotions of "debt," which are ascriptions of praise instead of blame. Our sense of justice (but not every people's sense of justice) places a premium on personal responsibility. Someone is to blame. Someone deserves praise. It is impossible to imagine a merit system without these notions, but, again, I think that we over-intellectualize the sometimes visceral attribution of responsibility.

There are also, of course, emotions of self-ascribed responsibility: shame, guilt, embarrassment, remorse, regret, and humiliation (all of which imply blame); pride, self-love, a sense of honor (which imply praise). How we feel about justice obviously depends, in part, on how we see ourselves and our roles in the world. John Rawls may apply the liberal principles of justice to a selfless situation of rational deliberation, but I think that conservative critics are much closer to the mark when they argue (ad hominem) that liberalism is first of all a keen sense of personal guilt about one's own privileged place in the world. We first of all feel uncomfortable about our comparative wealth, health, and opportunities; then we try to devise principles to give this discomfort some structure, to rationalize our privileges or at least allow us to live with them, to correct the inequities in some systematic way that is not wholly self-destructive at the same time. A big part of justice, in other words, is being able to blame (as well as praise) oneself, to admit one's responsibility for justice and not just delegate it to some system or social structure in which one is at most a contingent party or perhaps just an observer. The keenest sense of injustice, perhaps, is not our outrage at being slighted but rather our distress at finding that we ourselves are the beneficiaries of an injustice. It is there, perhaps, that our often childish sense of injustice turns into a sense of justice, not because we have learned to generalize our personal notions of rights and desert into an abstract theory but rather because we have learned to see ourselves in others' places and realize that we are never mere observers in injustice but almost always at least passive participants.

Finally, there are the vindictive emotions, especially vengefulness. Vengeance is often allied with emotions of offense, anger, and resentment, but it is something more in its core commitment to action and the extreme animus of its motivation. One can be angry or resentful and (contra Aristotle, for whom anger and the urge to revenge were one) not feel the necessity to get even—indeed, there may be no possibility of getting even. Even when anger and resentment lead to punishment, it is not necessary that the wronged person should get to carry out the punishment. But this personal involvement is essential to revenge. In the "spaghetti Western," *Once Upon a Time in the West*, the avenger (Charles Bronson) saves the life of the villain (wickedly played by Henry Fonda) just in order to be able to kill him at the climax of the movie. What is crucial to vengeance is one's own essential part of the process of justice (which is why, for all of us, "vengeance is mine"). And this is just what makes vengeance such anathema to the modern legal system, of course, for the system wants to retain justice, and in particular punishment, for itself.

An important note: there is a sense in which gratitude and its kin should be included here as well, not as vindictive, of course, but as emotions that "get even." It is extremely important—and in many societies essential to a person's honor, social standing, and self-esteem—to get even by returning good for good or kindness for kindness. And one must do this personally. It is not enough if someone else thanks or rewards your benefactor for the service he or she has given you, and it is of particular importance that the gift or reward that one gives in gratitude should be appropriate and commensurate, as is the punishment in revenge. It is well worth pondering why so much of the history of justice (in Western society) has taken vengeance as central to justice and placed gratitude on the periphery, and why so much of our current legal system is devoted to punishing wrongdoers but has little to say or do about rewarding those who help the system thrive. "Getting even" would seem to apply symmetrically in any system of desert, but it has often been noted that punishment and reward are too often treated as completely different concerns, and not similar or symmetrical at all.[13]

No discussion of vengeance, however brief, is complete without at least some mention of the emotions of forgiveness and mercy. It is worth noting that these are often contrasted with justice, for example, in the Old Testament, where mercy undercuts the claims of justice as vengeance and retaliation. Nietzsche, playing against this biblical tradition, takes mercy to be the hallmark of true justice, and available only to godlike beings (e.g., his *Übermensch*), and links the desire for vengeance with resentment, the emotion of the weak.[14] The New Testament, of course, makes much more of the virtue of forgiveness, but critics and commentators have often been perplexed about what sort of act or emotion this is supposed to be. Part of the problem, of course, is the more recent pairing of "forgiving and forgetting." Why does one need both? I would suggest that forgiving means giving up one's plans or hopes for vengeance and, where friends are concerned, trying to put the relationship back on an even keel. But forgetting is something quite different and usually a matter of imprudence where it isn't simply a distraction.[15]

Against the tradition that would distinguish mercy and justice (vengeance) and play them off against one another, however, I want to say that they are part of the same holistic package. Mercy and forgiveness do not deny or cancel an injustice but presuppose it and affirm it. They are contrasted because of an overly narrow conception of justice (i.e., as "getting even") instead of looking at the overall pattern of emotional and social relationships. One might show mercy because the crime does not really deserve the prescribed punishment, but one does not deny and thereby in effect affirm the crime itself. Or one shows mercy because even though the punishment fits the crime it does not fit the criminal. He or she has virtues that speak louder than the crime. One might show mercy not in order to say anything about the accused but rather to display something about oneself, one's power, one's kindness, even one's whimsicality and unpredictability. Mercy is not opposed to justice (or vengeance). It is, in the larger picture, an attempt to see that justice prevails, by way of a personal gesture instead of an abstract ruling or principle.

Sometimes an emotion may itself constitute an injustice. We have been talking about emotions through which the feeling of injustice is disclosed, but there are also what we might just call "bad feelings," such as fear, grief, disgust, and humiliation. If there were no suffering, no pain, no possibility of deprivation, it is hard to see why we would ever have a sense of injustice or how the emotions of injustice could get a foothold. (This is one reason for distinguishing philosophers like

Hume who take scarcity as necessary for justice from those who see injustice as primarily a violation of principle—whatever the circumstances or whether or not anyone suffers as a consequence.) But we do suffer, and some of our suffering—indeed most of our suffering—is emotional. There are particularly unpleasant emotions which, although they are not constitutive of our sense of justice as such, are often the subject matter of concerns about justice, notably fear and humiliation. Preventing people from living in fear is one of the purposes (some philosophers, following Hobbes and Locke, would say *the* purpose) of justice. Robert Nozick has an illuminating discussion of how one's rights are violated, say in an armed robbery, even if no goods or cash are lost,[16] just by virtue of the intrinsic unpleasantness of the fear involved. Similarly, one of the purposes of any code of justice must be to minimize humiliation except when humiliation is prescribed as a part of the punishment. (Indeed, humiliation is and always has been one of the essential ingredients in punishment and is often its sole ingredient.) Saving people from disgust is one of the aims of "legislating morality" even when, in a strict sense, the crimes thus condemned are "victimless." (Of course, the variability and subjectivity of people's threshold of disgust becomes a notorious problem, and as with fear and humiliation there is a very plausible argument that some disgust is not only unavoidable but essential to the moral life.) Grief, of course, is unpleasant mainly because of the loss it represents, but one could argue that there is something unjust about causing a person grief even if, in fact, the loss is nonexistent. Fooling someone into thinking that her cat has been run over by a car is cruel and unjust even if, in fact, the cat has been continuously cuddled and pampered and not harmed in any way.

One might categorize all of these emotions as "undeserved suffering" or simply "mental pain," but this fails to take into account that many of these painful emotions are directly involved in justice and thus a matter of desert (or lack of it). Thus remorse may be an extremely unpleasant emotion, but no one would say that it is the purpose of a system of justice to make sure that people don't feel remorse. So too with a wide variety of emotions such as shame and guilt, even humiliation. This category of emotions also includes those which refer to the loss of those affections that make justice possible, for instance, grief as the loss of love (or more accurately, of love's "object") and embarrassment as a loss of dignity.[17] In fact, there are some good arguments for understanding grief in particular as a devastation of emotion rather than as an emotion in its own right. One gets angry, but one suffers grief, when, for instance, a loved one dies and that love no longer has its beloved. Casting our net widely enough we would find that almost every human emotion has something to do with justice, whether as an ingredient in our sense of justice or as one of those forms of engagement in the social world that gives justice its content and concerns. I will only discuss a few of these in what follows, but I want to make the point that our sense of justice is not constituted by a few select feelings but is rather the composite synthesis of our overall emotional makeup. The mistake of the early moral sentiment theorists was to think that our sense of justice and injustice depended on just one or two special emotions: I want to argue that it is the product of virtually all of them.

RESENTMENT AND THE ORIGINS OF JUSTICE

As for Duhring's proposition that the home of justice is to be sought in the sphere of the reactive feelings, one is obliged for truth's sake to counter it with a blunt antithesis: the last *sphere to be conquered by the spirit of justice is the sphere of the reactive feelings!*   NIETZSCHE, ON THE GENEALOGY OF MORALS

. . . one must be careful not to conflate envy and resentment. For resentment is a moral feeling. If we resent our having less than others, it must be because we think that their being better off is the result of unjust institutions, or wrongful conduct on their part. Those who express resentment must be prepared to show why certain institutions are unjust or how others have injured them.   JOHN RAWLS, A THEORY OF JUSTICE

OF THE MANY EMOTIONS that go into our sense of justice, two in particular seem to play a primary role in our feelings of justice while getting especially short shrift in our various theories of justice. The two emotions I have in mind are both clearly "negative" on any of the standard Manichean modes of evaluating emotions, and many philosophers, including not only Socrates but also Friedrich Nietzsche, have contrasted them with justice and so dismissed them from the discussion. The first of these emotions is vengefulness, which I want to argue lies right at the historical if not also the visceral core of justice.[18] It is through the impulse to vengeance, not through the rules of fair distribution, that we get our primary sense of appropriate balance and of getting even. (I will discuss vengeance in the following section.) The other, equally "negative" emotion is resentment, which plays a spectacular role both in the evolution of justice and in the recent history of discussions about justice. Resentment has certainly earned its reputation as one of the nastier emotions, but it should also be said that it is one of the most clever, most philosophical of emotions, and at the heart of its philosophy is one key ingredient of our sense of justice. Granted, resentment always begins with a sort of self-absorption if not outright self-interest as well as a bitter sense of disappointment or humiliation, but it then tends to rationalize and generalize and so project its own impotence outward as a claim—even a theory—about injustice in the world. It is from this sense of being unfairly treated, along with a consequent feeling of vengefulness and, one hopes, a countermanding sense of compassion and other more generous sentiments, that our overall sense of justice develops. Indeed, even Rawls, who works so hard to make justice out as a matter of practical reason, acknowledges the significance of resentment in the psychological origins of justice. He notes that resentment is already the recognition that someone else's "being better off is the result of unjust institutions, or wrongful conduct on their part," and he presents that emotion as if it already contains the demands usually leveled against philosophical argument:[19] "Those who express resentment must be prepared to show why certain institutions are unjust or how others have injured them." I think that "must" is out of place there; resentment as such is not under any particular academic or conversational obligations. But it is true that resentment, in its urge to generalize and project itself and in its aim to undermine the status quo, tends to be quite articulate and outspoken, full of reasons if not reasonable or rational in the usual sense of dispassionate objectivity.

Of course, there are those people whose sense of justice is almost wholly obsessed with resentment, whose sense of oppression far outweighs any sense of compassion and eclipses any possible empathy with the oppressor. But even then, resentment rarely remains mere personal bitterness and almost always thinks of itself in terms of some larger injustice, not only to oneself but, typically, to an entire group of fellow-sufferers. This is not to say that resentment has embodied within it any principles of justice, but it certainly may contain such principles, and in any case it involves some appeal to expectations or implicit standards of fairness. These may be as simple and concrete as (in the case of my two sibling puppies) "that's for me, not you!" or as complex and abstract as "no one should get an ambassadorship on the basis of party politics alone" (when I, a foreign service professional, have just been passed over). Resentment always has a personal basis though not a personal focus or personal scope. One always feels somehow deprived or slighted oneself (or feels this for someone else) but the focus of one's complaint is the nature of the slight rather than just the slight itself, and the scope of the complaint, at least for articulate "rational" animals such as ourselves, is the whole class of deprivations and slights that have been instantiated here in this one. Resentment, one might say, is the class action suit among the emotions. Thus resentment, even if self-absorbed, typically becomes a social emotion, embracing others under its claws. One might note that it is resentment, not misery, that loves company. And with enough company and a little bit of courage, it can even start a revolution. It often has.

Resentment has been suggested to explain the origins of morality as such. One of the most radical and eye-opening attempts to analyze morality in terms of the negative emotions is by Friedrich Nietzsche, the late-nineteenth-century German philosopher who declared war in morality and, ever since, has been wrongly understood as a nihilist, one who thinks that there are no values and that anything goes.[20] The truth is that Nietzsche was quite the moralist himself, with a keen sense of justice and a devotion to a certain set of values—which one might summarize as Homeric. His attack on morality was in fact an attack on what he considered to be a particularly decadent set of values, values that encouraged mediocrity and brought out the worst rather than the best in us. His attack on justice was not in fact an attack on that keen sense of desert for excellence which he so admired but an attack on the purely vindictive, reactive emotions by which the weak and incompetent tried to get at those who were strong and successful.[21] Indeed, justice for Nietzsche—though not what most of us would call "justice"—was precisely that superior sense of being above all slights and beyond vindictiveness. Justice as we tend to understand it hinges on such notions as getting even and making sure that each person gets his or her due. But a sense of justice properly understood, according to Nietzsche, is very much akin in its expression (though not in its motivation) to the Christian virtues of mercy and forgiveness, not because one does not feel the right to judge or punish or because one ought to appeal to some greater court of justice, and emphatically not because one is afraid of the consequences of one's actions, but rather because one has much more important things to do with one's life than worry about the past and about those whom Nietzsche refers to with his usual flattering vocabulary as "parasites."[22] And as for the concern that each person should get his or her due, Nietzsche again insists that justice is not primarily the defense of the weak (though he even allows that those who are more fortunate have a duty to help them) but rather the cultivation and expression of one's own virtues.[23] One might draw a cautious parallel between Nietzsche's very elitist view of justice and the view that one finds today in some libertarian writings, such as Robert Shaeffer's *Resentment against Achievement*, where the author distinguishes between a "morality of achievement" and a morality of "resentment against achievement."[24] Of course, Nietzsche would have little tolerance for the obsession about "rights" that preoccupies so much of libertarian thinking, and he would be the first to point out the bitter resentment of many such authors against those who supposedly "resent achievement," but Nietzsche's emphasis on personal excellence and his condemnation of reactive mediocrity would strike a sympathetic chord in many modern thinkers.

What we call "morality," according to Nietzsche, is just this vengeance of the weak, this reactive mediocrity, and so, too, our ordinary sense of justice as fairness. What looks like rationality and the supposedly pure (and even a priori) ideals of moral thinking and justice turn out to be the expression of resentment. Nietzsche offers us a very condensed and rather mythic account of the history and evolution of morals from ancient times, the heart of which is a psychological hypothesis concerning the motives and mechanisms underlying that history and evolution. "The slave revolt in morality begins," Nietzsche tells us in his essay *On the Genealogy of Morals*, "when *ressentiment* itself becomes creative and gives birth to values."[25] (Nietzsche employs the somewhat more general French term for resentment in his discussion. "Genealogy," in general, means the historical search for origins.) Modern critics might well dismiss such speculation as yet another version of the genetic fallacy: that is, the question is supposed to be not the genealogy, genesis, or motivation of morality and justice but only, in neo-Kantian terms, the validity of our principles. Traditional theorists and Nietzsche expositors thus often talk past one another, the former focusing on arguments concerning the form and justification of moral precepts, the latter exposing the ulterior motives that underlie these supposedly noble, impersonal, and necessary ideals. How genealogy and psychology engage the concerns of current morality and moral philosophy is a large and still largely unanswered question. The more particular question I would like to discuss here has to do with the complex ethical nature of resentment: how does resentment give rise to ethical judgments in general and judgments about justice in particular, and what does this imply about those judgments?

Resentment, more than any other emotion, is primarily concerned with questions of power: who has it, who doesn't. Against the utilitarians and other, less systematic hedonists, Nietzsche suggests that the primary motive in our lives is not the search for pleasure (and avoidance of pain) but rather what he famously calls "the will to power."[26] We might well resist the idea that we are all basically motivated by any one passion, but it is by no means an unreasonable hypothesis that—to pick that passion which seems to dominate most of our lives—we live for power (or at least, not to be overpowered) rather than for pleasure, and most of us certainly seem to prefer some sense of self-importance to self-satisfaction, at least much of the time. Resentment is, above all, an emotion of power—or rather, of the lack of it. But lack of power is not the cause but the content of resentment, and resentment in turn is not the cause but the content of morality, as Nietzsche envisions it. It is not the soil from which morality and justice spring (one of Nietzsche's routine metaphors) but rather the structure of morals and justice as such. But, of course, on the thesis I am defending in this book (and for much of Nietzsche's own philosophy too) the personal virtues and in particular the virtue of justice depend very much on one's motives and personal character. Thus construed, Nietzsche's genealogy of resentment is not an instance of the genetic fallacy but a substantial moral insight.

An ethics of resentment, accordingly, is an expression of bad character—whatever its principles and their rationalizations. This is why abstract ethical theories, allegedly logical notions of universalizability, and models of practical reasoning are suspect; they distract us from questions of character, and, in addition, often provide not only a respectable façade for faulty character but an offensive weapon of resentment. And it is not far from this Nietzschean observation to the main thesis of this book, that any account of justice that does not include reference to and appreciation of the personal feelings that go into it is in danger of defending not justice as such but rather a rationalized sense of defensiveness.

Resentment—I will dispense with Nietzsche's use of the French in favor of the perfectly familiar and accurate English word—is an emotion that is distinguished, first of all, by its concern and involvement with power. It is not the same as self-pity, with which it often shares the subjective stage; it is not merely awareness of one's misfortune but involves a kind of personal outrage and an outward projection, an overwhelming sense of injustice. But neither is it just a version of hatred or anger, with which it is sometimes conflated, for both of these presume an emotional power base which resentment essentially lacks. Resentment is typically obsessive; "nothing on earth consumes a man more quickly," Nietzsche tells us, and its description often embodies such metaphors of duration and consumption as "smoldering," "simmering," "seething," and "fuming" rather than "raging," which would quickly burn itself out.[27] Resentment is also notable among the emotions for its lack of any specific desire. In this, it is not the same as envy—another kindred emotion—which has the advantage of being quite specific and based on desire. Envy wants, even if it cannot and has no right to obtain. If resentment has a desire, it is in its extreme form the total annihilation, prefaced by the utter humiliation, of its target—though the vindictive imagination of resentment is such that even that might not be enough. So too, resentment is quite different from spite, into which it occasionally degenerates, for resentment is nothing if not prudential, strategic, even ruthlessly clever. It has no taste at all for self-destruction; to the contrary, it is the ultimate emotion of self-preservation (we are not talking about survival) at any cost.[28]

Resentment is certainly among the most creative emotions. Insofar as language and insight, ruthless criticism and genealogy are worth praising—Nietzsche is willing to build an entire self out of them—then resentment would seem to be one of the most accomplished emotions as well, more articulate than even the most righteous anger, more clever than the most covetous envy, more critical than the indifferent spirit of reason would ever care to be.[29] Not surprisingly, our greatest critics and commentators are men and women of resentment. Nietzsche is surely right, that our most vocal and influential moralists are men and women of deep resentment—whether or not this is true of morality as such. Our revolutionaries are men and women of resentment. In an age deprived of passion—if Kierkegaard is to be believed—they alone have the one dependable emotional motive, constant and obsessive, slow-burning but totally dependable and durable. Through resentment, they get things done. Whatever else it may be, resentment is not ineffectual.

Resentment may be an emotion that begins with an awareness of its powerlessness, but by way of compensation, or what we call expression, resentment has forged the perfect weapon—an acid tongue and a strategic awareness of the world, which in most social contexts, excepting a few bars in Texas and San Bernardino, guarantees parity if not victory. The neo-Nietzschean stereotype is too often that of the cultivated master and the illiterate slave—perhaps because we cultivated ones cannot conceive of choosing slavery. But the typology that counts in the genealogy of resentment and morals is that of the articulate slave and the tongue-tied, even witless master. It is the slave who is sufficiently ingenious to do what even Nietzsche despairs of doing—invent new values.[30] And it is the master, not the slave, who becomes so decadent and unsure of himself that he allows himself to be taken in by this. Hegel had it right in his *Phenomenology of Spirit*; so did Joseph Losey in his 1963 movie, *The Servant*. Speech is the swordplay of the impotent, but in the absence of real swords it is often overpowering. Language may be the political invention of the herd (as Nietzsche suggests in his earlier book *The Gay Science*), but it is also the medium in which real power is expressed and exchanged. Irony is the ultimate weapon of resentment, because, as Socrates so ably demonstrated, it turns ignorance into power, personal weakness into philosophical strength. It is no wonder that Nietzsche had such mixed feelings about his predecessor in the weaponry of resentment, who created the "tyranny of reason" as the successful expression of his own will to power.[31]

Nietzsche famously tells us that certain emotions "drag us down with their stupidity," but resentment is surely not one of them.[32] No emotion is more clever, more powerful, more life-preserving if not "life-enhancing," no emotion more conducive to the grand act of revenge that Nietzsche himself wishes to perpetrate on modernity and the Christian world. Impotence, which is resentment's presupposition, would not be confused with its conclusion, which is a kind of arrogance, or with its practical results, which tend to be the most powerful motives around. So what Nietzsche despises about resentment—and an ethics built out of resentment—cannot be its conclusion or its results—whose power he often acknowledges and even admires (especially in the *Genealogy*); it must be that initial sense of impotence, the germ (not the soil) from which the whole plant grows. His complaint is not that resentment is vicious, even murderous, for it is the motive of viciousness that Nietzsche attacks, not viciousness as such. (Indeed he even praises cruelty, but limits his praise to cruelty out of strength, as if cruelty out of a sense of strength and cruelty out of a sense of weakness were easily distinguished.) Nietzsche can disparage resentment and its strategic expressions as hypocrisy but doing so leaves the values he wants to attack in place, indeed, even ennobles them. Hypocrisy, like imitation, can be a form of flattery.[33]

Resentment presupposes a sense of impotence, and it is often thought that Nietzsche's claim is that only the weak feel resentment. But the text of *Genealogy* makes it quite clear that this is not so. The strong feel resentment too, for they too find themselves facing a world that is not always in their control or to their liking. The most illuminating cases of resentment are to be found not in the pathetic digs of the underclass but in the highest rings of power. In Washington, for example, we are now used to the spectacle of some of the most powerful people on earth seething with resentment, every act expressing a sense of frustration and impotence. Nietzsche says that the difference between the weak and the strong is not the occurrence of resentment but its disposition and vicissitudes. A strong character may experience resentment but immediately discharges it in action; it does not poison him. But it then becomes clear that strength cannot be a public measure of power, for it is easy to see the wisdom of the Zen master and the Talmudic scholar who are never poisoned by resentment because they never allow themselves those desires and expectations which can be frustrated and lead to resentment. Here, of course, we remember Nietzsche's bitter criticism—"only the emasculated man is the good man"—but now we need a far more subtle ethics of emotion than some crude scale of intensity of passion. The man of resentment is hardly devoid of passion—even intense passion; his is the ultimate passion, which burns furiously without burning itself out. So what is wrong with resentment—and the ethics that is built upon it?

Nietzsche's attitude toward resentment was complex but too often sounded one-sided. It is not just a matter of good emotions and bad emotions, stupid emotions and life-enhancing emotions. And it is not just a matter of strength and weakness. Resentment is an emotion whose basis may be a sense of impotence but whose motivational power, creativity and strategic brilliance is unmatched in the realm of the passions. And that sense of impotence may be quite distinct from any objective measure of potency. Agamemnon was capable of resentment though he would also seem to be a paragon of ancient master morality. Napoleon, Nietzsche's most "untimely" exemplar of master morality in the Genealogy, was a cauldron of simmering resentment, more likely because he was Corsican and an outsider even as emperor rather than because he was short (he was actually 5'6"). Or, to take a more current example, Pete Rose, once of the Philadelphia Phillies, seems to express resentment even when he is one of the most physically powerful and successful men in America. (It has been pointed out that Rose was quite short in his formative years, and he never lost his defensiveness even when he filled out to size later on.)

Resentment, in other words, is based on an original perception of oneself, not—as Nietzsche seems to argue—on any natural or socially objective criterion. Strength and weakness ultimately have little to do with it, for the strong may be as capable of resentment (as "bad conscience") as the weak, who may well experience resentment as resignation or despair. Resentment is not the emotion of the lowly but an emotion of the demanding, the spoiled, the arrogant. Scheler, accordingly, tells us that Nietzsche's indictment of resentment applies best to bourgeois society, but this clearly contradicts Nietzsche's own genealogy, which traces the path of resentment back to the concept of the "other"—and only secondarily of oneself—as lowly, pathetic, contemptible. Resentment is quite independent of class and quite independent of power.[34] And yet, no emotion is more concerned with status and power, and no emotion is more keen in its social awareness and opinions.

At least in the Nietzschean context, we are so accustomed to thinking of resentment in its seething, vicious, most nasty embodiment that we fail to see that the same emotion invites a very different sort of interpretation. (Scheler, for instance, never took Nietzsche to task for being unfair to resentment; he only wanted to insist that Christianity and Christian morality were not necessarily based on this admittedly repulsive emotion.) Resentment is an extremely philosophical emotion. It is aware of the larger view. It has keen eyesight (the more Aristotelean analog of Nietzsche's sense of smell). It is quite conscious not only of how things are but of how they might be and, most important, how they ought to be. True, resentment always has a personal touch—one is always to some extent resentful for onself— but it also tends to open itself up to more general considerations, namely, those we call compassion and justice. It is a harsh and unfair analysis indeed that insists that the camaraderie of the resentful is only of the "misery loves company" variety. It is commiserative, can be mutually supportive and conspiratorial. Resentment is a sense of oppression. When I think of resentment, I think of Alexander Cockburn, pouring out brilliant invective in The Nation and L.A. Weekly— nasty, to be sure, but by no means impotent or ignoble. Would we rather have him write like John Kenneth Galbraith, or utter his theses in the saccharine platitudinous tone of an established mainstream politician? Resentment lies at the heart of democracy—Nietzsche was right about that—but it is not impotent resentment, not weakness, not slave or herd mentality. It is the will to power, not as mere reaction but as a keen sense of injustice, which is, in turn, the foundation of our sense of justice.

What Nietzsche ignores—in part because of his own sense of biological determinism but also, I expect, because of his own sense of rootlessness and social impotence—is the legitimacy of the felt need to change the world.[35] The sentiment of resentment may often be a legitimate sense of oppression. It is not the voice of mediocrity or incompetence but the passion of justice denied. None of this is to say that resentment isn't nasty. Of course it is. It is vindictive. It wants to change things. It looks vitriolically at those who are on top, who have the power. It wants to pull them down. But to pretend that this is mediocrity undermining excellence, the losers greasing the path of the winners, has no plausibility at all. It is in fact the dialectic of the modern world, perhaps the basic dialectic of all human competitive relations, as Hegel suggested (hardly argued) in the master-slave section of his *Phenomenology*.[36] It may not be the ideal form of human community, but it will inevitably be at least an ingredient in all social relations so long as our sense of self-importance—as opposed to a selfless sense of community—is the basis of our thinking. And then it is the dialectic of communities rather than individuals.

On this much more positive view, resentment is not just a selfish emotion, though it always has its self-interested element. It might even be said to depend on compassion, in that it insists on sharing and projecting its own sense of misfortune onto others. This is much more conceptually elevated than "herd mentality," which is unthinking, unreflective, imitative rather than compassionate. At the same time, I think that we should be cautious about concluding that this compassion amounts to a sense of community—I think that the notion of community is much more structured and less individualistic, but that isn't the crucial point here. Compassion lends itself to empathy, in that awareness of one's own suffering makes one prone to recognize suffering in others, and makes one capable of recognizing that other people are worse off than ourselves. One may feel resentful just for oneself and for some slight offense or failure of recognition, and, indeed, we usually consider this sort of resentment to be petty, selfish, and mean-spirited. But—and this is the crucial point—it is not resentment as such that deserves our criticism as a vice but rather its usual pettiness and personal limitations. We do not so criticize resentment when it is in the name of a much larger group. Cesar Chavez would not be a national folk hero if he had loudly proclaimed his own resentment about the way he was treated by employers. To the contrary, the predictable answer would have been, "Why do you think that you are different from anyone else?" But the grand scope of his resentment—and his political skills—make the case very different. It is not resentment as such that is discredited, but a merely personal, petty, disproportionate approach to the world. Our emotions betray our philosophies, whether they are petty, pathetic and narrowly self-serving or expansive, compassionate, principled, and bold. Thus I would argue that it is not ultimately resentment that Nietzsche attacks nor is it weakness but rather that particular combination of the two that so violates not just our sense of justice but our sense of what it is to be a decent human being as well.

Nietzsche separates justice from the "reactive emotions," defending justice as a rare and unusually noble sentiment. He also makes it clear that a keen sense of injustice—expressed through resentment—is the touchstone of morality for most of us. But we need not therefore disagree when Nietzche objects to the abuse of justice as the façade for the defense of one's own interests, whether in the name of "rights" or equality, and the consequent leveling effect of enforced mediocrity. What we call "justice" is too often hypocrisy. In the name of "justice" we adopt an egalitarian standpoint, for instance, but only in one direction. The bourgeoisie during the French Revolution only looked up at the aristocrats they wanted to replace; they never looked down at the rest of the "third estate" who were much worse off. Justice always begins with the self and the personal passions, but it need not and cannot therefore be selfish. Justice may begin with resentment, but resentment need not be petty or opposed to a noble sense of generosity and compassion. Indeed, given that we are not Nietzsche's much-fantasized Übermenschen, wholly satisfied and in charge of our world, it is hard even to imagine what justice would be without resentment.

JUSTICE AND THE PASSION FOR VENGEANCE

There is no denying the aesthetic satisfaction, the sense of poetic justice, that pleasures us when evil-doers get the comeuppance they deserve. . . . The satisfaction is heightened when it becomes possible to measure out punishment in exact proportion to the size and shape of the wrong that has been done.
ARTHUR LELYVELD, PUNISHMENT: FOR AND AGAINST

I think that the deterrent argument is simply a rationalization. The motive for punishment is revenge—not deterrence. . . . Punishment is hate.   A. S. NEILL, PUNISHMENT: FOR AND AGAINST

HOWEVER PROBLEMATIC ITS CURRENT role in justice may be, there is no doubt but that vengeance is the original passion for justice. The word *justice* in the Old Testament and in Homer too virtually always refers to revenge. Throughout most of history the concept of justice has been far more concerned with the punishment of crimes and the balancing of wrongs than it has been with the fair distribution of goods and services. "Getting even" is and has always been one of the most basic metaphors of our moral vocabulary, and the frightening emotion of righteous, wrathful anger is just as much a part of the emotional basis for our current sense of justice as benign compassion. Wrongdoing should be punished, and, especially, those who have wronged *us* should be punished, preferably by us or, at least, in our name. However intense our passion for justice, our resentment of injustice is necessarily its precondition and retributive anger its essential consequence. "Don't get mad, get even"—whether or not it is prudent advice—is conceptually confused. Getting even is just an effective way of being angry, and getting angry typically includes a lively desire for revenge.[37]

Like it or not, I think that we have to agree with Arthur Lelyveld's words in the epigraph at the head of this section. The immense pleasure, and aesthetic satisfaction to which he refers points to the depth of our passion, and the need for proportion indicates the intelligence involved in this supposedly most irrational and uncontrollable emotion. This is not to say, of course, that the motive of revenge is therefore legitimate or acts of revenge always justified. Sometimes vengeance is wholly called for, even obligatory. Sometimes it is not, notably when one is mistaken about the offender or the offense. But to seek vengeance for a grievous wrong, to revenge oneself against evil—that seems to lie at the very foundation of our sense of justice, indeed, of our very sense of ourselves, our dignity and our sense of right and wrong. Even Adam Smith writes, in his *Theory of the Moral Sentiments*, "The violation of justice is injury . . . it is, therefore, the proper object of resentment, and of punishment." We are not mere observers of the moral life, and the desire for vengeance seems to be an integral aspect of our recognition of evil. But it also contains—or can be cultivated to contain—the elements of its own control, a sense of its limits, a sense of balance. Thus the Old Testament instruction that revenge should be *limited to* "eye for eye, tooth for tooth, hand for hand, foot for foot, burning for burning, wound for wound, stripe for stripe" (the *lex talionis*, Exodus 21:24–5). The New Testament demands even more restraint, the abstention from revenge oneself and the patience to entrust it to God. Both the Old and New Testaments (more the latter than the former) also encourage forgiveness, but there can be no forgiveness if there is not first the desire (and the warrant) for revenge.

The desire for vengeance is not satisfied by harm to others alone no matter how harsh. It is a matter of emotion, and like punishment, it is always for some offense, not just hurting for its own sake. (We should stress here that retaliation and retribution should not be confused with mere reparation or compensation, which may in some cases undo the damage but in no case by themselves count as punishment.) Vengeance, then, always has its reasons (though, to be sure, these can be mistaken, irrelevant, out of proportion or otherwise bad reasons). Vengeance is not merely a matter of rational obligation, but neither is it opposed to a sense of obligation (e.g., in matters of family honor) or rationality (insofar as rationality is to be found in every emotion, even this one). Vengeance means getting even, putting the world back in balance, and these simple phrases already embody a whole philosophy of justice, even if (as yet) unarticulated and unjustified. Philosophers have been much too quick to attribute this sense of balance or retribution to reason, but I would want to argue that it is rather a function of emotion. Kant, for example, defends the need for "inequality" between crime and punishment but he, of course, immediately opts for reason, dismissing emotion virtually altogether.[38] Vengeance, he suggests, is purely subjective, wholly irrational, undependable, and unjustifiable. It is wholly without measure or reason, devoid of any sense of balance or justice. But I want to suggest that vengeance just is that sense of measure or balance that Kant (and so many other philosophers) attribute to reason alone. (Ultimately, the same old dichotomy is at fault here: the supposed antagonism between reason on the one side and passions on the other.) Where would our reasoning about punishment begin if not with our emotional sense of the need for retaliation and retribution? And what would our emotion be if it were not already informed and cultivated by a keen sense of its object and its target, as well as the mores and morals of the community in which the offense in question is deserving of revenge?

Vengeance, like justice, is said to be blind (though it is worth reminding ourselves which of the two is depicted in established mythology as blindfolded). Vengeance, it is said, knows no end. It is not just that it gets out of hand; it cannot be held "in hand" in the first place. And, of course, we agree that there is danger in vengeance: It is by its very nature violent, disrupting the present order of things in an often impossible attempt to get back to a prior order which has itself been violently disrupted. The impossibility of success breeds frustration and violence and this typically leads to more violence. Too often, an act of revenge (even if legitimate) results in a new offense to be righted. And when the act is perpetrated not against the same person who did the offense but against another who is part of the same family, tribe, or social group (as in a vendetta), the possibilities for escalation are endless. (Much of the traditional danger of escalating vengeance has been reduced or eliminated by our very strong contemporary notion of individual rather than collective responsibility, but at the same time the emphasis on individual responsibility has increasingly denied its attachments to vengeance.) It is because of the likelihood of escalation as well as the possibility of mistakes on a purely personal level (what John Locke called "the inconveniences" of rights enforcement in the state of nature) that the limitation of revenge through institutionalization becomes necessary.[39] But it does not follow that vengeance itself is illegitimate or without measure or of no importance in considerations of punishment. To the dangers of vengeance unlimited it must be countered that if punishment no longer satisfies the desire for vengeance, if it ignores not only the rights but the emotional needs of the victims of crime, then punishment no longer serves its primary purpose, even if it succeeds in rehabilitating the criminal and deterring other crime (which it evidently, in general, does not). The restriction of vengeance by law is entirely understandable, but, again, the wholesale denial of vengeance as a legitimate motive may be a psychological disaster.[40]

These preliminary comments are intended to unearth a number of bad arguments against vengeance (which are often generalized into even worse arguments concerning "negative" and violent emotions as a unified class):

(1) *Vengeance is (as such) irrational, and, consequently, it is never legitimate.* Ony a moment's reflection is necessary to realize that we all recognize (eventually if not immediately) the difference between justified and unjustified revenge. Vengeance is not just the desire to harm but the desire to harm for a reason, and a reason of a very particular sort. To flunk a student because he has an orange punk hairdo or because he disagreed with one's pet theory in class is not justified, but to expel him for burning down the department library is another matter. But what about the fact that sometimes, while in the grip of the passion for revenge, we fail to recognize or properly exercise the reason and warrant for our vengeance? But the point is the word *sometimes*, for there is nothing essential to vengeance that requires such failure. In indisputably rational contexts a decision-maker mistakes a means for an end, or becomes so distracted in his pursuit of the end that he neglects or simply misses the most appropriate means. In vengeance one can also get caught up in the means or obsessed and distracted by the end, but the logic of reasons and appropriateness is

nevertheless present as a standard. Accordingly, the question is not whether vengeance is ever legitmate but rather when it is legitimate.

(2) *There is no "natural" end to vengeance.* But, of course, there is. The idea that vengeance leads to a total loss of inhibition and control ignores the built-in and cultivated satisfactions of revenge, and seems to confuse the fact that mutually vengeful acts tend to escalate with the fact that a single act of vengeance typically has its very specific goals and, consequently, its own built-in standard of satisfaction.[41] I think that we are misled here by the conflation of vengeance, which is always aimed at some particular offense (or series of offenses) and the familiar feud, which is an ongoing form of personal, family or tribal hostility whose origins may well be forgotten. In other words, we conflate hatred (which may or may not be part of vengeance) with vengeance itself. We might note that one reason for the escalation of violence in vengeance, even when it seems that both sides have good reason to be vengeful, is that they may have, as Elizabeth Wolgast suggests, "different arithmetics."[42] That is, what seems to count as getting even to one side is evidently an overpayment according to the other, or else the frameworks in which the balance is calculated are themselves very different. One of Wolgast's examples is the debt of Agamemnon to Apollo, which he pays off by sacrificing his daughter Iphegenia. But Iphegenia's mother, Clytymnestra, does not recognize the legitimacy of that debt; she sees only the murder of her daughter. So she murders Agamemnon, and her other children Orestes and Electra then avenge him by murdering her. I do not deny that such horrible sequences are possible, but there is a reason why this particular sequence should have come down to us as a tragedy. It is not the ordinary course or complication of revenge, and while it is easy enough to identify conflicts of "arithmetics" in our own day (e.g., in the Middle East) I believe that it is an enormous mistake to see these as the paradigm or conceptual prototype of vengeance as such.

(3) *Vengeance is always violent.* The bloodthirsty acts of the Clint Eastwood character or the Ninja assassin may hold dramatic sway over our fantasies, but the more usual act of revenge is a negative vote in the next department meeting, a forty-five minute delay in arriving to dinner, or a hurtful comment or letter, delivered with a vicious twist of phrase, perhaps, but rarely the twist of a blade, except,

of course, metaphorically. One might, given the current tendency to inflate the meaning of words and numb our sensitivities to moral differences, argue that such acts do indeed constitute "violence," but this certainly drains the substance from this standard objection against vengeance. At stake here is the important if problematic distinction between actually doing harm to an offender and depriving him or her of some essential human good, like liberty, for example. It is probably true that vengeance generally aims at harm whereas the cooler claims of the law tend to prefer punishments by way of deprivation—the payment of fines, for example, or depriving the criminal of certain privileges or freedoms (to drive a car, for example, or to use the university library), or even depriving him of freedom as such. The continuing ruckus over the death penalty is, in part, due to the fact that it is one of the few punishments today that is designed to inflict harm—indeed the ultimate harm—rather than impose some deprivation. But, then, it is obvious that this important distinction will not stand too much scrutiny, and it would be hard to insist for very long that sending a man to prison is not in fact actually harming him. And by the same token, there is much that counts as punishment, and consequently satisfies the desire for revenge, but is not violent.

(4) *It takes the law "into our own hands."* (The use of "in hand" metaphors seem to abound in such discussions.) Historically, punishing the perpetrator for almost any offense against an individual, from an obscene gesture to rape and murder, rested with the family, and it was considered not only inappropriate but unjustifiable intrusion into private matters for the state to step in. It is a relatively recent development—and an obviously very political move—that punishment of such crimes should have become the exclusive province of the state. Moral objections against vengeance and the desire for public order seem to me to have far less to do with this than the state's usual arrogance in abrogating individual rights and its desire for control. Indeed, it is a point worth pondering that major crimes against the person are construed by the law as crimes against the state. When current criminal law reduces the victim of such crimes to a mere bystander (if, that is, the victim has survived the crime), the problem is not that in vengeance we take the law "into our own hands" but rather that without vengeance justice seems not only to be taken out

of our hands but eliminated as a consideration altogether. Current concerns with punishment, even those that claim to take "retribution" seriously, seem to serve the law and sanction respect for the law (or reason) rather than the need for justice. Not that the law and respect for the law are unimportant, of course, but one should not glibly identify these with justice and dismiss the passion for vengeance as something quite different and wholly illegitimate.

Retribution is the pivotal term in all arguments about punishment. On the one hand, "backward-looking" retribution is juxtaposed against the "forward-looking" utilitarian concerns of deterrence and rehabilitation. That is, retribution is characterized in terms of its "undoing" a past offense; deterrence and criminal reform are concerned with preventing future offenses. Much of this dispute, I would argue, is purely academic; it is almost impossible to imagine an instance in which both responsibility for the offense and concern for the future are not at stake. (It is to get around this practical point that Kant shocks us by insisting: "even if a civil society were to dissolve itself by common agreement of all its members, the last murderer remaining in prison must first be executed.")[43] What gets left out of the argument, except marginally, is the all-important question of character—which obviously refers both to one's past behavior and one's disposition to future behavior. Punishment theorists, like so many theorists of justice, are too caught up in the abstractions—"punishment," "deterrence"—and too dismissive of the personal motives and character of both the criminal and those who do the punishing; but judges virtually always use "discretion"—which means, essentially, that they weigh many factors, past and future, in determining punishments. Thus retribution in actual practice is not just "getting even" and "blind" to the future but roundly concerned with the whole question of the personalities involved in guilt and punishment.

How did our passion for retribution—our need for vengeance— come about? I think that my evolutionary speculations in Chapter 3 go a long way in answering this question. In that chapter, I was primarily concerned to account for our "natural" sympathies and our sense of fellowship with others, as opposed to the antagonistic, competitive view of the "state of nature" described by writers like Hobbes. But I hope that I was sufficiently careful not to give the impression that we are naturally "nice" in any ridiculous sense. Without retreating to the too-prevalent presumptions of self-interest I nevertheless wanted to show that there is some demonstrable advantage for groups and species—if not always for individuals—in the evolution of cooperation. But cooperation has two sides: first of all the willingness to cooperate, but also the resentment and punishment of those who do not cooperate. One cannot imagine the evolution of cooperation without the evolution of punishment, and Kenneth Axelrod's now-classic "tit for tat" model of the former explains as well the latter. In a repetitive "prisoner's dilemma" type situation, or in any ongoing situation in which one person frequently has the ability to "cheat" the others, an optimum strategy for discouraging such cheating is to respond, dependably, with retribution. A creature endowed only with compassion, who would "understand" the motives of the criminal in every case, would be just as much of an evolutionary failure as a creature who did nothing but watch out for his or her own advantage and cheated every time. Swift and dependable retaliation is thus in the nature of social animals as well as the lesson of game theory. Vengeance is not the antagonist to rationality but its natural manifestation. To breed a social animal who has "the right to make promises," which according to Nietzsche is nature's "paradoxical task," is to breed a creature who has the natural urge to punish as well as natural sympathy and a sense of social solidarity.

The desire for vengeance is our natural need for retribution. Needless to say, few philosophers have acknowledged this kinship. Kant, notably, defends retribution as a rational necessity but insists that it is wholly rational and not at all emotional. Virtually all "retributivists," in fact, insist on separating retribution from vengeance.[44] They insist that notion of retribution lies right at the heart of punishment—indeed, they often argue that it is just another word for punishment. Thus retributivists defend as a product of reason, even a matter of metaphysics, the undoing of some "corrupt" or "unnatural" state caused by crime. But even retribution has often been called barbaric, and it remains, as R. S. Gerstein has recently written, "the most unfashionable theory in philosophical and other circles" and is "frequently dismissed with contempt."[45] So why do we punish? Why not forget about the past misdeeds—which after all cannot be undone—

and move on to the future? The usual argument is this: if punishment were essentially a way of preventing future crime rather than punishment for a particular past crime, then wouldn't it be justifiable to punish a wholly innocent man just as a warning to potential lawbreakers? The obvious answer to this (usually) rhetorical question is, "No! That would be the height of injustice." So even if retribution is "barbaric," "unfashionable," and "dismissed with contempt," it has long held the dominant position against its rival theories (which emphasize deterrence and rehabilitation respectively). Too often it is defended in a purely trivial way, as the very meaning of the word "punishment," and too often it is defended with great obscurity in metaphysical terms that are not intelligible to most people. But, without assuming that what is natural is therefore desirable, I think we can argue persuasively that our natural desire for vengeance—even if it requires careful correction and containment under the auspices of reason and tradition and through the machinery of the law—already gives us good grounds for punishment, even if, while in the thrall of the emotion itself, we cannot articulate those grounds.

The argument that vengeance and retribution are "backward-looking" does not, I think, hold up to scrutiny. The "tit for tat" strategy may be a response to a past offense, but it is a strategy just insofar as it is a way of planning a future. Thus retributivists need not deny the importance or desirability of deterring crime or changing the character or at least the behavior of criminals, but such activities, no matter how well-intended or conceived, do not by themselves count as punishment. But, again, why punish? I do not think that we can answer this question without reference to that supposedly primitive passion for vengeance and its implicit strategy. The idea of "evening the score" is also a way of "teaching the offender a lesson." This phrase does, of course, capture something of deterrence and rehabilitation theories as well as the idea of getting back at the offender, but the key point is that punishment is not primarily motivated by either deterrence or rehabilitation or even the rationality of retribution. As Nietzsche tells us in his *Genealogy*, "the urge to punish" comes first; the reasons and attempts at justification come later.

The rationale of retribution, the "intelligence" embodied in vengeance, is the idea that "the punishment should fit the crime." This is an idea that goes back (at least) to the biblical "eye for an eye" injunction, but it has long been under fire as well. Since ancient times, there has been Socrates' oft-repeated objection—that punishment is the return of evil for evil and so is never legitimate, no matter how horrendous the crime. So conceived, of course, punishment is just another wrong, whether carried out as a personal act of revenge or under the cool, deliberate auspices of the state legal system. (The argument that "murder is wrong, no matter who does it" has often been used as a central argument against capital punishment.) But punishment is not the return of "evil for evil." The German philosopher Hegel argued, I think convincingly, that this is one sure way to misunderstand the nature of punishment.[46] "Harm for harm" perhaps, but it is justified and legitimate harm in return for unjustified and illegitimate harm. The hard question is, how does one get one harm to "fit" another? What does "an eye for an eye" really mean, and is it ultimately intelligible?

How does one calculate how many years in prison it will take to "equal" the crime of armed robbery, even after we decide to take into account the history and character of the criminal and the circumstances of the crime? In what conceivable sense does time in prison "equal" the harm inflicted by the offender on his victims or on the community? My favorite objection to the "eye for an eye" formulation was leveled against retributivism by Lord Blackstone back in the eighteenth century. He queried, "What is the equivalent harm when a two-eye'd man knocks out the eye of a one-eye'd man?"[47] Cute, to be sure, but hardly a knock-down argument against the idea that the punishment should fit the crime. Granting the gruesomeness of the concept, we might well feel an embarrassing satisfaction if a vicious criminal who has intentionally blinded his innocent victim were blinded himself in an accident. To be sure, few of us would suggest that the law should inflict such a punishment, but the "fit" is evident enough to us.

Kant puts the case for retribution succinctly: "only the law of retribution (*jus talionis*) can determine exactly the kind and degree of punishment," though (he carefully adds) such a determination must be made in a court of justice and not as a private judgment. It is this "equality" (Kant's word) that makes punishment rational, the idea of "fitting" the crime. If a man has committed a murder, Kant argues, he must die; "there is no substitute that will satisfy the requirements of legal justice. There is no sameness of kind between death and remaining alive even under the most miserable conditions."[48] We may not agree. But we must agree that a serious crime such as murder demands a serious punishment, while a minor crime does not. Hanging a poor man for stealing a loaf of bread now strikes us as barbaric, not because we reject the idea of retribution (and not just because we feel compassion for the man's plight) but because we accept it. Hanging a man for stealing food is barbaric because it doesn't "fit." It is monstrously excessive. And that means that we do indeed use the standard of "equality" in making such judgments; we would not understand the meaning of "punishment" without it.

The reader will no doubt discern that much of the language with which we describe both our passion for vengeance and the concept of retribution consists largely of an interrelated group of metaphors—notably the images of "equality," "balance," and "fit." These are too often thrown together as one, and too often treated as if they were not metaphors at all but literal truths. I want to wrap up this section by distinguishing and discussing briefly four such metaphors.

(1) The *debt* metaphor: to punish is to "repay" a wrong. There is some dispute (for example, in Nietzsche, *Genealogy*, Essay II) whether the notion of legal obligation preceded or rather grew out of this idea of a debt, but with regard to punishment, the metaphorical character of "repayment" is quite clear. The suggestion that there is an implicit contract (whether via Hobbes and Locke or Plato's *Crito*) is just another approach to the same metaphor. To link it with the other metaphors, punishment does not "balance the books" nor does it "erase" the wrong in question, as repayment of a debt surely does. The "debt" metaphor, by the way, is not restricted to capitalist societies; "debt" is not the same as "consumer debt" and applies as well to the New Guinea custom of giving a pig for a wrongful death as to the problem of paying off one's MasterCard. In most societies, debt is a moral measure rather than a monetary arrangement.

(2) The *fit* metaphor is the popular idea that the punishment should "fit" the crime (W. S. Gilbert's *Mikado*: "My object all sublime . . . To make the punishment fit the crime"). Punishment must "fit"

the crime, we are told, going back to the easy formulation of the *lex talionis*: "Eye for eye, tooth for tooth," etc. But as many critics of retributivism have pointed out, such punishments are administered— or even make sense—only for a very limited number of crimes, such as intentional murder. But even then, as Albert Camus has famously pointed out, "For there to be equivalence, the death penalty would have to punish a criminal who had warned his victim of the date at which he would inflict a horrible death on him and who, from that moment onward, had confined him at his mercy for months. Such a monster is not encountered in private life."[49]

Defenders of retributivism gladly weaken the demands of "fit," suggesting, for instance, that it provides only a general measure, that the crucial concept is "proportion"—so that petty theft is not (as it once was) punished with the harshness of a violent crime. With this, of course, we all agreed, but "proportion" too misleadingly suggests quantification where there often is none, and it summarizes rather than solves the problem of punishment. To be sure, it is somehow fitting to trade a life for a life (or more accurately, "a death for a death"), but is it just? And given the many extenuating circumstances that qualify each and every case, does "fit" make sense? Of course, we recognize the lack of fit: witness our horror, for example, when Afghan tribesmen summarily behead the hapless tourist involved in an automobile accident, even one in which the driver, if given a trial, might have been proclaimed faultless. In eighteenth-century British law, responsible for the burgeoning white population of Australia, was astonishing in its lack of fit and harsh penalties, as were the punishments meted out to those who arrived on the "fatal shore."[50]

(3) The *balance* metaphor: punishment makes things "even" again. It is through punishment that one "gets even." In epic literature, it is by punishing the villain that one balances the forces of good and evil. One problem is that this moral balance is often simply equated, in the crudest utilitarian fashion, with a balance of pleasure and pain, as if the application to the villain of an amount of pain equal to the amount of pain he or she has caused balances the scales. (We should remember again the standard allegorical figure of justice, this time with her scales.) Where the crime is strictly pecuniary, it might seem that balance (like the repayment of a debt) might be literally appropri-

ate, but this, of course, isn't so. One can pay back the amount of money stolen or otherwise taken, but this does not yet take into account the offense itself. As soon as one must pay back even an extra penny, the literalness of the "balance" again comes into question. Granted the original sum has been repaid, but now what is the "cost" or the "price" of the crime? Again, my point is not that the metaphor of "balance" isn't applicable or revealing of how we think about justice, but it underscores rather than solves our problems.

(4) The *erasure* metaphor: the idea that we can "annul the evil" through punishment. Vendetta cultures talk about "blood marks" (also "blood debts") not as a sign of guilt but rather of unrevenged wrong. But the obvious question is, can we undo a crime—for instance, rape or murder—in any sense whatever? In financial crimes, again, one can "erase" the debt by paying it back, but not the crime itself. For example, how could the terror suffered in an armed robbery be erased, even if the money were to be politely returned? ("Here you are, Miss; I'm a student at the local police academy and I wanted to experience what the criminal felt like.") Indeed, how can we measure the fear suffered in such crimes, quite apart from any more substantial harm? And yet, the idea of annulment looms large in the history of theories of punishment, from the ancient world (in which one quite literally made the offender disappear through exile and obliteration, for example) to modern conceptions in Hegel, Bosanquet, and others. The punishment doesn't literally eliminate the crime, of course, but Bosanquet's suggestion that it eliminates it as a precedent has the virtue of showing us how this metaphor too, hardly intelligible when taken literally, can nonetheless be given an intelligible interpretation that is not strictly retributivist but takes future behavior into account as well.[51]

Retributivism, I want to argue, is primarily a set of concepts and judgments embodied in a feeling, not a theory. Perhaps it was overstated in the majority opinion in United States Supreme Court decision in the case of *Gregg* vs. *Georgia* (1976):

> the instinct for retribution is part of the nature of man, and channeling that instinct in the administration of criminal justice serves an important purpose in promoting the stability of a society governed by law. When

people begin to believe that organized society is unwilling or unable to impose upon criminal offenders the punishment they "deserve," then there are sown the seeds of anarchy—of self-help, vigilante justice, and lynch law.

But at least the justices took vengeance seriously and did not urge that it be wholly sacrificed to the dispassionate authority of the law. Retributive justice, however rationalized, is not as such a purely rational matter—but neither is it irrational. But in the end, it is perhaps not just a question of whether revenge is rational or not, but whether it is—at the bottom of our hearts as well as off the top of our heads— an undeniable aspect of the way we react to the world, not as an instinct but as such a basic part of our world-view and our moral sense of ourselves that it is, in that sense, unavoidable.

I have not tried here to defend vengeance as such, but my claim is that vengeance deserves its central place in any theory of justice and, whatever else we are to say about punishment, the desire for revenge must enter into our deliberations along with such emotions as compassion, caring, and love. Any system of legal principles that does not take such emotions into account, which does not motivate itself on their behalf, is not—whatever else it may be—a system of justice. But vengeance as such, I do not deny, is in any case dangerous. As the Chinese used to say (and no doubt still do), "If you seek vengeance, dig two graves." But I think that the dangers and destructiveness of vengeance are much overblown, and its importance for a sense of one's own self-esteem and integrity ignored. Many people believe that vengeance is the primary cause of the world's troubles today, causing unending feuds and vendettas that block every rational effort at resolution and peace. But in addition to my insistence that vengeance is not the same as vendetta and feuds are not the same as vengeance, I would argue that the passionate hostilities of the world that are fueled by revenge are only secondary. In many cases they are caused or at any rate aggravated and rendered unresolvable not by passion so much as by supposedly rational ideology. It is ideology that abstracts and elevates personal prejudices to the status of absolute truths and gives vengeance a set of reasons far less negotiable than any feud or mere urge to "get even." Vengeance, at least, has its measure. Ideology, however "reasonable," may not.

Vengefulness, no doubt, is a vice, and because vengeance is so often dangerous and destructive it makes perfectly good sense for moralists to urge us to rise "above" the urge to vengeance. But the argument behind this need not involve forgiveness and mercy, nor need it appeal to Nietzschean "master" morality and "self-overcoming." Neither need it be anything so detached and saintly as "turning the other cheek." The argument is that instead of following that often narrow path to personal retribution we would much better embrace that expansive form of social conciousness in which we become more aware of the real desperation of others than we are of our own (usually petty) complaints. To transcend revenge is to become keenly aware of the suffering of others with an urgency that eclipses the blows to our own fragile egos and gives our sense of compassion priority over the urge to vengeance. But it is not to give up vengeance as such and, as in tit for tat, it is the ready willingness to retaliate that provides stability to both the social system and one's personal sense of integrity and control. Despite volumes of propaganda to the contrary, experience seems to show that to see oneself as a helpless victim makes one less, and not more, likely to open one's heart to others. But we do not have to be or see ourselves as victims, and it is vengeance or at least fantasies of vengeance that make this possible. Our concept of injustice is inextricably tied up with the concept of blame and with the concept of punishment, and where the injustice is personal, so is the felt need for retribution. In a world in which justice is getting ever more impersonal and statistical, vengeance retains the virtue of being personal. But so, of course, does compassion, which commands not the impersonal but a more expanded sense of the personal. Between vengeance and compassion there is no doubt which is the greater virtue, but vengeance is nevertheless necessary and compassion for one's own offender (the object of one's revenge) is often foolish rather than noble. Justice is not forgiveness nor even forgetting but rather it is getting one's emotional priorities right, putting blame aside in the face of so much other human suffering and thereby giving up vengeance for the sake of larger and more noble emotions.

THE PASSIONS OF A LARGER SELF: REGAINING LOYALTY, HONOR, AND SHAME

*Loyalty has its domestic, its religious, its commercial, its profes-
sional forms, and many other forms as well. The essence of it,
whatever forms it may take is . . . this: Since no man can find a
plan of life by merely looking within his own chaotic nature, he
has to look without, to the world of social conventions, deeds and
causes.*   JOSIAH ROYCE, THE PHILOSOPHY OF LOYALTY

Where there is no shame, there is no honor.
                                    ETHIOPIAN PROVERB

I HAVE ARGUED THAT justice must be understood first of
all as a matter of emotions, and I have briefly discussed a number of
those "moral sentiments" that go into our sense of justice, especially
caring, compassion, resentment, and revenge. But these emotions still
give us an only partial picture of the emotional geography of justice,
and in particular they lack what we might call "the enlarged sense of
self" that goes along with the sense of justice. Too often it is assumed
without argument or discussion that the emotions are merely personal
and subjective, exclusively of concern to the feeling subject and
merely a matter of subjective self-worth. But emotions can be "about"
all sorts of things and significant to both the individual and the society. Many emotions are concerned with society (as when one resents
one's place in society or feels morally indignant about the latest government scandal). And some emotions are not only "about" society
(as their "object") but involve society in the very identity of their
subject. They are emotions that would be unintelligible without this
larger sense of self.

Of particular interest here is a mixed set of emotions that, with
the rise of radical individualism, has all but dropped out of most discussions of justice. That set includes loyalty, honor, and shame (as
distinct from guilt, which is not part of the set). Loyalty is a kind of
integrity, not within oneself (conceived of as a self-sufficient, integral

whole) but rather with oneself conceived as a part of a larger self, a group, a community, an organization, or an institution. Most philosophers today don't talk about it, since they think that justice has to do with individual selves, individual rights, and the drawing up of grand agreements. So long as we respect one another's rights, or so long as we respect contracts, what is the point of a superfluous and perhaps childish emotion like loyalty? An employee has signed a three-year contract; why does she have to be loyal as well? What's more, many theorists—like our politicians—feel much more comfortable talking about what people should receive rather than what they are and what they should do. Loyalty shifts the attention from what we need and deserve from society (or any institution) to what we should give and what we owe. Loyalty forces us to reject (or at least suspend indefinitely) the ideal of autonomy and renders heteronomy not only respectable but virtuous. No wonder that the many followers of Kant find loyalty (as opposed to respect) quite foreign to the moral enterprise and certainly no part of justice.

Of course, loyalty (like patriotism, one special variant of it) can be a refuge from responsibility or a forum for venal self-righteousness, but it does not follow—as many people seem to think it does—that it is an emotion that has no place in a democratic society, that our loyalties should always be first and foremost to ourself, or to our conscience, or to some set of "higher" standards. The most frequently used example, in case anyone has any doubts, is the instance of the loyal Nazi. Doesn't that show for sure that loyalty is an emotion of scoundrels and amoralists, that loyalty is an emotion contrary to justice and not part of it? But the need for critical self-awareness in one's loyalties and the possibility that some loyalties may go sour (or worse) is not an argument against loyalty as such, any more than the dangers of love are an argument against love. (Loyalty would not be wrongly conceived as a variety of love, appropriate to groups and institutions as well as to individuals.) The virtue of a democracy is not that it eliminates the need for loyalties but that it compounds that need by making loyalty an element of personal choice, and that choice a primary feature of a person's identity. The neighborhood one lives in, the company one works for, the friends and colleagues one collects, the teams one supports—it is through such "identifications" that we build our sense of self. Any one of these might be of merely instrumental importance (one simply houses one's bed and books in a neighborhood, as in many urban apartment buildings, or one simply "needs the job" but is already looking elsewhere). But if all or even most of one's identifications are merely instrumental—if one has no loyalties—then one has a greatly impoverished self, if indeed it makes sense to say that such naked and "unencumbered" agency is a self at all.

In the history of recent ethics, there is little discussion of loyalty, and when it enters the picture at all, it is usually in the guise of a "bias" that interferes with, rather than forms the basis of, moral judgment. And yet, what could be more central to a decent conception of the world than the legitimacy of acting out of loyalty to a friend, one's family, or some special organization? The problem in understanding justice is the excessive and even obsessive emphasis on general principles and universal policies and the rejection of all particular feelings and inclinations. There are "personal" decisions, on the one hand, and then there are (much more important, and always trump) decisions made on the basis of moral principle or the principles of justice. The assumption is further made that such personal decisions are based merely on feelings which are "subjective" and, therefore, a species of self-interest or egoism or perhaps sheer irrationality. But this is an extremely poor argument, and its result is to eliminate much if not most of what ordinary people—not philosophers—call justice.

Subjectivity is not as such either egoistic or irrational. For instance, subjectivity is often interpreted as meaning that feelings are phenomenological, that is, that they are experienced by a particular person (or, perhaps, millions of particular persons) and can be described in the first person. But there is no reason why a first person account cannot be objectively correct. The fact that the same emotion can be had by millions is an argument against the usual idea that emotions are merely personal and not an argument for mass irrationality. There is also the tendency to project one's own emotions onto the world, as when someone in love (not unreasonably) finds the beloved lovable, or when a people at war finds the enemy hateful, and so on.[52] To be sure, such projection is sometimes dangerous and often biased, but it is not therefore unwarranted or illegitimate. Indeed, what would the world look like without a projection of attitudes—if there were no love, no respect, no pity, as well as no hatred and anger? The fact that we project our attitudes does not mean that these projections are distorted or wrong, and it does not mean that the "object" of our emotion doesn't deserve the attitude we project upon it. What would it mean to have a sense of justice if one felt no loyalty to anyone?

It is in response to loyalties—not to general principles or policies—that people willingly sacrifice their interests, their happiness, or even their lives. One dies for one's child, or perhaps for one's country, but dying for a principle strikes many people as fatally foolish inflexibility. (Not even Socrates did that: he died for the sake of his "soul.") Loyalty is an emotion which displays just that local, particular, personal attachment and identity that the abstract notion of justice—and with it "morality"—tends to miss. Loyalties provide powerful motives. Loyalty, after all, provides a concrete sense of self, a tangible membership in a family, organization, or group with many faces and voices of support. Compared to the promptings of loyalty, rational principles provide thin encouragement indeed, and self-interest seems merely pathetic.

One might still insist that group loyalty—even patriotism—is a bias, the source of all of the conflicts in the world from intertribal rivalry in East Africa and militant nationalism in the Middle East to the confrontations of the superpowers. What about racism? Isn't that ultimately just another brand of loyalty—to one's race instead of one's family or country? Racism, I would argue, is far more concerned with hatred of others than with pride in one's own race and may well reflect feelings of inferiority.[53] The fact that loyalty is a virtue doesn't mean that all loyalties are of equal value, or that some loyalties are not virtues at all. Racism isn't loyalty to one's own race (as white supremacists often claim); it is untutored hostility towards others. The difference here might seem slim, but it is nevertheless a crucial difference. Loyalty is affinity for one's group, not the manufacture of a group in order to join ranks against another. So, too, nationalism may necessarily be exclusive, and it may often be divisive, but it is not as such competitive or hostile. Hostility arises not from group loyalties but from other pressures, such as scarcity of land or overlapping homeland claims.

Loyalty also accounts for the justifiable inconsistency (which is certainly not "irrationality") in our treating similar cases differently just because some of them happen to involve our loyalty. Michael Walzer employs his concept of "spheres of justice" to explain how we universalize and treat equally all members within a family, or a group, or a community but don't employ the same rules at these different levels. (In times of scarcity, I look after my family first, but I treat all family members equally.) Morality and justice are essentially and first of all interpersonal but then become intertribal as well. The problem is, perhaps, that we are members of so many tribes at once.

There seem to be size limits to loyalty. Loyalty to the earth or to "humanity" doesn't seem much like loyalty at all, no matter how noble it may sound. (Of course, there is always the oft-mentioned possibility of invasion from another planet.) Indeed, we see even loyalty to giant nation-states as being a bit contrived, which is another one of the many reasons why patriotism is so often treated with suspicion. Family loyalties make perfectly good sense, of course; indeed, the family is no doubt the origin of the concept. Loyalty to one's community and local leaders makes equally good sense, and even loyalty to the local baseball or basketball team seems to me to be perfectly bona fide. Even large but concrete organizations like religious congregations make perfectly good sense as objects of loyalty. But I get very nervous when people start talking about loyalty as one more grand abstraction, a substitute for (or a rejection of) the usual canons of justice and morality. "My country, right or wrong" is not an expression of loyalty. It is more often the desperate refuge of those who have no real loyalties and, consequently, no honor of their own to defend.

Honor is another grand emotion of the larger self, and another emotion that is an endangered species in radical individualist thinking. Honor, when we use the term at all, usually means "pride," or even "vanity"—both of which are actually very different from honor. (Nixon's "peace with honor" in Vietnam meant "avoid political humiliation," not "doing what is honorable.") Pride is a highly individual emotion; it has to do (as Hume argued in his *Treatise*) with a sense of personal accomplishment, and its main focus is the individual self. Of course, it is possible to be proud of someone else by way of a slightly enlarged notion of self, as when we are proud of our children or our parents or our team; but pride is too personal and too concerned with accomplishment. Honor, by contrast, need not involve accomplishment at all (though it certainly may and often does) and makes very little sense as a purely personal notion. (That is why, when people say that they are defending their honor but are obviously nursing their pride we find such behavior not only foolish but pretentious as well.) Vanity, of course, is even farther from honor. It is typically defensive and often superficial (involving matters of appearance rather than the core of the self as such). Honor first of all requires a sense of belonging, a sense of membership, a sense of self that is inseparable from one's group identity. Honor involves living up to the expectations of the group—whether these are spelled out as a code of honor or a set of moral rules or simply implicit in the practices and goals of the group. (It is not obeying moral rules that makes one honorable, however; it is obeying the rules because they are the rules of one's group— very un-Kantian.) One's honor, in other words, is never one's own honor alone. It is the honor of the group that one represents and stands up for, and defending one's own honor necessarily entails defending it as a representative of the group.

There are honor societies (Japan, Brazil), but they are markedly different from our own. Of course, what is called "honor" there can also be pride—but this confusion is typically recognized not only as self-deception but as dishonorable as well. And then there is that particularly atavistic and brutal sense of male honor called "machoism" which casts a dark shadow on some honor societies. (In Brazil, wives are often beaten and more than occasionally murdered for challenging their husbands' "honor," not by commiting adultery but by simple disobedience, or perhaps expressing a desire to start a career or get a new hairdo. Inadequate sexual performance, of course, tops the list of offenses to "honor.") But although honor (like any emotion or virtue) can be miscast and abused, we would be wise to take it more seriously. It is, I think, much of what Alasdair MacIntrye and Charles Taylor are after in their long defenses of "tradition" in ethics. It is not so much community as such, with all of the dangers to individuality therein, but a sense of primal, shared values and expectations, something to live up to rather than just rules to obey. One's sense of justice, accordingly, can be almost indistinguishable from a sense of honor, for as the standards and expectations of justice are built into the concept of the group, living up to those standards already includes being just—although not, as in Kant and Rawls, for justice's sake. Thus Aristotle thought that justice in its general sense was no particular virtue but the sum of all the virtues, equivalent in particular to honor. And good Christians have often believed, rightly I think, that just by being good Christians they would also satisfy the demands of justice. (Why would they need another set of reasons, a special set of principles, to do that?) We can see that honor, like loyalty, is not a particularly philosophical virtue. Honor presupposes a kind of tribal sensibility, a certain lack of reflection and acceptance of group values without critical reasoning, but this is not yet an argument against it. (Of course, it can be in certain circumstances, but the mistake is to think that it ought to be reflective and critical all the time.)

Honor should not be thought of as a set of personal constraints defined by one's membership in a group. The notion of "constraints" is appropriate rather to a nonmember of a group or, perhaps, to one who is a member of a group only by chance or was a member and now desperately wants to get out. One's sense of honor is, if not voluntary at least personally acceptable, part and parcel of one's sense of self. It is, in this sense, a species of merit, although it is very different from any sense of desert or achievement. Merit in the context of honor has to do with who one is—namely a member of the group in good standing—and not particularly with anything that one has done (or not done) except insofar as such acts are part of one's membership in the group. So, too, there is a natural affinity between honor and self-esteem; one's self-esteem depends on one's sense of honor (though not vice versa), and one's standing in the group becomes the criterion of self-esteem. One cannot be much of a member if one can be humiliated in the group and nevertheless have a solid sense of self-worth. So, too, the contemporary idea that one's main objective after public humiliation is to "get over it" makes any sense of honor—which presupposes that one doesn't just "get over it"—impossible. We might note that one symptom of our collective loss of honor is the fact that no one seems to believe in the concept of a "ruined life" anymore. Even earlier in this century (and still in many small communities) there were some violations or breaches of honor that could not be undone. We think, on the other hand, that one just moves to another town or gets married again and "starts over." The difference between self-respect and self-esteem may be relevant here. One gets self-respect from being a member of the group, but one's self-esteem is a function of one's status within it. Of course, the two cannot be entirely untangled, for one can hardly feel good about being a member of a group in which one is not of good standing.

The opposite of honor is shame. Thus Rawls is not entirely wrong when he insists that shame is the opposite of self-esteem, since honor can be the criterion for self-esteem.[54] But not all societies are honor societies, and not everyone's self-esteem is tied to their sense of honor. And shame, not self-esteem, necessarily presupposes a sense of honor. Shame is not, as Rawls says, failing to live up to one's potential; it is, much more specifically, failing to live up to the standards of the group through which one gains one's self-identity. (In Korea, a student recently committed ritual suicide after failing his exams the third time, despite the fact that he had done his best. He had let his family down, and that was shameful.) In an achievement-oriented society, failing to live up to one's potential may indeed be equivalent to failing to live up to the standards of the group, but even in a non-achievement society, a person may well feel ashamed because he or she has made a commitment that cannot be kept or set a goal that cannot be met. But personal achievement and failure as such are not essential and often not relevant to honor and shame. Rather, one fails to be acceptable to the group and in this way damages one's own essential sense of identity. To feel shame (not quite the same as our "being ashamed") is quite literally to fail oneself, but only in the context of the group that defines one's larger self, the self that includes and identifies with one's group or association.

It is in this sense that shame is contrasted to guilt, for it is guilt that defines the appropriate attitude in our nonhonor society, not shame. Shame is always defined in a group context; guilt (that is, the emotion of guilt) is borne by one alone. It is not surprising that the Scriptures talk mainly of sin and guilt when concerned with an individual's wrongdoing before God. Guilt permeates the self, but other people, one's peers, play no clear role in its workings. We feel guilty, not shamed, for failing to live up to our own goals and standards. We feel guilty, not shamed, for breaking the rules or commiting a moral infelicity. Guilt is appropriate to isolated individuals; shame is possible only in groups. Guilt ties in nicely with the traditional concept of the individual soul; shame is essentially a tribal emotion. It has often been said (by Nietzsche and Freud most famously) that there is too much guilt in our society. I would like to suggest that, while this is probably true, there isn't nearly enough shame. Indeed, the "payoff" for public humiliation in current-day America seems to be a fat book advance and profitable public appearances, not repentance, apology, and retribution. We may have more guilt than we ought to have, but part of the reason may be that we don't have enough room for honor—or shame.

There are other points of comparison between guilt and shame. Shame typically involves some particular (possibly very serious) transgression while guilt, notoriously, may consume one's entire self on the basis of no particular (or no memorable) misdeed at all. (The notion of "original sin" brilliantly captures this odd metaphysical feature of guilt, whatever else one makes of the Adam and Eve story that is usually used to explain it.) This distinction is obscured by our use of the term *guilt* not only as the name of an emotion but also as a causal term ("He was the guilty one! He did it") and as a legal concept ("I find you guilty as charged"). One may *feel* guilty because one *is* guilty, but one need not feel anything. (A good play on these three different senses is Camus's treatment of Meursault's guilt in *The Stranger*. His causal guilt is in question, since the murder was hardly his doing; his legal guilt is settled by the court; but the real action is his coming to realize what it means to be guilty—and then getting over it.)[55] But the real problem with guilt is not so much the fact that it is hard to pin down (much less the fact that it is an emotion) but rather that it presupposes a sort of detachment and a sense of oneself that it is my whole object in this book to shake down. When we fail in this world (and inevitably we often do) we do not just fall short of our principles, and we do not just fail ourselves—the focus of all too much of our attention. We fail each other, and we fail ourselves ultimately only in terms of the others. Loyalty, honor, and the potential for shame are not just curious emotions, appropriate only for earlier epochs and societies, that have dropped out of our emotional repertoire. They are essential to that sense of justice that begins (perhaps also ends) with the realization that we are all in this together.

CONCLUSION

I never think in terms of a crowd, only of one person. When some-one argues that the sisters have done no enormous task, I answer that even if they helped only one human being, it would have been enough. MOTHER THERESA (1988)

WHEN I MENTIONED TO friends and acquaintances that I was writing a book on justice, I was often met with the question, "Do you believe in justice?" It was much the same tone of personal probing and sophisticated disbelief with which one asks, "Do you be-lieve in true love?" if not quite "Do you still believe in Santa Claus?" But the critical question is not, I reply, a matter of "believing in" justice, if by that one means that life is fair and we all get what we deserve. There are too many tragedies and, if we only open our eyes, too many tens of millions who never even get the chance to see what they might "deserve" or not. We entertain our quasi-theological or utopian ("nowhere") fantasies of a world of plenty and undisturbed happiness, but reality rudely intrudes. We carefully think out our po-licies and expectations and even develop them into a theory of justice, but, inevitably, we bump into the obstinacy of personalities and tradi-tions as well as fate and collide with other theories traveling in the opposite direction. Whether or not one believes in God and Heaven and Hell and Ultimate Deserts, it is the knowing sensibility of the age that there is no justice. Of course, there may be justice in certain carefully defined and controlled contexts (e.g., games), which is why we may be so fanatically drawn to them—as if to refute or in any case temporarily eclipse that awful realization. But the larger picture is the one spelled out half a century ago by Albert Camus, in his often referred to (if less read) *Myth of Sisyphus*. Camus calls it "the Absurd," this devastating sense of disappointment and outrage that the world is indifferent to our just demands and expectations. And yet, we can-not give up those demands and expectations, the pursuit of which Camus defends somewhat misleadingly as "keeping the Absurd alive." So, too, in an important but ultimately depressing recent study, social psychologist Melvin J. Lerner has catalogued various forms of self-deception concerning the "fundamental delusion" of the "belief in a just world." He shows, in painful detail, how we tend to misperceive or reinterpret the world in order to maintain this belief, and he shows in considerable detail how far we will go in attributing unseen virtues to recipients of rewards and evident vices to victims of injustice to do so.[56] For Lerner as for Camus—and for most of my friends and acquaintances too—believing in justice is a "delusion." So what, then, is there to write about?

It is that cynicism, common to the most sensitive and compassion-ate people as well as to those with an ideological ax to grind, that brought me back to the ancient question, "What is justice?" If the belief in a just world really was a delusion, then that was no reason to give up on justice but rather a good reason to relocate it. If our expectations and ideals do not match up to reality—and who would deny this?—why should we blame reality? But should we blame our-selves? Certainly not for our failure to do the impossible, to right the world, save the starving, assure just rewards and punishments in every instance—but we can and should blame ourselves for blocking out the realities of the world, for trading our recognition of the "delusion" for an equally (or more) tragic sense of hopelessness. Or, what is ulti-mately the same, we can and should blame ourselves for creating new versions of the delusion, new rationalizations, new abstract ideals to be argued about in place of concrete feelings and specific actions to rectify or at least modify particular wrongs and injustices. It is on such grounds that I argue, perhaps perversely, for the superior virtues of vengeance in opposition to the abstract and lofty debates about the theory of punishment, and, without apology, for the importance of compassion in contrast to the cleverness of philosophical theory. It is not that I reject theories and debates, needless to say; but it is on the high plain of theories and debates that the sentimentality of our feelings and the pointlessness of our actual actions becomes so seemingly undeniable. And as Marx argued (against Feuerbach) over a hundred years ago, the point is not just to understand the awfulness of the world; it is rather to change it. But not the way he (or his nominal followers) did, with a new set of theories and a new ideology and a new series of rationalizations for brutality and bloodshed. The way to change the world is bit by bit, one small act of generosity after another, hundreds of millions of them adding up to some real global difference. And if the world is not just and never will be, and even if it is true that few of us will ever "do our most and best," at least we will not have been guilty of the accusation, all too appropriate nowadays, that "as citizens of the richest nation on earth, . . . we were unwilling to be good and faithful stewards of our resources, that we deliberately decided not to use our resources to try to improve the human condition." (Ray Marshall) The world may not be just but we ourselves can be, and that begins with the acceptance of all of those mawkish clichés that in our worldly wisdom we have learned to loathe—"opening up one's heart" and "weeping for humanity." There is nothing wrong with being a "bleeding heart," and an intellectual or a politician with a heart (even without an ideology) is never defenseless. That, after all, is what that remarkable organ is for.[1] There is a sensibility that is more fundamental to morality and politics than the intellectual prominence of the ideologue and the moral superiority of the uninvolved. That is the passion for justice which is neither naive nor merely sentimental, but natural and engaged in the world and which alone can justify our good fortunes.

NOTES

Preface

1. *Newsweek*, January 23, 1988.

Introduction

1. Rousseau, *Discourse on the Origins of Inequality*, 35.
2. The feminist opposition between justice and caring has received its most persuasive defense by Cheshire Calhoun in her essay, "Justice, Care and Gender Bias." The classic statement is Carol Gilligan's *In a Different Voice*. A particularly belligerent and divisive argument is Nell Noddings's *Caring*. See also Sara Ruddick, *Maternal Thinking*.
3. John Rawls, *A Theory of Justice*, 567. As always, Rawls covers the bases and excludes virtually no relevant topic, including the moral sentiments, from his overall analysis. But it would take a particularly uncritical reader to miss the overwhelmingly rationalistic frame of Rawls's basic theory, as opposed to the cosmetic plaster that he adds between the structural struts to give his deductive theory some sense of humanity. So too Kant defends compassion and the moral sentiments in his *Doctrine of Virtue*, but there can be little doubt about their merely secondary place in the overall scheme of his ethics. For the most extreme current defense of this purely rationalist trend, see Stephen L. Darwall, *Impartial Reason*.
4. Homer, *Iliad* 6.51—65, trans. R. Lattimore, 2d ed. (Chicago: Univ. of Chicago Press, 1975).
5. So too, we are shocked by the idea of Abraham's killing his own son Isaac, until we realize that the sacrifice of the eldest son was standard fare in Abraham's world, and God's intervention was a message to end the practice. So much for Kierkegaard's worrisome "teleological suspension of the ethical," in which God's behavior is thought to be incomprehensible because it opposes divine obedience to morality.
6. Aristotle, *Nichomachean Ethics* 5.1, trans. T. Irwin.
7. Friedrich von Hayek, *The Mirage of Social Justice*.
8. Adam Smith, *The Wealth of Nations*, book 4, especially chapter 7.
9. *New York Times*, Aug. 21, 1988.
10. Figures according to Amnesty International, Sept. 22, 1988.
11. *Newsweek*, Oct. 9, 1989.
12. Elizabeth Wolgast, *A Grammar of Justice*; E. Dupreel, *Treatise of Morals* (translated and quoted in Chaim Perelman, *The Rhetoric of Justice*).

13. The phrase "spheres of justice" is from Michael Walzer, *Spheres of Justice.*
14. *Newsweek*, Oct. 20, 1986.
15. This would follow from the very definitions of justice in many authors (e.g., Rawls, "justice is the first virtue of institutions"), but Bernard Williams, whose ethical writings are very much in sympathy with the general position defended here, also argues that the particular notion of justice as a virtue is a kind of category mistake, especially in Aristotle, whom he discusses on this matter at considerable length in "Justice as a Virtue," in Amelie Rorty, ed., *Essays on Aristotle's Ethics* (Univ. of California Press, 1980), 189–99.
16. The life of the Ik tribe in Africa is described in detail by Colin Turnbull in his now famous book, *The Mountain People.*

Chapter 1

1. Rawls, *A Theory of Justice*, 74, 300; Robert Nozick, *Anarchy, State and Utopia*, 167.
2. Shula Sommers taught psychology at the University of Massachusetts–Boston and was the author of several cross-cultural studies of emotion and the variable distinction between "positive" and "negative" emotions. See, e.g., "Adults Evaluating Their Emotions."
3. Helmut Schoek, *Envy: A Theory of Social Behavior.*
4. Susan Jacoby, *Wild Justice.* (New York: Harper and Row, 1983)
5. See, for example, the variety of essays on retributive punishment in H. B. Acton's book, *The Philosophy of Punishment*, and Robert S. Gerstein's essay on retribution, "Capital Punishment: A Retributivist Response" and R. S. Downie in Tom Donaldson, ed., 341.
6. Robert Nozick distinguishes between retribution and revenge by noting that the first can be impersonal while the second is not. But, of course, the range of the "personal" is just what I am calling into question here. See his very good discussion in *Philosophical Explanations*, 366–74.
7. Pietro Marongiu and Graeme Newman, *Vengeance.* (Toronga, N.J.: Rowman and Littlefield, 1987)
8. Buck Shiefflin, lecture at the University of Texas, anthropology series, 1988.
9. The failure of deterrence, with particular regard to the death penalty, is discussed in Ernst van den Haag, "Deterrence and Uncertainty." Even the foremost deterrence theorists, e.g., Hugh Bedau in his essay "Capital Punishment and Retributive Justice," acknowledge the data.

10. Kant discusses punishment in his *Philosophy of Law*, especially 195–202.
11. Robert Nozick, *Anarchy, State and Utopia*, ix–x.
12. Peter Singer, *The Expanding Circle*.
13. Jonathan Kozol, *Rachel's Children* (New York: Crown, 1988).
14. Lorraine Code, *Epistemic Responsibility*.
15. Paul Woodruff has interpreted the ancient skeptics as holding such a view. Pyrrho and his followers refused to accept any "beliefs," a view that subjected them to ridicule and a charge of obvious self-contradiction, for how could they function in everyday life without beliefs? (And didn't they thereby hold beliefs about their beliefs, etc.?) But it is necessary to distinguish between everyday beliefs (such as, that the milk is in the ice chest) and Beliefs, with a capital B, of the sort that make up most political ideologies and much of official religion. The skeptics rejected the latter, not the former. So, too, David Hume, a latter day skeptic, did not reject the "natural" inclinations and beliefs that guided him through life, only the big Beliefs that philosophers defended as the product of pure reason. Thus he could say, at his polemical best (in his *Treatise on Human Nature*, pg. 416), "it is not irrational for me to prefer the destruction of half the world to the pricking of my little finger," intending to underscore the moral impotence of reason, not any insensitivity on his part.
16. Edmund Pincoffs, *Quandaries and Virtues*.
17. Robert Nozick, *Anarchy, State and Utopia*, 35–36.
18. Plato, *The Apology*; Sextus Empiricus, *Works*.
19. Hobbes, *Leviathan*.
20. Rousseau, *Discourse on the Origins of Inequality*.

Chapter 2

1. Plato, *The Republic*, 2.359–60.
2. Plato, *Crito*.
3. In his *Ethics and the Limits of Philosophy* (Cambridge: Harvard Univ. Press, 1985), Bernard Williams argues a similar thesis regarding ethics and philosophy in general, emphasizing considerations of character and noting that "it is a mistake of morality to try to make everything into obligations" (180).
4. Fyodor Dostoevsky, *Notes from Underground*.
5. Plato, *The Republic*, book 4; Smith, *Wealth of Nations*, book 1.
6. *Playboy*, Mar. 1988, 146.
7. K. Hanson and R. Solomon, *It's Good Business*, and R. Solomon, *Ethics and Excellence* (New York: Oxford Univ. Press, forthcoming).

8. My understanding of the continuity between Smith's two works owes much to Patricia Werhane's unpublished manuscript, "The Legacy of Adam Smith for Modern Capitalism."

9. *Washington Post*, Jan. 18, 1988, 23.

10. Many examples of such generosity in the wake of tragedy were reported following the October 1989 earthquake in San Francisco, and, of course, there are thousands of wartime stories and tales of spontaneous altruism in the face of the most desperate personal circumstances.

11. R. Solomon, *About Love*.

12. R. Solomon, *The Passions*.

13. Nozick defends the notion of rights in this way as providing "side constraints," not goals for action but rather limits to goals and actions (*Anarchy, State and Utopia*, especially 28–35).

14. Mary Douglas, *The World of Goods*. (New York: Norton, 1979)

15. This is the underlying argument in Alasdair MacIntyre, *After Virtue*, and in Michael Sandel, *Liberalism and the Limits of Justice*.

16. Michael Walzer in *The New Republic*, Dec. 13, 1982.

17. MacIntyre, for instance, rejects the label "communitarian" on the grounds that a community by itself is not necessarily a good thing. There are good and there are bad communities.

18. Michael Sandel gives a preliminary analysis of how this creation takes place, through conscious reflection and dialogue (*Liberalism*, chapter 4).

Chapter 3

1. "Now justice is a moral virtue, merely because it has that tendency to the good of mankind; and, indeed, is nothing but an artificial invention to that purpose. . . [but] once established, it is naturally attended with a strong sentiment of morals" (David Hume, *Treatise*, 577, 579).

2. German shepherd–chow mix, born Nov. 1, 1987, named after their personality prototypes, Friedrich Nietzsche ("Fritz") and Lou Andreas-Salome.

3. Peter Singer, *The Expanding Circle*, 4.

4. Mary Midgely, *Beast and Man*, quoted in Singer, op. cit.

5. In contrast to Nietzsche: "I am afraid that we are not rid of God because we still have faith in grammar" (*Twilight of the Idols*, III, 5 in W. Kaufmann, trans. and ed., *Viking Portable Nietzsche*, 483).

6. MacIntyre, *After Virtue*, especially chapter 17.

7. Edward O. Wilson, *Sociobiology* (Cambridge: Harvard University Press, 1975).

8. Richard Dawkins, *The Selfish Gene*. (New York: Oxford University Press, 1976)
9. Charles Darwin, *The Descent of Man*, quoted in Singer, *The Expanding Circle*, 10–11.
10. Hillel, Babylonian Talmud, I, xiv.
11. Singer, op. cit.
12. Thomas J. Peters and Robert S. Waterman, *In Search of Excellence* (New York: Warner, 1982).
13. Robert M. Kenneth, *The Evolution of Cooperation* (New York: Basic Books, 1984).
14. Wilson, *Sociobiology*, 246.
15. Wilson, op. cit.
16. Mark Murphy, "The Art of Justice."
17. Wilson, *Sociobiology*, 247; L. Michael Mech, *The Wolves of Isle Royale*.
18. Wilson, op. cit.
19. R. Fox, "The Cultural Animal," in J. F. Eisenberg and W. S. Dillon, eds., *Man and Beast* (Washington: Smithsonian, 1971), 20.
20. Wilson, *Sociobiology*, 268.
21. Jane Goodall, *In the Shadow of Man*.
22. Gregory Bateson, "A Theory of Play and Fantasy."
23. Wilson, *Sociobiology*, 98.
24. Goodall, *In the Shadow of Man*, 300–1.
25. Robert Nozick, *Anarchy, State and Utopia*, part 1, chapter 2.

Chapter 4

1. David Miller, *Social Justice*, 270–71.
2. There is a familiar objection against Rawls and his "original position" here, that insofar as a broad and noncommittal characterization of rationality is allowed (thus blunting the objection, for instance, that the original choice situation presumes self-interest on the part of the participants) the lack of cultural context then makes determination of any principle of justice impossible.
3. Plato, *The Republic*, book 1; Aristotle, *Nicomachean Ethics*, book 5.
4. Michael Walzer, *Spheres of Justice*.
5. Joel Feinberg on "comparative" and "non-comparative" justice, in (among other books) *Doing and Deserving*.
6. Peter Singer, *Practical Ethics*, especially chapter 2.
7. Last year a van Gogh painting fetched almost forty million dollars at an auction in New York. The artist could never sell the painting (or any other, save one) during his lifetime.
8. MacIntyre, *After Virtue*, (Notre Dame: Notre Dame Univ. Press, 1981).

9. MacIntyre, *Whose Justice? Which Rationality?* (Notre Dame: Notre Dame Univ. Press, 1988).
10. MacIntyre, *After Virtue*, chapter 17.
11. Rawls, *A Theory of Justice*, especially 103*f*, 310–11.
12. This is not the argument pursued by most "deontologists" and utilitarians, for whom the emphasis remains on the rationality of principles rather than the self-esteem and personal role of the participants (except derivatively: Rawls considers "self-respect" and "self-esteem"—which he does not adequately distinguish—in his discussion of "the good," not in his derivation of the principles of justice as such).
13. Ronald Dworkin, *Taking Rights Seriously*, 81; Nozick, *Anarchy, State and Utopia*, ix.
14. MacIntyre, *After Virtue*, 67.
15. MacIntyre, loc. cit.; Elizabeth Wolgast, "Wrong Rights," in *A Grammar of Justice*.
16. Albert Camus, *The Myth of Sisyphus*; *The Stranger*, pg. 154.
17. For a fascinating but ultimately depressing empirical study of these rationalizations and their strategies, see Melvin J. Lerner, *Belief in a Just World*.
18. See Wolgast, *A Grammar of Justice*, especially chapter 7.

Chapter 5

1. Again, it is not insignificant that Rawls gives considerable attention to the sentiments surrounding justice—including, especially, resentment—but only as a secondary concern, developmentally prior to justice and motivationally significant in some cases, perhaps, but clearly not part of the sense of justice as such. For Rawls as for so many earlier thinkers, sympathy and compassion are praiseworthy but not sufficiently universal or dependable to serve as bases for a theory.
2. I have benefited in this discussion from Cheryl H. (Cheshire) Calhoun, "Feeling and Value." It should be noted that both Shaftesbury and Hutcheson (as well as Hume and Smith) considered themselves very much in tune with the ancients, as opposed to the moral philosophies of their own time. Alasdair MacIntyre challenges their pagan pretensions (*Whose Justice? Which Rationality?*, especially 268–9).
3. Kant, *Grounding for the Metaphysics of Morals*, 442.
4. Schopenhauer, *On the Basis of Morality*.
5. Max Scheler, *The Nature of Sympathy*, trans. P. Heath (London: 1954).

6. "Emotivism" was best represented by Charles Stevenson of the University of Michigan in his book *Ethics and Language* (New Haven: Yale Univ. Press, 1944), but the best-known presentation is probably still A. J. Ayer's polemic in *Language, Truth and Logic* (New York: Dover, 1952). The theory states, in effect, that ethical utterances are nothing but expressions of emotion—as opposed to declarations of belief—and so are neither true nor false, cannot be verified and are therefore "meaningless." The presumption for the most part is that emotions themselves are meaningless and devoid of cognitive content.

7. Adam Smith, *Theory of the Moral Sentiments*, II, ii, 2, 1.

8. For example, Corey Venning, "The World of Adam Smith Revisited" in *Studies in Burke and His Time*, vol. 19, 197. See also Milton Friedman, "Adam Smith's Relevance for 1976," in *Selected Papers of the Graduate School of Business*, no. 50 (University of Chicago, 1977); and Patricia Werhane's unpublished manuscript, "The Legacy of Adam Smith for Modern Capitalism."

9. Hume, *Treatise*, 235; but see also 577, 579, quoted above in note 1 to chapter 3.

10. This conception of nausea may not include the rather philosophical variety suffered some years ago by Jean-Paul Sartre, or at least by one of his most famous characters, Antoine Roquentin, in *Nausea* (translated by A. Lloyd, [New York: New Directions, 1959]). That variety of nausea is clearly more than mere physiology and is intimately connected with a deep philosphical penetration of the world.

11. William James's theory of the emotions is best summarized in his 1884 article, "What Is an Emotion?" which is reprinted in Calhoun and Solomon, eds., *What Is an Emotion?* (New York: Oxford Univ. Press, 1984).

12. Philosophers call this technical property of emotions (and other acts of consciousness) "intentionality." Two good discussions of intentionality are A. Kenny, *Action, Emotion and Will* (London: Routledge and Kegan Paul, 1963) and Daniel Dennett, *Content and Consciousness* (Boston: Routledge, 1970). I have discussed the intentionality of emotions in particular in my "Emotions Mysterious Objects" (Irani and Myers, eds. *Emotions*) and "Nothing to be Proud Of" in *Understanding Human Emotions* (Bowling Green, 1982).

13. An excellent analysis of the rationality of emotions is Ronald de Sousa, *The Rationality of Emotion*, especially chapter 7, where he talks about the variety of meanings given to the notion of "subjectivity" in these contexts.

14. See also Bernard Williams, "Morality and the Emotions," in his *Problems of the Self* (New York: Cambridge Univ. Press, 1973).
15. On the intractability of the emotions, see Amelie Rorty, "Explaining Emotions," in her book, *Explaining Emotions*, 103–126. See also Patricia Greenspan, "A Case of Mixed Feelings: Ambivalence and the Logic of Emotion," in the same volume, 223–50.
16. John Stuart Mill, *Utilitarianism*.
17. Ibid, 46. The phrase is Jeremy Bentham's, *Introduction to the Principles Concerning Morals and Legislation*.
18. Again, such an obviously absurd counterexample has been anticipated by the illustrious proponents of any serious ethical theory. Similar examples have been raised against Kant, for instance, by Charles Fried in his *Right and Wrong* (Cambridge: Harvard Univ. Press, 1978). The question is not whether the theorist under attack can respond to such examples but whether the general thrust and structure of the theory is capable of capturing their absurdity, not just qualifying the theory to "handle" them.
19. Solomon, *The Passions*.
20. Jean-Paul Sartre, *The Emotions*. trans. Frechtman (New York: Citadel, 1971).
21. Robert Levy, *The Tahitians*. (University of Chicago Press, 1973)
22. Milton Mayeroff, *On Caring*. (New York: Harper and Row, 1971)
23. Nell Noddings, *Caring*, e.g., 6.
24. Lawrence Blum, "Compassion" in A. Rorty, ed., *Explaining Emotions*, 507–18.
25. Ibid., 511.
26. Ibid., 513f. Cf. Schopenhauer, *The Basis of Morality*, 148f.
27. Aristotle, *Nicomachean Ethics*, book 4, chapter 9.
28. Blum, "Compassion," 509; see also Max Scheler, *The Nature of Sympathy*.
29. Blum, op. cit., 510f.
30. For instance, see Schiller's letter to Goethe, Aug. 23, 1794, and his *Letters on the Aesthetic Education of Man*, trans. R. Snell (New York: Ungar, 1965), letter 9.
31. Robert Southey, quoted in Mark Jefferson, "What's Wrong with Sentimentality," 519.
32. Michael Tanner, "Sentimentality."
33. I have argued this point at length in my "Literacy and the Education of the Emotions," in E. Kieran, et al., eds., *Literature and Schooling* (Cambridge: Cambridge Univ. Press, 1984).
34. Mary Midgley, "Brutality and Sentimentality," 386.
35. Mark Jefferson, "What's Wrong with Sentimentality," 526.

36. Mary Midgely, "Brutality and Sentimentality." On the connection between charges of "sentimentality" and sexism, see Jane Tompkins, *Sensational Designs.*

Chapter 6

1. A good case is made for the importance of some of the "negative" emotions by Laurence Thomas in "Morals, the Self and Our Natural Sentiments" and in his book, *Living Morally.*
2. Rawls, *A Theory of Justice*, 533n.
3. Wolgast, *A Grammar of Justice*, who also takes injustice as the "grammatically" prior concept and argues, with shifting conviction, that justice is an often inappropriate extrapolation.
4. The image of "rational man"—for whom the sense of justice is inescapable—and the "indifferent universe" (in *The Stranger*, "the benign indifference of the universe") forms the central image of "the Absurd" in Camus's *Myth of Sisyphus*, but rather than yield to despair, he encourages us to "keep the absurd alive."
5. Rawls, *A Theory of Justice*, 310–15.
6. R. D. Laing, *The Divided Self* (London: Tavistock, 1960). Gregory Bateson is famous for his conception of "the double-bind" theory of schizophrenia.
7. Robert Gordon, *The Structure of Emotions* (Cambridge: Cambridge Univ. Press, 1987) especially 47–50.
8. Michael Walzer, *Spheres of Justice*, 12–14.
9. Nietzsche insisted the first attribute of the moral philosopher ought to be a keen sense of smell, and he had, perhaps, the best nose among the great philosophers. See, e.g., his various olfactory accusations in *Beyond Good and Evil*, and especially in *The Antichrist*.
10. Pride is an emotion of accomplishment; vanity involves some (real or imagined) virtue but need not involve accomplishment and typically suggests exaggerated self-admiration rather than achievement. I have analyzed the difference in *The Passions*, especially 344–47, 363–65.
11. For an excellent analysis of the relations and differences between jealousy and envy, see Jerome Neu, "Jealous Thoughts," in Amelie Rorty, *Explaining Emotions*, 425–63.
12. Rawls briefly discusses envy and resentment in *A Theory of Justice*, 530–41; Robert Nozick analyzes these emotions in *Anarchy, State and Utopia*, 239–46.
13. The asymmetry of distributive justice and punishment is suggested, but not stated or argued, in Rawls, op. cit., 314–15, 575.
14. Nietzsche writes about justice in *On the Genealogy of Morals*, book 2, and suggests that it is, indeed, a virtue of character but a very, very

rare one, based on strength and "overflowing" rather than compassion.

15. The best analytic discussion of justice in terms of mercy and forgiveness is Jean Hampton and Jeffrey Murphy, *Mercy and Forgiveness* (Cambridge: Cambridge Univ. Press, 1988).

16. Robert Nozick provides an insightful accounting of the relevance of fear to justice in *Anarchy, State and Utopia*, 65–71. A very different account was defended by G.W.F. Hegel in his *Phenomenology of Spirit* (1807) as an essential aspect of social development and self-identity (in the famous section on "Master and Slave," Miller translation [New York: Oxford Univ. Press, 1977] especially paragraphs 190–196).

17. Donald Gustafson, "Grief," in *Nous*, (Fall, 1989).

18. The syntax of "vengeance" is rather awkward in that the grammar of the word depicts a scheme of intentional action rather than a motive or an emotion as such. I have sometimes used "vengefulness" to indicate what I take to be the relevant emotion, but this has implications (of a general trait rather than a particular emotion) that make it less than adequate. "Revenge" is even less adequate, referring as it does to the accomplished act and only secondarily to the motive. So, with reservations, I sometimes use "vengeance" to refer to an emotion. Could our aversion to this emotion be revealing itself in the absence of an adequate word to refer to it?

19. Rawls, *A Theory of Justice*, 533n.

20. Nietzsche is often thought to be a "nihilist," but a reading of his works—including his unpublished notes (now published as *The Will to Power*, translated and edited by W. Kaufmann [New York: Random House, 1967])—shows that he is a persistent enemy of nihilism. Nihilism—and in particular the "life-denying" values of established morality—is what he attacks, not what he defends. The often-noted parallel between his announcement that nihilism is a "specter haunting Europe" (in *The Will to Power*) and Marx and Engels's similar warning concerning communism is therefore quite misleading. Marx and Engels were clearly enthusiastic about the prospect. Nietzsche was horrified.

21. It is worth noting that Walter Kaufmann, one of Nietzsche's first and best defenders in recent philosophy, attacks the concept of justice as Nietzsche himself does not, particularly in his *Without Guilt and Justice*.

22. With his usual tact, Nietzsche refers to the "parasites" who cry out for justice in self-defense (*On the Genealogy of Morals*, book 2).

23. Nietzsche suggests that ethics, in the final analysis, consists of "giving

style to one's character" (*The Gay Science*, [New York: Random House, 1986] 290).

24. Nietzsche, *On the Genealogy of Morals*, book 1, paragraph 10.

25. Ibid, pg. 36.

26. Nietzsche, especially *The Will to Power*.

27. Nietzsche's "combustion" metaphors are part of a long tradition of physical energy metaphors, often concerned with heat and hydraulics, of "pressure" (*cathexis*) and "emptying out" (*catharsis*), of "exploding" and being "overwhelmed." But do such metaphors already bias analysis against the passions and lead us to underestimate their importance and their intelligence?

28. In *The Gay Science* and elsewhere, Nietzsche insists (against Darwin) that all living creatures, far from tending to preserve their existence, strive to enhance themselves, even at great risk to their own lives.

29. Alexander Nehamas has written an intriguing and ingenious analysis of Nietzsche as his own creator (much as Socrates was created in the writings of Plato): *Nietzsche: Life as Literature* (Cambridge: Harvard Univ. Press, 1985).

30. Nietzsche insists on "new values," for example, in *Beyond Good and Evil* (paragraph 44), where he declares "philosophers must be legislators!"

31. For Nietzsche's conflicted views about Socrates, see W. Kaufmann, *Nietzsche: Philosopher, Psychologist, Antichrist* 4th ed. (Princeton: Princeton Univ. Press, 1974), chapter 13, and Nehamas, *Nietzsche*, especially 24–34.

32. Nietzsche: "All passions have a phase when they are merely disastrous, when they drag down their victim with the weight of stupidity—and a later phase when they wed the spirit, when they "spiritualize" themselves. . . Destroying the passions and cravings, merely as a preventive measure against their stupidity, today this itself strikes us as a merely another acute form of stupidity" ("Morality as Anti-Nature," in *Twilight of the Idols*).

33. See, for example, Frithjof Bergmann on Nietzsche's *Genealogy* in Higgins and Solomon, eds., *Reading Nietzsche* (New York: Oxford Univ. Press, 1988).

34. Max Scheler upholds Nietzsche's condemnation of resentment in modern bourgeois morality, but he rejects the indictment concerning Christian morality (Scheler, *Ressentiment*).

35. Nietzsche is sarcastic about the "improvers of mankind," *Twilight of the Idols*, chapter 7.

36. Hegel, *Phenomenology of Spirit* (1807).

37. Aristotle's analysis of anger as including the desire for revenge is in his *Rhetoric*, 1378–80.

38. Kant, *Philosophy of Law.*
39. Cf. John Locke on the need for punishment, in his second *Treatise on Government*, ed. Peter Laslett (Indianapolis: Hackett, 1983), especially sections 124–25.
40. Cf. Jacoby, *Wild Justice*, especially chapter 1.
41. In Eisenstein's *Ivan the Terrible, Part II*, one of the outraged Russians responds to the slaughter of the innocents by insisting, "even beasts are rational in their anger." Considering the intervening centuries of human slaughter, we might well choose to side with the beasts.
42. Wolgast, "Getting Even."
43. Kant, *Philosophy of Law.*
44. On vengeance versus retribution, see Gerstein, "Capital Punishment"; and Robert Nozick, *Philosophical Explanations* 366–74. J. D. Mabbott summarizes what we might call the standard position: "In the theory of punishment retribution has been defended by no philosopher of note except [F. H.] Bradley. . . . Retributive punishment is only a polite name for revenge; it is vindictive, inhumane, barbarous, and immoral" ("The Humanitarian Theory of Punishment," in *Twentieth Century*, March 1949.) But cf. K. G. Armstrong, "The Retributivist Hits Back" in Acton, ed., *The Philosophy of Punishment.*
45. Robert S. Gerstein, "Capital Punishment: A Retributivist Response."
46. Hegel on punishment: *Philosophy of Right*, translated by T. M. Knox (New York: Oxford Univ. Press, 1967), 140–41.
47. Blackstone is quoted in Acton, *The Philosophy of Punishment*, 13.
48. Kant, *Philosophy of Law.*
49. Camus, "Reflections on the Guillotine," in *Resistance, Rebellion and Death* (New York: Vintage, 1961).
50. Robert Hughes, *The Fatal Shore* (New York: Knopf, 1987).
51. Bernard Bosanquet defends a "therapeutic" theory of punishment in his *Philosophical Theory of the State.*
52. For the sometimes horrible ways in which we encourage such distortions, see, e.g., Sam Keen, *Faces of the Enemy* (Harper & Row, 1986).
53. Jean-Paul Sartre argues, in *Anti-Semite and Jew*, that racism and prejudice are always a façade for serious self-deception and cowardice. One projects onto others traits and vices that betray one's own bad character.
54. Rawls discusses self-respect at some length in *A Theory of Justice*, part 3, 440–46, but confuses it with self-esteem and defends an overly achievement-oriented "Aristotelean" conception. So too Robert Nozick analyzes self-esteem (*Anarchy, State and Utopia*, 239–46) in terms of achievement, contrasts it with envy, and offers an even

more competitive conception than that of Rawls ("the Harvard Syndrome"?). Little attention is devoted to anything quite so common and noncompetitive as "just feeling good about oneself." One wonders, in the midst of all of this frenzy for self-realization (a California not Cambridge term), where one finds the room for compassion or an adequate concept of justice (as opposed to writing famous books about justice).

Conclusion

1. Melvin Lerner, *Belief in a Fair World.*
2. Ray Marshall, former Secretary of Labor (under President Carter).
3. Charles Siebert, "The Rehumanization of the Heart," *Harper's*, Feb., 1990.

BIBLIOGRAPHY

Ackerman, B. A. *Social Justice in the Liberal State.* New Haven: Yale Univ. Press, 1980.

Acton, H. B., ed. *The Philosophy of Punishment.* London: Macmillan, 1969.

Ardrey, Robert. *The Social Contract.* New York: Atheneum, 1970.

——. *Territorial Imperative.* New York: Atheneum, 1966.

Aristotle. *Nicomachean Ethics.* Translated by T. Irwin. Indianapolis: Hackett, 1985.

——. *Politics.* Translated by B. Jowett. New York: Modern Library, 1943.

——. *Rhetoric.* Translated by Keith Erickson. Metuchen, N. J.: Scarecrow Press, 1974.

Arrow, Kenneth. *Social Choice and Individual Values.* 2d ed. New Haven: Yale Univ. Press, 1970.

Axelrod, Robert M. *The Evolution of Cooperation.* New York: Basic Books, 1984.

Bateson, Gregory. "A Theory of Play and Fantasy." *Psychiatric Research and Reports* 2 (1955): 39–51.

Becker, Lawrence. *Reciprocity.* Boston: Routledge & Kegan Paul, 1986.

Bedau, Hugh. "Capital Punishment and Retributive Justice." In *Matters of Life and Death: New Essays in Moral Philosophy,* edited by Tom Regan. New York: Random House, 1980.

Bellah, Robert, et al. *Habits of the Heart.* Berkeley: Univ. of California Press, 1985.

Bentham, Jeremy. *Introduction to the Principles of Morals and Legislation.* New York: Hafner, 1948.

Bergmann, Frithjof. *On Being Free.* Notre Dame: Univ. of Notre Dame Press, 1977.

Blum, Lawrence A. "Compassion." In *Explaining Emotions,* edited by A. Rorty.

Blum, Lawrence A. *Friendship, Altruism and Morality.* Boston: Routledge & Kegan Paul, 1980.

Bonevac, Daniel, and Thomas Seung. "Conflicts of Values." *Philosophical Studies* (1988).

Bosanquet, Bernard. *The Philosophical Theory of the State.* London: Macmillan, 1899.

Brandt, Richard. "The Psychology of Benevolence and its Implications for Philosophy." *Journal of Philosophy* 23 (1976): 429–53.

Brandt, Richard, ed. *Social Justice.* Englewood Cliffs: Prentice Hall, 1962.

Brickman, Philip. "Models of Helping and Coping." *American Psychologist* 37 (Apr. 1982): 368–84.

Briggs, Jean L. *Never in Anger.* Cambridge: Harvard Univ. Press, 1970.

Broad, C. D. *Five Types of Ethical Theory.* London: Routledge & Kegan Paul, 1971.

Calhoun, Cheryl H. "Feeling and Value." Ph.D. diss., Univ. of Texas, 1981.

Calhoun, Cheshire. "Justice, Care and Gender Bias." *Journal of Philosophy* 85 (Sept. 1988): 451–463.

Campbell, C. A. *In Defense of Free Will.* Glasgow: Jackson, 1938.

Camus, Albert. *The Myth of Sisyphus.* Translated by Justin O'Brien. New York: Vintage, 1960.

———. *Resistance, Rebellion and Death.* Translated by Justin O'Brien. New York: Vintage, 1961.

———. *The Stranger.* Translated by S. Gilbert. New York: Vintage, 1946.

Code, Lorraine. *Epistemic Responsibility.* Providence, R.I.: University Press of New England, 1987.

Collard, David. *Altruism and Economics.* Oxford: Oxford Univ. Press, 1978.

Cooper, John M. *Reason and Human Good in Aristotle.* Cambridge: Harvard Univ. Press, 1975.

Coopersmith, Stanley. *The Antecedents of Self Esteem.* San Francisco: W. H. Freeman, 1967.

Corning, Peter. *The Synergism Hypothesis.* New York: McGraw-Hill, 1983.

Daniels, Norman. *Reading Rawls.* New York: Basic Books, 1975.

Darwall, Stephen L. *Impartial Reason.* Ithaca: Cornell Univ. Press, 1983.

Dawkins, Richard. *The Selfish Gene.* New York: Oxford Univ. Press, 1976.

d'Emilio, John, and Estelle B. Freedman. *Intimate Matters.* New York: Harper & Row, 1987.

Deigh, John. "Shame and Self-esteem: A Critique." *Ethics* 93 (Jan. 1983): 225–245.

de Sousa, Ronald. *The Rationality of Emotion.* Cambridge: MIT Press, 1987.

Dostoevsky, Fyodor. *Notes from Underground.* Translated by Ralph Matlaw. New York: Dutton, 1960.

Douglas, Mary. *The World of Goods.* New York: Norton, 1979.

Dworkin, Ronald, "Liberalism" In *Public and Private Morality,* edited by Stuart Hampshire. New York: Cambridge Univ. Press, 1978.

Dworkin, Ronald. *Taking Rights Seriously.* London: Duckworth, 1977.

Else, Gerald F. *Aristotle's Poetics.* Cambridge: Harvard Univ. Press, 1957.

Feinberg, Joel. *Doing and Deserving.* Princeton: Princeton Univ. Press, 1970.

Feinberg, Joel. "The Nature and Value of Rights." *The Journal of Value Inquiry* 4 (1970).

Feinberg, Joel. *Social Philosophy.* Englewood Cliffs, N.J.: Prentice-Hall, 1973.

Firth, Roderick. "Ethical Absolutism and the Ideal Observer." *Philosophy and Phenomenological Research* 12 (Mar. 1952): 317–345.

Flew, Antony. *The Politics of Procrustes*. Buffalo: Prometheus, 1981.

Fox, R. "The Cultural Animal" in Eisenberg and Dillon, eds., *Man and Beast*. Washington: Smithsonian, 1971.

French, P., T. Uehling, and H. Wettstein, eds. *Ethical Theory: Character and Virtue*. Midwest Studies in Philosophy XIII. Minneapolis: Univ. of Minnesota Press, 1988.

———. *Social and Political Philosophy*. Midwest Studies in Philosophy VII. Minneapolis: Univ. of Minnesota Press, 1982.

Galston, William. "Equal Opportunity and Liberal Theory" In *Justice and Equality: Here and Now*, edited by F. Lucasch. 89–107. Ithaca: Cornell Univ. Press, 1986.

Gerstein, Robert S. "Capital Punishment: A Retributivist Response." *Ethics* 85 (1974–75): 75–79).

Gilligan, Carol. *In a Different Voice*. Cambridge: Harvard Univ. Press, 1982.

Goodall, Jane. *In the Shadow of Man*. Boston: Houghton-Mifflin, 1971.

Grice, G. P. "Moral Theories and Received Opinion." *Proceedings of the Aristotelean Society*, Supplement 52 (1978).

Hampshire, Stuart. *Morality and Conflict*. Cambridge: Harvard Univ. Press, 1983.

Hanson, Kristine R., and Robert C. Solomon. *It's Good Business*. New York: Atheneum/Harper & Row, 1985.

Harrison, Jonathan. "Some Comments on Firth." *Philosophy and Phenomenological Research* 12 (1956): 256–62.

Hegel, G. W. F. *The Phenomenology of Spirit*. Translated by A. V. Miller. Oxford: Oxford Univ. Press, 1977.

Heschel, Abraham. *The Prophets*. New York: Harper & Row, 1962.

Hobbes, Thomas. *Leviathan*. New York: Hafner, 1926.

Hochschild, Jennifer. *What's Fair?* Cambridge: Harvard Univ. Press, 1981.

Holmes, Stephen. "The Community Trap." *The New Republic*, Nov. 29, 1988, 24–28.

Homans, G. C. *Social Behavior: Its Elementary Forms*. New York: Harcourt Brace World, 1961.

Hospers, John. *Human Conduct: An Introduction to the Problems of Ethics*. San Diego: Harcourt Brace Jovanovich, 1961.

Hume, David. *A Treatise of Human Nature*. Edited by L. A. Selby-Bigge. Oxford: Oxford Univ. Press, 1978.

———. *Inquiry Concerning the Principles of Morals*. Edited by L. A. Selby-Bigge. Oxford: Oxford Univ. Press, 1978.

Hutcheson, Francis. *A System of Moral Philosophy*. 1755. 2 vols. New York: A. M. Kelly, 1968.

Irani, K. S., and Gerald Myers. *Emotion: Philosophical Studies*. New York: Haven, 1983.

Jackson, W. W. *Matters of Justice.* London: Croom Helm, 1986.

Jacoby, Susan. *Wild Justice.* New York: Harper & Row, 1983.

James, William. *Principles of Psychology.* New York: Dover, 1950.

———. "What is an Emotion?" *Mind* (1884).

Jefferson, Mark. "What's Wrong with Sentimentality" *Mind* 92 (1983): 519–29.

Kant, Immanuel. *The Critique of Practical Reason.* Translated by Lewis W. Beck. Indianapolis: Bobbs-Merrill, 1956.

———. *Grounding for the Metaphysics of Morals.* Translated by James W. Ellington. Indianapolis: Hackett, 1981.

———. *The Metaphysical Elements of Justice.* Translated by John Ladd. Indianapolis: Bobbs-Merrill, 1965.

——— *Philosophy of Law.* Translated by W. Hastie. Edinburgh: Clark, 1889.

Kaufmann, Walter. *Without Guilt and Justice.* New York: Wyden, 1973.

Kekes, John. "Moral Sensitivity." *Philosophy* 59 (1984).

Kohlberg, Lawrence. "From Is to Ought." In *Cognitive Development and Epistemology*, edited by T. Mischel. New York: Academic Press, 1971.

Lapham, Lewis. *Money and Class in America.* London: Weidenfeld & Nicolson, 1988.

Lelyveld, Arthur. "Punishment: For and Against." In *Punishment: For and Against*, edited by A. S. Neill. (New York: Hart, 1971).

Lerner, Melvin J. *Belief in a Fair World.* New York: Plenum, 1980.

Levy, Robert. *The Tahitians.* Chicago: Univ. of Chicago Press, 1973.

Locke, John. *Second Treatise on Government.* Indianapolis: Hacket, 1983.

Lucasch, Frank, ed. *Justice and Equality: Here and Now.* Ithaca: Cornell Univ. Press, 1986.

Luce, R. D. and Howard Raiffa. *Games and Decisions.* New York: Wiley, 1957.

Macaulay, J. R., and L. Berkowitz, eds. *Altruism and Helping Behavior.* (New York: Academic Press, 1970).

MacIntyre, Alasdair. *After Virtue.* Notre Dame: Univ. of Notre Dame Press, 1981.

———. *Whose Justice? Which Rationality?* Notre Dame: Univ. of Notre Dame Press, 1988.

McFall, Lynn. "Integrity." *Ethics* 98 (Oct. 1987): 5–20.

McGregor, Douglas A. *The Human Side of Enterprise.* New York: McGraw-Hill, 1960.

Mandeville, Bernard. *The Fable of the Bees.* London, 1705.

Marongiu, Pietro and Graeme Newman. *Vengeance.* Toronga, N. J.: Rowman & Littlefield, 1987.

Marx, Karl. *Selected Writings.* Edited by David McClellan. New York: Oxford Univ. Press, 1977.

Massey, Stephen J. "Is Self-Respect a Moral or a Psychological Concept?" *Ethics* 93 (Jan. 1983):246–261.

Mayeroff, Milton. *On Caring.* New York: Harper & Row, 1971.

Maynard-Smith, John. *The Evolution of Social Behavior.* London: King's College Sociobiology Group, 1982.

Mech, L. Michael. *The Wolves of Isle Royale.* Washington: U. S. Government Printing Office, 1966.

Melden, A. *Rights and Persons.* Berkeley: Univ. of California Press, 1977.

Mencius. *The Mind of Mencius* Translated by P. Lau. New York: Penguin, 1970.

Midgley, Mary. *Beast and Man.* Ithaca: Cornell Univ. Press, 1978.

——. "Brutality and Sentimentality." *Philosophy* 54 (July 1979).

Mill, John Stuart. *On Liberty.* Indianapolis: Hackett, 1978.

——. *Utilitarianism.* Indianapolis: Hackett, 1981.

Miller, David. *Social Justice.* Oxford: Oxford Univ. Press, 1976.

Moore, G. E. *Principia Ethica.* Cambridge: Cambridge Univ. Press, 1903.

Morgan, Edmund. *Inventing the People.* New York: Norton, 1987.

Marongiu, Pietro, and Graeme Newman. *Vengeance.* Toronga, N. J.: Rowman & Littlefield, 1987.

Murphy, Mark. "The Art of Justice," Plan II honors thesis, Univ. of Texas, 1988.

Murray, Charles. *In Pursuit of Happiness and Good Government.* New York: Simon & Schuster, 1988.

Nagel, Thomas, "Fragmentation of Values." In *Mortal Questions.* Cambridge: Cambridge Univ. Press, 1979.

Nagel, Thomas. Review of *A Theory of Justice,* by John Rawls. *Philosophical Review* 82 (Apr. 1973): 220, 222–31.

Nagel, Thomas. *The View from Nowhere.* New York: Oxford Univ. Press, 1986.

Natsoulas, T. "Sympathy, Empathy and the Stream of Consciousness. *Journal of the Theory of Social Behavior* 18 (June 1988).

Neill, A. S. *Punishment: For and Against.* New York: Hart, 1971.

Nietzsche, Friedrich. *On the Genealogy of Morals.* Translated by W. Kaufmann. New York: Random House, 1967.

Noddings, Nell. *Caring.* Berkeley: Univ. of California Press, 1984.

Nozick, Robert. *Anarchy, State and Utopia.* New York: Basic Books, 1974.

——. *Philosophical Explanations.* Cambridge: Harvard Univ. Press, 1981.

Nussbaum, Martha. *The Fragility of Goodness.* New York: Cambridge Univ. Press, 1985.

Oldenquist, Andrew. "Loyalties." *Journal of Philosophy* 79 (April 1982): 173–193.

Parfit, Derek. *Reasons and Persons.* Oxford: Oxford Univ. Press, 1984.

Pincoffs, Edmund. *Quandaries and Virtues*. Lawrence: Univ. Press of Kansas, 1986.

Plato. *The Apology*, in *The Trial and Death of Socrates*, translated by Grube, (Indianapolis: Hackett, 1982).

Plato. *Crito*, in The *Trial and Death of Socrates*, translated by Grube (Indianapolis: Hackett, 1980).

Plato. The *Republic*. Translated by E. M. A. Grube. Indianapolis: Hackett, 1974.

Rapacynski, Andrzej. *Nature and Politics*. Ithaca: Cornell Univ. Press, 1987.

Raphael, D. D. *Moral Philosophy*. Oxford: Oxford Univ. Press, 1981.

Rawls, John. *A Theory of Justice*. Cambridge: Harvard Univ. Press, 1971.

Rawls, John. "Justice as Fairness." *Philosophical Review* (1971).

Redfield, Robert. "How Human Society Operates." In *The Science of Man in the World Crisis*. New York: Columbia Univ. Press, 1945.

Rescher, Nicholas. *Unselfishness*. Pittsburgh: Univ. of Pittsburgh Press, 1975.

Rorty, Amelie. *Explaining Emotions*. Berkeley: Univ. of California Press, 1980.

Rosaldo, Michelle. *Woman, Culture and Society*. Stanford: Stanford Univ. Press, 1974.

Rosenthal, David. "Emotions and the Self." In *Emotions*, edited by K. S. Irani and Gerald Myers.

Rousseau, Jean-Jacques. *Discourse on the Origins of Inequality*. Translated by D. Cress. Indianapolis: Hackett, 1983.

———. *Emile*. Translated by A. Bloom. New York: Basic Books, 1979.

———. *The Social Contract*. Translated by D. Cress. Indianapolis: Hackett, 1983.

Royce, Josiah. *The Philosophy of Loyalty*. New York: Macmillan, 1908.

Ruddick, Sara. *Maternal Thinking*. Boston: Beacon, 1988.

Ryan, Alan. *J. S. Mill*. London: Routledge & Kegan Paul, 1974.

Sahlins, Marshall. "Origin of Society." *Scientific American*, Sept. 1960, 76–87.

Sandel, Michael. *Liberalism and the Limits of Justice*. Cambridge, Cambridge Univ. Press, 1982.

Sartre, Jean-Paul. *Being and Nothingness*. Translated by H. Barnes. New York: Philosophical Library, 1956.

———. *The Emotions*. Translated by B. Frechtman. New York: Citadel, 1971.

———. *Transcendence of the Ego*. Translated by F. Williams and R. Kirkpatrick. New York: Noonday, 1957.

Scheler, Max. *The Nature of Sympathy*. Translated by P. Heath. New Haven: Yale Univ. Press, 1954.

Scheler, Max. *Ressentiment.* New York: Free Press, 1961.

Schelling, Thomas C. *The Strategy of Conflict.* Cambridge: Harvard Univ. Press, 1960.

Schoeck, Helmut. *Envy: A Theory of Social Behavior.* New York: Harcourt Brace World, 1970.

Schopenhauer, Arthur. *On the Basis of Morality.* Translated by E. F. Payne. Indianapolis: Bobbs-Merrill, 1965.

Schott, Robin. *Cognition and Eros.* Boston: Beacon, 1988.

Scruton, Roger. "Emotion, Practical Knowledge and Common Culture." In *Explaining Emotions,* edited by A. Rorty.

Sen, A. K. *Collective Choice and Social Welfare.* San Francisco: Holden-Day, 1970.

Sextus Empiricus. *Philosophical Works.* Cambridge: Harvard Univ. Press, 1947.

Sheaffer, Robert. *Resentment Against Achievement.* New York: Libertarian Books, 1987.

Shore, Bradd. *Sala'ilua, A Samoan Mystery.* New York: Columbia Univ. Press, 1971.

Sidgwick, Henry. *Methods of Ethics,* 2d ed. London: Macmillan, 1907.

Singer, Irving. *The Nature of Love.* 3 vols. Chicago: Univ. of Chicago Press, 1966–87.

Singer, Peter. *The Expanding Circle.* New York: Farrar Straus & Giroux, 1981.

Singer, Peter. *Practical Ethics.* Cambridge: Cambridge Univ. Press, 1979.

Smith, Adam. *The Theory of Moral Sentiments.* London: George Bell & Sons, 1880.

——. *The Wealth of Nations.* New York: Hafner, 1948.

Smith, Roger W., ed. *Guilt, Man and Society.* New York: Doubleday, 1971.

Solomon, Leonard. "The Influence of Some Types of Power Relationships and Game Strategies on the Development of Interpersonal Trust." *Journal of Abnormal and Social Psychology* (1960).

Solomon, Robert C. *About Love.* New York: Simon & Schuster, 1988.

Solomon, Robert C. "Emotions and Anthropology." *Inquiry,* 1979.

Solomon, Robert C. *In the Spirit of Hegel.* New York: Oxford Univ. Press, 1983.

Solomon, Robert C. "On Emotions as Judgments." *American Philosophical Quarterly* 25 (Apr. 1988); 183–91.

Solomon, Robert C. *The Passions.* New York: Doubleday, 1976.

Soltan, Karol. *The Causal Theory of Justice.* Berkeley: Univ. of California Press, 1987.

Sommers, Shula. "Adults Evaluating Their Emotions." In *Emotion in Adult Development,* edited by Carole Z. Malatesta and Carroll E. Isard. (Newbury Park, Calif.: Sage, 1984).

——. "Unamerican Emotions." Unpublished manuscript, 1985.
——. "An Approach to the Study of Emotion in Adulthood." Unpublished manuscript, 1985.
Spelman, Elizabeth V. *Inessential Woman.* Boston: Beacon, 1988.
Stocker, Michael. "The Schizophrenia of Modern Ethical Theories." *Journal of Philosophy* 78, 747–765.
Strawson, P. F. *Freedom and Resentment and Other Essays.* London: Methuen, 1974.
Suits, G. *The Grasshopper.* Toronto: Univ. of Toronto Press, 1971.
Tanner, Michael "Sentimentality." *Proceedings of the Aristotelean Society* 77 (1976–77).
Tavris, Carol *Anger: The Misunderstood Emotion.* 2d ed. New York: Simon & Schuster, 1989.
Tawney, R. H. *Equality.* New York: Barnes & Noble, 1964.
Taylor, Charles. "The Nature and Scope of Distributive Justice." In *Justice and Equality: Here and Now,* edited by F. Lucasch.
Thomas, Laurence. "Ethical Egoism and Our Psychological Dispositions." *American Philosophical Quarterly* 17 (1980): 73–78.
Thomas, Laurence. *Living Morally.* Philadelphia: Temple Univ. Press, 1989.
——. "Love and Morality: The Possibility of Altruism." In *Sociobiology and Epistemology,* edited by J. Fetzer. Norwell, Mass.: Reidel, 1985.
——. "Morals, the Self and Our Natural Sentiments." In *Emotion,* edited by K. S. Irani and Gerald Myers.
Thomas, Lewis. *Lives of a Cell and The Medusa and the Snail.* New York: Viking, 1974.
Tompkins, Jane. *Sensational Designs: The Cultural Work of American Fiction, 1790–1860.* New York: Oxford Univ. Press, 1985.
Trivers, Robert. "The Evolution of Reciprocal Altruism," *Quarterly Review of Biology* 46 (1971).
Turnbull, Colin. *The Mountain People.* New York: Simon & Schuster, 1974.
Van den Haag, Ernst. "Deterrence and Uncertainty." *Journal of Criminal Law, Criminology, and Police Science* 60 (1969): 141–47.
Vlastos, Gregory. "Justice and Equality." In *Social Justice,* edited by Richard Brandt.
von Hayek, Friedrich. *The Mirage of Social Justice.* London: Routledge & Kegan Paul, 1976.
Wallace, James. *Virtues and Vices.* Ithaca: Cornell Univ. Press, 1978.
Walzer, Michael. "Justice Here and Now." In *Justice and Equality: Here and Now,* edited by F. Lucasch.
——. Review of *Liberalism and the Limits of Justice,* by Michael Sandel. *New Republic,* Dec. 13, 1982.
——. *Spheres of Justice.* New York: Basic Books, 1983.

Wasserstrom, Richard. "Racism, Sexism and Preferential Treatment." *U.C.L.A. Law Review* 24 (Feb. 1977):

Weiner, Annette. *Women of Value, Men of Renown.* Univ. of Texas Press, 1980.

Westermarck, Edward. *The Origin and Development of the Moral Ideas.* 2 vols. London: Macmillan, 1912.

Williams, Bernard. "The Idea of Equality." In *Problems of the Self.* New York: Cambridge Univ. Press, 1973. (Originally published in *Philosophy, Politics and Society,* edited by P. Laslett and W. C. Runciman. Oxford: Blackwell, 1964.)

Williams, Bernard. "Justice as a Virtue." In *Essays on Aristotle's Ethics,* edited by Amelie Rorty. Berkeley: Univ. of California Press, 1980.

Wilson, Edward O. *Sociobiology.* Cambridge: Harvard Univ. Press, 1975.

Winfield, Richard. *Reason and Justice.* Buffalo: SUNY Press, 1988.

Wispé, L. "The Distinction between Sympathy and Empathy." *Journal of Personality and Social Psychology* 50 (1986):314–21.

Wolff, Robert Paul. *Understanding Rawls.* Princeton: Princeton Univ. Press, 1977.

Wolgast, Elizabeth. *A Grammar of Justice.* Ithaca: Cornell Univ. Press, 1987.

——. "Getting Even." Unpublished essay.

Zweig, Paul. *The Heresy of Self-love.* Princeton: Princeton Univ. Press, 1980.

Index